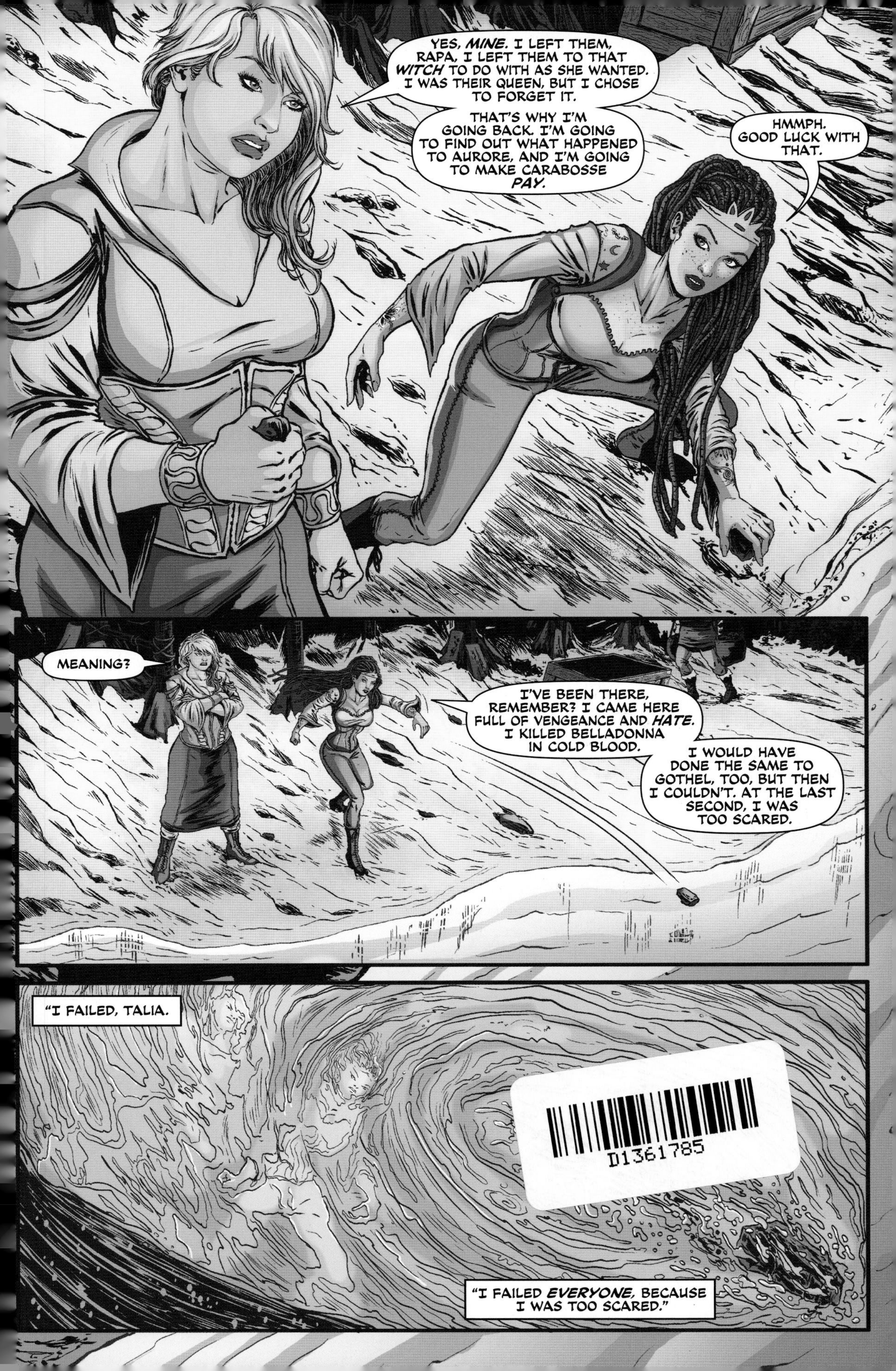
YES, *MINE*. I LEFT THEM, RAPA, I LEFT THEM TO THAT *WITCH* TO DO WITH AS SHE WANTED. I WAS THEIR QUEEN, BUT I CHOSE TO FORGET IT.
THAT'S WHY I'M GOING BACK. I'M GOING TO FIND OUT WHAT HAPPENED TO AURORE, AND I'M GOING TO MAKE CARABOSSE *PAY*.
HMMPH. GOOD LUCK WITH THAT.
MEANING?
I'VE BEEN THERE, REMEMBER? I CAME HERE FULL OF VENGEANCE AND *HATE*. I KILLED BELLADONNA IN COLD BLOOD.
I WOULD HAVE DONE THE SAME TO GOTHEL, TOO, BUT THEN I COULDN'T. AT THE LAST SECOND, I WAS TOO SCARED.
"I FAILED, TALIA.
"I FAILED *EVERYONE*, BECAUSE I WAS TOO SCARED."

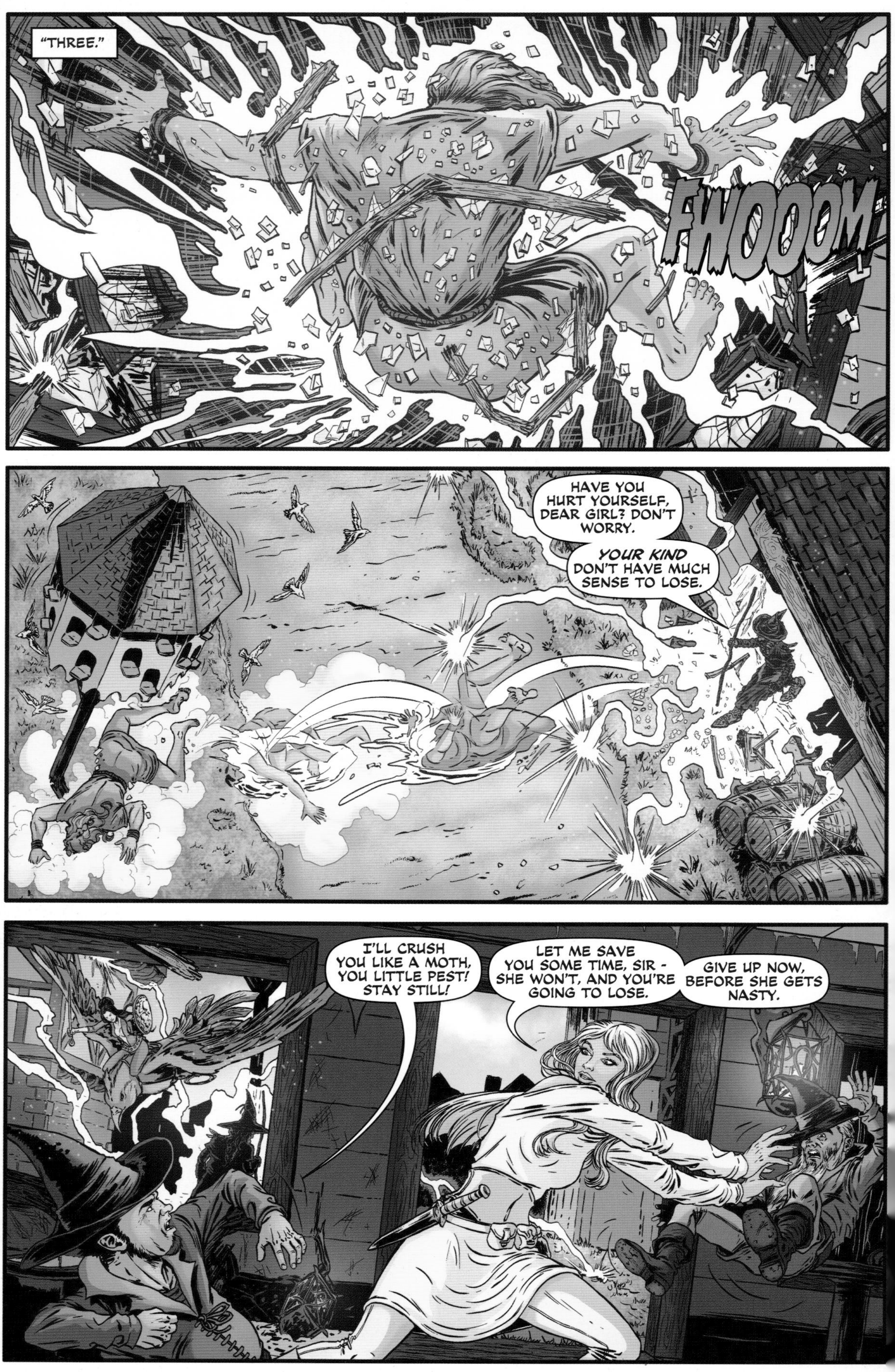
"THREE."
FWOOOM
HAVE YOU HURT YOURSELF, DEAR GIRL? DON'T WORRY.
YOUR KIND DON'T HAVE MUCH SENSE TO LOSE.
I'LL CRUSH YOU LIKE A MOTH, YOU LITTLE PEST! STAY STILL!
LET ME SAVE YOU SOME TIME, SIR - SHE WON'T, AND YOU'RE GOING TO LOSE.
GIVE UP NOW, BEFORE SHE GETS NASTY.

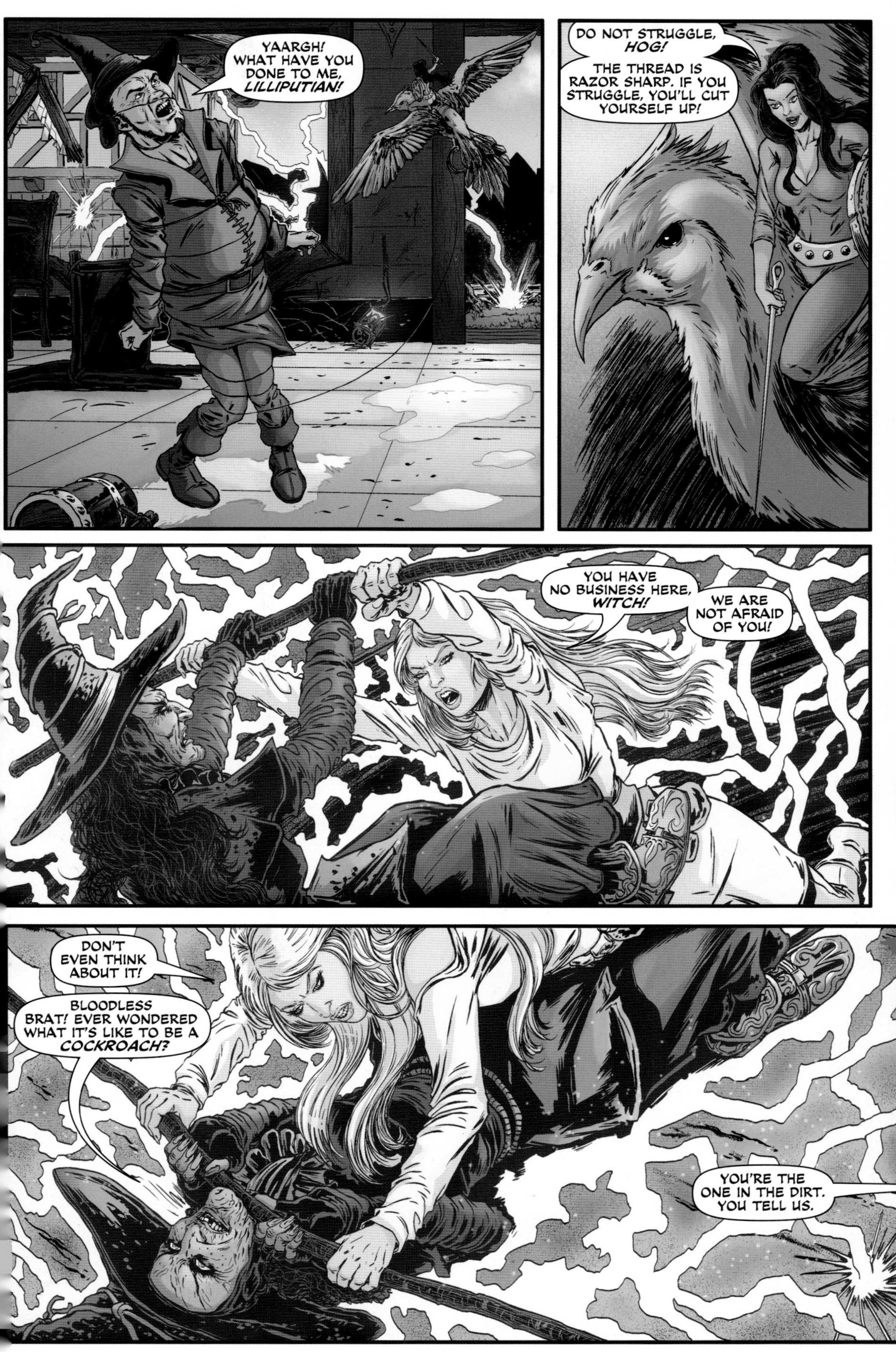
YAARGH! WHAT HAVE YOU DONE TO ME, LILLIPUTIAN!
DO NOT STRUGGLE, HOG!
THE THREAD IS RAZOR SHARP. IF YOU STRUGGLE, YOU'LL CUT YOURSELF UP!
YOU HAVE NO BUSINESS HERE, WITCH!
WE ARE NOT AFRAID OF YOU!
DON'T EVEN THINK ABOUT IT!
BLOODLESS BRAT! EVER WONDERED WHAT IT'S LIKE TO BE A COCKROACH?
YOU'RE THE ONE IN THE DIRT. YOU TELL US.

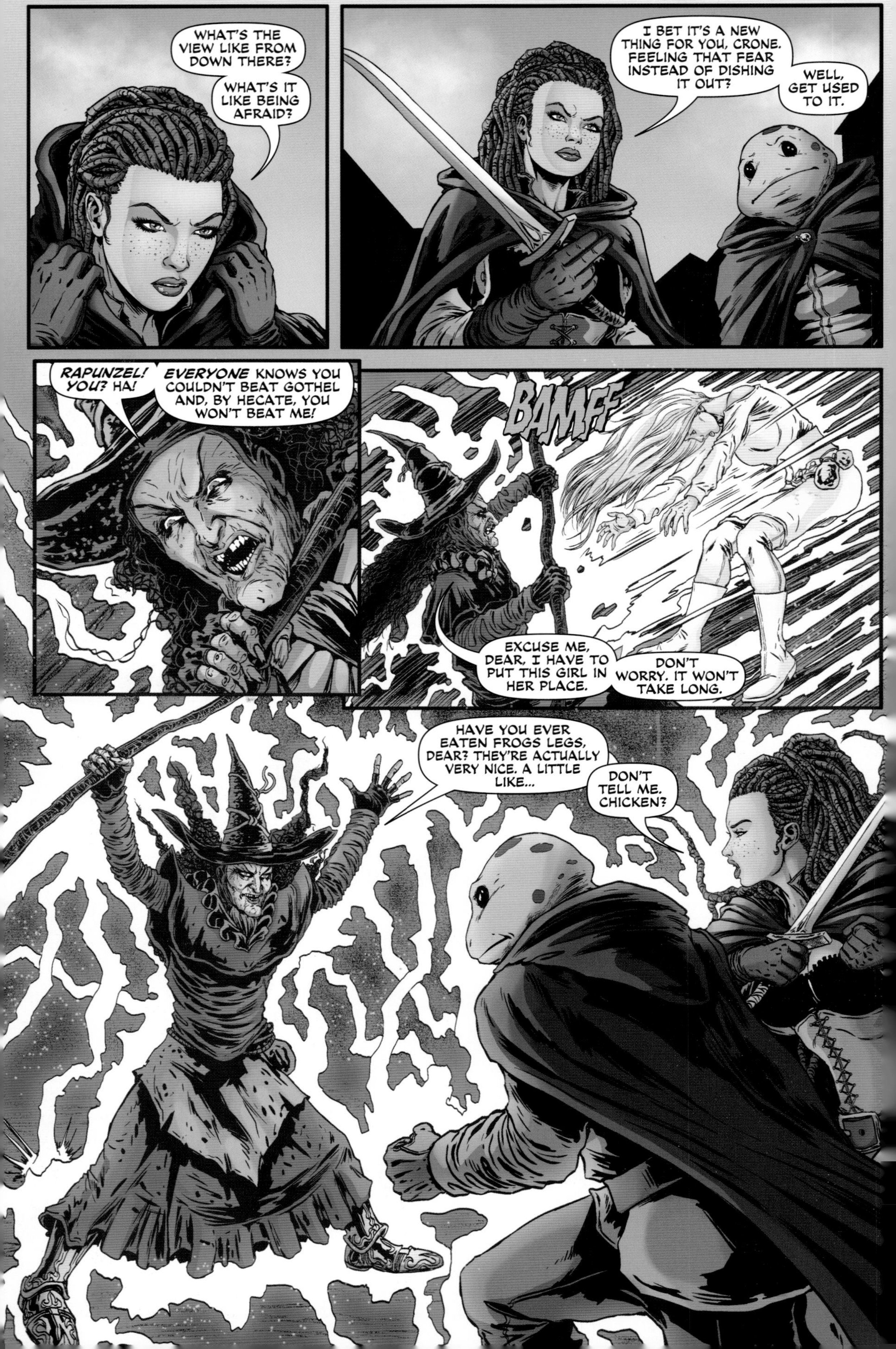
WHAT'S THE VIEW LIKE FROM DOWN THERE?
WHAT'S IT LIKE BEING AFRAID?
I BET IT'S A NEW THING FOR YOU, CRONE. FEELING THAT FEAR INSTEAD OF DISHING IT OUT?
WELL, GET USED TO IT.
RAPUNZEL! YOU? HA!
EVERYONE KNOWS YOU COULDN'T BEAT GOTHEL AND, BY HECATE, YOU *WON'T* BEAT ME!
BAMFF
EXCUSE ME, DEAR, I HAVE TO PUT THIS GIRL IN HER PLACE.
DON'T WORRY. IT WON'T TAKE LONG.
HAVE YOU EVER EATEN FROGS LEGS, DEAR? THEY'RE ACTUALLY VERY NICE. A LITTLE LIKE...
DON'T TELL ME. CHICKEN?

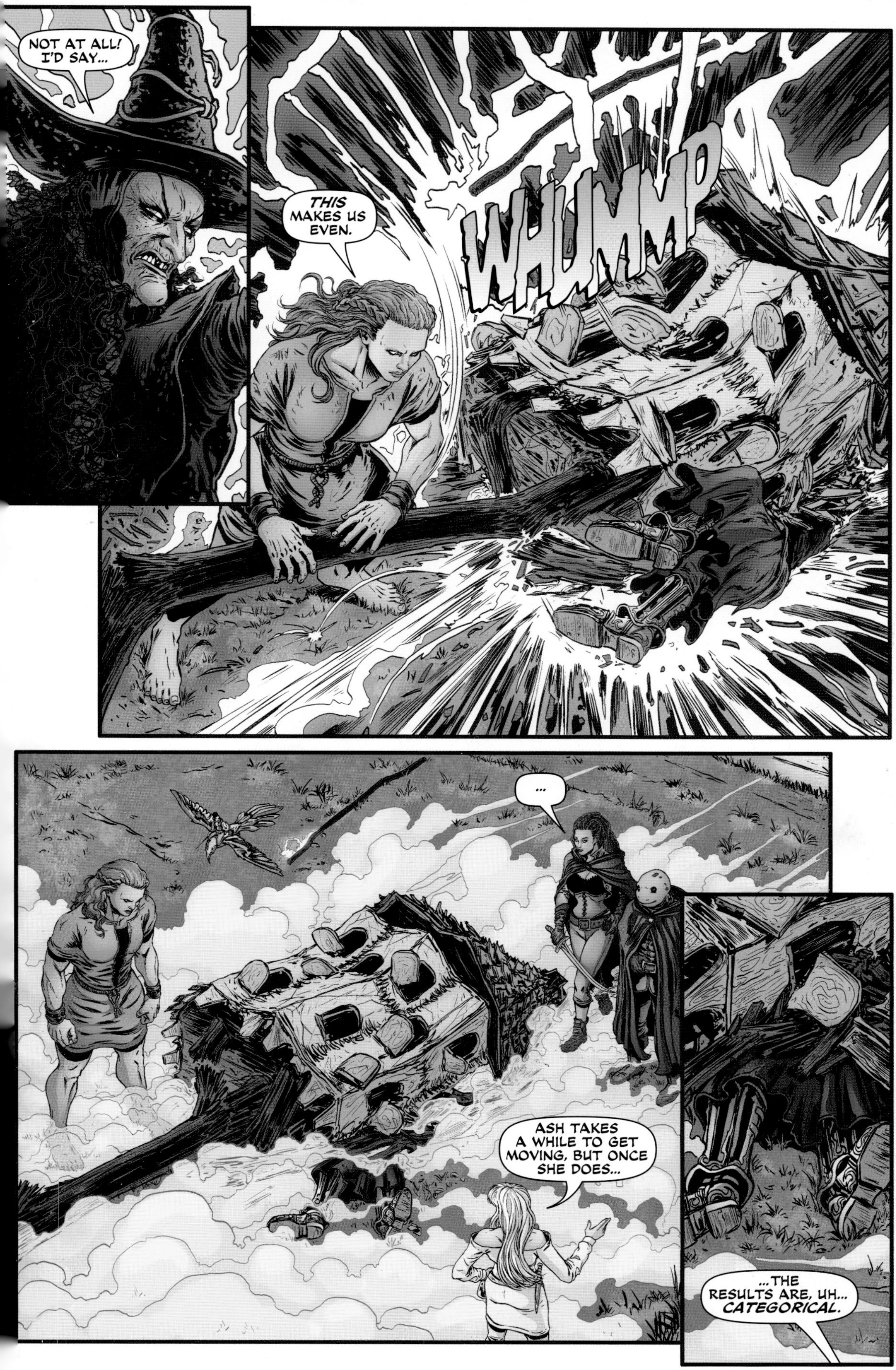
NOT AT ALL! I'D SAY...
THIS MAKES US EVEN.
WHUMMP
...
ASH TAKES A WHILE TO GET MOVING, BUT ONCE SHE DOES...
...THE RESULTS ARE, UH... *CATEGORICAL.*

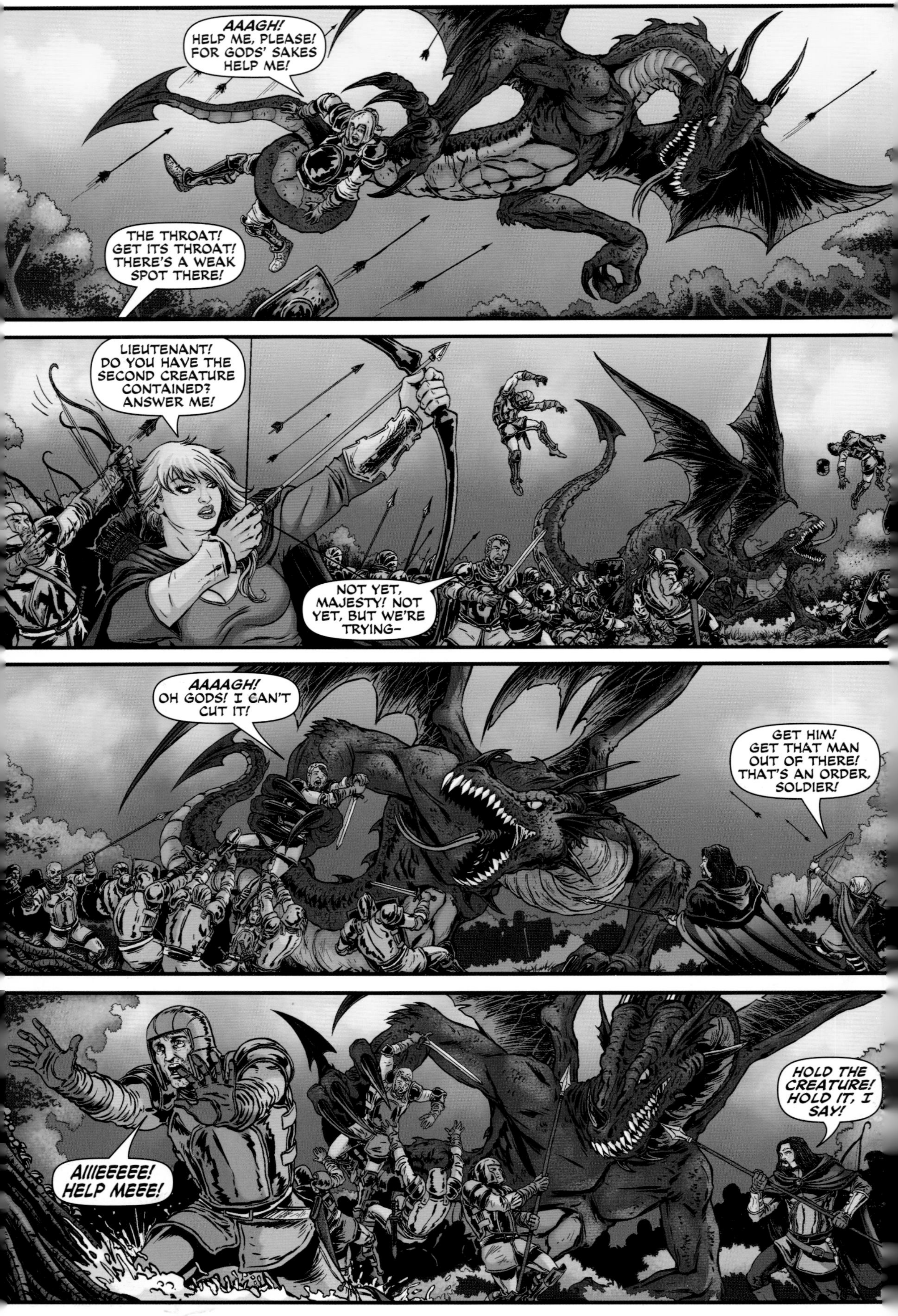

AAAGH! HELP ME, PLEASE! FOR GODS' SAKES HELP ME!
THE THROAT! GET ITS THROAT! THERE'S A WEAK SPOT THERE!
LIEUTENANT! DO YOU HAVE THE SECOND CREATURE CONTAINED? ANSWER ME!
NOT YET, MAJESTY! NOT YET, BUT WE'RE TRYING–
AAAAGH! OH GODS! I CAN'T CUT IT!
GET HIM! GET THAT MAN OUT OF THERE! THAT'S AN ORDER, SOLDIER!
AIIIEEEEE! HELP MEEE!
HOLD THE CREATURE! HOLD IT, I SAY!

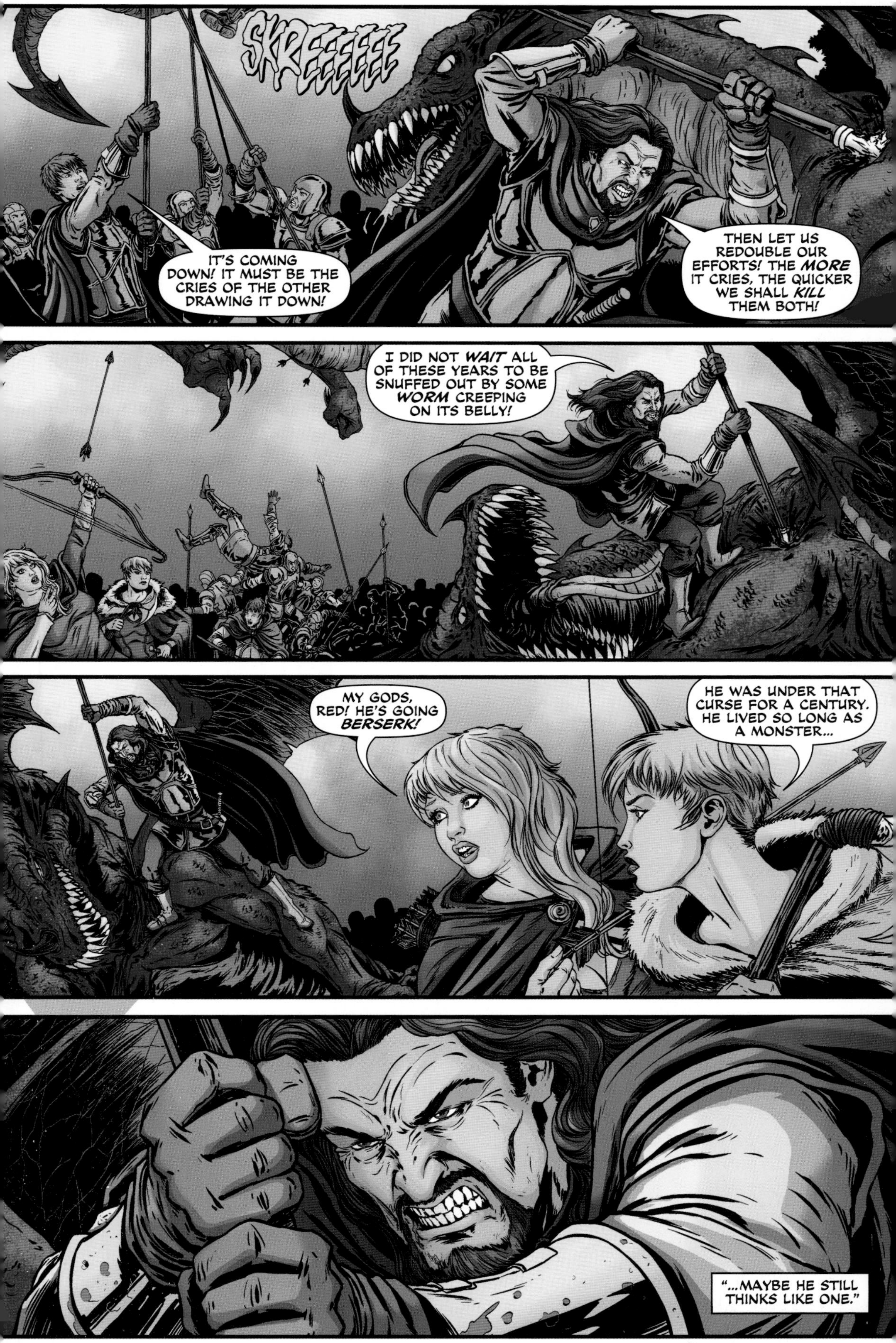
SKREEEEEEE
IT'S COMING DOWN! IT MUST BE THE CRIES OF THE OTHER DRAWING IT DOWN!
THEN LET US REDOUBLE OUR EFFORTS! THE MORE IT CRIES, THE QUICKER WE SHALL KILL THEM BOTH!
I DID NOT WAIT ALL OF THESE YEARS TO BE SNUFFED OUT BY SOME WORM CREEPING ON ITS BELLY!
MY GODS, RED! HE'S GOING BERSERK!
HE WAS UNDER THAT CURSE FOR A CENTURY. HE LIVED SO LONG AS A MONSTER...
"...MAYBE HE STILL THINKS LIKE ONE."

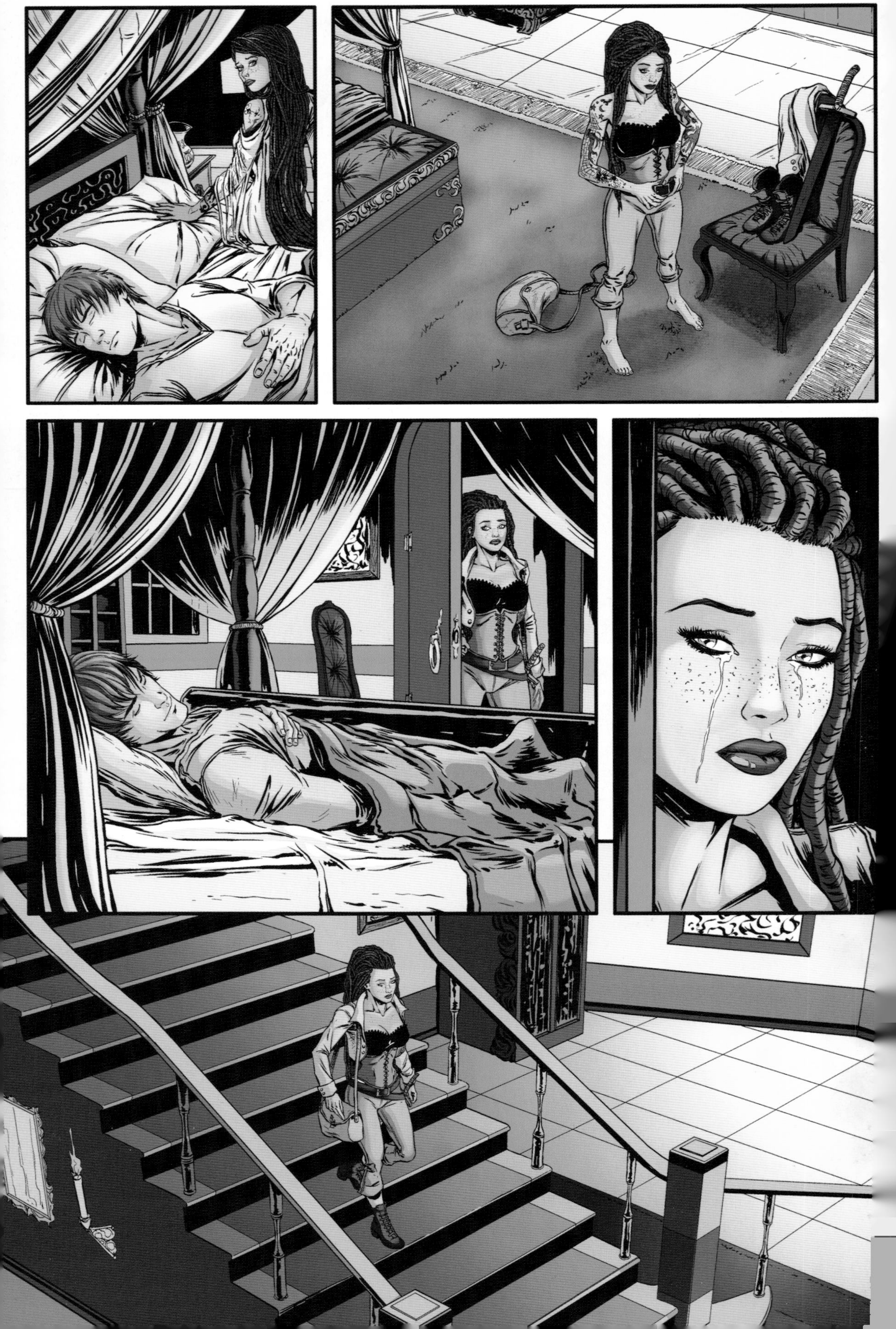

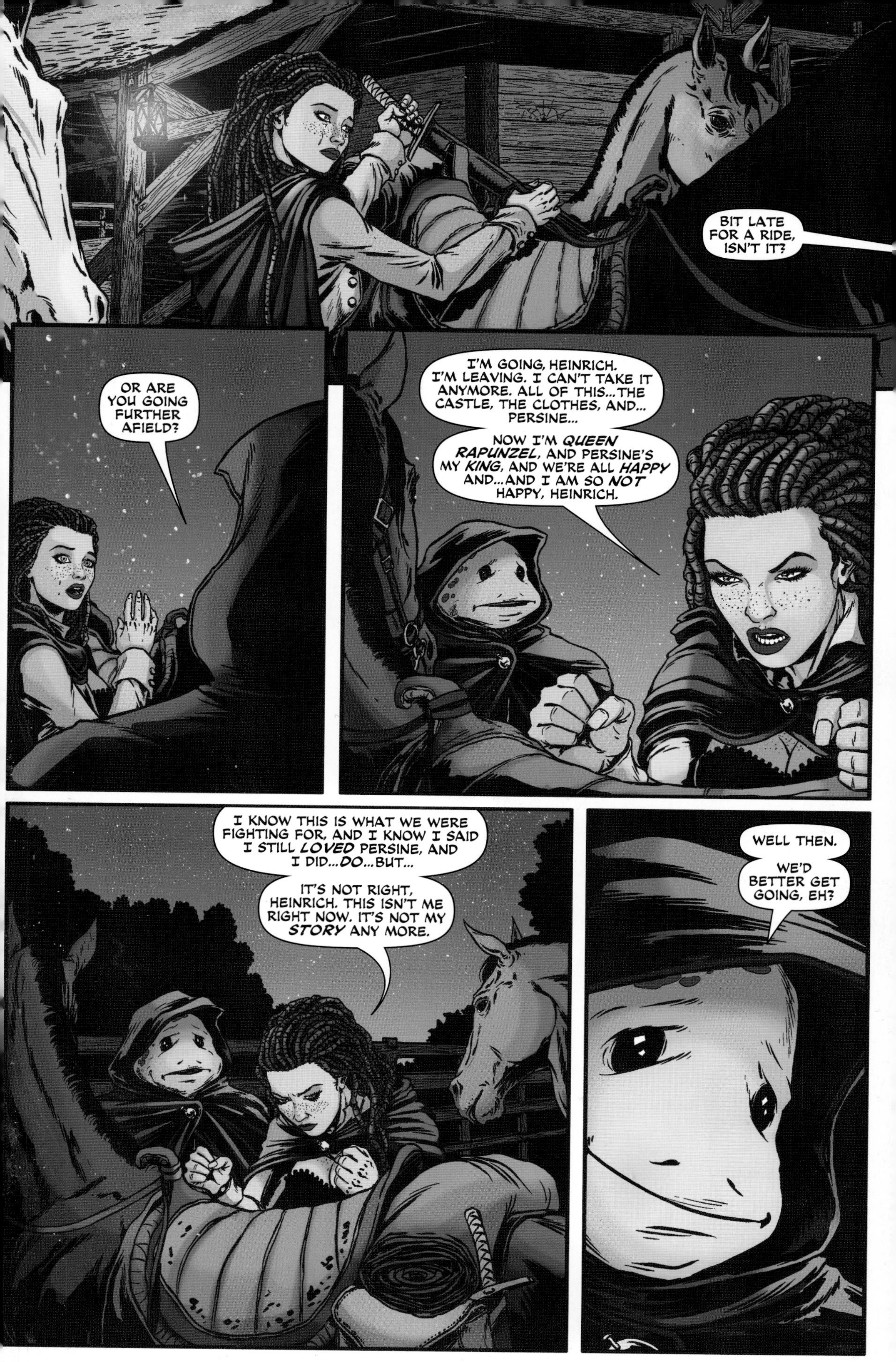
BIT LATE FOR A RIDE, ISN'T IT?
OR ARE YOU GOING FURTHER AFIELD?
I'M GOING, HEINRICH. I'M LEAVING. I CAN'T TAKE IT ANYMORE. ALL OF THIS...THE CASTLE, THE CLOTHES, AND... PERSINE...
NOW I'M *QUEEN RAPUNZEL*, AND PERSINE'S MY *KING*, AND WE'RE ALL *HAPPY* AND...AND I AM SO *NOT* HAPPY, HEINRICH.
I KNOW THIS IS WHAT WE WERE FIGHTING FOR, AND I KNOW I SAID I STILL *LOVED* PERSINE, AND I DID...*DO*...BUT...
IT'S NOT RIGHT, HEINRICH. THIS ISN'T ME RIGHT NOW. IT'S NOT MY *STORY* ANY MORE.
WELL THEN.
WE'D BETTER GET GOING, EH?

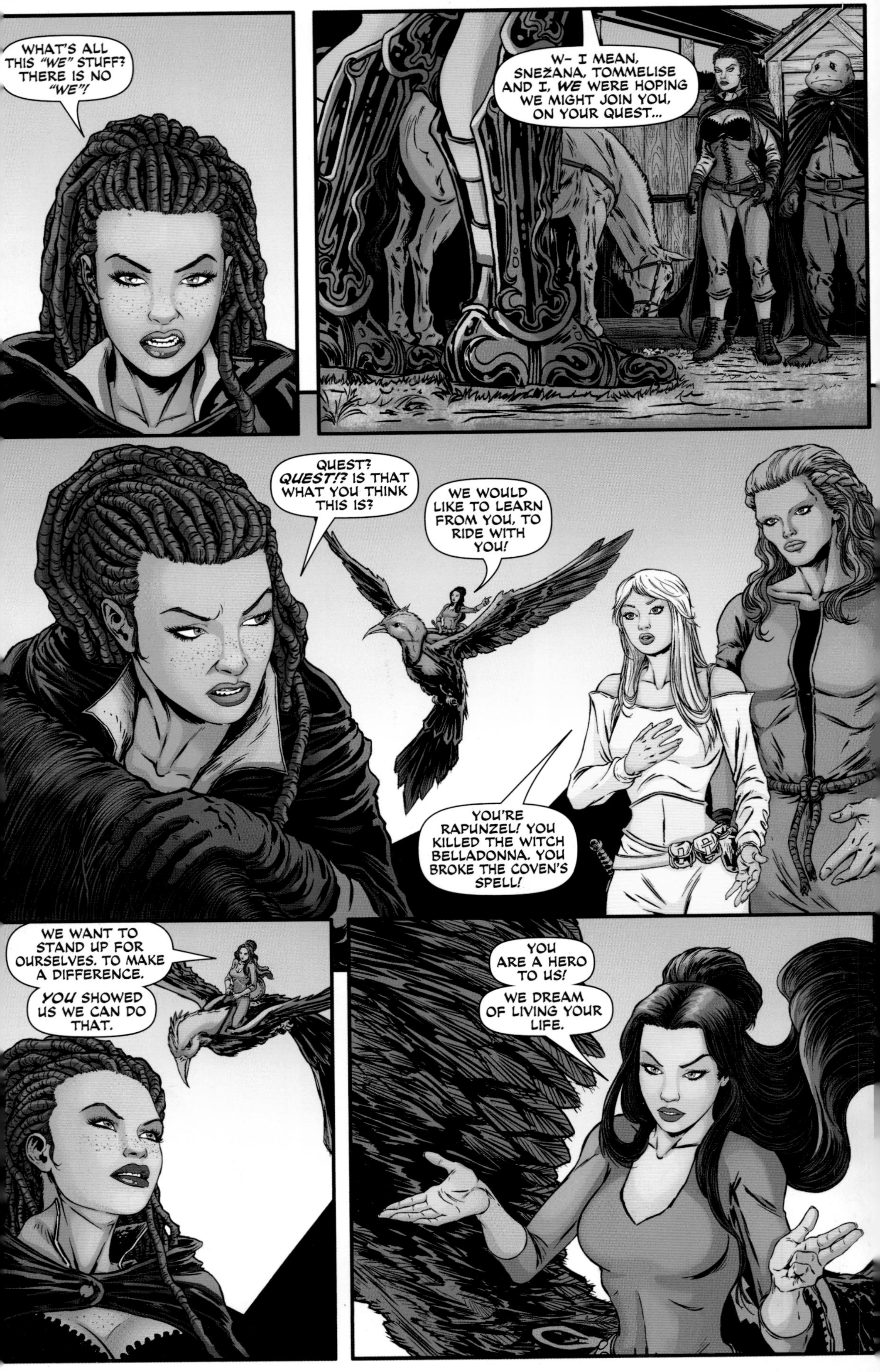
WHAT'S ALL THIS "WE" STUFF? THERE IS NO "WE"!
W- I MEAN, SNEŽANA, TOMMELISE AND I, WE WERE HOPING WE MIGHT JOIN YOU, ON YOUR QUEST...
QUEST? QUEST!? IS THAT WHAT YOU THINK THIS IS?
WE WOULD LIKE TO LEARN FROM YOU, TO RIDE WITH YOU!
YOU'RE RAPUNZEL! YOU KILLED THE WITCH BELLADONNA. YOU BROKE THE COVEN'S SPELL!
WE WANT TO STAND UP FOR OURSELVES. TO MAKE A DIFFERENCE.
YOU SHOWED US WE CAN DO THAT.
YOU ARE A HERO TO US!
WE DREAM OF LIVING YOUR LIFE.

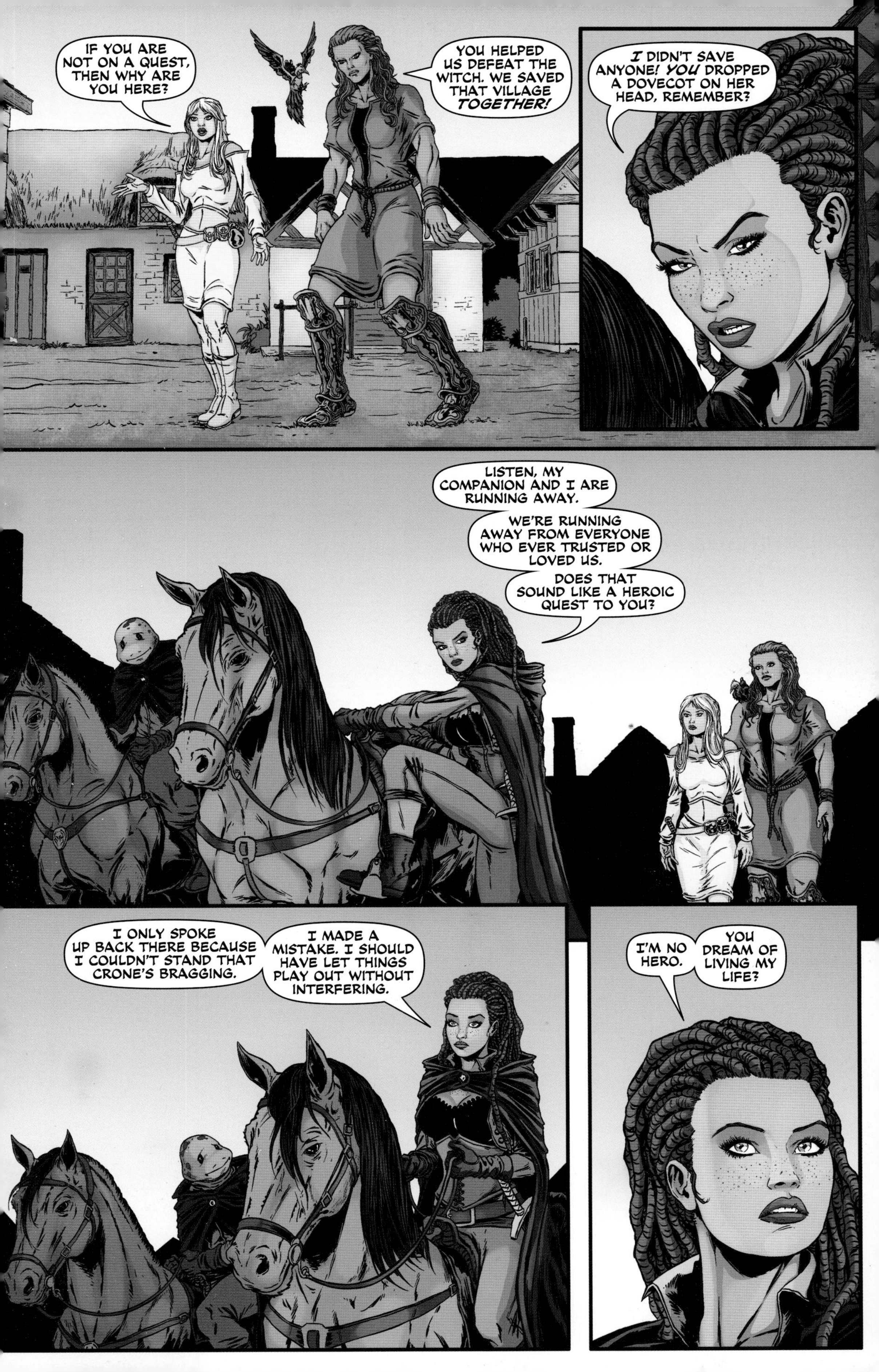
IF YOU ARE NOT ON A QUEST, THEN WHY ARE YOU HERE?
YOU HELPED US DEFEAT THE WITCH. WE SAVED THAT VILLAGE *TOGETHER!*
I DIDN'T SAVE ANYONE! *YOU* DROPPED A DOVECOT ON HER HEAD, REMEMBER?
LISTEN, MY COMPANION AND I ARE RUNNING AWAY.
WE'RE RUNNING AWAY FROM EVERYONE WHO EVER TRUSTED OR LOVED US.
DOES THAT SOUND LIKE A HEROIC QUEST TO YOU?
I ONLY SPOKE UP BACK THERE BECAUSE I COULDN'T STAND THAT CRONE'S BRAGGING.
I MADE A MISTAKE. I SHOULD HAVE LET THINGS PLAY OUT WITHOUT INTERFERING.
I'M NO HERO.
YOU DREAM OF LIVING MY LIFE?

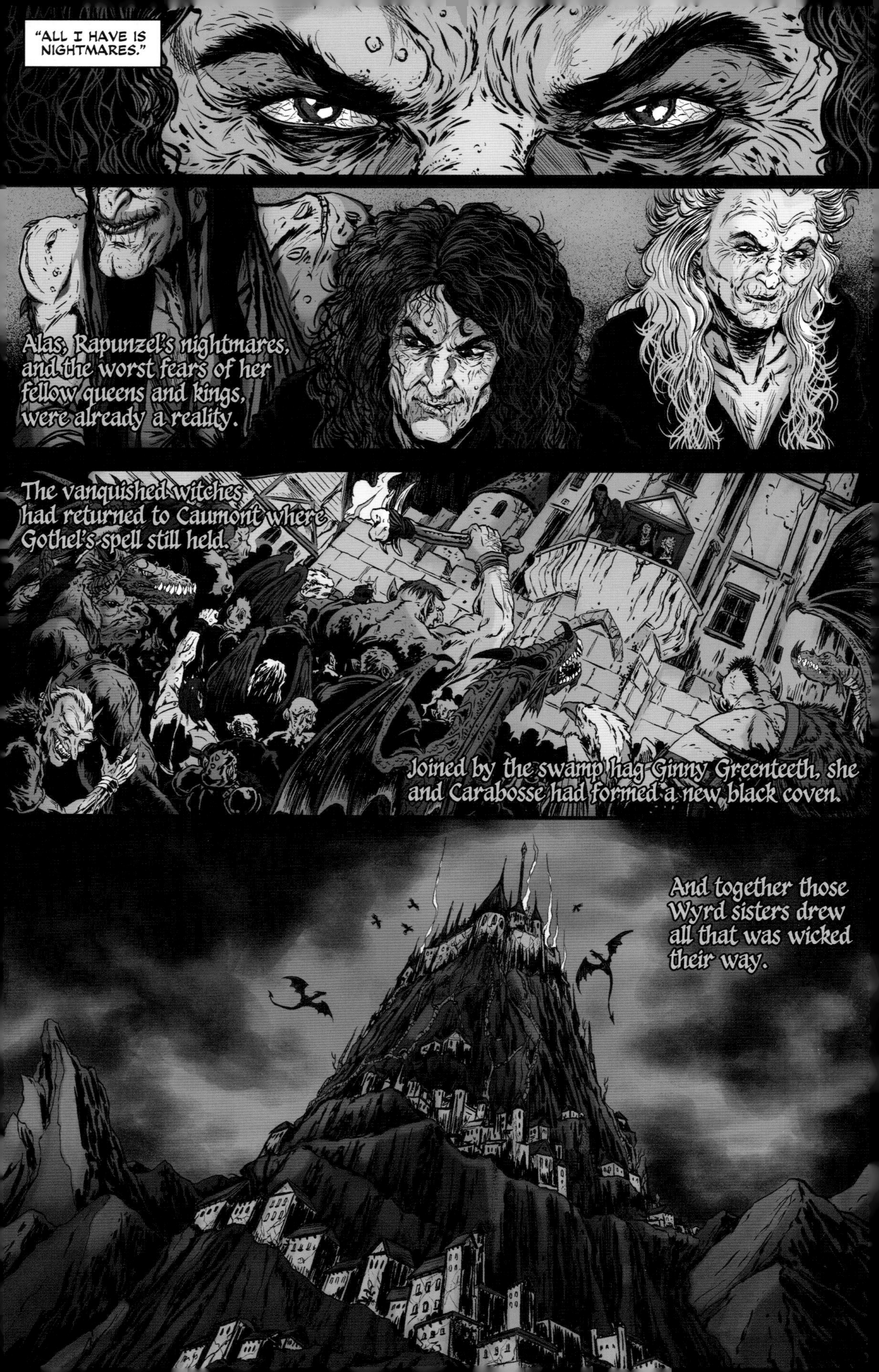
"ALL I HAVE IS NIGHTMARES."
Alas, Rapunzel's nightmares, and the worst fears of her fellow queens and kings, were already a reality.
The vanquished witches had returned to Caumont where Gothel's spell still held.
Joined by the swamp hag Ginny Greenteeth, she and Carabosse had formed a new black coven.
And together those Wyrd sisters drew all that was wicked their way.

Chapter

10

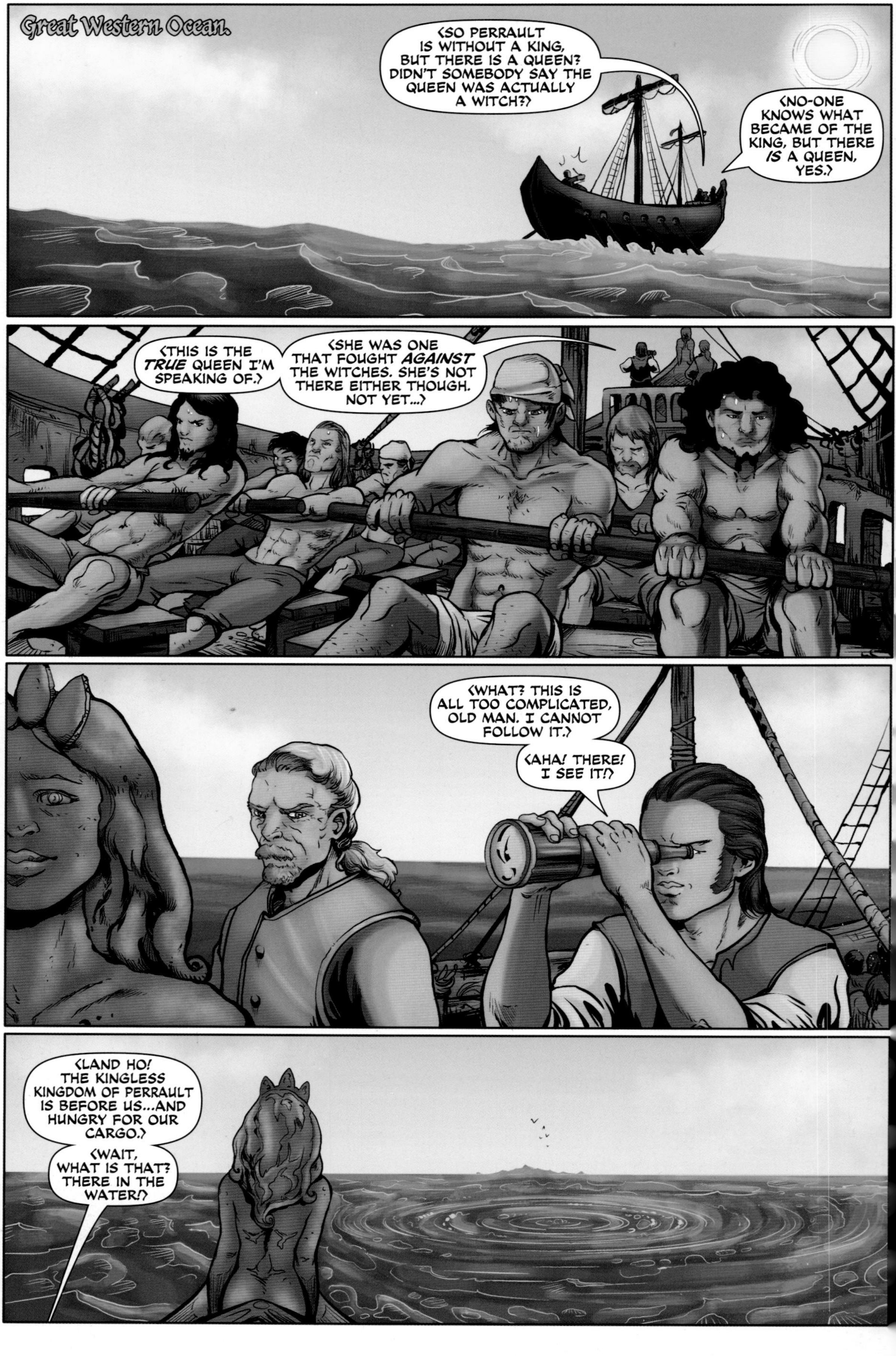
Great Western Ocean.
<SO PERRAULT IS WITHOUT A KING, BUT THERE IS A QUEEN? DIDN'T SOMEBODY SAY THE QUEEN WAS ACTUALLY A WITCH?>
<NO-ONE KNOWS WHAT BECAME OF THE KING, BUT THERE *IS* A QUEEN, YES.>
<THIS IS THE ***TRUE*** QUEEN I'M SPEAKING OF.>
<SHE WAS ONE THAT FOUGHT ***AGAINST*** THE WITCHES. SHE'S NOT THERE EITHER THOUGH. NOT YET...>
<WHAT? THIS IS ALL TOO COMPLICATED, OLD MAN. I CANNOT FOLLOW IT.>
<AHA! THERE! I SEE IT!>
<LAND HO! THE KINGLESS KINGDOM OF PERRAULT IS BEFORE US...AND HUNGRY FOR OUR CARGO.>
<WAIT, WHAT IS THAT? THERE IN THE WATER!>

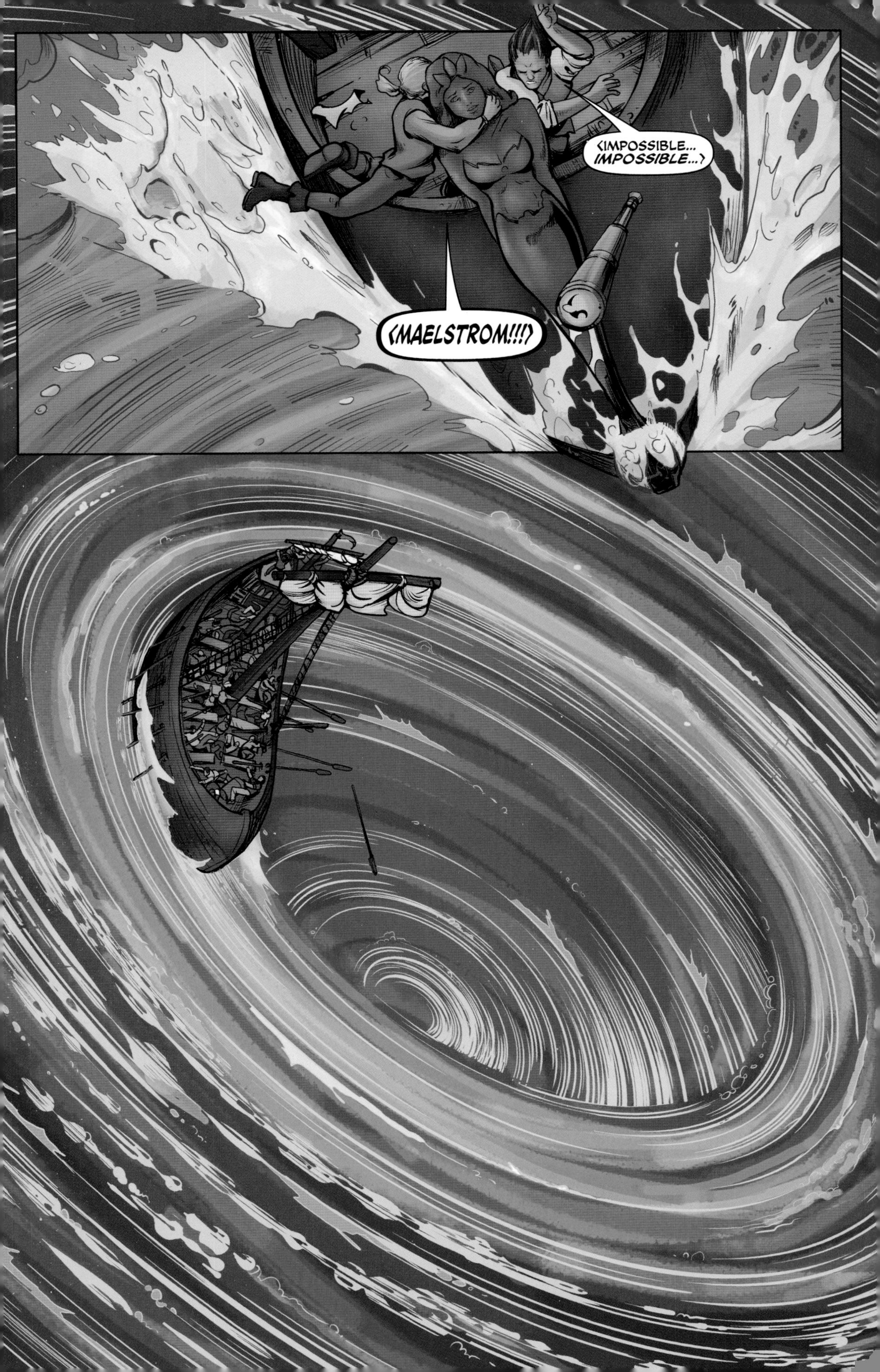
<IMPOSSIBLE... IMPOSSIBLE...>
<MAELSTROM!!!>

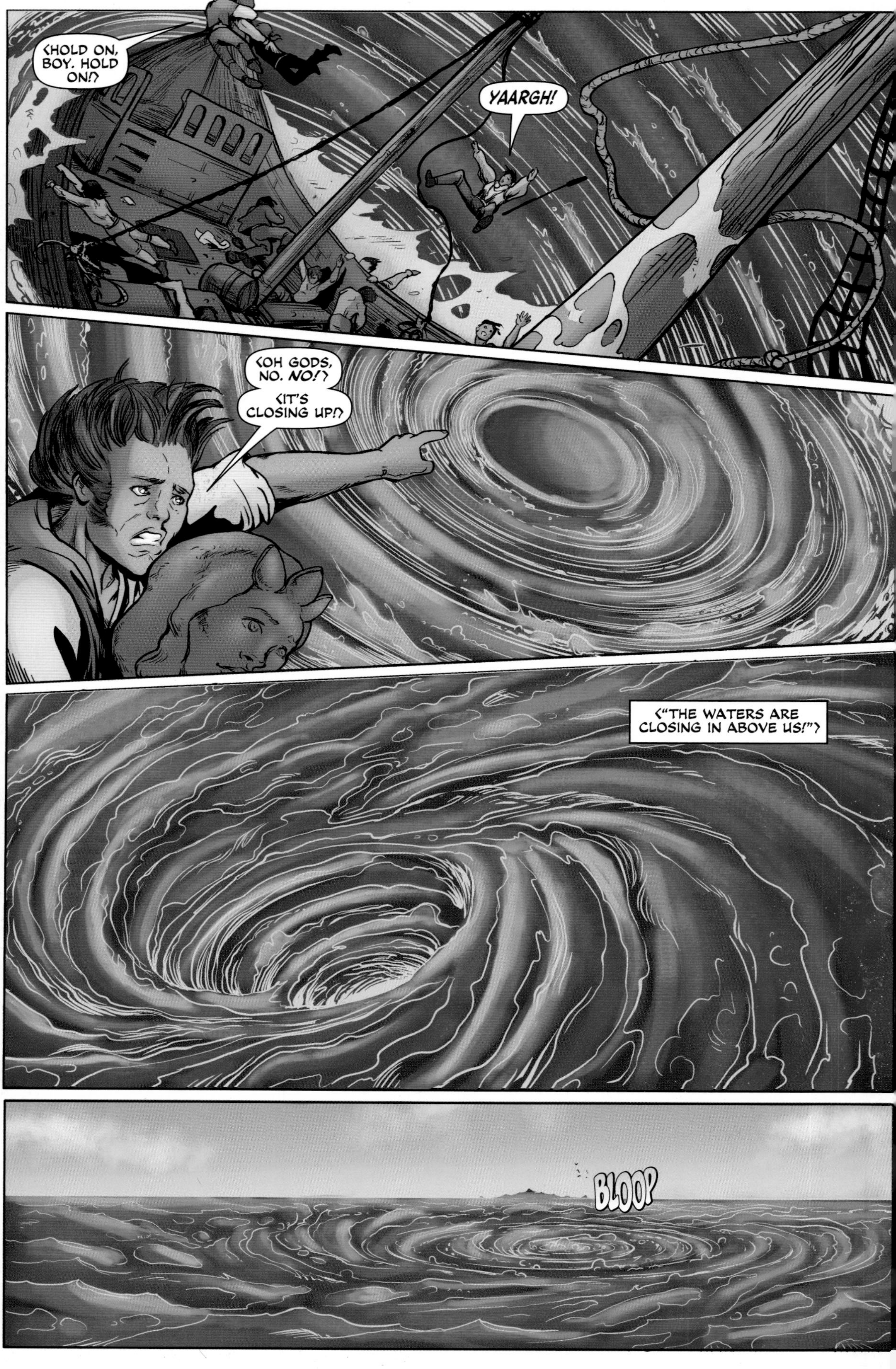

<HOLD ON, BOY. HOLD ON!>
YAARGH!
<OH GODS, NO. NO!>
<IT'S CLOSING UP!>
<"THE WATERS ARE CLOSING IN ABOVE US!">
BLOOP

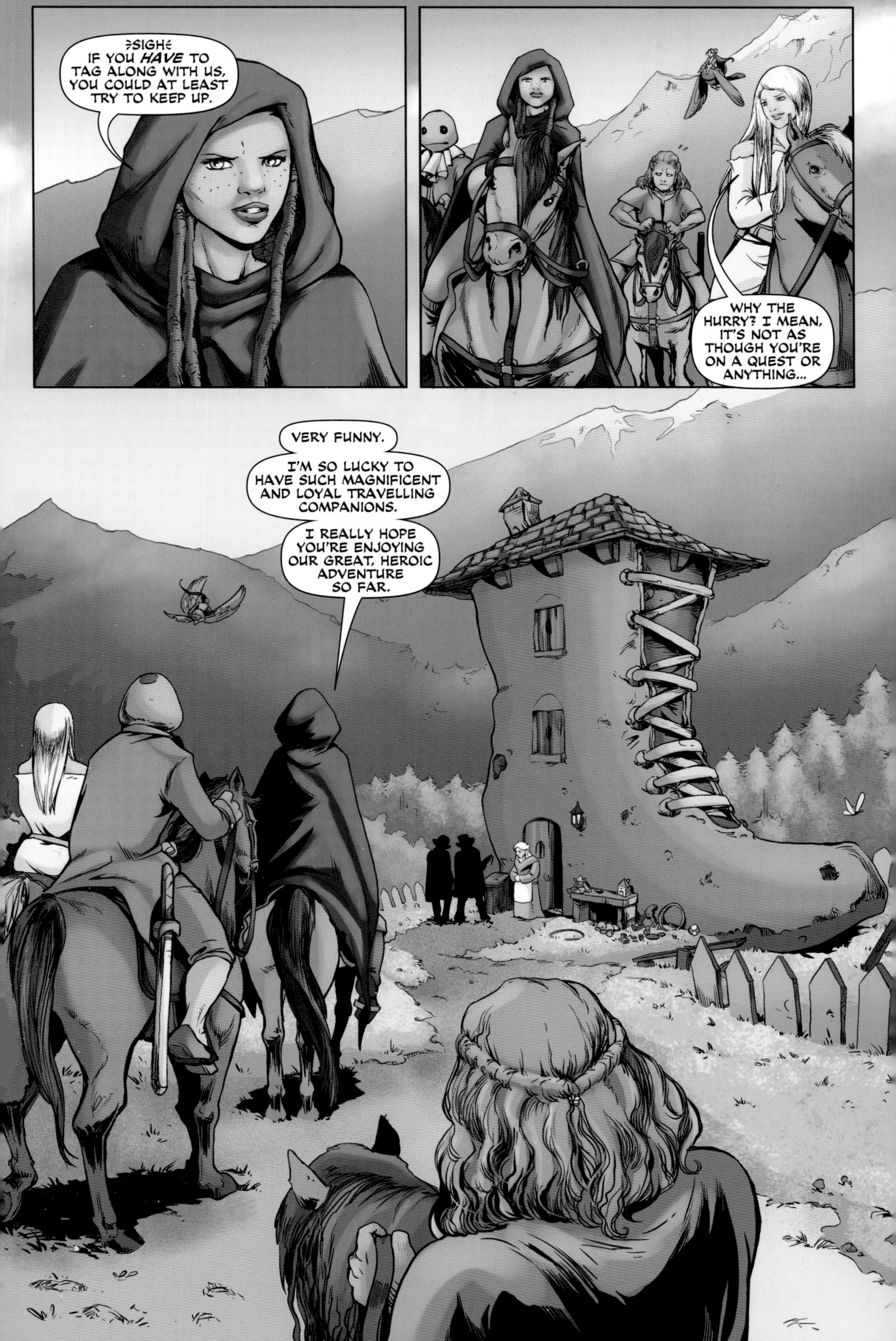

⋟SIGH⋞ IF YOU *HAVE* TO TAG ALONG WITH US, YOU COULD AT LEAST TRY TO KEEP UP.
WHY THE HURRY? I MEAN, IT'S NOT AS THOUGH YOU'RE ON A QUEST OR ANYTHING...
VERY FUNNY.
I'M SO LUCKY TO HAVE SUCH MAGNIFICENT AND LOYAL TRAVELLING COMPANIONS.
I REALLY HOPE YOU'RE ENJOYING OUR GREAT, HEROIC ADVENTURE SO FAR.

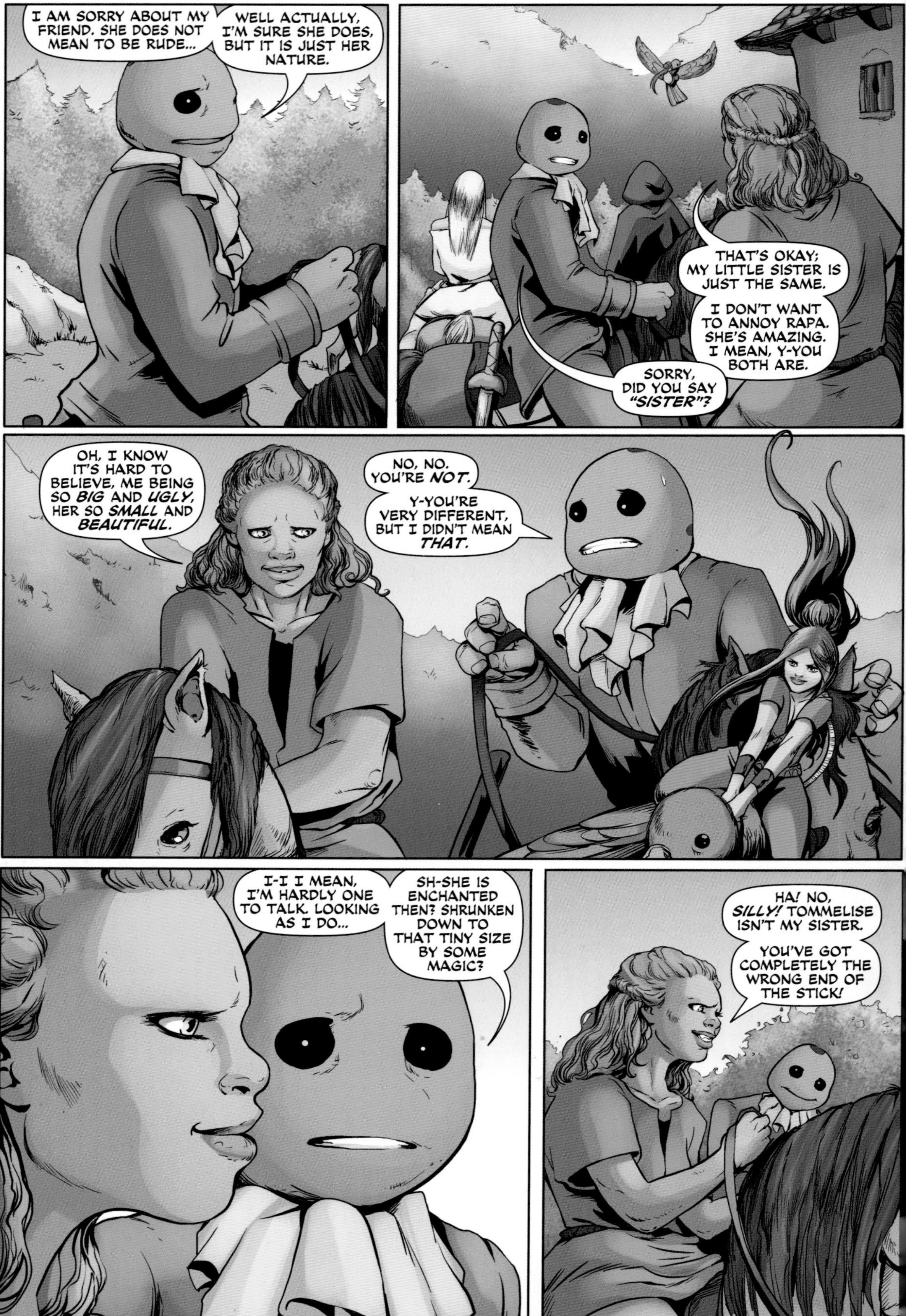
I AM SORRY ABOUT MY FRIEND. SHE DOES NOT MEAN TO BE RUDE...
WELL ACTUALLY, I'M SURE SHE DOES, BUT IT IS JUST HER NATURE.
THAT'S OKAY; MY LITTLE SISTER IS JUST THE SAME.
I DON'T WANT TO ANNOY RAPA. SHE'S AMAZING. I MEAN, Y-YOU BOTH ARE.
SORRY, DID YOU SAY *"SISTER"*?
OH, I KNOW IT'S HARD TO BELIEVE, ME BEING SO *BIG* AND *UGLY*, HER SO *SMALL* AND *BEAUTIFUL*.
NO, NO. YOU'RE *NOT*.
Y-YOU'RE VERY DIFFERENT, BUT I DIDN'T MEAN *THAT*.
I-I I MEAN, I'M HARDLY ONE TO TALK. LOOKING AS I DO...
SH-SHE IS ENCHANTED THEN? SHRUNKEN DOWN TO THAT TINY SIZE BY SOME MAGIC?
HA! NO, *SILLY!* TOMMELISE ISN'T MY SISTER.
YOU'VE GOT COMPLETELY THE WRONG END OF THE STICK!

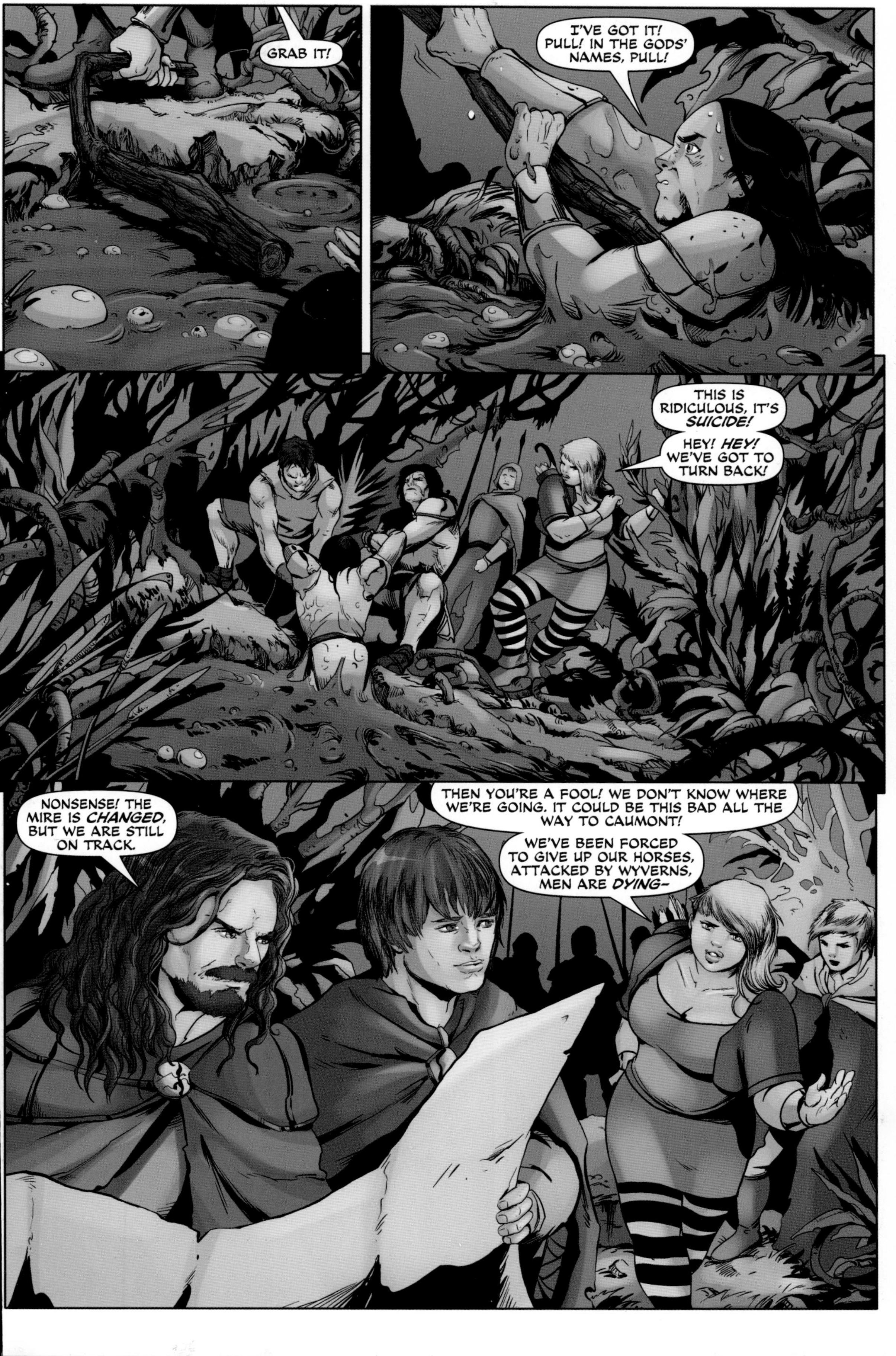
GRAB IT!
I'VE GOT IT! PULL! IN THE GODS' NAMES, PULL!
THIS IS RIDICULOUS, IT'S *SUICIDE!*
HEY! *HEY!* WE'VE GOT TO TURN BACK!
NONSENSE! THE MIRE IS *CHANGED*, BUT WE ARE STILL ON TRACK.
THEN YOU'RE A FOOL! WE DON'T KNOW WHERE WE'RE GOING. IT COULD BE THIS BAD ALL THE WAY TO CAUMONT!
WE'VE BEEN FORCED TO GIVE UP OUR HORSES, ATTACKED BY WYVERNS, MEN ARE *DYING*-

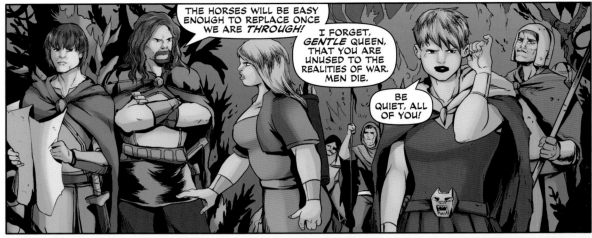

THE HORSES WILL BE EASY ENOUGH TO REPLACE ONCE WE ARE *THROUGH!*

I FORGET, *GENTLE* QUEEN, THAT YOU ARE UNUSED TO THE REALITIES OF WAR. MEN DIE.

BE QUIET, ALL OF YOU!

LISTEN...

WHAT HAVE WE HERE?

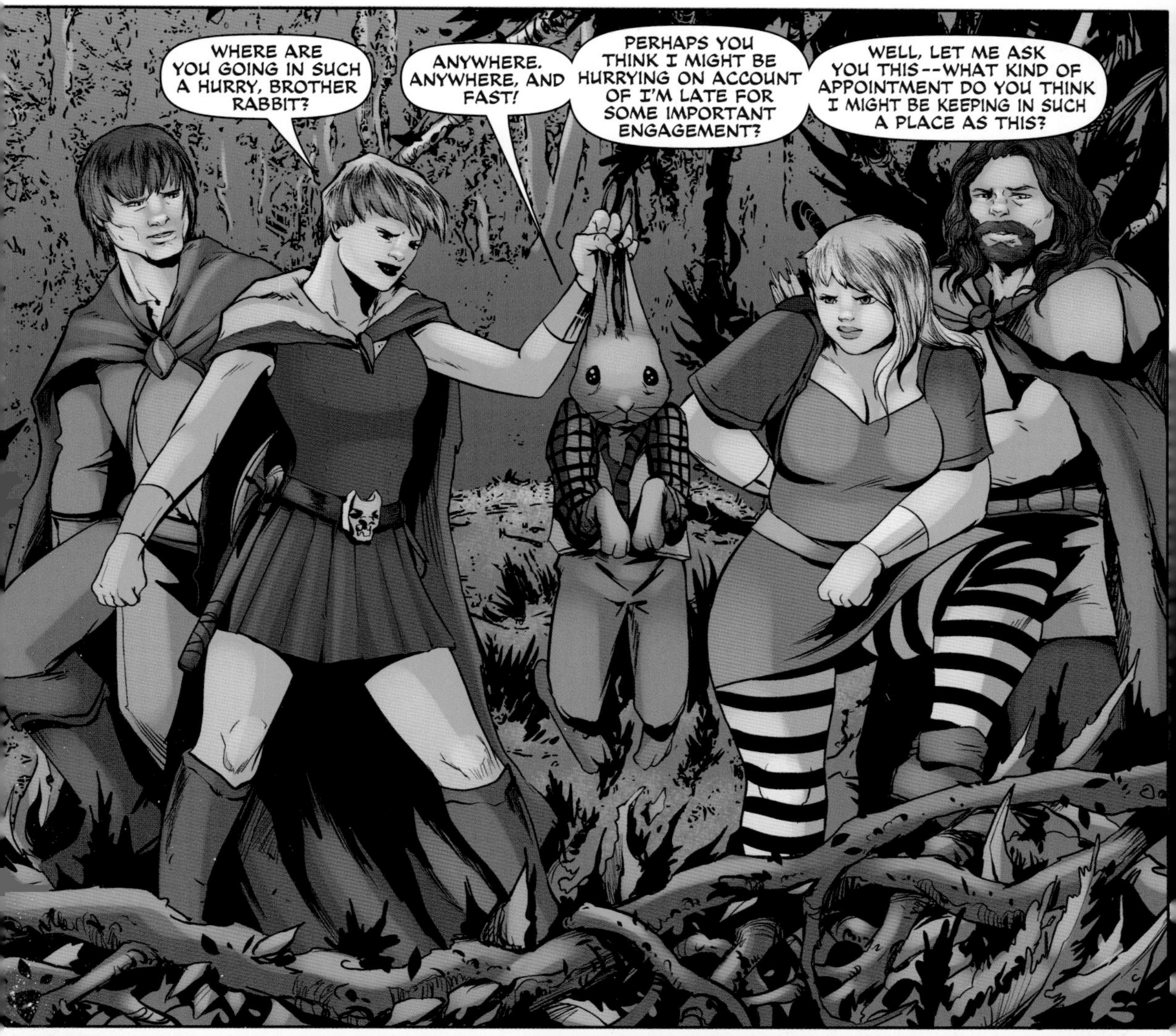
WHERE ARE YOU GOING IN SUCH A HURRY, BROTHER RABBIT?
ANYWHERE. ANYWHERE, AND FAST!
PERHAPS YOU THINK I MIGHT BE HURRYING ON ACCOUNT OF I'M LATE FOR SOME IMPORTANT ENGAGEMENT?
WELL, LET ME ASK YOU THIS--WHAT KIND OF APPOINTMENT DO YOU THINK I MIGHT BE KEEPING IN SUCH A PLACE AS THIS?
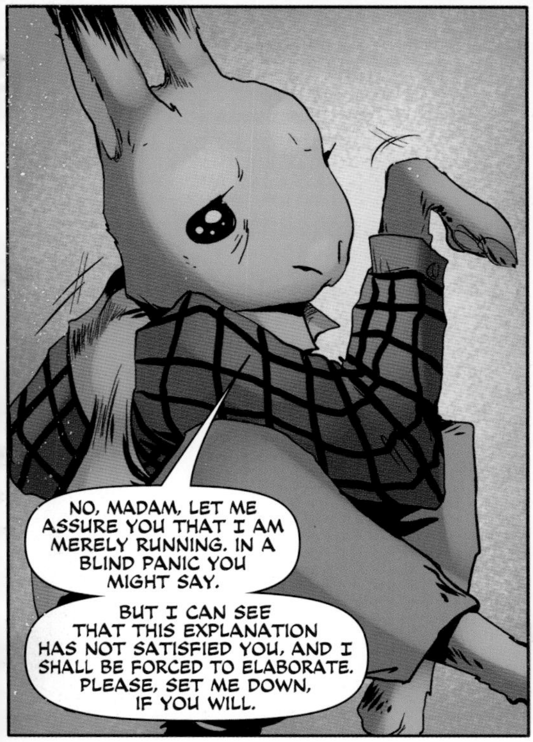
NO, MADAM, LET ME ASSURE YOU THAT I AM MERELY RUNNING. IN A BLIND PANIC YOU MIGHT SAY.
BUT I CAN SEE THAT THIS EXPLANATION HAS NOT SATISFIED YOU, AND I SHALL BE FORCED TO ELABORATE. PLEASE, SET ME DOWN, IF YOU WILL.
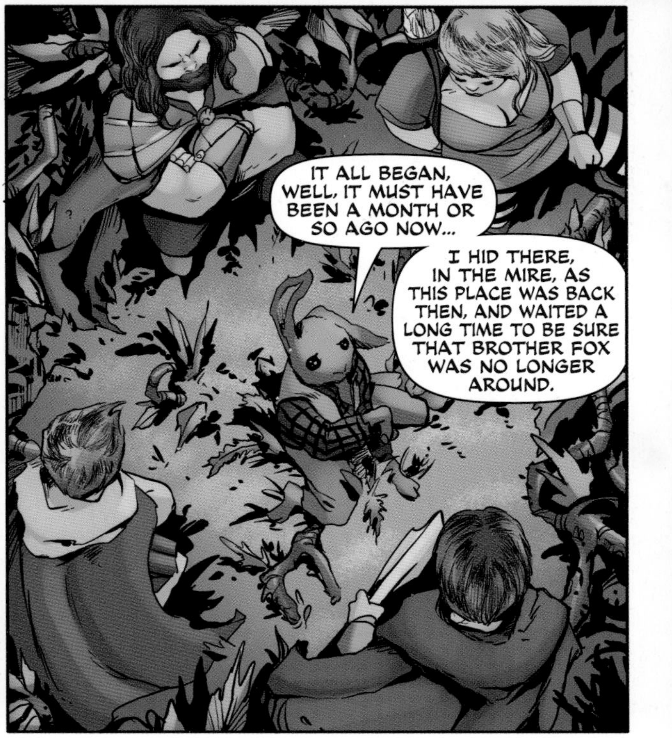
IT ALL BEGAN, WELL, IT MUST HAVE BEEN A MONTH OR SO AGO NOW...
I HID THERE, IN THE MIRE, AS THIS PLACE WAS BACK THEN, AND WAITED A LONG TIME TO BE SURE THAT BROTHER FOX WAS NO LONGER AROUND.

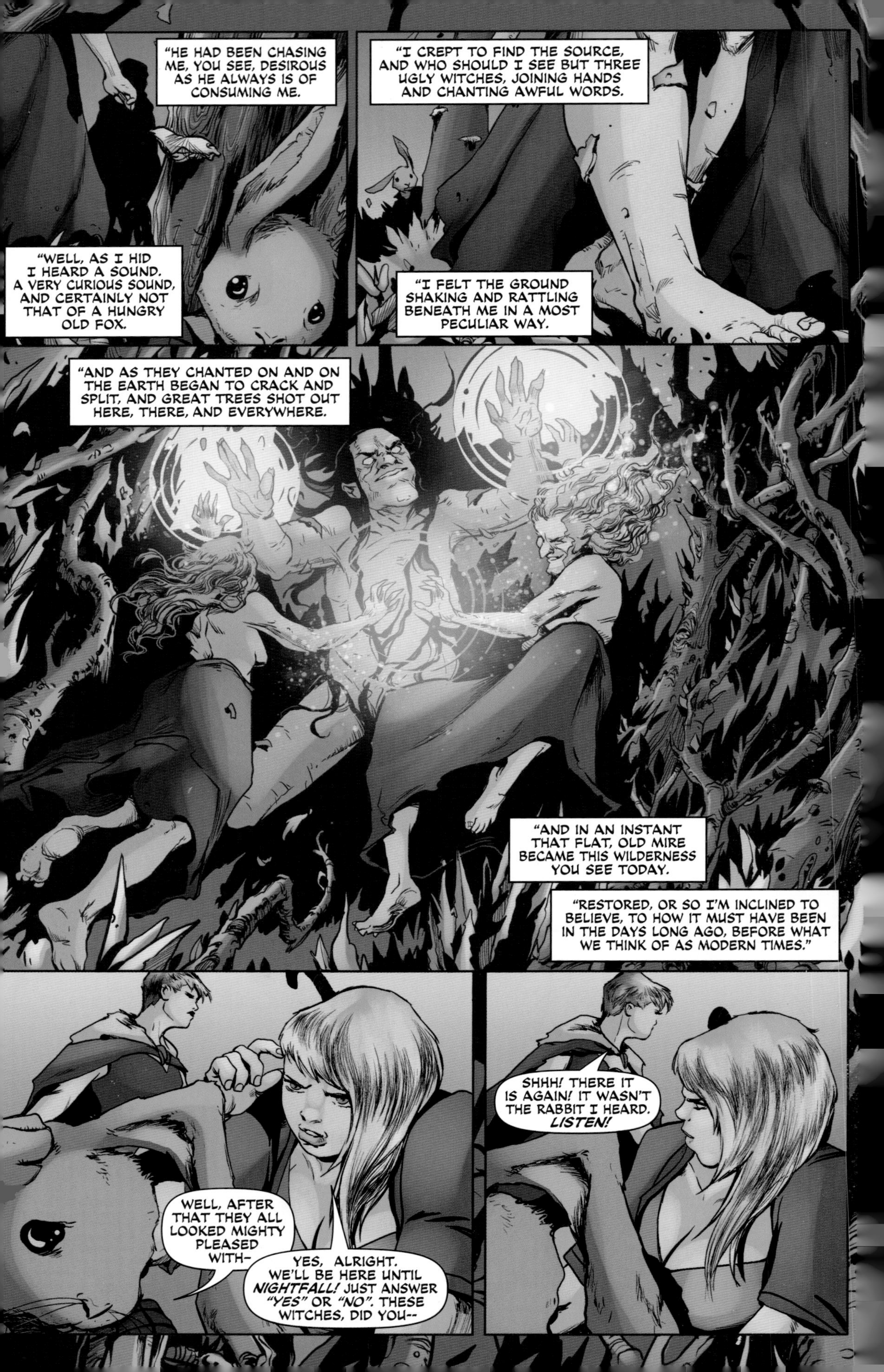

"HE HAD BEEN CHASING ME, YOU SEE, DESIROUS AS HE ALWAYS IS OF CONSUMING ME.
"WELL, AS I HID I HEARD A SOUND. A VERY CURIOUS SOUND, AND CERTAINLY NOT THAT OF A HUNGRY OLD FOX.
"I CREPT TO FIND THE SOURCE, AND WHO SHOULD I SEE BUT THREE UGLY WITCHES, JOINING HANDS AND CHANTING AWFUL WORDS.
"I FELT THE GROUND SHAKING AND RATTLING BENEATH ME IN A MOST PECULIAR WAY.
"AND AS THEY CHANTED ON AND ON THE EARTH BEGAN TO CRACK AND SPLIT, AND GREAT TREES SHOT OUT HERE, THERE, AND EVERYWHERE.
"AND IN AN INSTANT THAT FLAT, OLD MIRE BECAME THIS WILDERNESS YOU SEE TODAY.
"RESTORED, OR SO I'M INCLINED TO BELIEVE, TO HOW IT MUST HAVE BEEN IN THE DAYS LONG AGO, BEFORE WHAT WE THINK OF AS MODERN TIMES."
WELL, AFTER THAT THEY ALL LOOKED MIGHTY PLEASED WITH–
YES, ALRIGHT. WE'LL BE HERE UNTIL *NIGHTFALL!* JUST ANSWER *"YES"* OR *"NO"*. THESE WITCHES, DID YOU--
SHHH! THERE IT IS AGAIN! IT WASN'T THE RABBIT I HEARD. *LISTEN!*

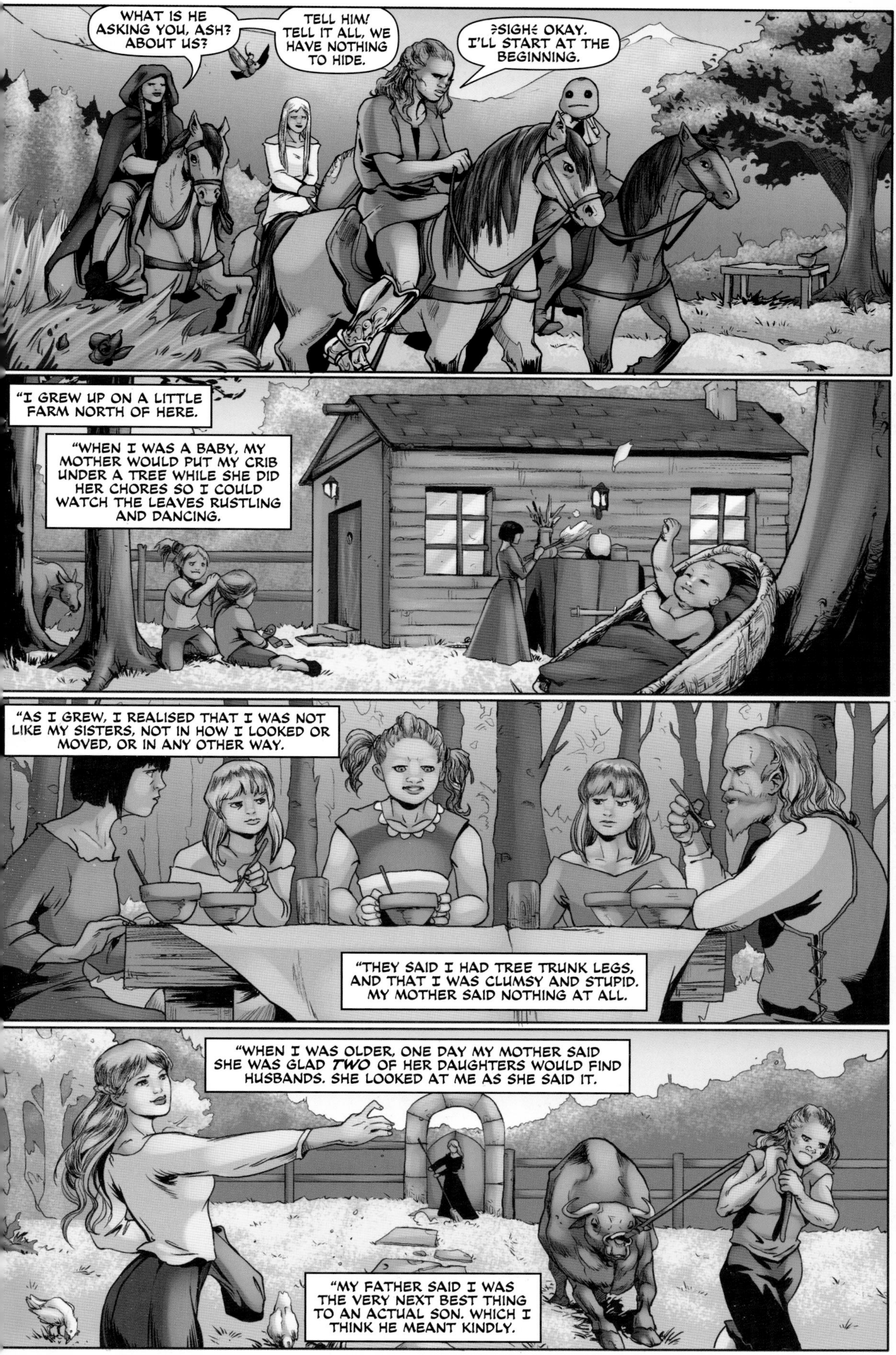
WHAT IS HE ASKING YOU, ASH? ABOUT US?
TELL HIM! TELL IT ALL, WE HAVE NOTHING TO HIDE.
ᗒSIGHᗕ OKAY. I'LL START AT THE BEGINNING.
"I GREW UP ON A LITTLE FARM NORTH OF HERE.
"WHEN I WAS A BABY, MY MOTHER WOULD PUT MY CRIB UNDER A TREE WHILE SHE DID HER CHORES SO I COULD WATCH THE LEAVES RUSTLING AND DANCING.
"AS I GREW, I REALISED THAT I WAS NOT LIKE MY SISTERS, NOT IN HOW I LOOKED OR MOVED, OR IN ANY OTHER WAY.
"THEY SAID I HAD TREE TRUNK LEGS, AND THAT I WAS CLUMSY AND STUPID. MY MOTHER SAID NOTHING AT ALL.
"WHEN I WAS OLDER, ONE DAY MY MOTHER SAID SHE WAS GLAD *TWO* OF HER DAUGHTERS WOULD FIND HUSBANDS. SHE LOOKED AT ME AS SHE SAID IT.
"MY FATHER SAID I WAS THE VERY NEXT BEST THING TO AN ACTUAL SON. WHICH I THINK HE MEANT KINDLY.

"EVENTUALLY, WORRIED I WOULD NEVER STOP GETTING LARGER AND UGLIER, MOTHER TOOK ME TO A WISE WOMAN.

SHE LAUGHED. IT WAS OBVIOUS I WAS 'HILDEBRAN', A CHANGELING CHILD LEFT BY TROLLS.

"SHE SAID SHE WOULD SUMMON THEM, THEN THEY COULD TRADE ME FOR THEIR REAL DAUGHTER.

"WHEN THEY SAW ME, THE TROLLS AGREED I WAS THEIRS.

"BUT THEY TOLD MY PARENTS THEIR BABY HAD BEEN LOST.

"AND, AS THEY COULD NOT EXCHANGE US, THE TROLLS SAID MY PARENTS SHOULD KEEP ME. I WOULD BE USEFUL, THEY SAID.

"I SLEPT IN THE ASHES OF THE FIRE FROM THEN ON.

"THEIR CHILD NO LONGER, A MERE BEAST OF BURDEN.

"STILL, I DID MY BEST FOR THEM, I WORKED HARD.

"AND EVERY NIGHT, I CRIED MYSELF TO SLEEP AMONG THE CINDERS."

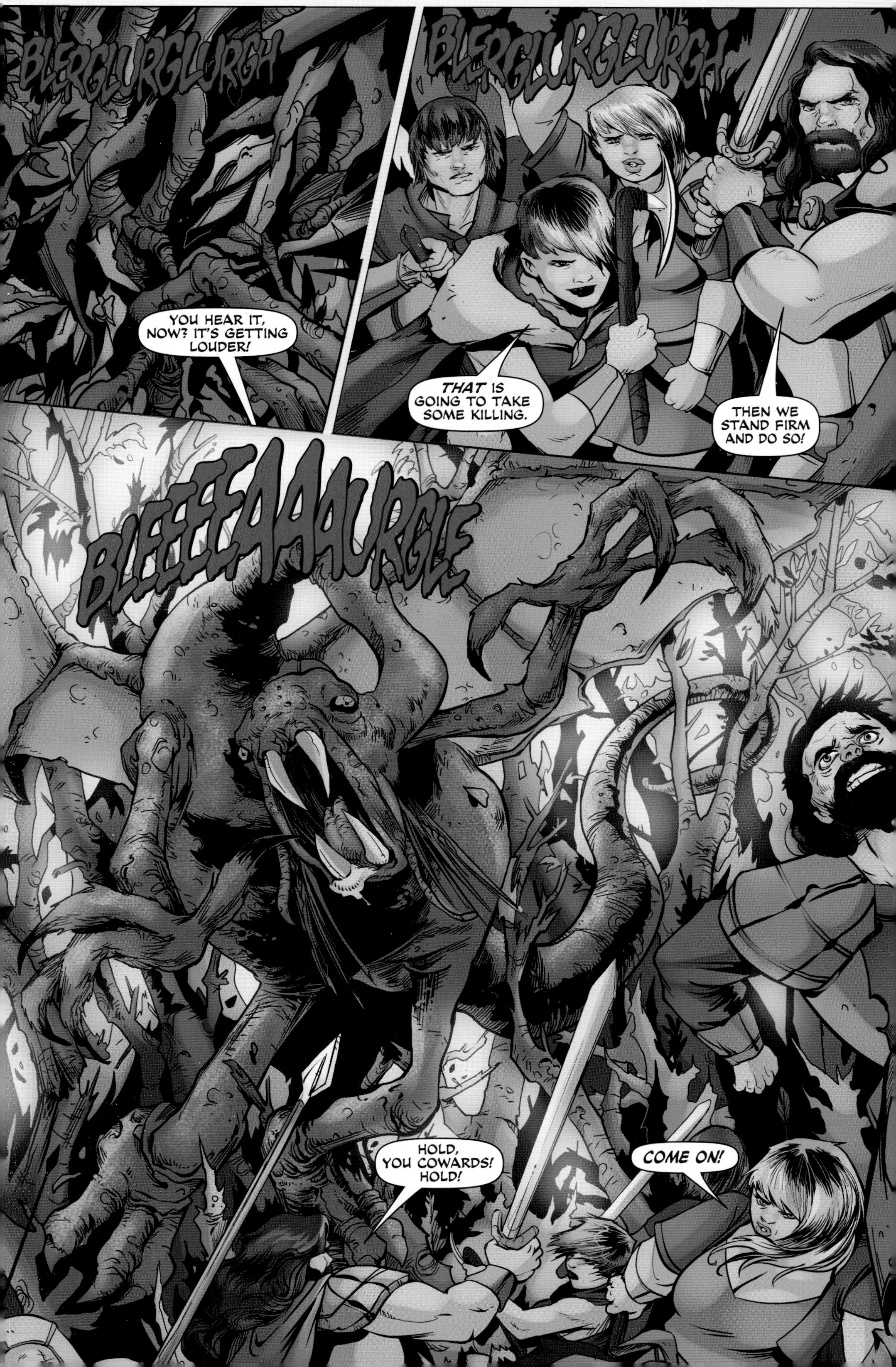
BLERGLURGLURGH
YOU HEAR IT, NOW? IT'S GETTING LOUDER!
BLERGLURGLURGH
THAT IS GOING TO TAKE SOME KILLING.
THEN WE STAND FIRM AND DO SO!
BLEEEEAAAAURGLE
HOLD, YOU COWARDS! HOLD!
COME ON!

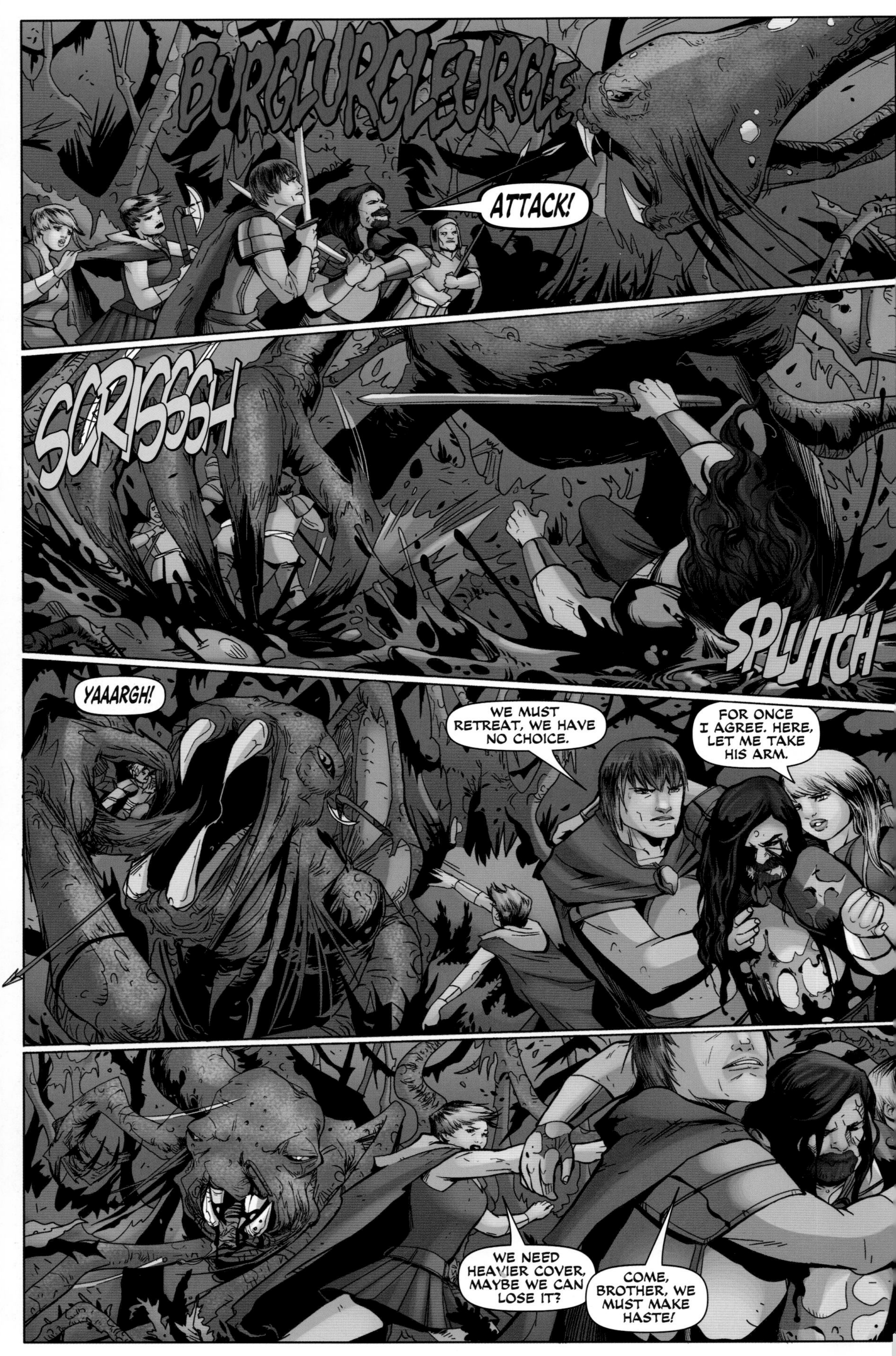
BURGLURGLEURGLE
ATTACK!
SCRISSSH
SPLUTCH
YAAARGH!
WE MUST RETREAT, WE HAVE NO CHOICE.
FOR ONCE I AGREE. HERE, LET ME TAKE HIS ARM.
WE NEED HEAVIER COVER, MAYBE WE CAN LOSE IT?
COME, BROTHER, WE MUST MAKE HASTE!

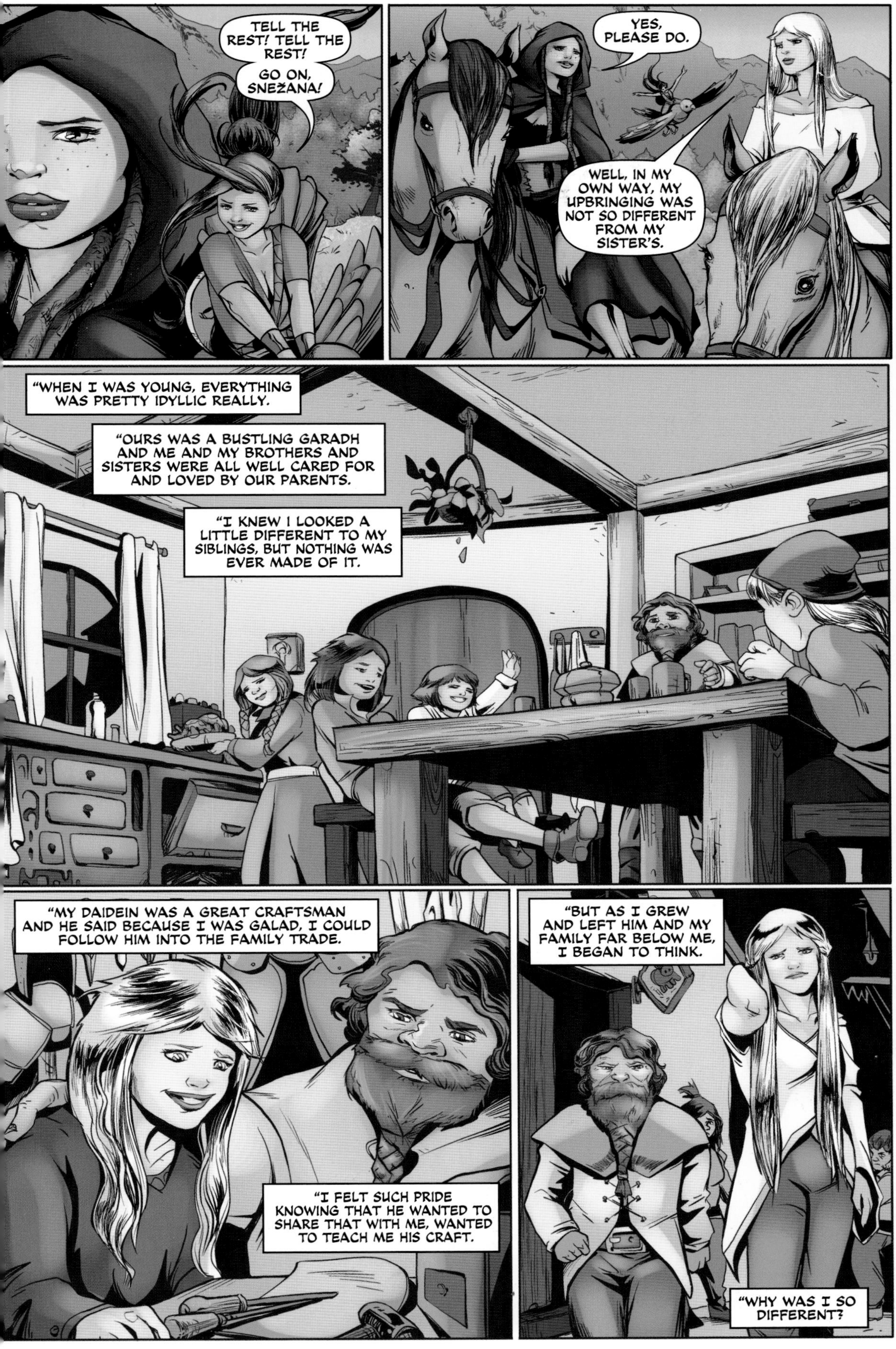
TELL THE REST! TELL THE REST!
GO ON, SNEŽANA!
YES, PLEASE DO.
WELL, IN MY OWN WAY, MY UPBRINGING WAS NOT SO DIFFERENT FROM MY SISTER'S.
"WHEN I WAS YOUNG, EVERYTHING WAS PRETTY IDYLLIC REALLY.
"OURS WAS A BUSTLING GARADH AND ME AND MY BROTHERS AND SISTERS WERE ALL WELL CARED FOR AND LOVED BY OUR PARENTS.
"I KNEW I LOOKED A LITTLE DIFFERENT TO MY SIBLINGS, BUT NOTHING WAS EVER MADE OF IT.
"MY DAIDEIN WAS A GREAT CRAFTSMAN AND HE SAID BECAUSE I WAS GALAD, I COULD FOLLOW HIM INTO THE FAMILY TRADE.
"I FELT SUCH PRIDE KNOWING THAT HE WANTED TO SHARE THAT WITH ME, WANTED TO TEACH ME HIS CRAFT.
"BUT AS I GREW AND LEFT HIM AND MY FAMILY FAR BELOW ME, I BEGAN TO THINK.
"WHY WAS I SO DIFFERENT?

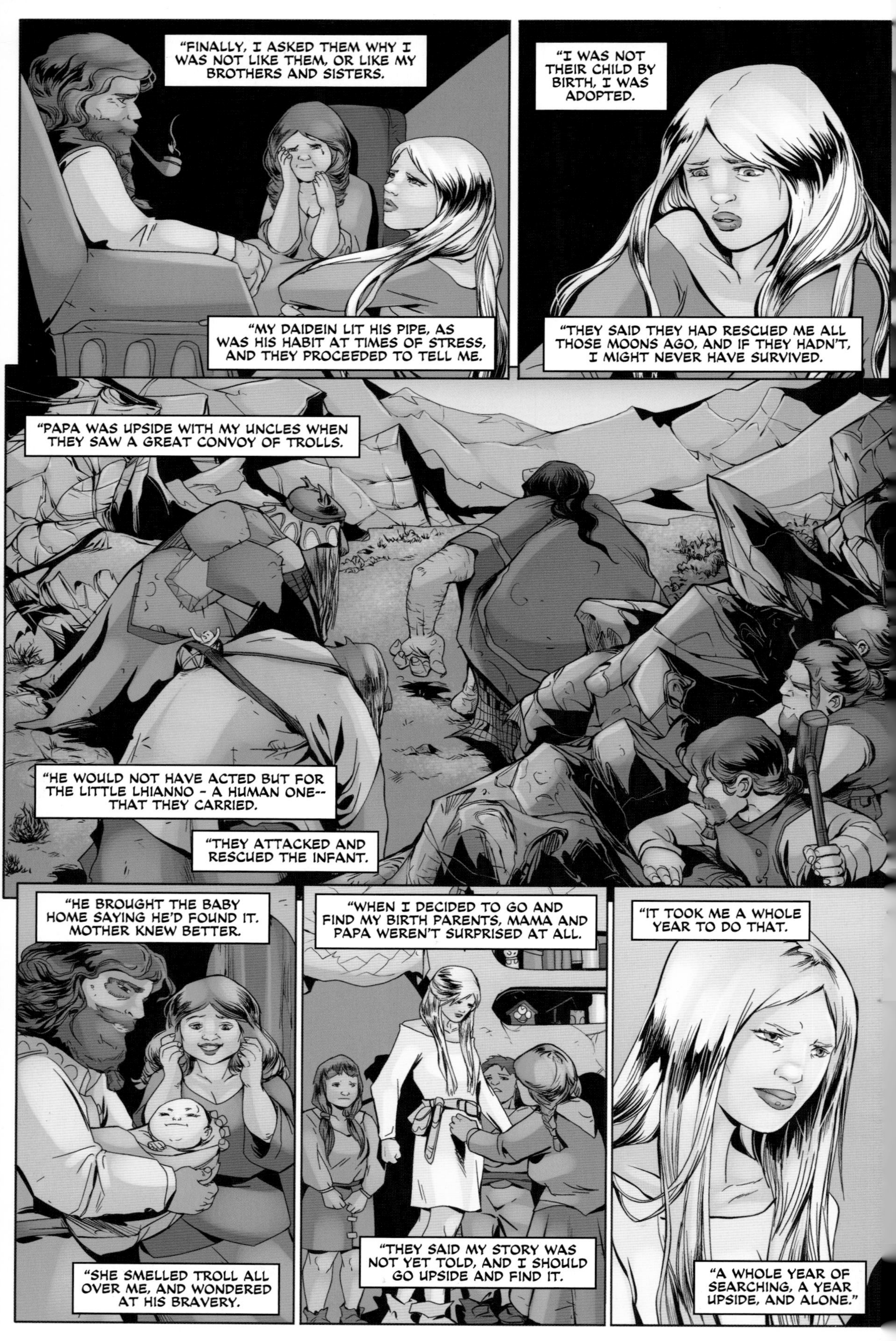
"FINALLY, I ASKED THEM WHY I WAS NOT LIKE THEM, OR LIKE MY BROTHERS AND SISTERS.
"MY DAIDEIN LIT HIS PIPE, AS WAS HIS HABIT AT TIMES OF STRESS, AND THEY PROCEEDED TO TELL ME.
"I WAS NOT THEIR CHILD BY BIRTH, I WAS ADOPTED.
"THEY SAID THEY HAD RESCUED ME ALL THOSE MOONS AGO, AND IF THEY HADN'T, I MIGHT NEVER HAVE SURVIVED.
"PAPA WAS UPSIDE WITH MY UNCLES WHEN THEY SAW A GREAT CONVOY OF TROLLS.
"HE WOULD NOT HAVE ACTED BUT FOR THE LITTLE LHIANNO - A HUMAN ONE-- THAT THEY CARRIED.
"THEY ATTACKED AND RESCUED THE INFANT.
"HE BROUGHT THE BABY HOME SAYING HE'D FOUND IT. MOTHER KNEW BETTER.
"SHE SMELLED TROLL ALL OVER ME, AND WONDERED AT HIS BRAVERY.
"WHEN I DECIDED TO GO AND FIND MY BIRTH PARENTS, MAMA AND PAPA WEREN'T SURPRISED AT ALL.
"THEY SAID MY STORY WAS NOT YET TOLD, AND I SHOULD GO UPSIDE AND FIND IT.
"IT TOOK ME A WHOLE YEAR TO DO THAT.
"A WHOLE YEAR OF SEARCHING, A YEAR UPSIDE, AND ALONE."

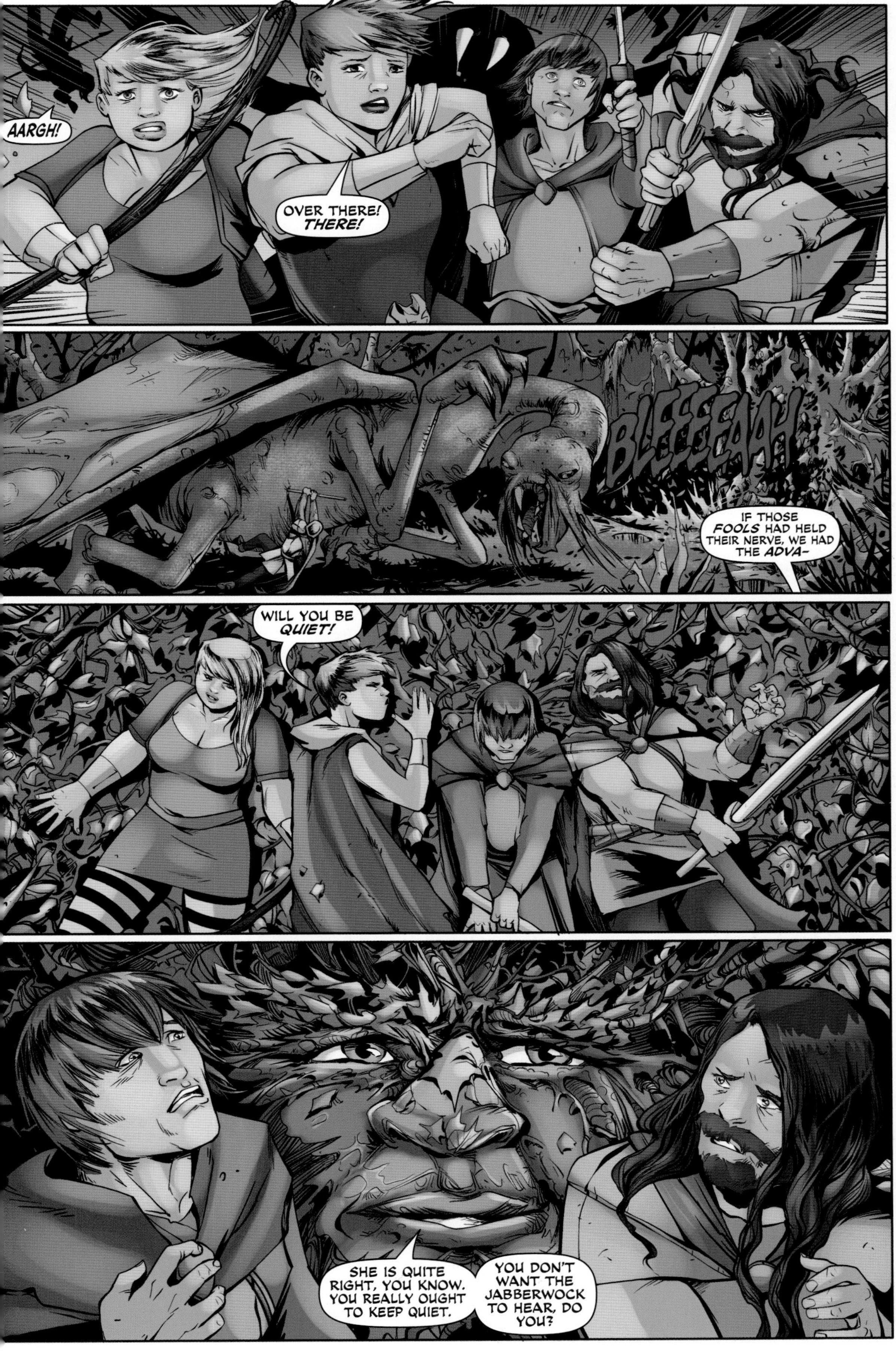
AARGH!
OVER THERE! THERE!
BLEEEEAAH
IF THOSE FOOLS HAD HELD THEIR NERVE, WE HAD THE ADVA-
WILL YOU BE QUIET!
SHE IS QUITE RIGHT, YOU KNOW. YOU REALLY OUGHT TO KEEP QUIET.
YOU DON'T WANT THE JABBERWOCK TO HEAR, DO YOU?

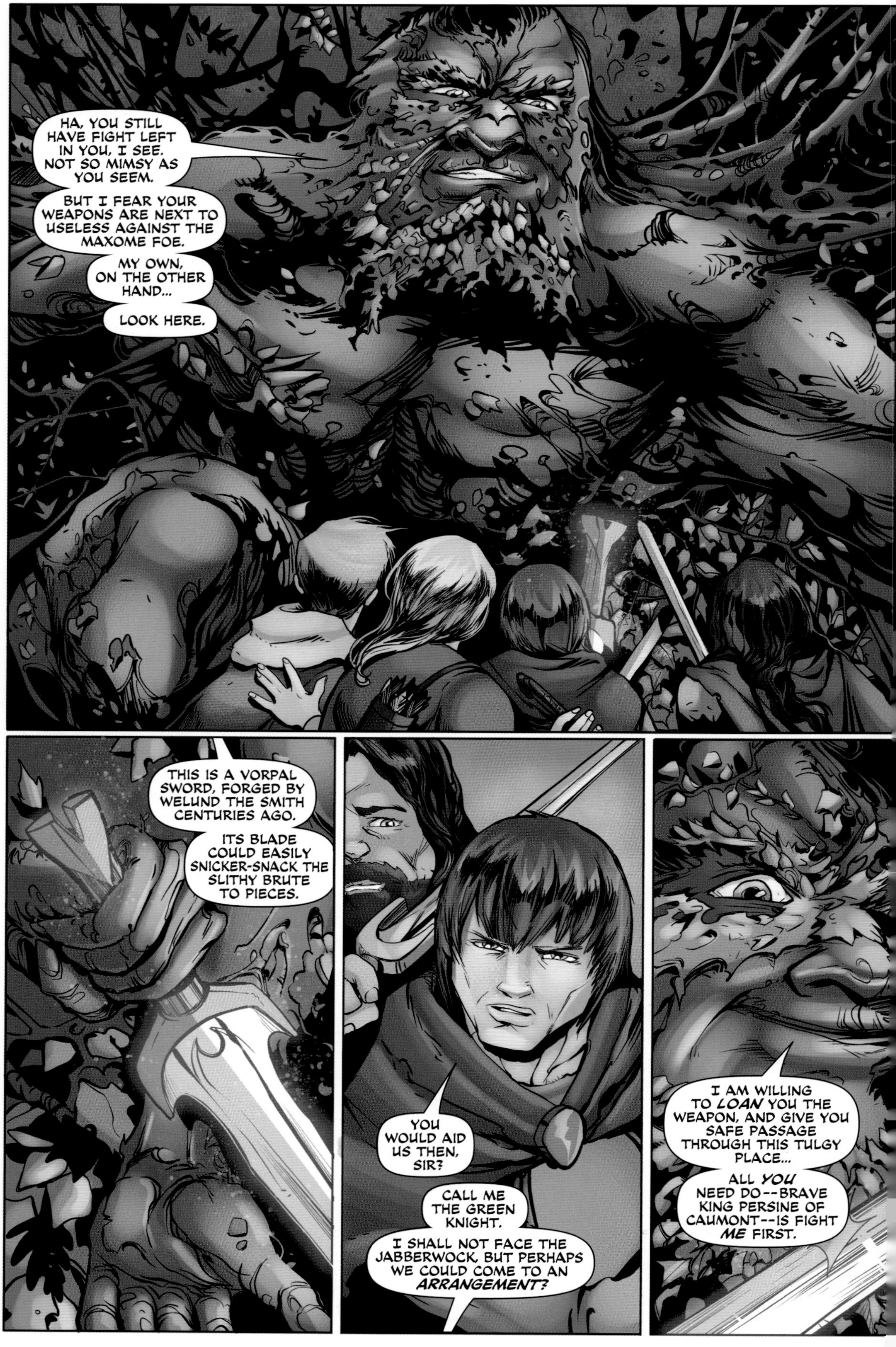
HA, YOU STILL HAVE FIGHT LEFT IN YOU, I SEE. NOT SO MIMSY AS YOU SEEM.
BUT I FEAR YOUR WEAPONS ARE NEXT TO USELESS AGAINST THE MAXOME FOE.
MY OWN, ON THE OTHER HAND...
LOOK HERE.
THIS IS A VORPAL SWORD, FORGED BY WELUND THE SMITH CENTURIES AGO.
ITS BLADE COULD EASILY SNICKER-SNACK THE SLITHY BRUTE TO PIECES.
YOU WOULD AID US THEN, SIR?
CALL ME THE GREEN KNIGHT.
I SHALL NOT FACE THE JABBERWOCK, BUT PERHAPS WE COULD COME TO AN *ARRANGEMENT*?
I AM WILLING TO *LOAN* YOU THE WEAPON, AND GIVE YOU SAFE PASSAGE THROUGH THIS TULGY PLACE...
ALL *YOU* NEED DO--BRAVE KING PERSINE OF CAUMONT--IS FIGHT *ME* FIRST.

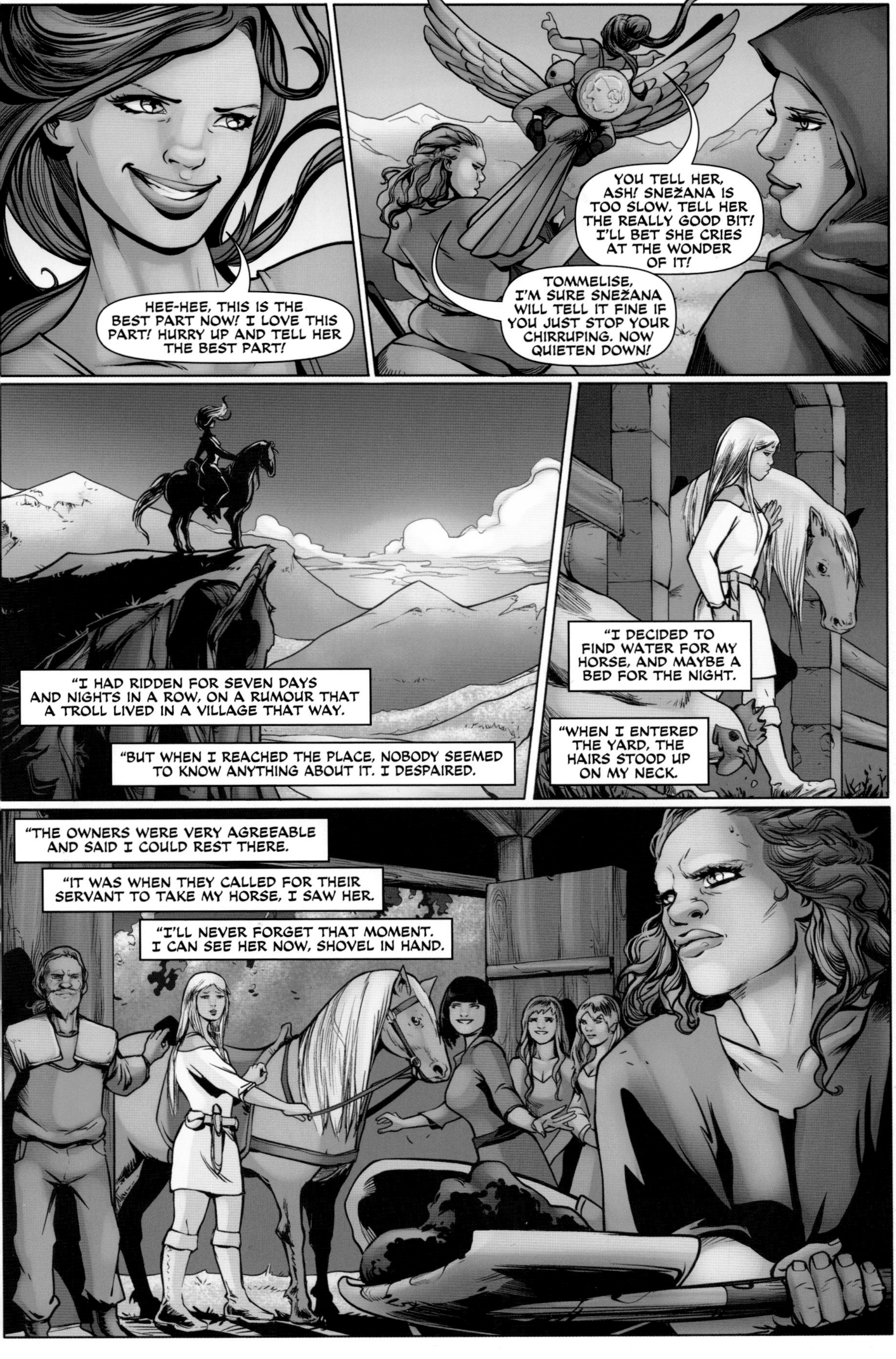
HEE-HEE, THIS IS THE BEST PART NOW! I LOVE THIS PART! HURRY UP AND TELL HER THE BEST PART!
YOU TELL HER, ASH! SNEŽANA IS TOO SLOW. TELL HER THE REALLY GOOD BIT! I'LL BET SHE CRIES AT THE WONDER OF IT!
TOMMELISE, I'M SURE SNEŽANA WILL TELL IT FINE IF YOU JUST STOP YOUR CHIRRUPING. NOW QUIETEN DOWN!
"I HAD RIDDEN FOR SEVEN DAYS AND NIGHTS IN A ROW, ON A RUMOUR THAT A TROLL LIVED IN A VILLAGE THAT WAY.
"BUT WHEN I REACHED THE PLACE, NOBODY SEEMED TO KNOW ANYTHING ABOUT IT. I DESPAIRED.
"I DECIDED TO FIND WATER FOR MY HORSE, AND MAYBE A BED FOR THE NIGHT.
"WHEN I ENTERED THE YARD, THE HAIRS STOOD UP ON MY NECK.
"THE OWNERS WERE VERY AGREEABLE AND SAID I COULD REST THERE.
"IT WAS WHEN THEY CALLED FOR THEIR SERVANT TO TAKE MY HORSE, I SAW HER.
"I'LL NEVER FORGET THAT MOMENT. I CAN SEE HER NOW, SHOVEL IN HAND.

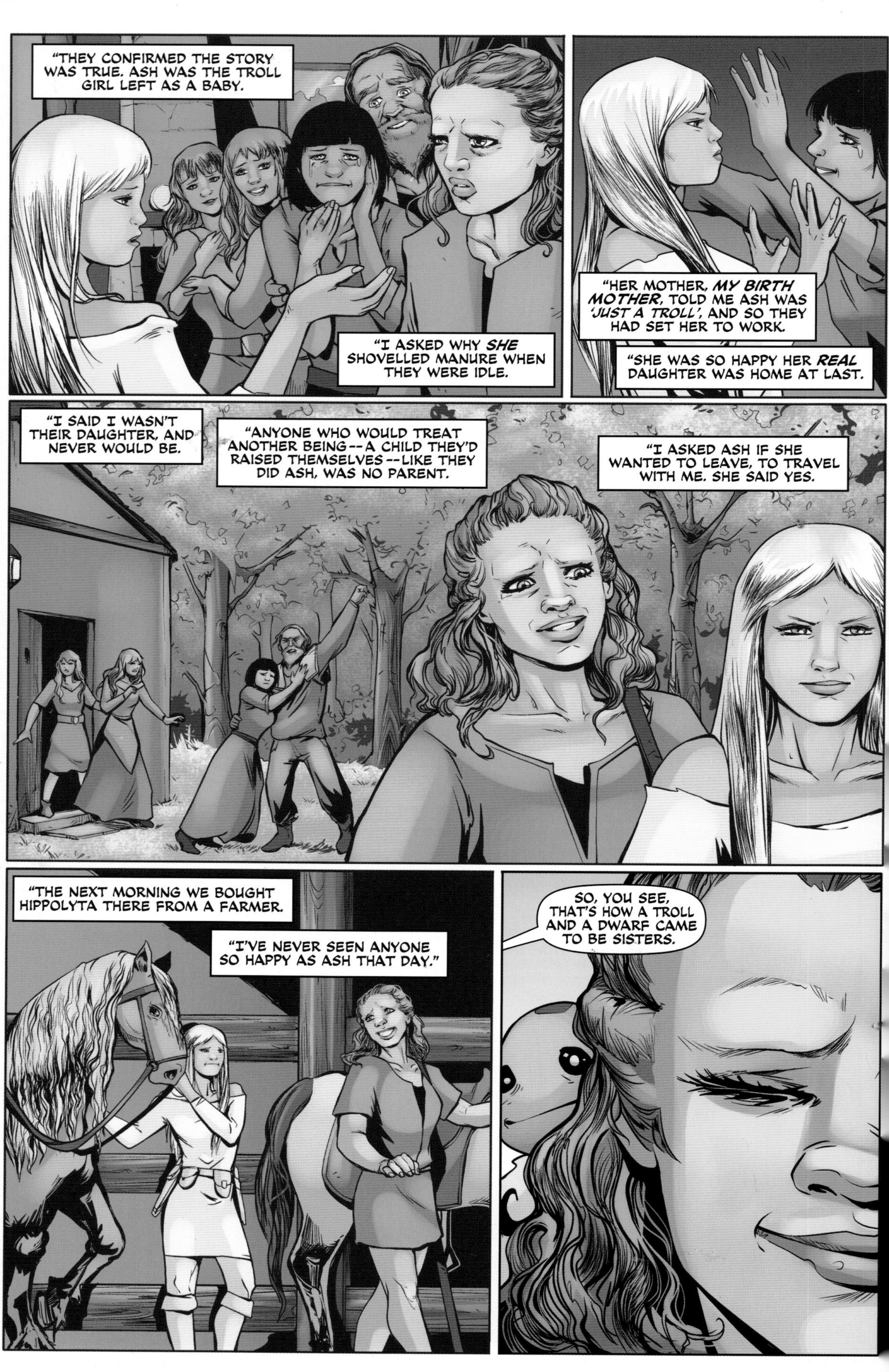
"THEY CONFIRMED THE STORY WAS TRUE. ASH WAS THE TROLL GIRL LEFT AS A BABY.
"I ASKED WHY *SHE* SHOVELLED MANURE WHEN THEY WERE IDLE.
"HER MOTHER, *MY BIRTH MOTHER*, TOLD ME ASH WAS *'JUST A TROLL'*, AND SO THEY HAD SET HER TO WORK.
"SHE WAS SO HAPPY HER *REAL* DAUGHTER WAS HOME AT LAST.
"I SAID I WASN'T THEIR DAUGHTER, AND NEVER WOULD BE.
"ANYONE WHO WOULD TREAT ANOTHER BEING--A CHILD THEY'D RAISED THEMSELVES--LIKE THEY DID ASH, WAS NO PARENT.
"I ASKED ASH IF SHE WANTED TO LEAVE, TO TRAVEL WITH ME. SHE SAID YES.
"THE NEXT MORNING WE BOUGHT HIPPOLYTA THERE FROM A FARMER.
"I'VE NEVER SEEN ANYONE SO HAPPY AS ASH THAT DAY."
SO, YOU SEE, THAT'S HOW A TROLL AND A DWARF CAME TO BE SISTERS.

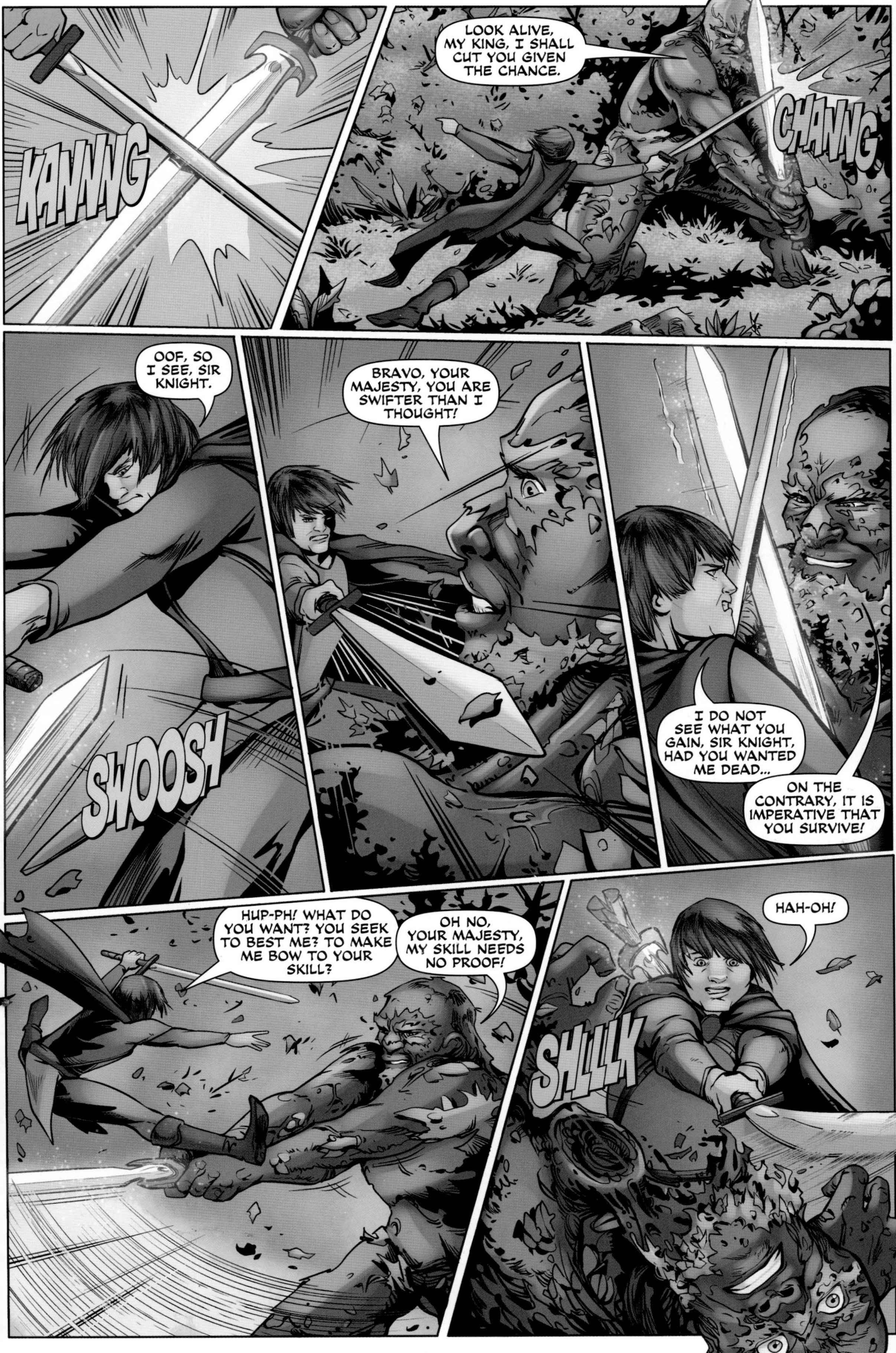
KANNNG
LOOK ALIVE, MY KING, I SHALL CUT YOU GIVEN THE CHANCE.
CHANNG
OOF, SO I SEE, SIR KNIGHT.
SWOOSH
BRAVO, YOUR MAJESTY, YOU ARE SWIFTER THAN I THOUGHT!
I DO NOT SEE WHAT YOU GAIN, SIR KNIGHT, HAD YOU WANTED ME DEAD...
ON THE CONTRARY, IT IS IMPERATIVE THAT YOU SURVIVE!
HUP-PH! WHAT DO YOU WANT? YOU SEEK TO BEST ME? TO MAKE ME BOW TO YOUR SKILL?
OH NO, YOUR MAJESTY, MY SKILL NEEDS NO PROOF!
HAH-OH!
SHLLLK

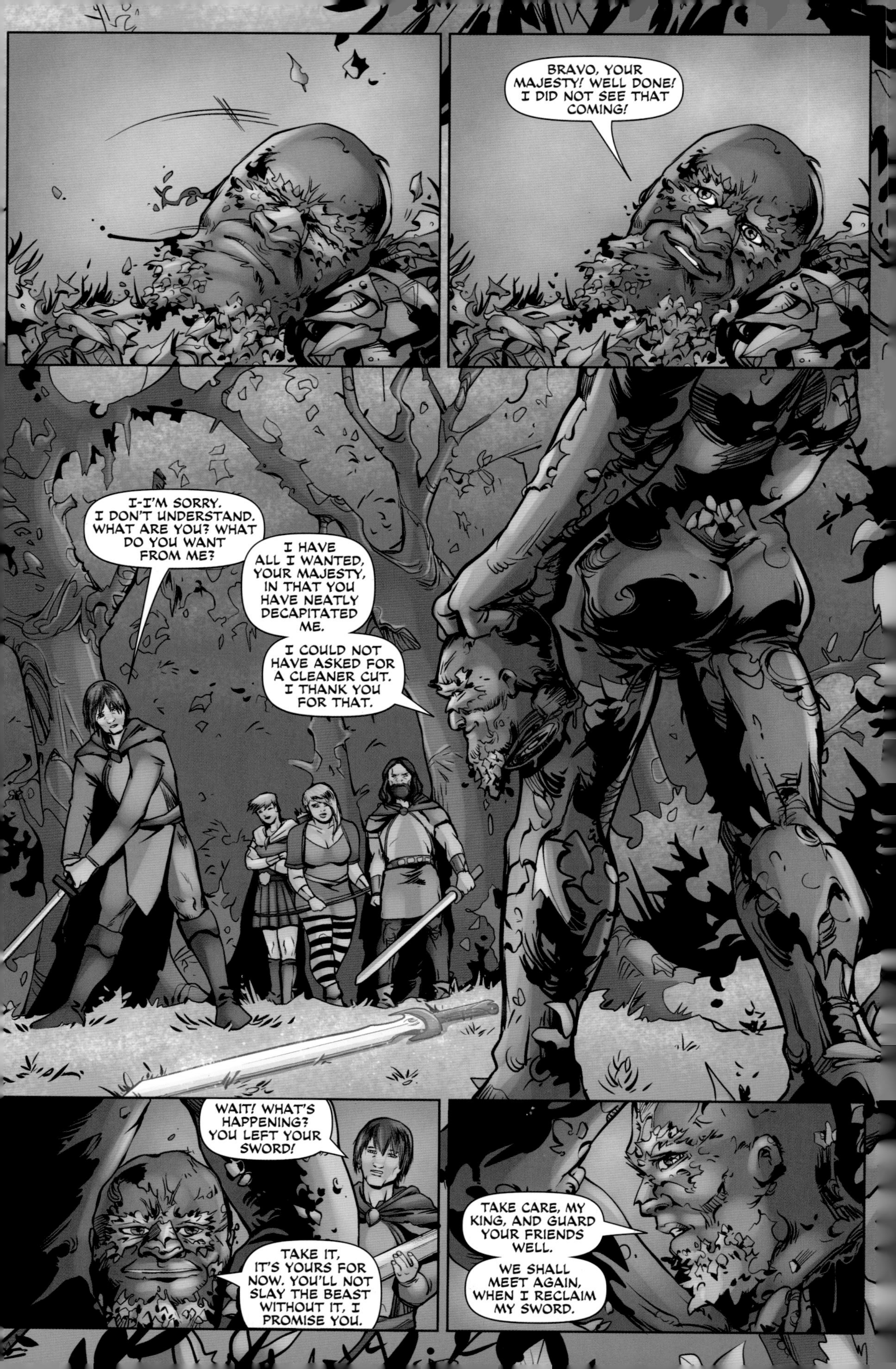
BRAVO, YOUR MAJESTY! WELL DONE! I DID NOT SEE THAT COMING!
I-I'M SORRY. I DON'T UNDERSTAND. WHAT ARE YOU? WHAT DO YOU WANT FROM ME?
I HAVE ALL I WANTED, YOUR MAJESTY, IN THAT YOU HAVE NEATLY DECAPITATED ME.
I COULD NOT HAVE ASKED FOR A CLEANER CUT. I THANK YOU FOR THAT.
WAIT! WHAT'S HAPPENING? YOU LEFT YOUR SWORD!
TAKE IT, IT'S YOURS FOR NOW. YOU'LL NOT SLAY THE BEAST WITHOUT IT, I PROMISE YOU.
TAKE CARE, MY KING, AND GUARD YOUR FRIENDS WELL.
WE SHALL MEET AGAIN, WHEN I RECLAIM MY SWORD.

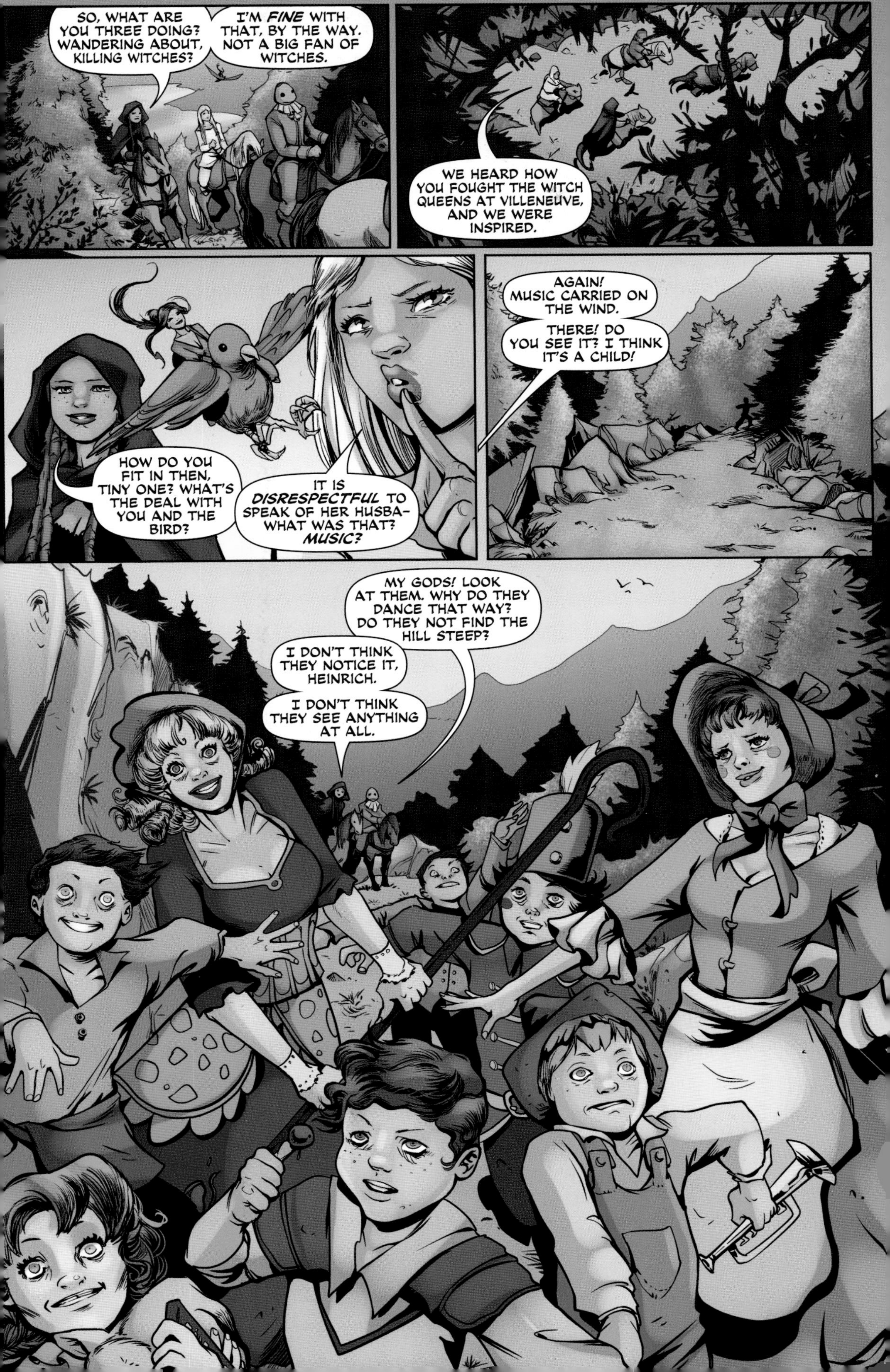
SO, WHAT ARE YOU THREE DOING? WANDERING ABOUT, KILLING WITCHES?
I'M *FINE* WITH THAT, BY THE WAY. NOT A BIG FAN OF WITCHES.
WE HEARD HOW YOU FOUGHT THE WITCH QUEENS AT VILLENEUVE, AND WE WERE INSPIRED.
HOW DO YOU FIT IN THEN, TINY ONE? WHAT'S THE DEAL WITH YOU AND THE BIRD?
IT IS *DISRESPECTFUL* TO SPEAK OF HER HUSBA- WHAT WAS THAT? *MUSIC?*
AGAIN! MUSIC CARRIED ON THE WIND.
THERE! DO YOU SEE IT? I THINK IT'S A CHILD!
MY GODS! LOOK AT THEM. WHY DO THEY DANCE THAT WAY? DO THEY NOT FIND THE HILL STEEP?
I DON'T THINK THEY NOTICE IT, HEINRICH.
I DON'T THINK THEY SEE ANYTHING AT ALL.

Chapter

11

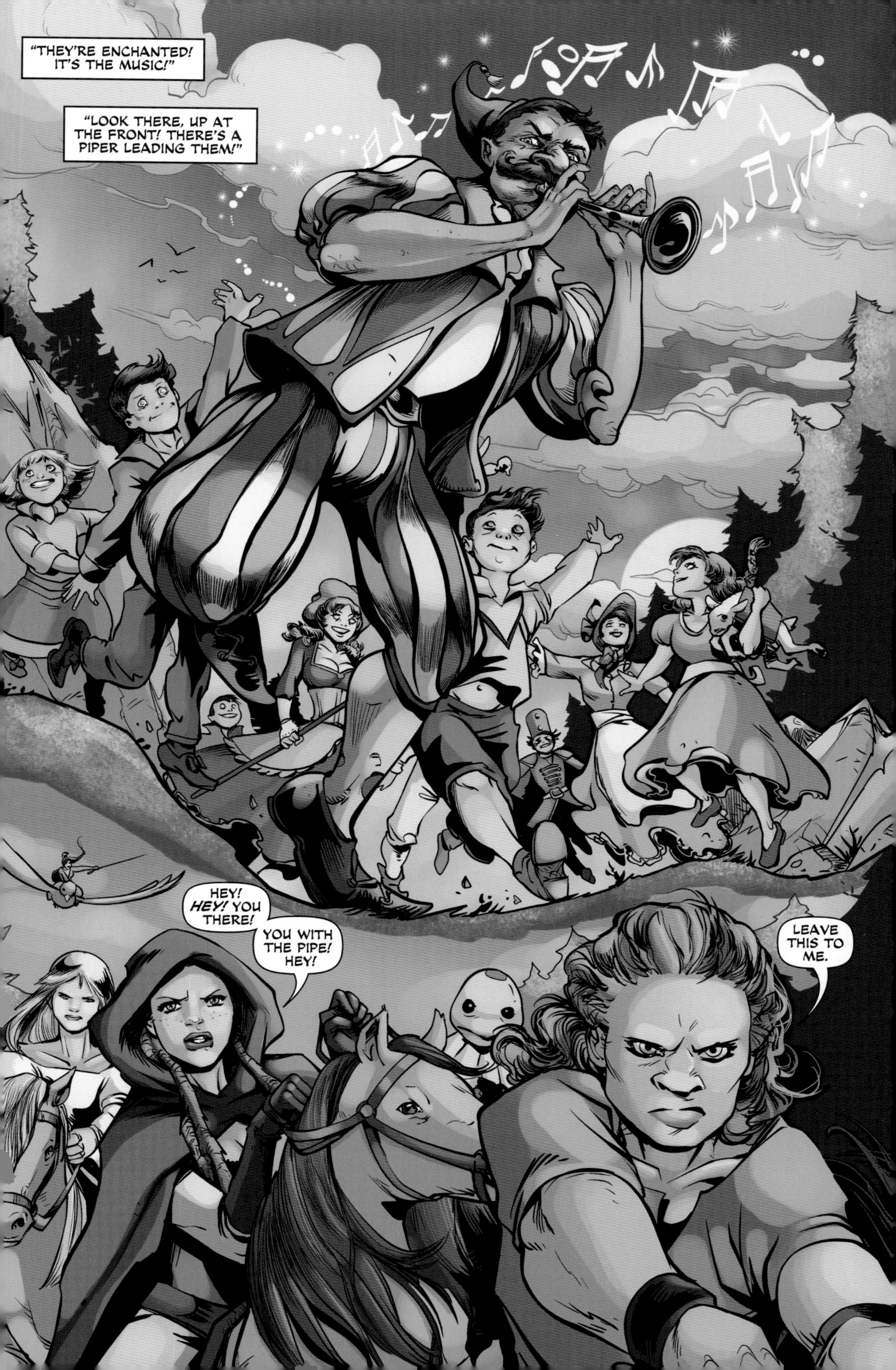
"THEY'RE ENCHANTED! IT'S THE MUSIC!"
"LOOK THERE, UP AT THE FRONT! THERE'S A PIPER LEADING THEM!"
HEY! *HEY!* YOU THERE!
YOU WITH THE PIPE! HEY!
LEAVE THIS TO ME.

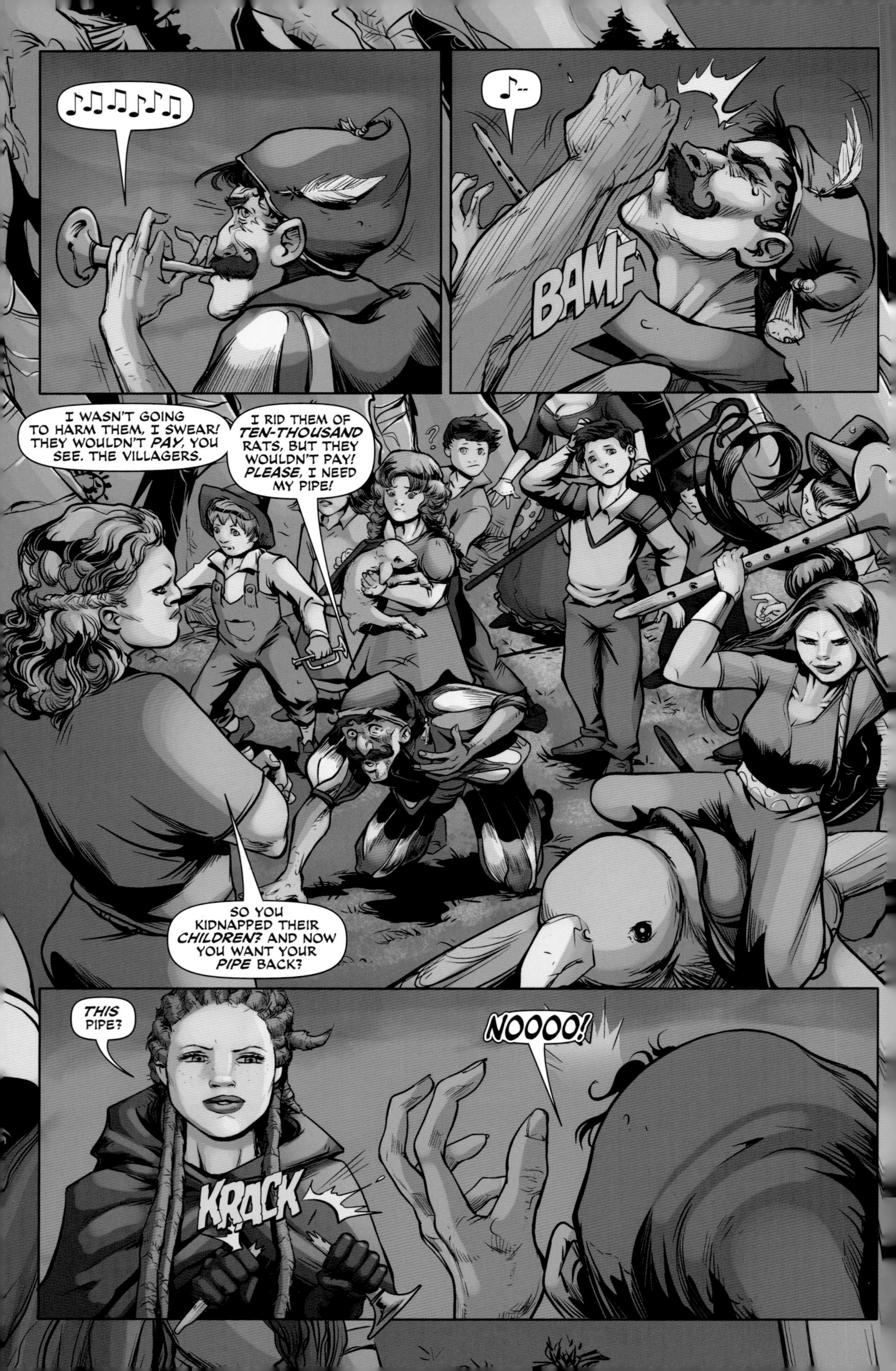
♪♫♫♪♪♫
♪--
BAMF
I WASN'T GOING TO HARM THEM, I SWEAR! THEY WOULDN'T *PAY*, YOU SEE. THE VILLAGERS.
I RID THEM OF *TEN-THOUSAND* RATS, BUT THEY WOULDN'T PAY! *PLEASE*, I NEED MY PIPE!
?
SO YOU KIDNAPPED THEIR *CHILDREN?* AND NOW YOU WANT YOUR *PIPE* BACK?
THIS PIPE?
NOOOO!
KRACK

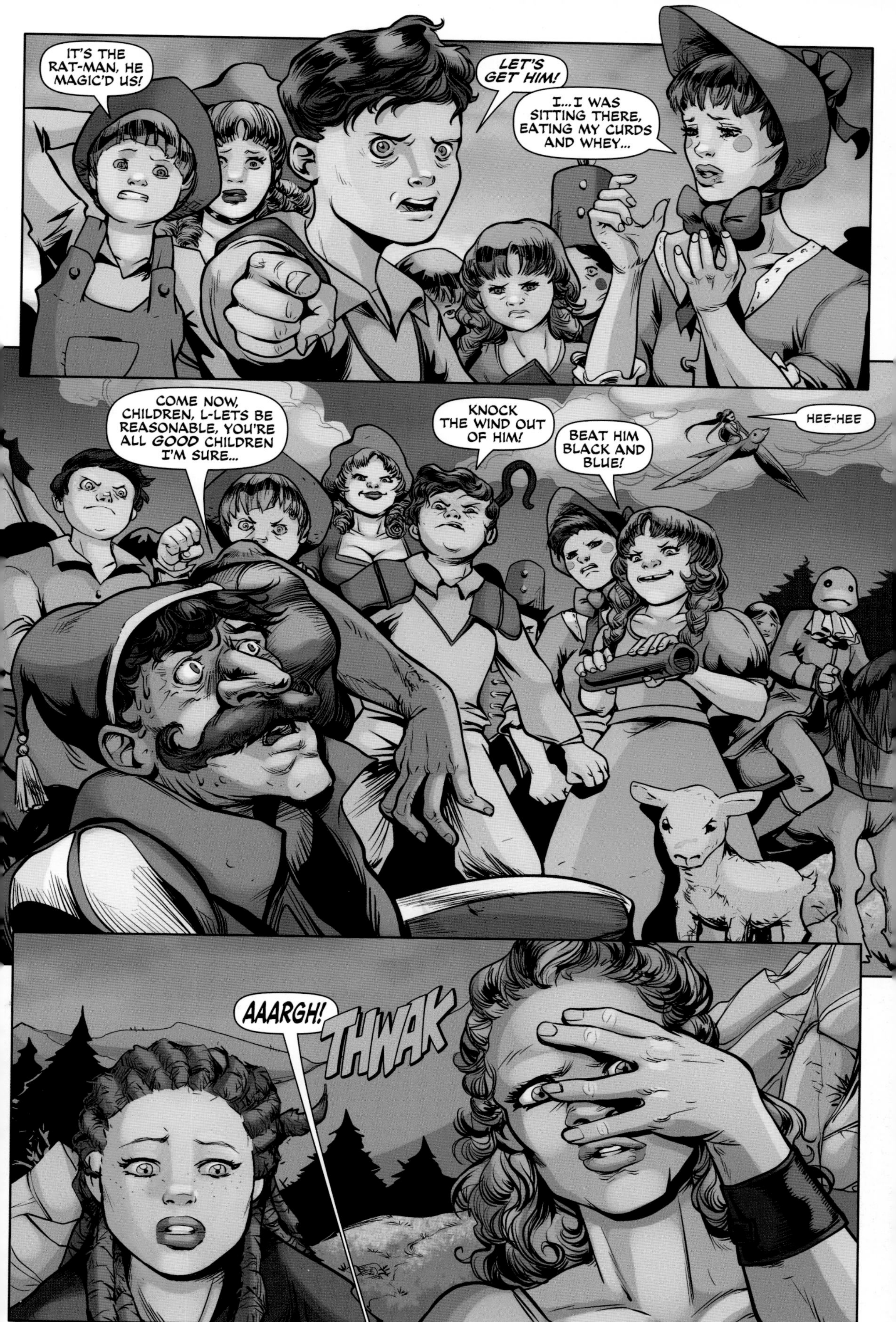
IT'S THE RAT-MAN, HE MAGIC'D US!
LET'S GET HIM!
I... I WAS SITTING THERE, EATING MY CURDS AND WHEY...
COME NOW, CHILDREN, L-LETS BE REASONABLE, YOU'RE ALL GOOD CHILDREN I'M SURE...
KNOCK THE WIND OUT OF HIM!
BEAT HIM BLACK AND BLUE!
HEE-HEE
AAARGH!
THWAK

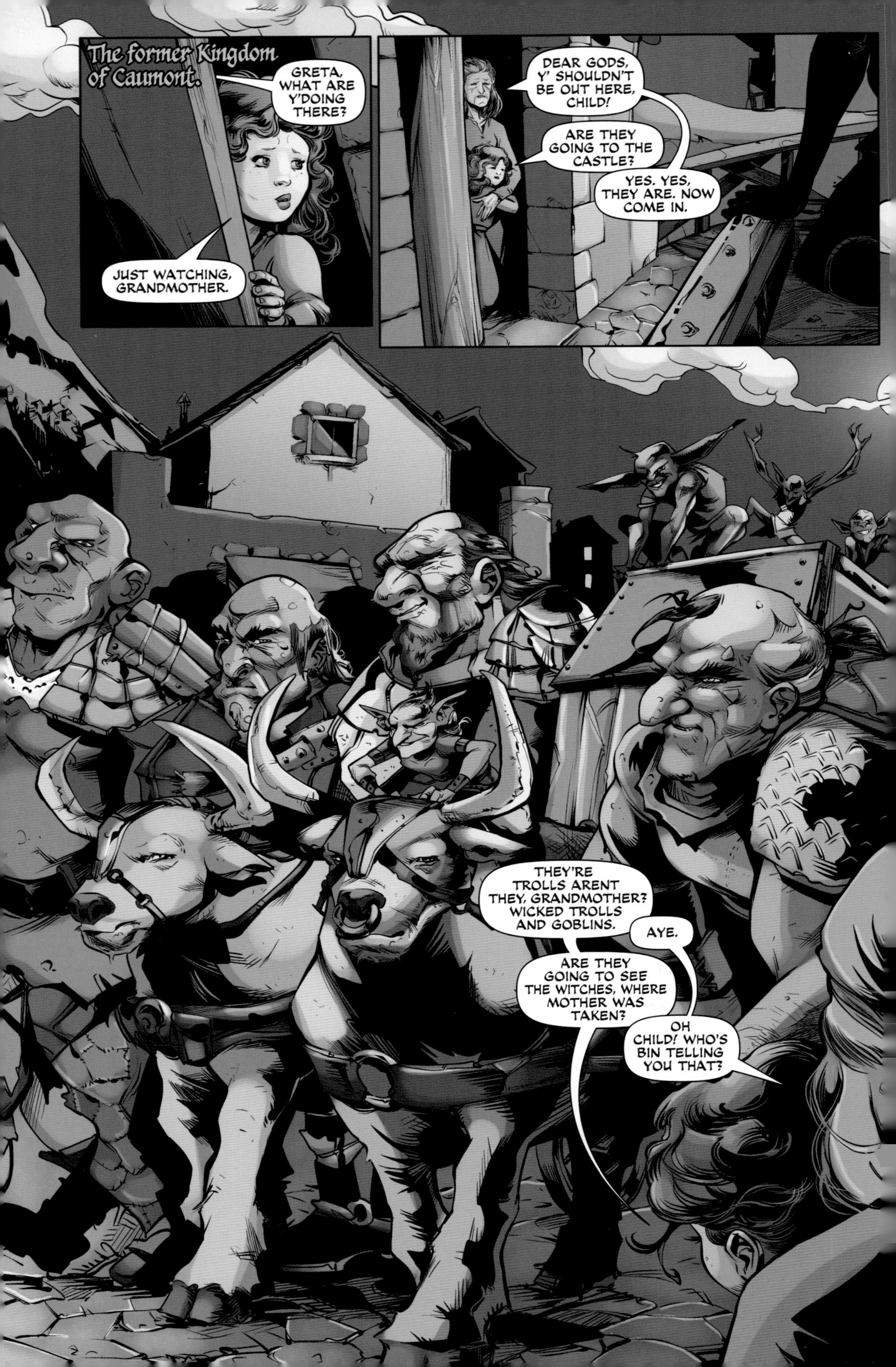
The former Kingdom of Caumont.
GRETA, WHAT ARE Y'DOING THERE?
JUST WATCHING, GRANDMOTHER.
DEAR GODS, Y' SHOULDN'T BE OUT HERE, CHILD!
ARE THEY GOING TO THE CASTLE?
YES. YES, THEY ARE. NOW COME IN.
THEY'RE TROLLS ARENT THEY, GRANDMOTHER? WICKED TROLLS AND GOBLINS.
AYE.
ARE THEY GOING TO SEE THE WITCHES, WHERE MOTHER WAS TAKEN?
OH CHILD! WHO'S BIN TELLING YOU THAT?

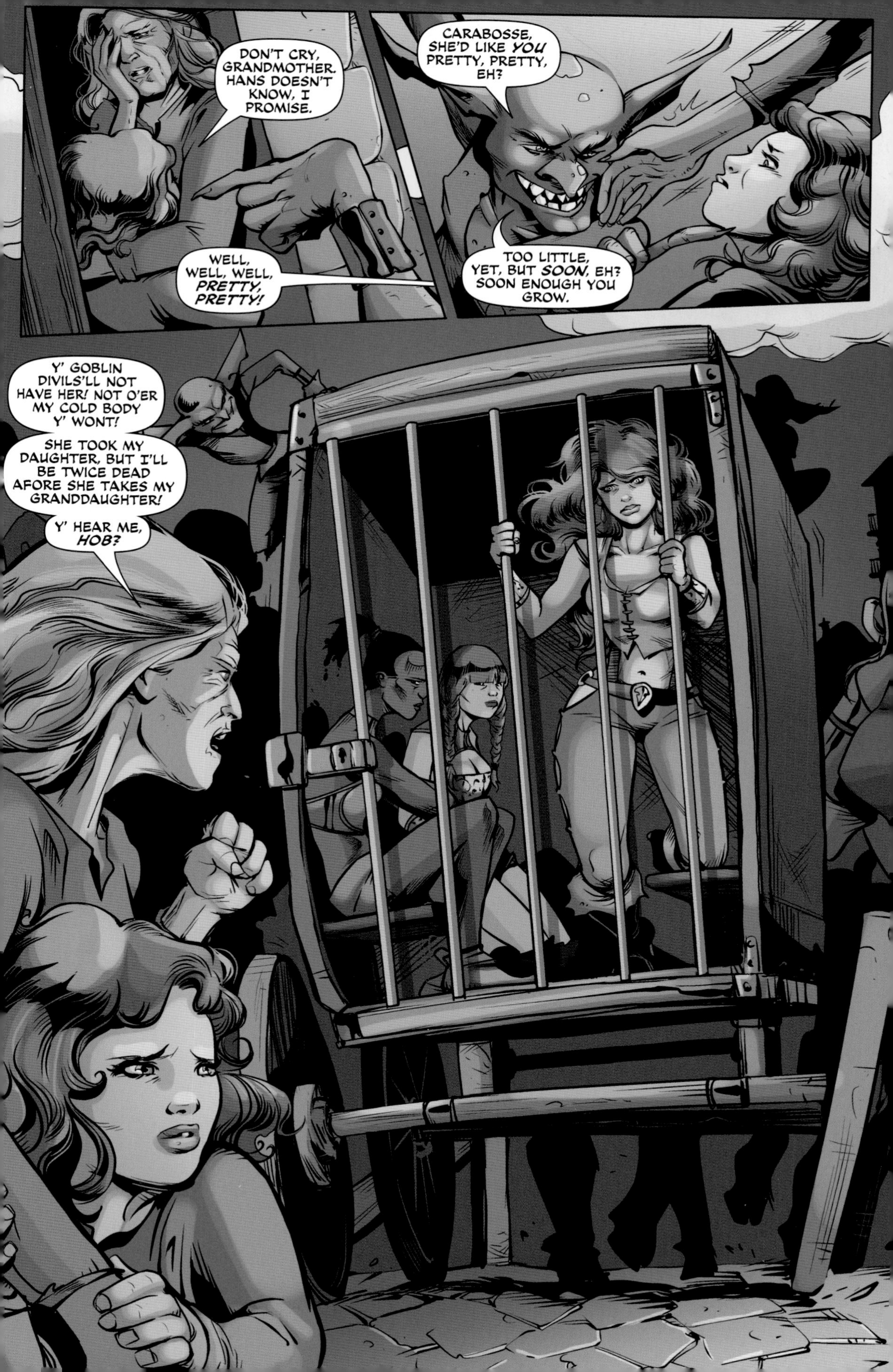
DON'T CRY, GRANDMOTHER. HANS DOESN'T KNOW, I PROMISE.
WELL, WELL, WELL, PRETTY, PRETTY!
CARABOSSE, SHE'D LIKE YOU PRETTY, PRETTY, EH?
TOO LITTLE, YET, BUT SOON, EH? SOON ENOUGH YOU GROW.
Y' GOBLIN DIVILS'LL NOT HAVE HER! NOT O'ER MY COLD BODY Y' WONT!
SHE TOOK MY DAUGHTER, BUT I'LL BE TWICE DEAD AFORE SHE TAKES MY GRANDDAUGHTER!
Y' HEAR ME, HOB?

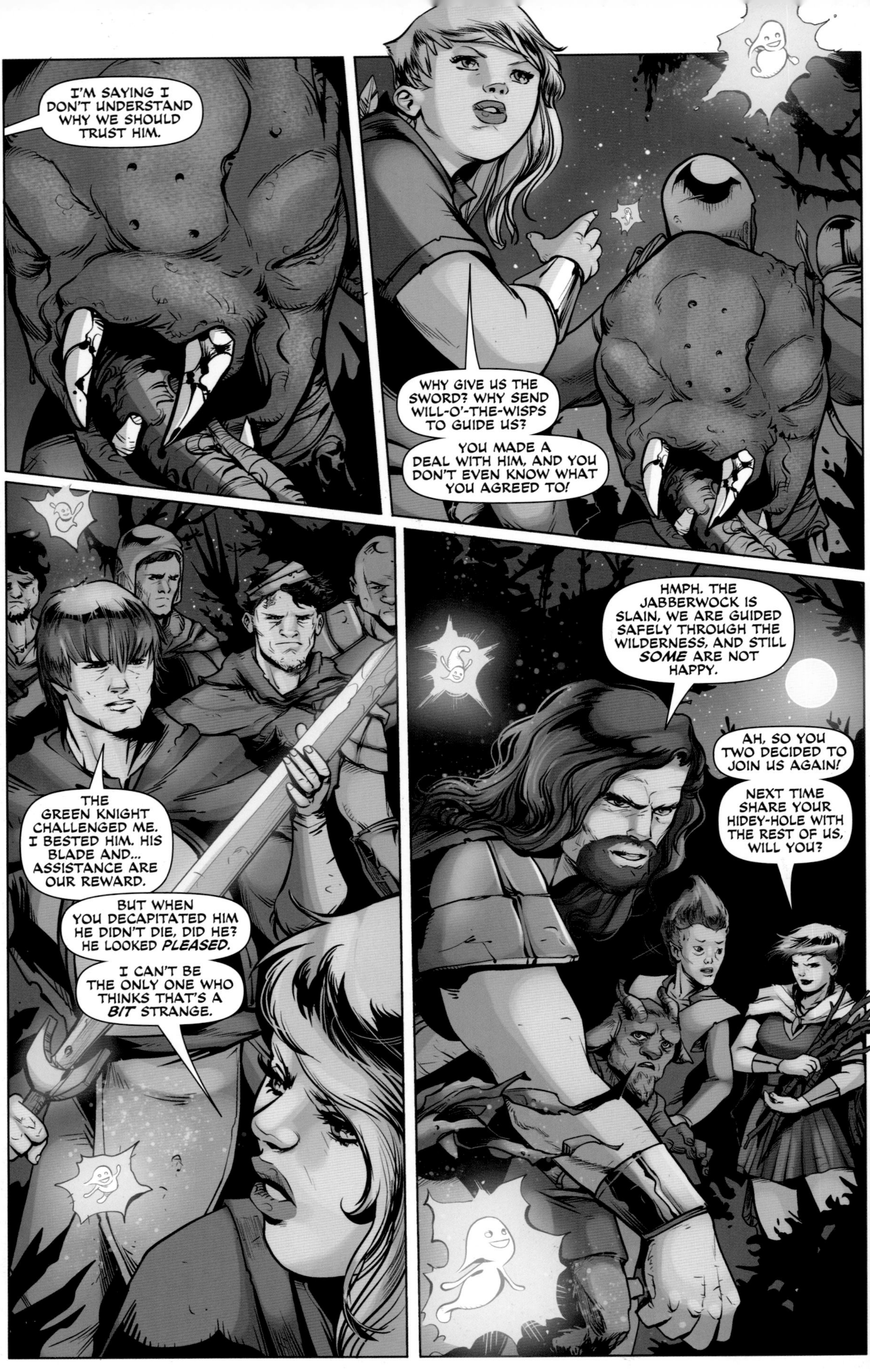
I'M SAYING I DON'T UNDERSTAND WHY WE SHOULD TRUST HIM.
WHY GIVE US THE SWORD? WHY SEND WILL-O'-THE-WISPS TO GUIDE US?
YOU MADE A DEAL WITH HIM, AND YOU DON'T EVEN KNOW WHAT YOU AGREED TO!
THE GREEN KNIGHT CHALLENGED ME. I BESTED HIM. HIS BLADE AND... ASSISTANCE ARE OUR REWARD.
BUT WHEN YOU DECAPITATED HIM HE DIDN'T DIE, DID HE? HE LOOKED *PLEASED.*
I CAN'T BE THE ONLY ONE WHO THINKS THAT'S A *BIT* STRANGE.
HMPH. THE JABBERWOCK IS SLAIN, WE ARE GUIDED SAFELY THROUGH THE WILDERNESS, AND STILL *SOME* ARE NOT HAPPY.
AH, SO YOU TWO DECIDED TO JOIN US AGAIN!
NEXT TIME SHARE YOUR HIDEY-HOLE WITH THE REST OF US, WILL YOU?

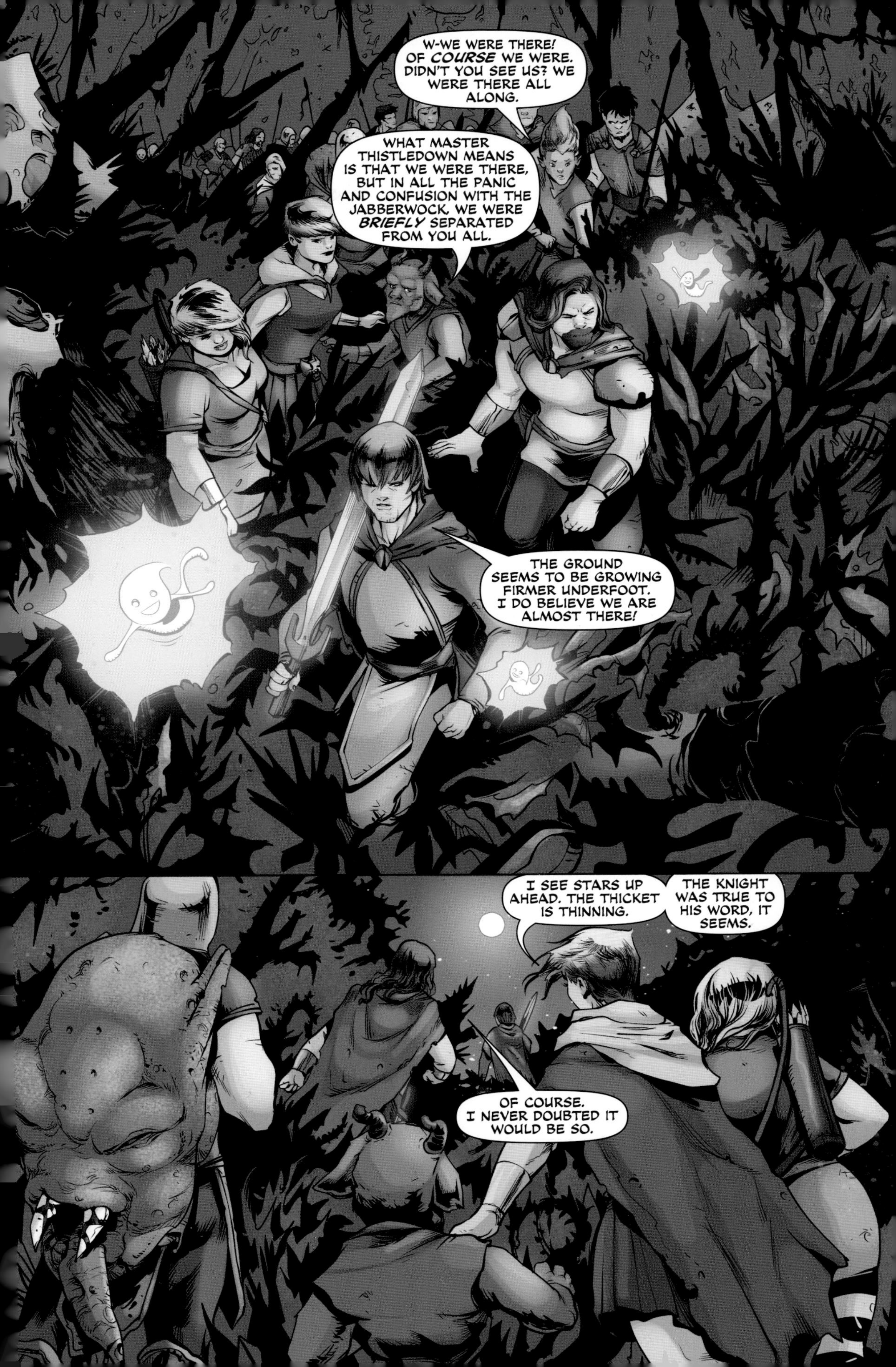
W-WE WERE THERE! OF *COURSE* WE WERE. DIDN'T YOU SEE US? WE WERE THERE ALL ALONG.
WHAT MASTER THISTLEDOWN MEANS IS THAT WE WERE THERE, BUT IN ALL THE PANIC AND CONFUSION WITH THE JABBERWOCK, WE WERE *BRIEFLY* SEPARATED FROM YOU ALL.
THE GROUND SEEMS TO BE GROWING FIRMER UNDERFOOT. I DO BELIEVE WE ARE ALMOST THERE!
I SEE STARS UP AHEAD. THE THICKET IS THINNING.
THE KNIGHT WAS TRUE TO HIS WORD, IT SEEMS.
OF COURSE. I NEVER DOUBTED IT WOULD BE SO.

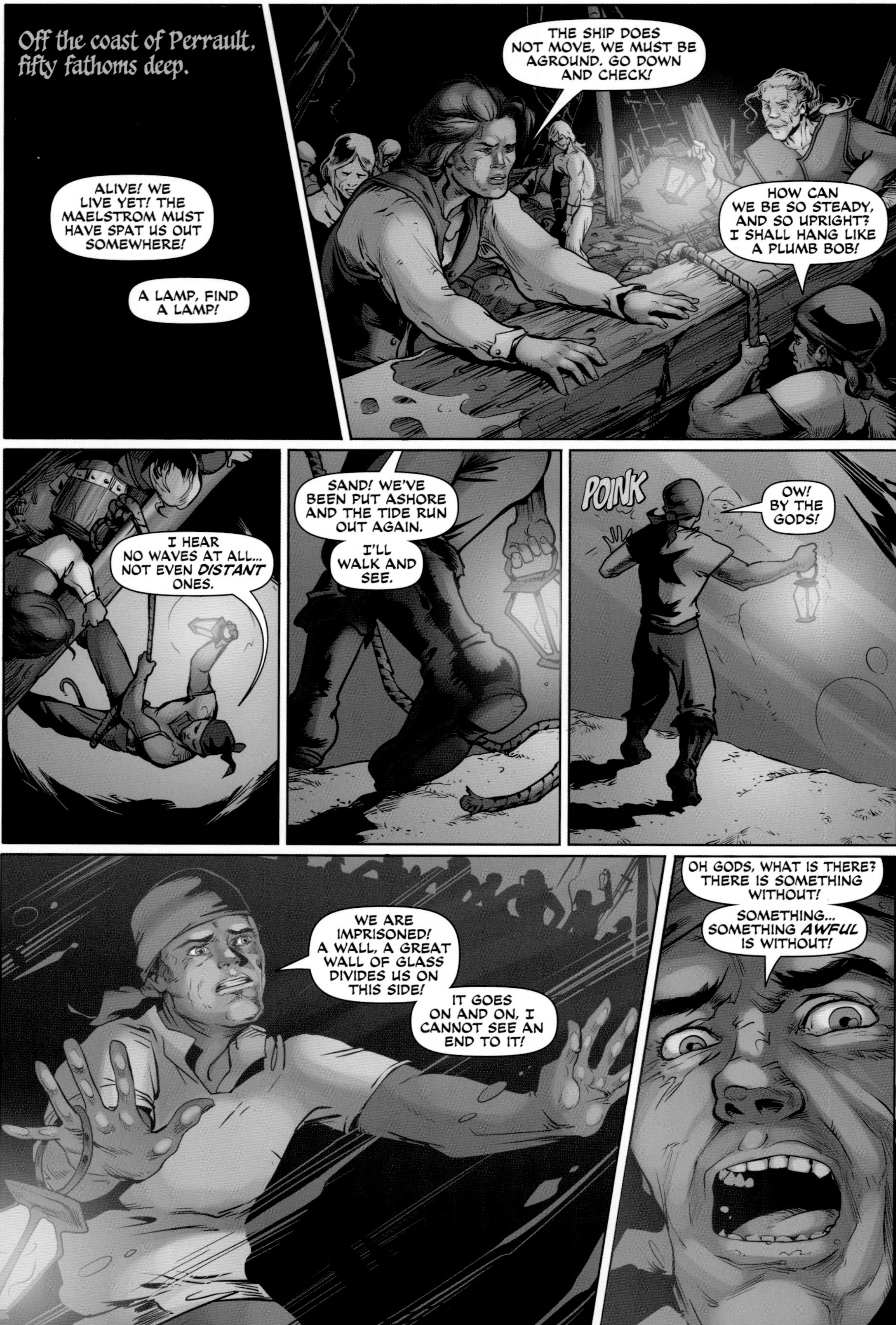
Off the coast of Perrault, fifty fathoms deep.
ALIVE! WE LIVE YET! THE MAELSTROM MUST HAVE SPAT US OUT SOMEWHERE!
A LAMP, FIND A LAMP!
THE SHIP DOES NOT MOVE, WE MUST BE AGROUND. GO DOWN AND CHECK!
HOW CAN WE BE SO STEADY, AND SO UPRIGHT? I SHALL HANG LIKE A PLUMB BOB!
I HEAR NO WAVES AT ALL... NOT EVEN *DISTANT* ONES.
SAND! WE'VE BEEN PUT ASHORE AND THE TIDE RUN OUT AGAIN.
I'LL WALK AND SEE.
POINK
OW! BY THE GODS!
WE ARE IMPRISONED! A WALL, A GREAT WALL OF GLASS DIVIDES US ON THIS SIDE!
IT GOES ON AND ON, I CANNOT SEE AN END TO IT!
OH GODS, WHAT IS THERE? THERE IS SOMETHING WITHOUT!
SOMETHING... SOMETHING *AWFUL* IS WITHOUT!

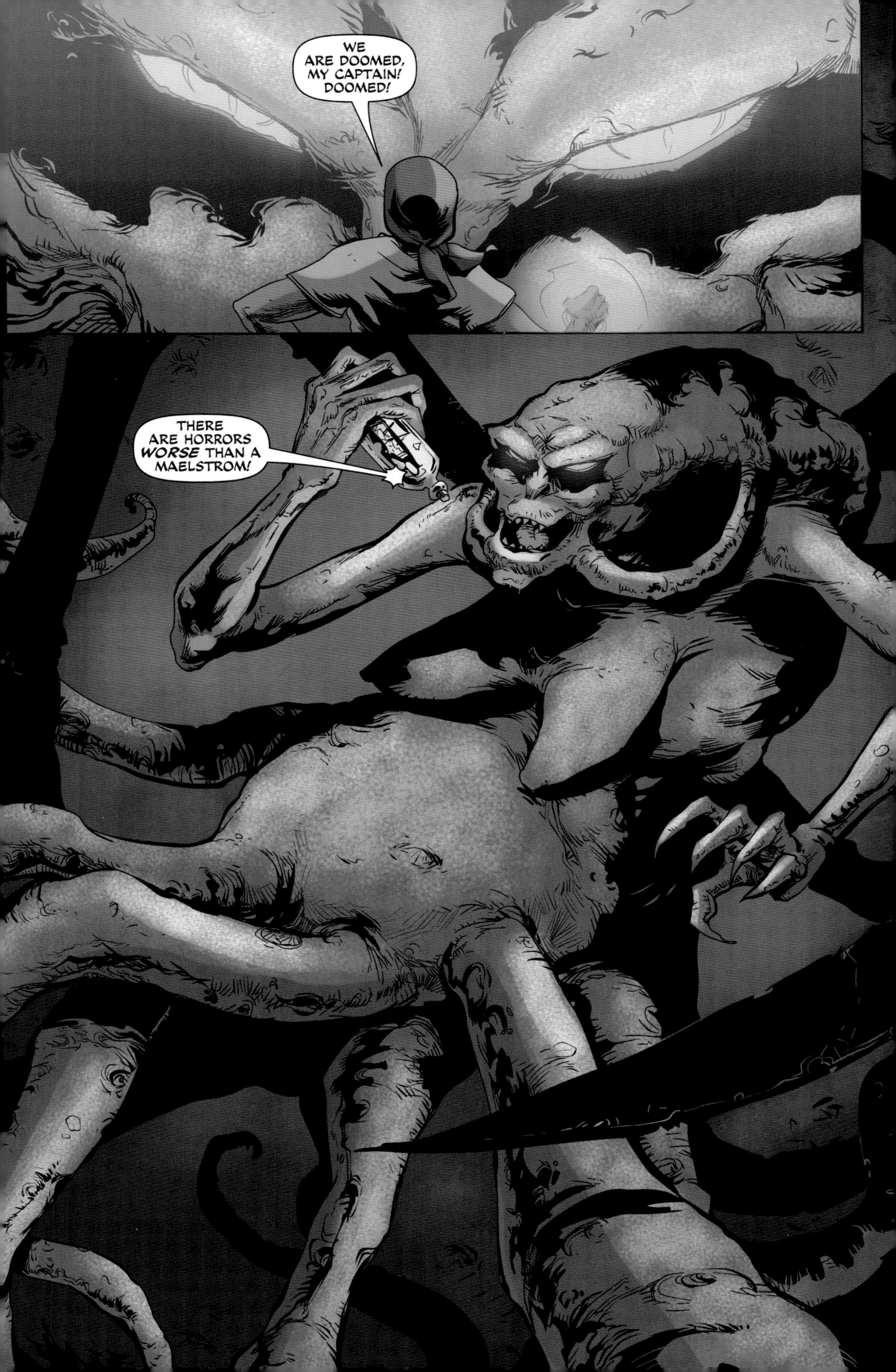
WE ARE DOOMED, MY CAPTAIN! DOOMED!
THERE ARE HORRORS *WORSE* THAN A MAELSTROM!

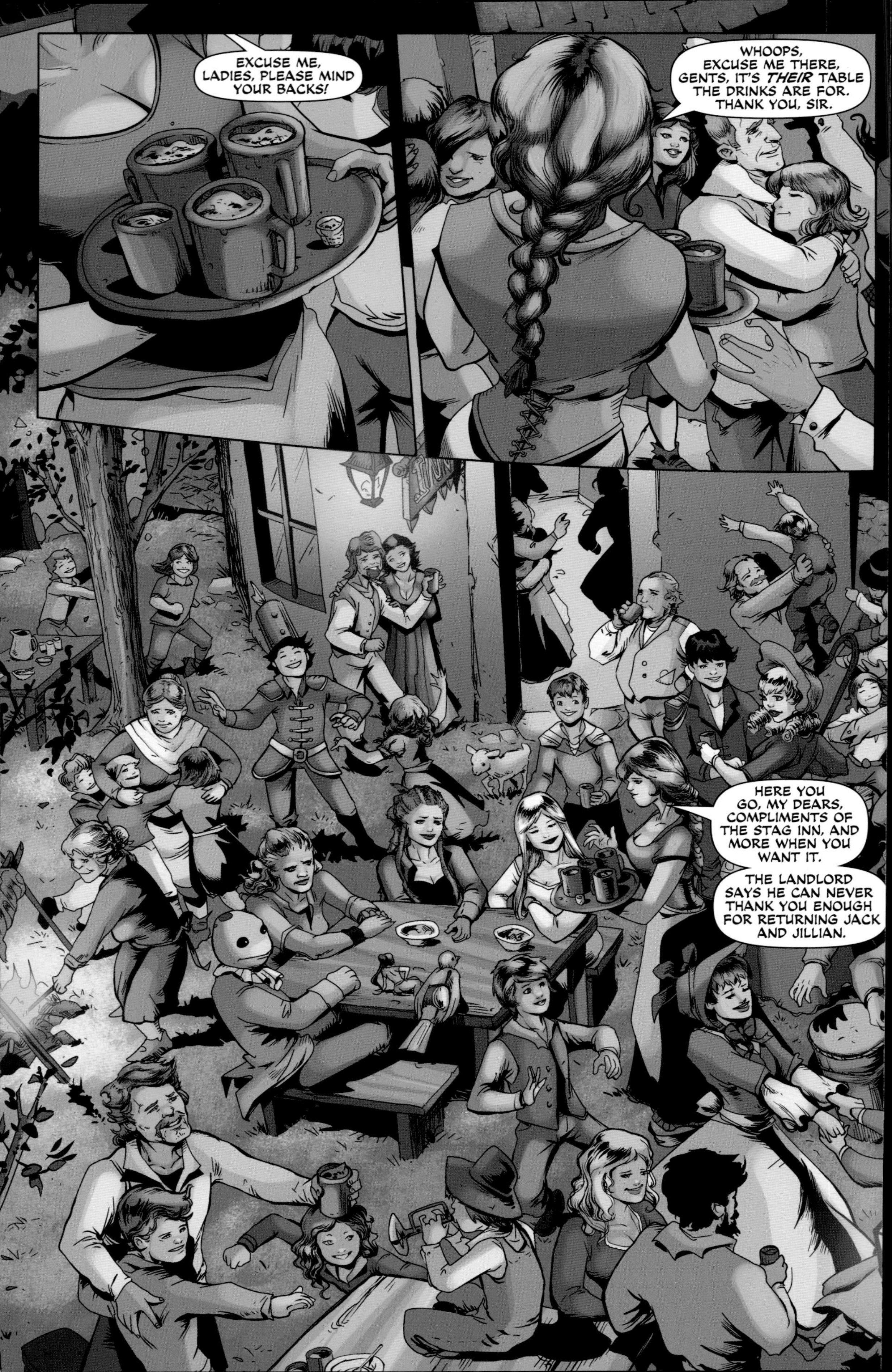
EXCUSE ME, LADIES, PLEASE MIND YOUR BACKS!
WHOOPS, EXCUSE ME THERE, GENTS, IT'S *THEIR* TABLE THE DRINKS ARE FOR. THANK YOU, SIR.
HERE YOU GO, MY DEARS, COMPLIMENTS OF THE STAG INN, AND MORE WHEN YOU WANT IT.
THE LANDLORD SAYS HE CAN NEVER THANK YOU ENOUGH FOR RETURNING JACK AND JILLIAN.

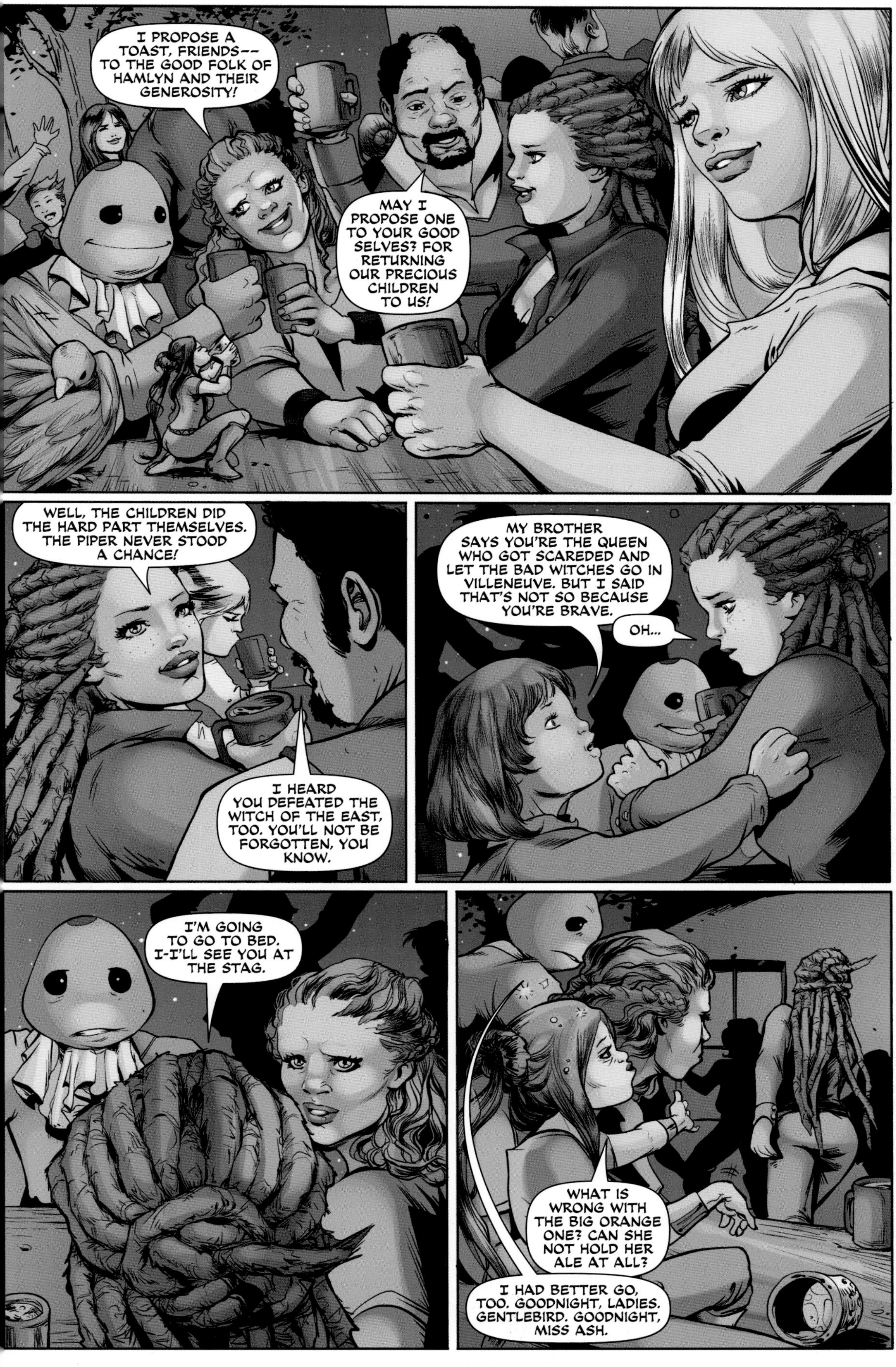
I PROPOSE A TOAST, FRIENDS-- TO THE GOOD FOLK OF HAMLYN AND THEIR GENEROSITY!
MAY I PROPOSE ONE TO YOUR GOOD SELVES? FOR RETURNING OUR PRECIOUS CHILDREN TO US!
WELL, THE CHILDREN DID THE HARD PART THEMSELVES. THE PIPER NEVER STOOD A CHANCE!
I HEARD YOU DEFEATED THE WITCH OF THE EAST, TOO. YOU'LL NOT BE FORGOTTEN, YOU KNOW.
MY BROTHER SAYS YOU'RE THE QUEEN WHO GOT SCAREDED AND LET THE BAD WITCHES GO IN VILLENEUVE. BUT I SAID THAT'S NOT SO BECAUSE YOU'RE BRAVE.
OH...
I'M GOING TO GO TO BED. I-I'LL SEE YOU AT THE STAG.
WHAT IS WRONG WITH THE BIG ORANGE ONE? CAN SHE NOT HOLD HER ALE AT ALL?
I HAD BETTER GO, TOO. GOODNIGHT, LADIES. GENTLEBIRD. GOODNIGHT, MISS ASH.

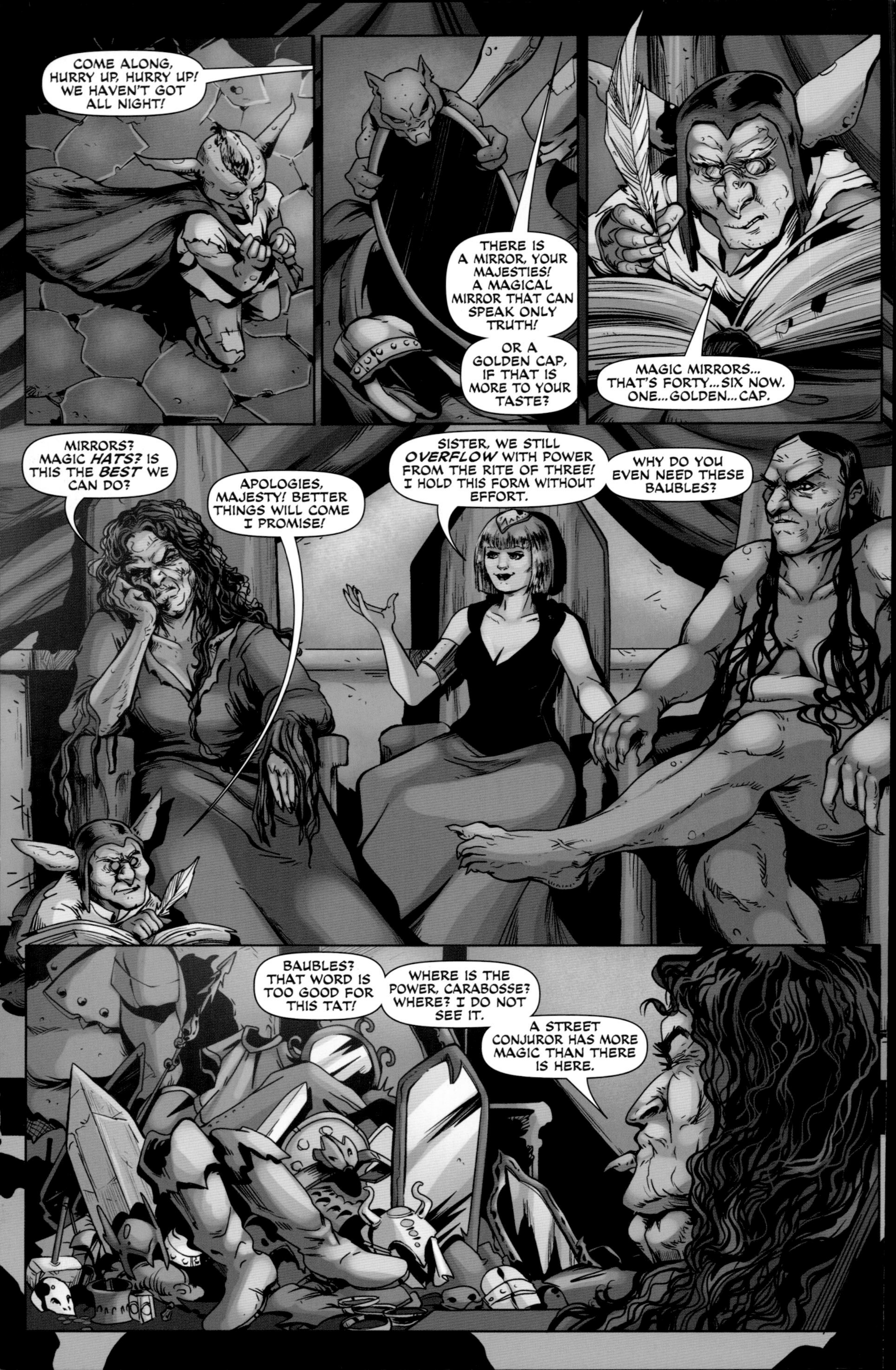
COME ALONG, HURRY UP, HURRY UP! WE HAVEN'T GOT ALL NIGHT!
THERE IS A MIRROR, YOUR MAJESTIES! A MAGICAL MIRROR THAT CAN SPEAK ONLY TRUTH!
OR A GOLDEN CAP, IF THAT IS MORE TO YOUR TASTE?
MAGIC MIRRORS... THAT'S FORTY...SIX NOW. ONE...GOLDEN...CAP.
MIRRORS? MAGIC *HATS?* IS THIS THE *BEST* WE CAN DO?
APOLOGIES, MAJESTY! BETTER THINGS WILL COME I PROMISE!
SISTER, WE STILL *OVERFLOW* WITH POWER FROM THE RITE OF THREE! I HOLD THIS FORM WITHOUT EFFORT.
WHY DO YOU EVEN NEED THESE BAUBLES?
BAUBLES? THAT WORD IS TOO GOOD FOR THIS TAT!
WHERE IS THE POWER, CARABOSSE? WHERE? I DO NOT SEE IT.
A STREET CONJUROR HAS MORE MAGIC THAN THERE IS HERE.

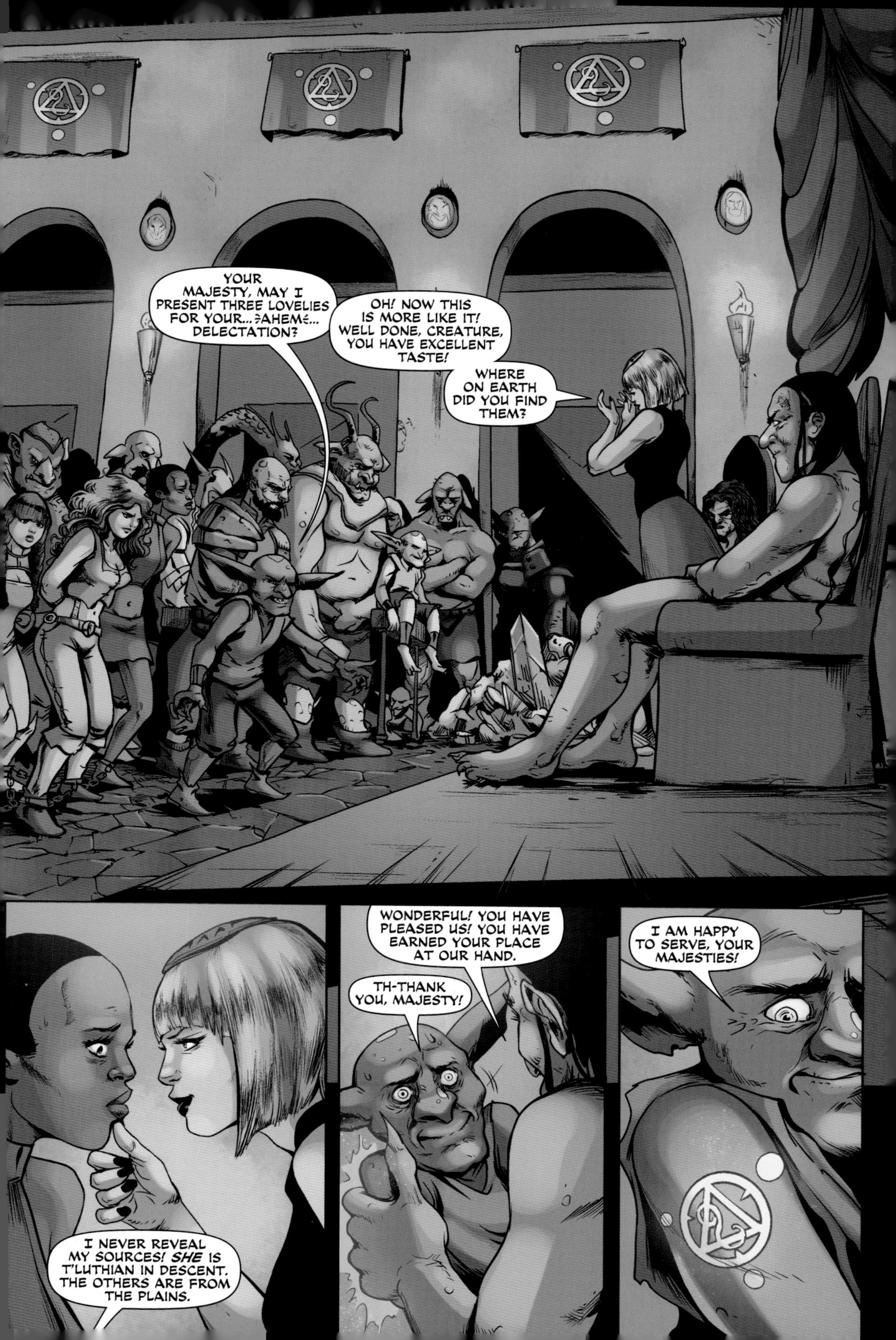
YOUR MAJESTY, MAY I PRESENT THREE LOVELIES FOR YOUR... ≥AHEM≤... DELECTATION?
OH! NOW THIS IS MORE LIKE IT! WELL DONE, CREATURE, YOU HAVE EXCELLENT TASTE!
WHERE ON EARTH DID YOU FIND THEM?
I NEVER REVEAL MY SOURCES! SHE IS T'LUTHIAN IN DESCENT. THE OTHERS ARE FROM THE PLAINS.
WONDERFUL! YOU HAVE PLEASED US! YOU HAVE EARNED YOUR PLACE AT OUR HAND.
TH-THANK YOU, MAJESTY!
I AM HAPPY TO SERVE, YOUR MAJESTIES!

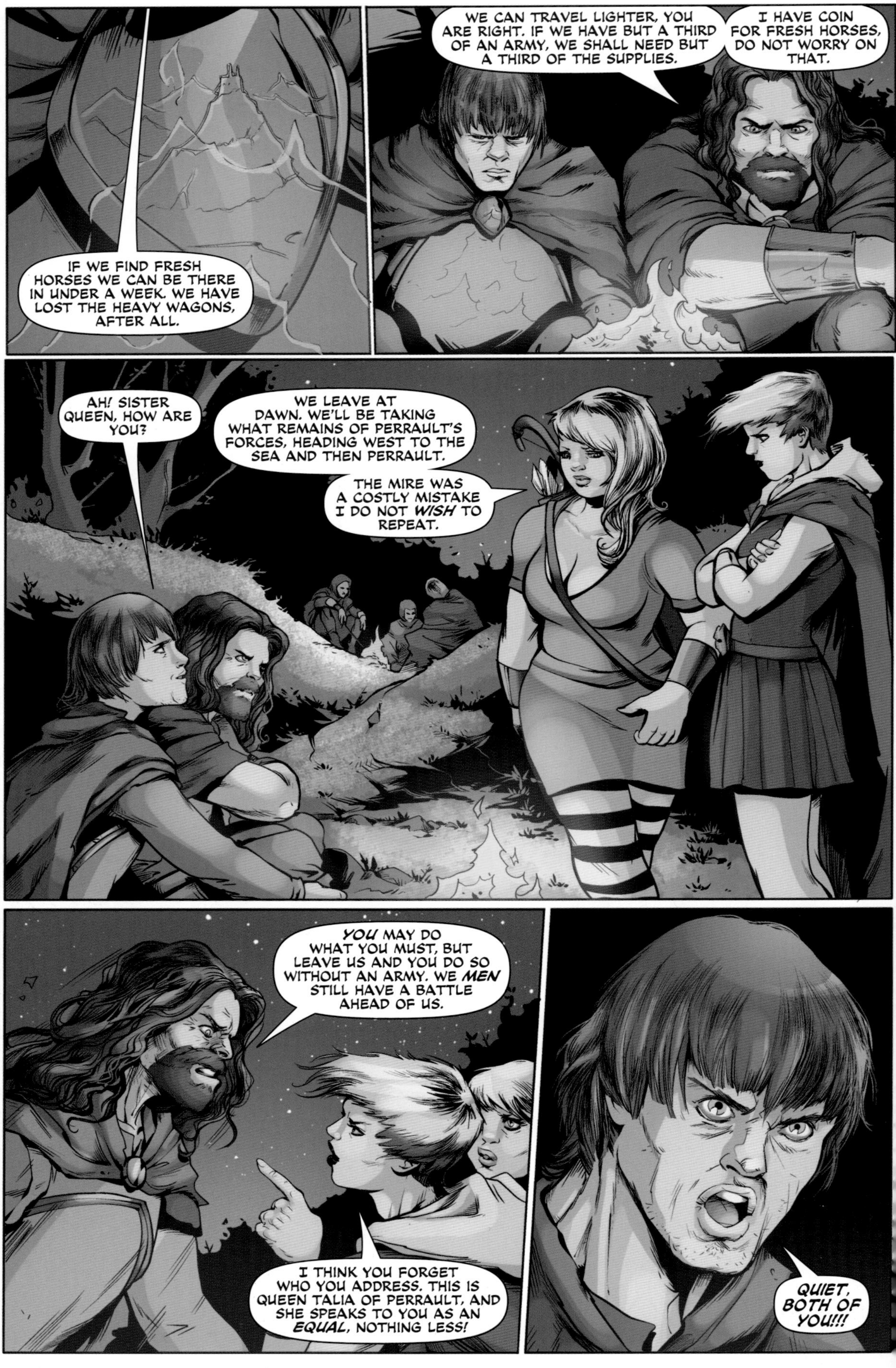
IF WE FIND FRESH HORSES WE CAN BE THERE IN UNDER A WEEK. WE HAVE LOST THE HEAVY WAGONS, AFTER ALL.
WE CAN TRAVEL LIGHTER, YOU ARE RIGHT. IF WE HAVE BUT A THIRD OF AN ARMY, WE SHALL NEED BUT A THIRD OF THE SUPPLIES.
I HAVE COIN FOR FRESH HORSES, DO NOT WORRY ON THAT.
AH! SISTER QUEEN, HOW ARE YOU?
WE LEAVE AT DAWN. WE'LL BE TAKING WHAT REMAINS OF PERRAULT'S FORCES, HEADING WEST TO THE SEA AND THEN PERRAULT.
THE MIRE WAS A COSTLY MISTAKE I DO NOT *WISH* TO REPEAT.
YOU MAY DO WHAT YOU MUST, BUT LEAVE US AND YOU DO SO WITHOUT AN ARMY. WE *MEN* STILL HAVE A BATTLE AHEAD OF US.
I THINK YOU FORGET WHO YOU ADDRESS. THIS IS QUEEN TALIA OF PERRAULT, AND SHE SPEAKS TO YOU AS AN *EQUAL*, NOTHING LESS!
QUIET, BOTH OF YOU!!!

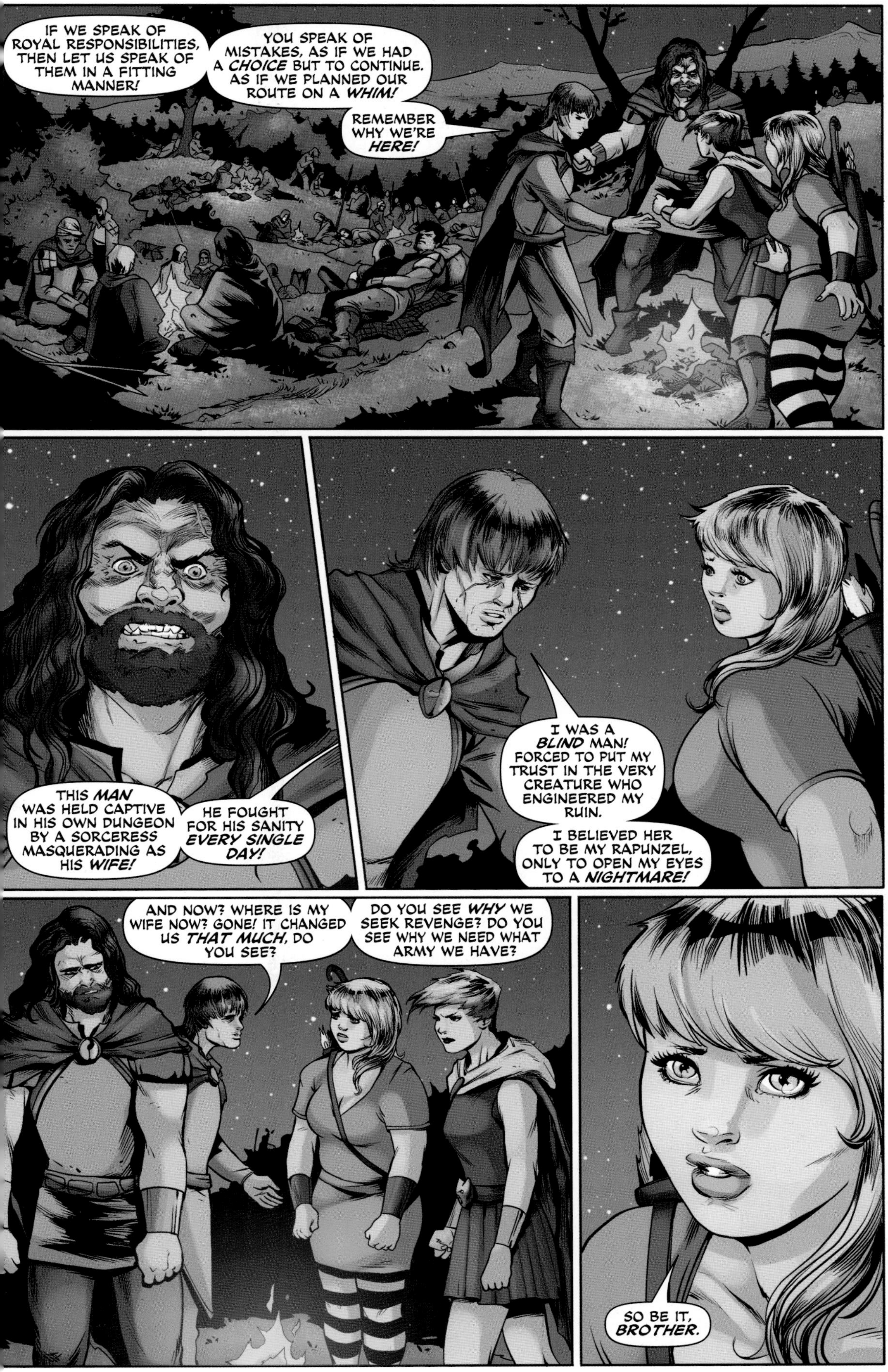

IF WE SPEAK OF ROYAL RESPONSIBILITIES, THEN LET US SPEAK OF THEM IN A FITTING MANNER!
YOU SPEAK OF MISTAKES, AS IF WE HAD A *CHOICE* BUT TO CONTINUE. AS IF WE PLANNED OUR ROUTE ON A *WHIM!*
REMEMBER WHY WE'RE *HERE!*
THIS *MAN* WAS HELD CAPTIVE IN HIS OWN DUNGEON BY A SORCERESS MASQUERADING AS HIS *WIFE!*
HE FOUGHT FOR HIS SANITY *EVERY SINGLE DAY!*
I WAS A *BLIND MAN!* FORCED TO PUT MY TRUST IN THE VERY CREATURE WHO ENGINEERED MY RUIN.
I BELIEVED HER TO BE MY RAPUNZEL, ONLY TO OPEN MY EYES TO A *NIGHTMARE!*
AND NOW? WHERE IS MY WIFE NOW? GONE! IT CHANGED US *THAT MUCH*, DO YOU SEE?
DO YOU SEE *WHY* WE SEEK REVENGE? DO YOU SEE WHY WE NEED WHAT ARMY WE HAVE?
SO BE IT, *BROTHER.*

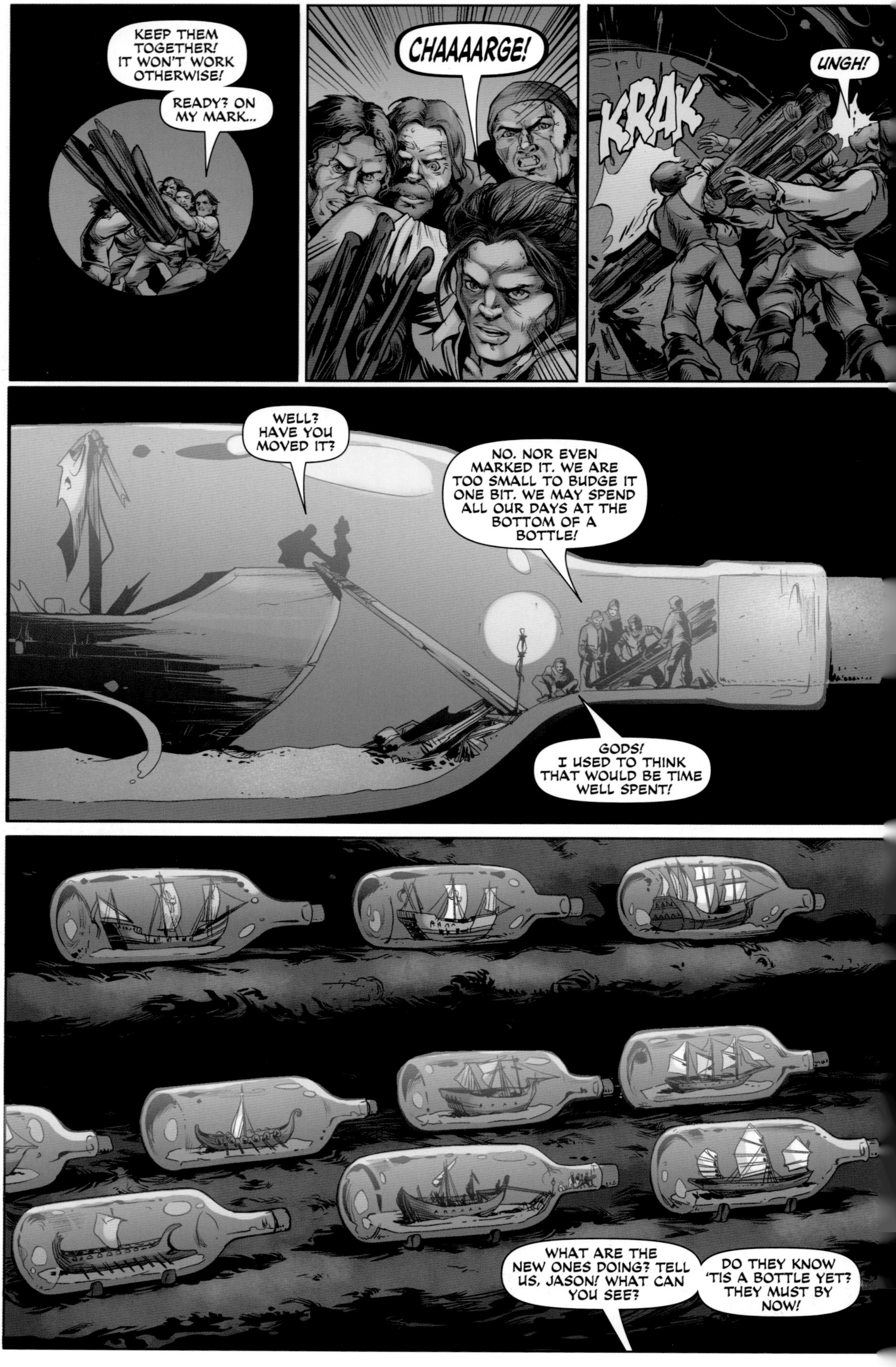
KEEP THEM TOGETHER! IT WON'T WORK OTHERWISE!
READY? ON MY MARK...
CHAAAARGE!
KRAK
UNGH!
WELL? HAVE YOU MOVED IT?
NO. NOR EVEN MARKED IT. WE ARE TOO SMALL TO BUDGE IT ONE BIT. WE MAY SPEND ALL OUR DAYS AT THE BOTTOM OF A BOTTLE!
GODS! I USED TO THINK THAT WOULD BE TIME WELL SPENT!
WHAT ARE THE NEW ONES DOING? TELL US, JASON! WHAT CAN YOU SEE?
DO THEY KNOW 'TIS A BOTTLE YET? THEY MUST BY NOW!

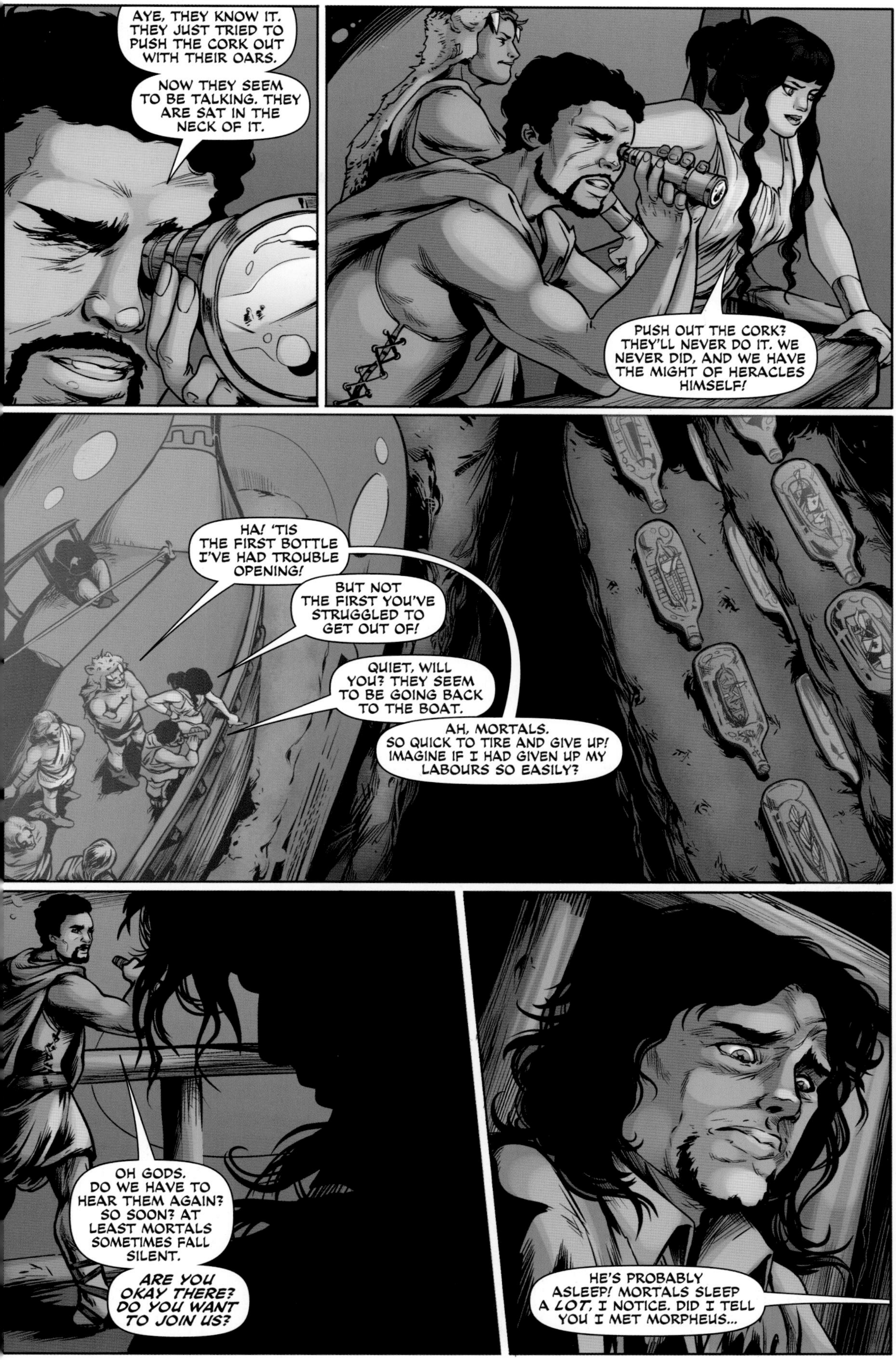
AYE, THEY KNOW IT. THEY JUST TRIED TO PUSH THE CORK OUT WITH THEIR OARS.
NOW THEY SEEM TO BE TALKING. THEY ARE SAT IN THE NECK OF IT.
PUSH OUT THE CORK? THEY'LL NEVER DO IT. WE NEVER DID, AND WE HAVE THE MIGHT OF HERACLES HIMSELF!
HA! 'TIS THE FIRST BOTTLE I'VE HAD TROUBLE OPENING!
BUT NOT THE FIRST YOU'VE STRUGGLED TO GET OUT OF!
QUIET, WILL YOU? THEY SEEM TO BE GOING BACK TO THE BOAT.
AH, MORTALS. SO QUICK TO TIRE AND GIVE UP! IMAGINE IF I HAD GIVEN UP MY LABOURS SO EASILY?
OH GODS. DO WE HAVE TO HEAR THEM AGAIN? SO SOON? AT LEAST MORTALS SOMETIMES FALL SILENT.
ARE YOU OKAY THERE? DO YOU WANT TO JOIN US?
HE'S PROBABLY ASLEEP! MORTALS SLEEP A *LOT*, I NOTICE. DID I TELL YOU I MET MORPHEUS...

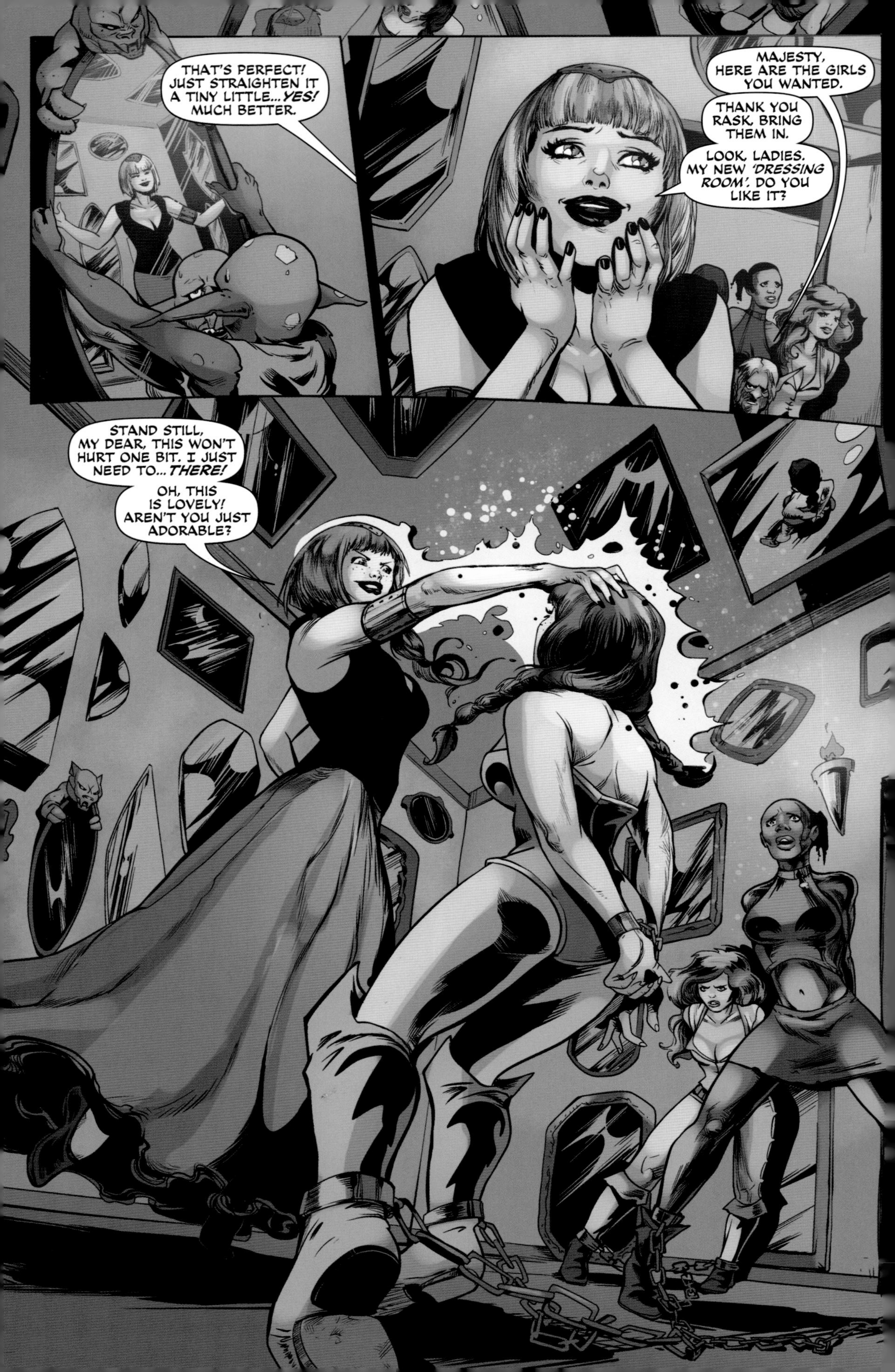
THAT'S PERFECT! JUST STRAIGHTEN IT A TINY LITTLE...*YES!* MUCH BETTER.
MAJESTY, HERE ARE THE GIRLS YOU WANTED.
THANK YOU RASK, BRING THEM IN.
LOOK, LADIES. MY NEW *'DRESSING ROOM'*. DO YOU LIKE IT?
STAND STILL, MY DEAR, THIS WON'T HURT ONE BIT. I JUST NEED TO...*THERE!*
OH, THIS IS LOVELY! AREN'T YOU JUST ADORABLE?

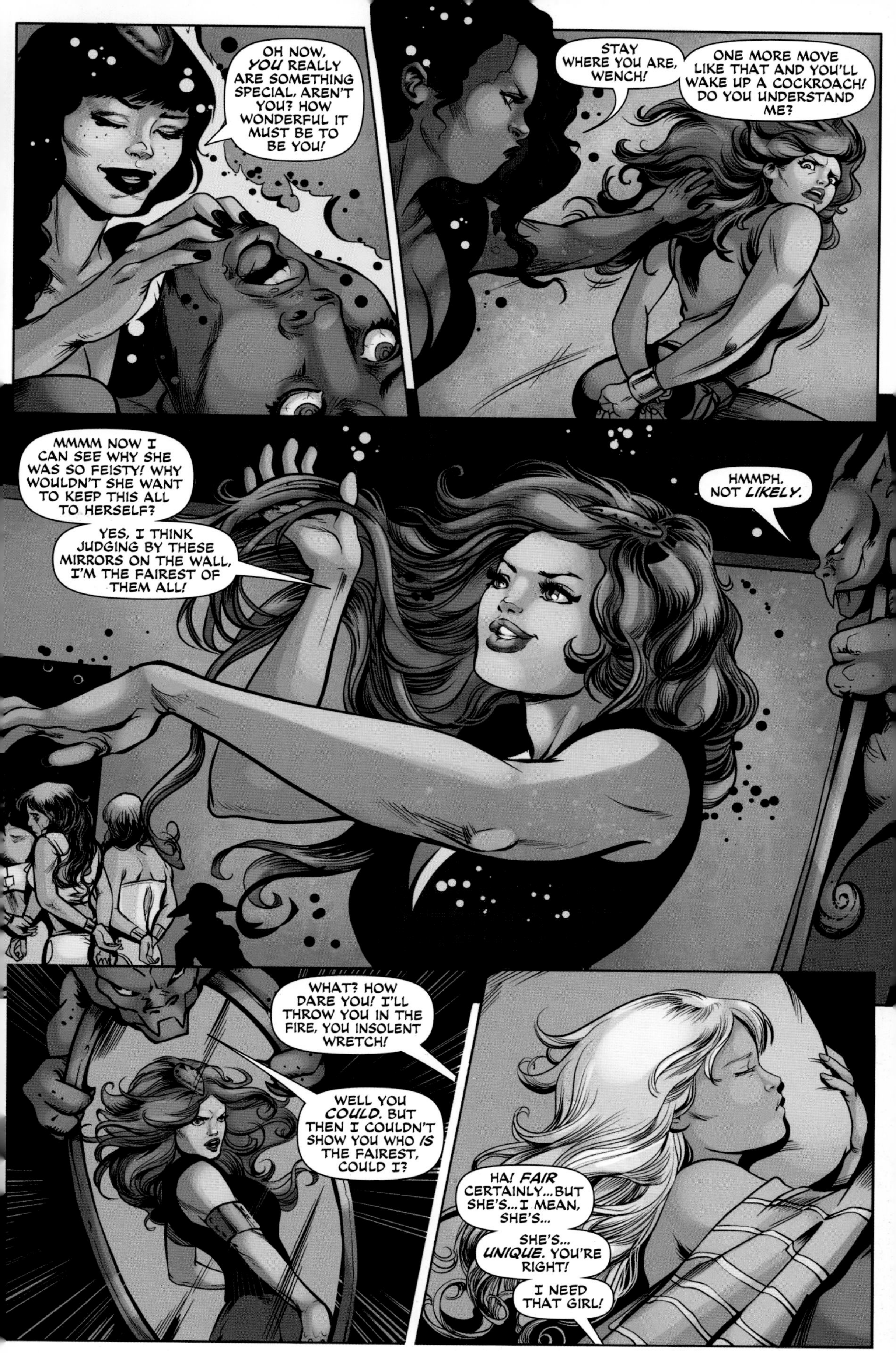
OH NOW, *YOU* REALLY ARE SOMETHING SPECIAL, AREN'T YOU? HOW WONDERFUL IT MUST BE TO BE YOU!
STAY WHERE YOU ARE, WENCH!
ONE MORE MOVE LIKE THAT AND YOU'LL WAKE UP A COCKROACH! DO YOU UNDERSTAND ME?
MMMM NOW I CAN SEE WHY SHE WAS SO FEISTY! WHY WOULDN'T SHE WANT TO KEEP THIS ALL TO HERSELF?
YES, I THINK JUDGING BY THESE MIRRORS ON THE WALL, I'M THE FAIREST OF THEM ALL!
HMMPH. NOT *LIKELY*.
WHAT? HOW DARE YOU! I'LL THROW YOU IN THE FIRE, YOU INSOLENT WRETCH!
WELL YOU *COULD*. BUT THEN I COULDN'T SHOW YOU WHO *IS* THE FAIREST, COULD I?
HA! *FAIR* CERTAINLY...BUT SHE'S...I MEAN, SHE'S...
SHE'S... *UNIQUE*. YOU'RE RIGHT!
I NEED THAT GIRL!

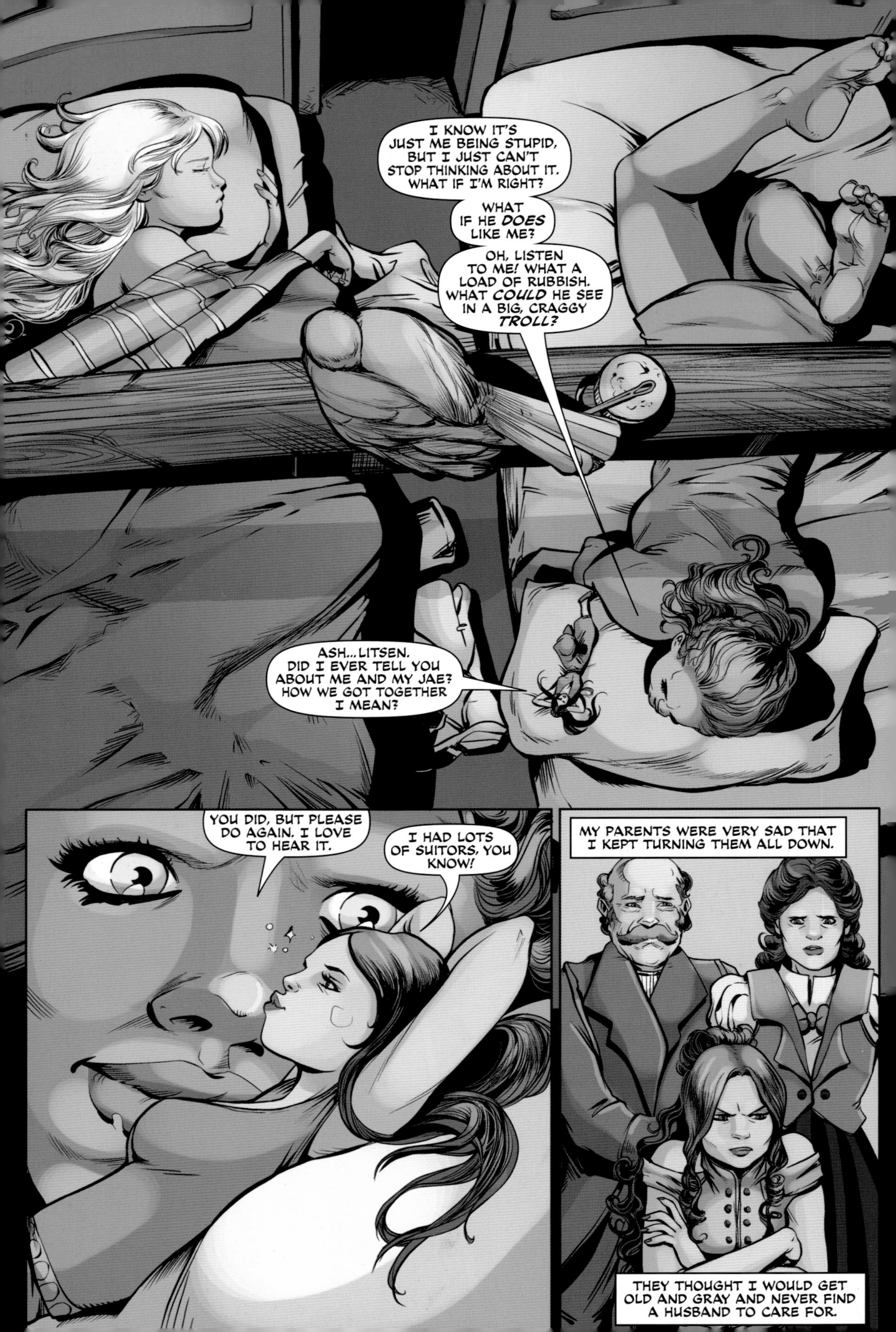
I KNOW IT'S JUST ME BEING STUPID, BUT I JUST CAN'T STOP THINKING ABOUT IT. WHAT IF I'M RIGHT?
WHAT IF HE DOES LIKE ME?
OH, LISTEN TO ME! WHAT A LOAD OF RUBBISH. WHAT COULD HE SEE IN A BIG, CRAGGY TROLL?
ASH... LITSEN. DID I EVER TELL YOU ABOUT ME AND MY JAE? HOW WE GOT TOGETHER I MEAN?
YOU DID, BUT PLEASE DO AGAIN. I LOVE TO HEAR IT.
I HAD LOTS OF SUITORS, YOU KNOW!
MY PARENTS WERE VERY SAD THAT I KEPT TURNING THEM ALL DOWN.
THEY THOUGHT I WOULD GET OLD AND GRAY AND NEVER FIND A HUSBAND TO CARE FOR.

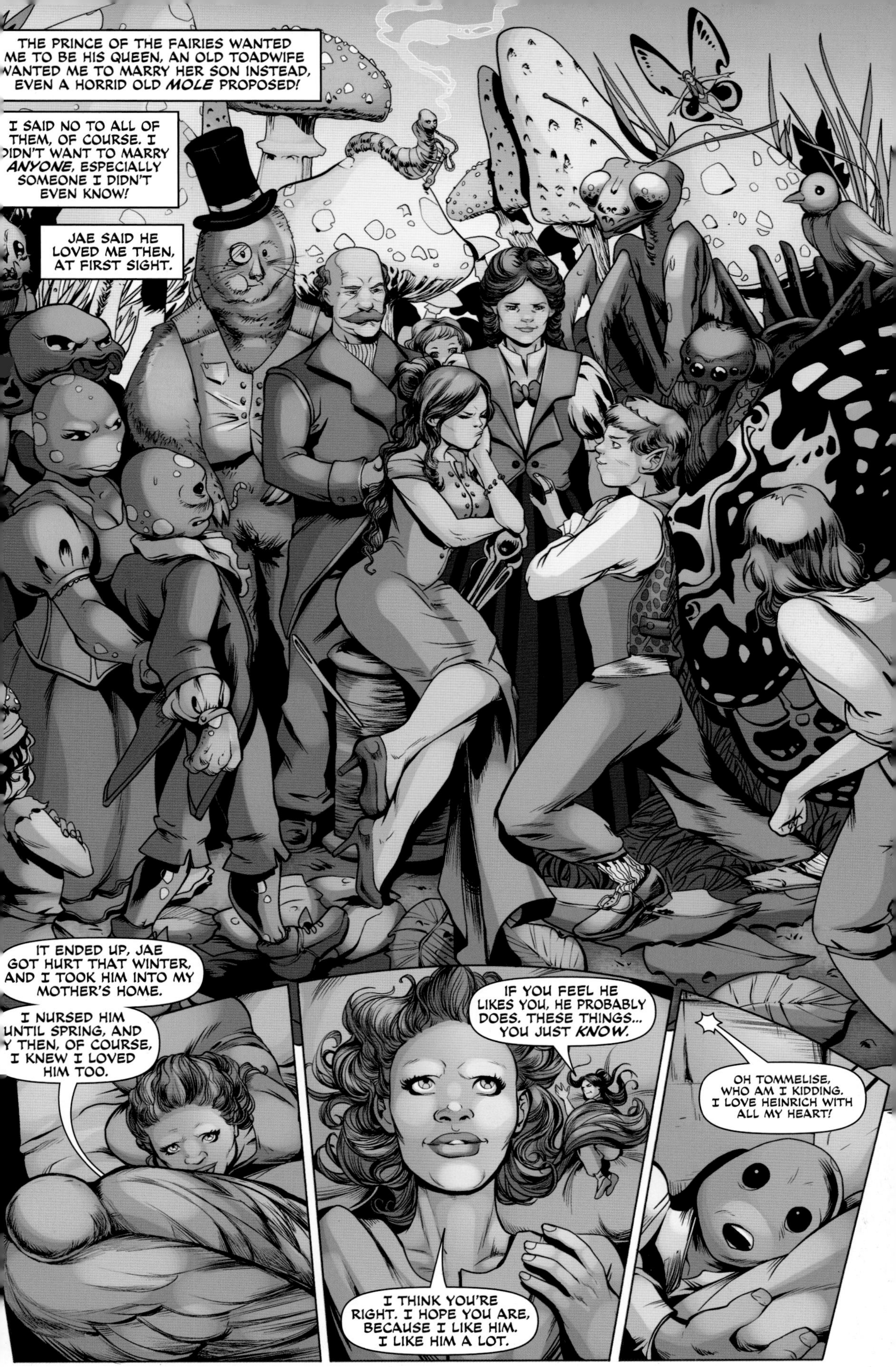

THE PRINCE OF THE FAIRIES WANTED ME TO BE HIS QUEEN, AN OLD TOADWIFE WANTED ME TO MARRY HER SON INSTEAD, EVEN A HORRID OLD *MOLE* PROPOSED!
I SAID NO TO ALL OF THEM, OF COURSE. I DIDN'T WANT TO MARRY *ANYONE*, ESPECIALLY SOMEONE I DIDN'T EVEN KNOW!
JAE SAID HE LOVED ME THEN, AT FIRST SIGHT.
IT ENDED UP, JAE GOT HURT THAT WINTER, AND I TOOK HIM INTO MY MOTHER'S HOME.
I NURSED HIM UNTIL SPRING, AND BY THEN, OF COURSE, I KNEW I LOVED HIM TOO.
IF YOU FEEL HE LIKES YOU, HE PROBABLY DOES. THESE THINGS... YOU JUST *KNOW*.
I THINK YOU'RE RIGHT. I HOPE YOU ARE, BECAUSE I LIKE HIM. I LIKE HIM A LOT.
OH TOMMELISE, WHO AM I KIDDING. I LOVE HEINRICH WITH ALL MY HEART!

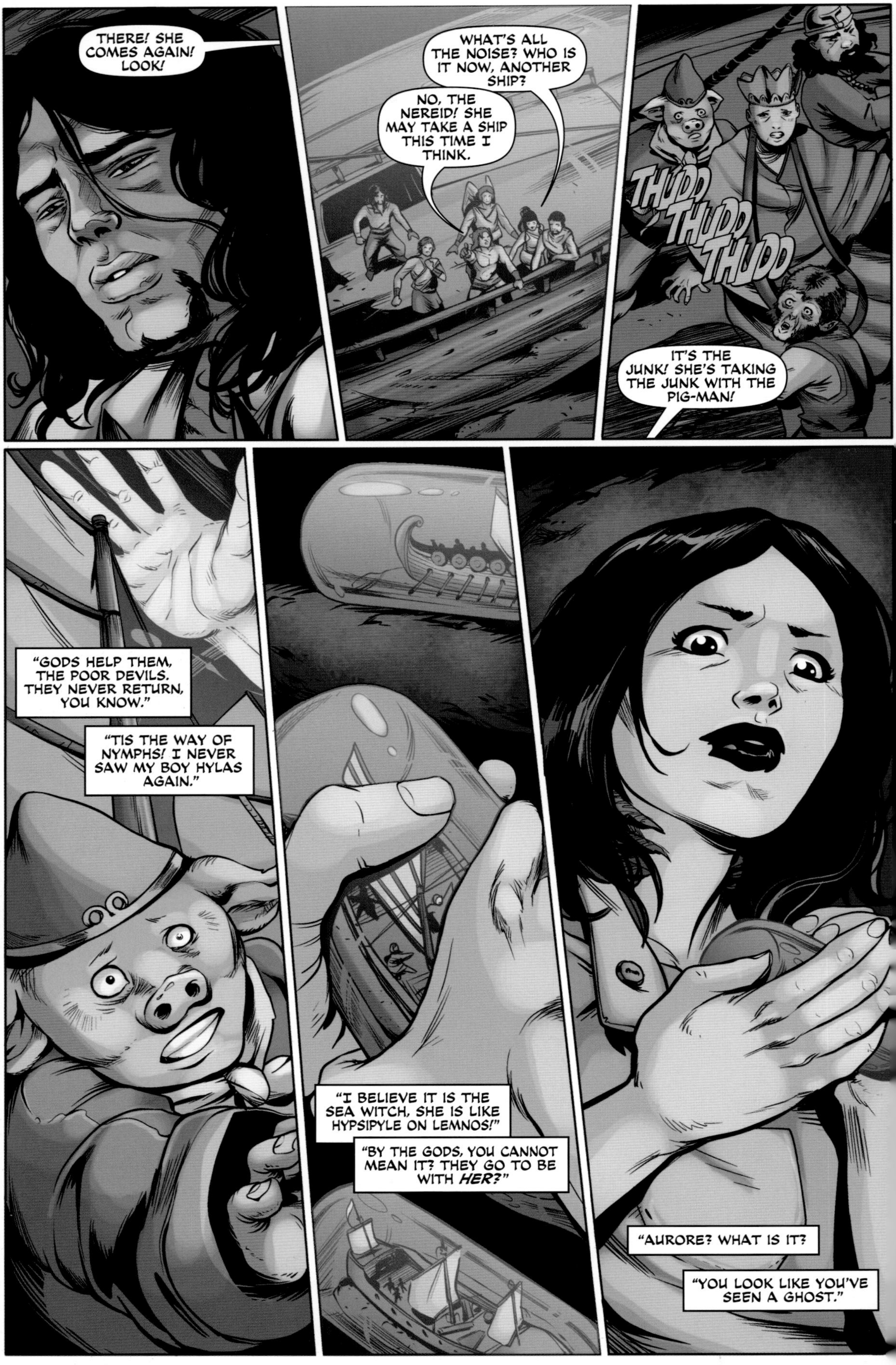
THERE! SHE COMES AGAIN! LOOK!
WHAT'S ALL THE NOISE? WHO IS IT NOW, ANOTHER SHIP?
NO, THE NEREID! SHE MAY TAKE A SHIP THIS TIME I THINK.
THUDD THUDD THUDD
IT'S THE JUNK! SHE'S TAKING THE JUNK WITH THE PIG-MAN!
"GODS HELP THEM, THE POOR DEVILS. THEY NEVER RETURN, YOU KNOW."
"TIS THE WAY OF NYMPHS! I NEVER SAW MY BOY HYLAS AGAIN."
"I BELIEVE IT IS THE SEA WITCH, SHE IS LIKE HYPSIPYLE ON LEMNOS!"
"BY THE GODS, YOU CANNOT MEAN IT? THEY GO TO BE WITH HER?"
"AURORE? WHAT IS IT?
"YOU LOOK LIKE YOU'VE SEEN A GHOST."

Chapter

12

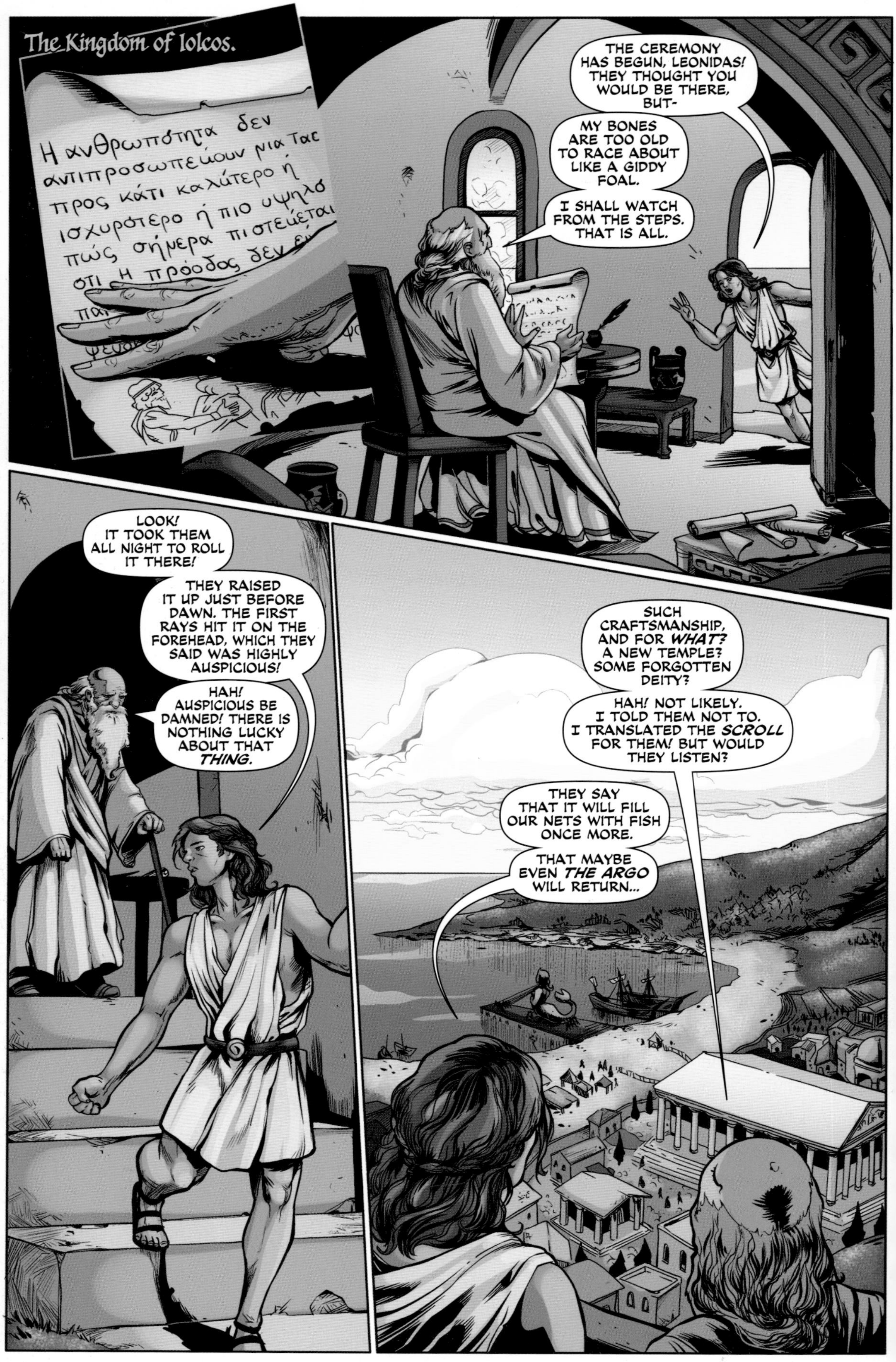

The Kingdom of Iolcos.
Η ανθρωπότητα δεν
αντιπροσωπεύουν μια τας
προς κάτι καλύτερο ή
ισχυρότερο ή πιο υψηλό
πώς σήμερα πιστεύεται
οτι η πρόοδος δεν
THE CEREMONY HAS BEGUN, LEONIDAS! THEY THOUGHT YOU WOULD BE THERE, BUT-
MY BONES ARE TOO OLD TO RACE ABOUT LIKE A GIDDY FOAL.
I SHALL WATCH FROM THE STEPS. THAT IS ALL.
LOOK! IT TOOK THEM ALL NIGHT TO ROLL IT THERE!
THEY RAISED IT UP JUST BEFORE DAWN. THE FIRST RAYS HIT IT ON THE FOREHEAD, WHICH THEY SAID WAS HIGHLY AUSPICIOUS!
HAH! AUSPICIOUS BE DAMNED! THERE IS NOTHING LUCKY ABOUT THAT *THING*.
SUCH CRAFTSMANSHIP, AND FOR *WHAT?* A NEW TEMPLE? SOME FORGOTTEN DEITY?
HAH! NOT LIKELY. I TOLD THEM NOT TO. I TRANSLATED THE *SCROLL* FOR THEM! BUT WOULD THEY LISTEN?
THEY SAY THAT IT WILL FILL OUR NETS WITH FISH ONCE MORE.
THAT MAYBE EVEN *THE ARGO* WILL RETURN...

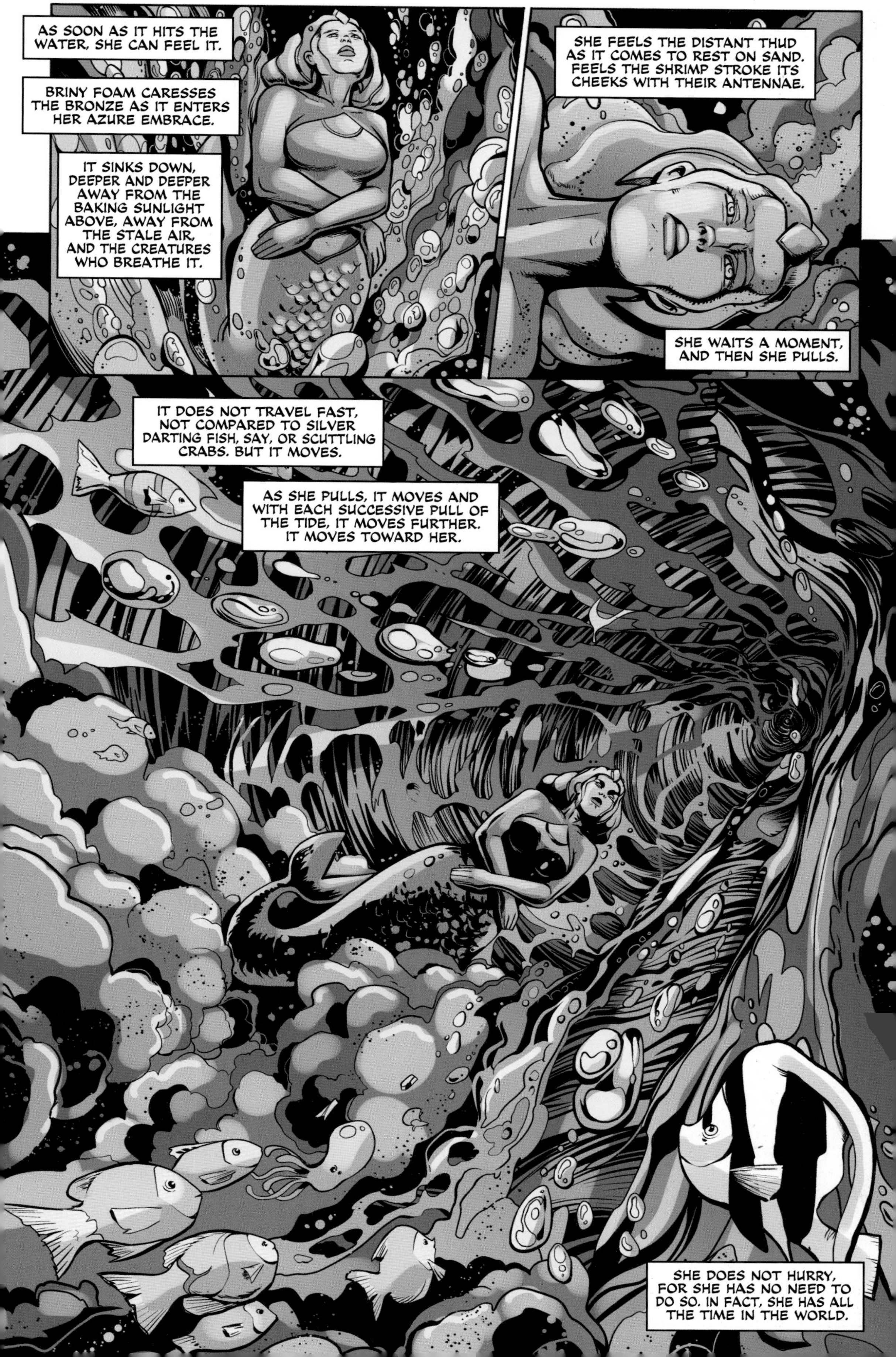
AS SOON AS IT HITS THE WATER, SHE CAN FEEL IT.
BRINY FOAM CARESSES THE BRONZE AS IT ENTERS HER AZURE EMBRACE.
IT SINKS DOWN, DEEPER AND DEEPER AWAY FROM THE BAKING SUNLIGHT ABOVE, AWAY FROM THE STALE AIR, AND THE CREATURES WHO BREATHE IT.
SHE FEELS THE DISTANT THUD AS IT COMES TO REST ON SAND. FEELS THE SHRIMP STROKE ITS CHEEKS WITH THEIR ANTENNAE.
SHE WAITS A MOMENT, AND THEN SHE PULLS.
IT DOES NOT TRAVEL FAST, NOT COMPARED TO SILVER DARTING FISH, SAY, OR SCUTTLING CRABS. BUT IT MOVES.
AS SHE PULLS, IT MOVES AND WITH EACH SUCCESSIVE PULL OF THE TIDE, IT MOVES FURTHER. IT MOVES TOWARD HER.
SHE DOES NOT HURRY, FOR SHE HAS NO NEED TO DO SO. IN FACT, SHE HAS ALL THE TIME IN THE WORLD.

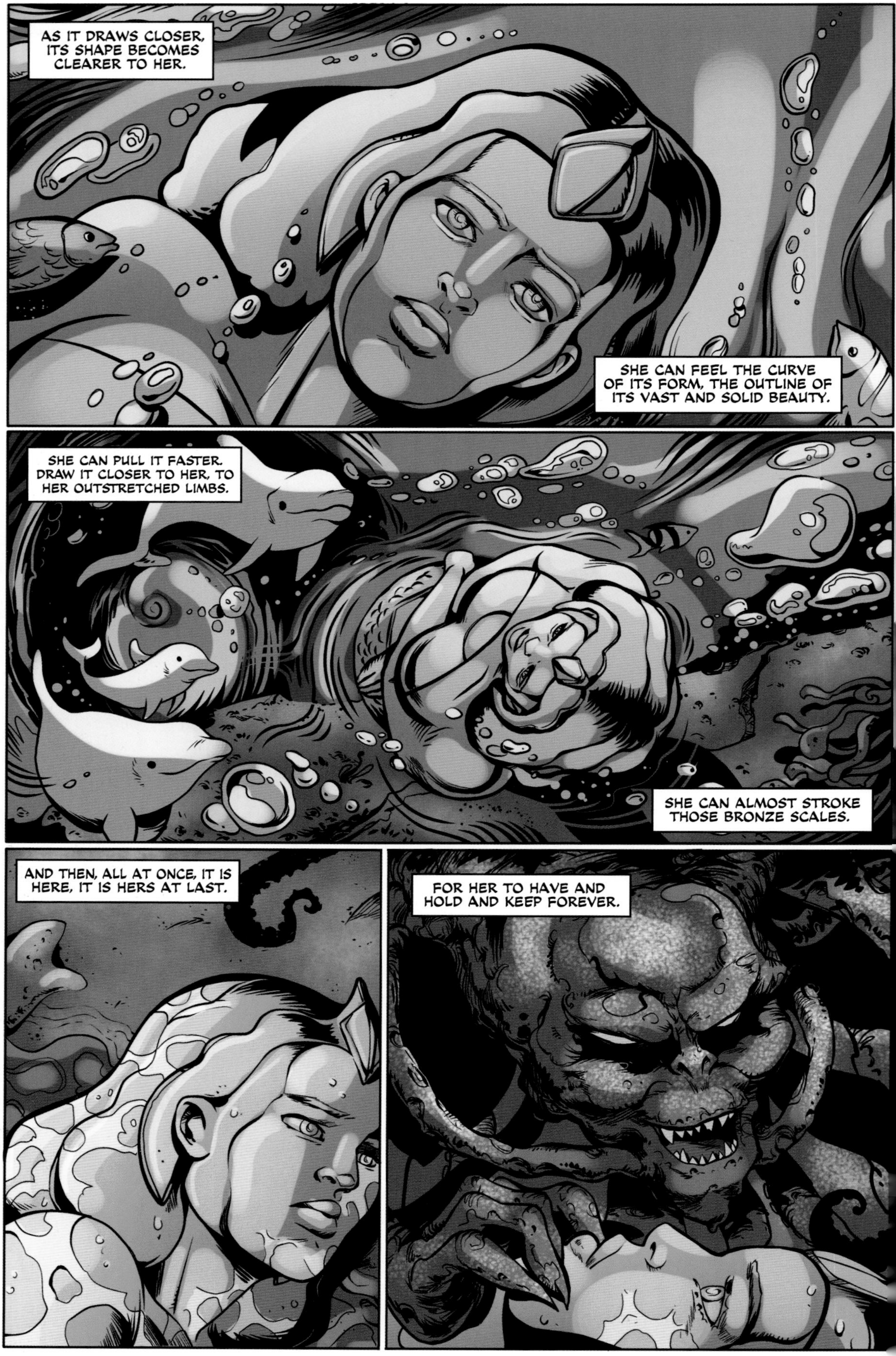
AS IT DRAWS CLOSER, ITS SHAPE BECOMES CLEARER TO HER.
SHE CAN FEEL THE CURVE OF ITS FORM, THE OUTLINE OF ITS VAST AND SOLID BEAUTY.
SHE CAN PULL IT FASTER. DRAW IT CLOSER TO HER, TO HER OUTSTRETCHED LIMBS.
SHE CAN ALMOST STROKE THOSE BRONZE SCALES.
AND THEN, ALL AT ONCE, IT IS HERE, IT IS HERS AT LAST.
FOR HER TO HAVE AND HOLD AND KEEP FOREVER.

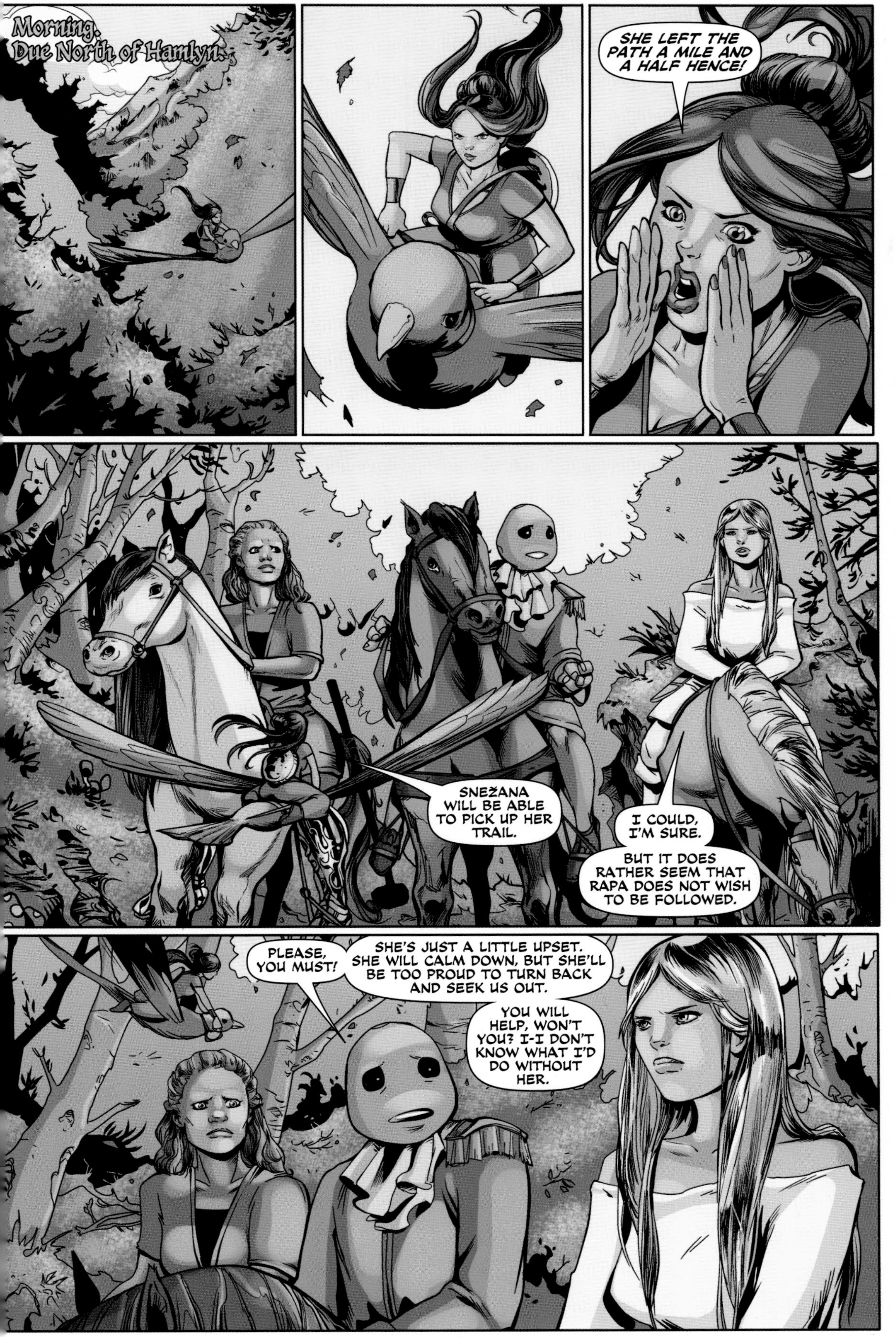
Morning. Due North of Hamlyn.
SHE LEFT THE PATH A MILE AND A HALF HENCE!
SNEŽANA WILL BE ABLE TO PICK UP HER TRAIL.
I COULD, I'M SURE.
BUT IT DOES RATHER SEEM THAT RAPA DOES NOT WISH TO BE FOLLOWED.
PLEASE, YOU MUST!
SHE'S JUST A LITTLE UPSET. SHE WILL CALM DOWN, BUT SHE'LL BE TOO PROUD TO TURN BACK AND SEEK US OUT.
YOU WILL HELP, WON'T YOU? I-I DON'T KNOW WHAT I'D DO WITHOUT HER.

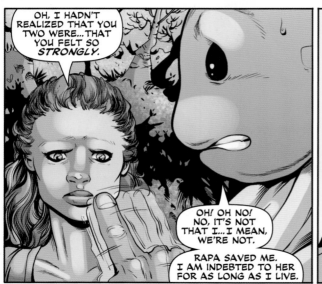

OH, I HADN'T REALIZED THAT YOU TWO WERE...THAT YOU FELT SO *STRONGLY.*

OH! OH NO! NO, IT'S NOT THAT I... I MEAN, WE'RE NOT.

RAPA SAVED ME. I AM INDEBTED TO HER FOR AS LONG AS I LIVE.

B-BUT I DO FEEL *STRONGLY* ABOUT SOMEONE.

MISS ASH, I THINK I–

LOOK, THERE!

WHAT'S HAPPENING? WHAT *ARE* THOSE THINGS?

PREPARE YOURSELVES.

WE ARE UNDER ATTACK...

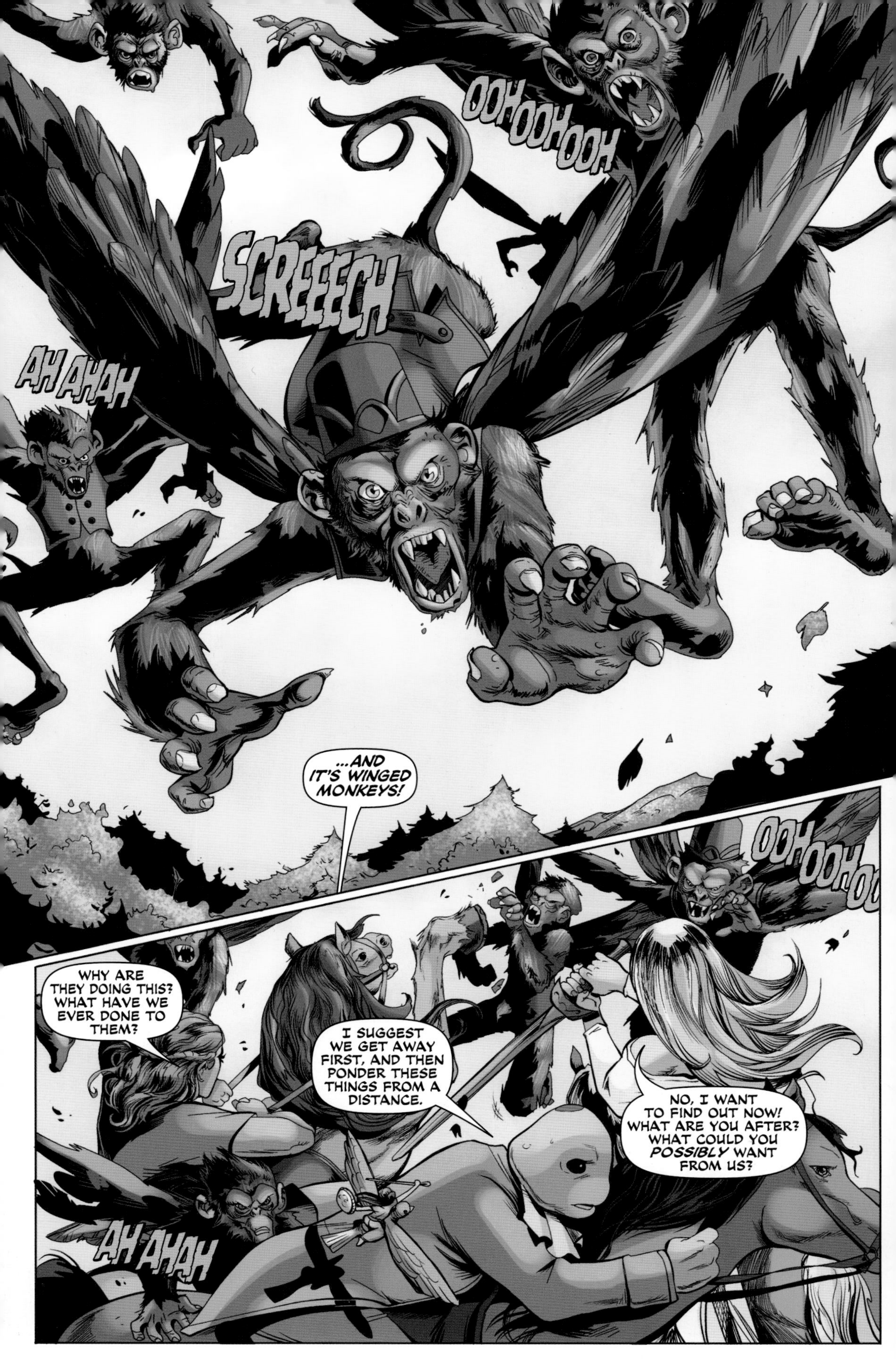
OOHOOHOOH
SCREEECH
AH AHAH
...AND IT'S WINGED MONKEYS!
OOHOOHOO
WHY ARE THEY DOING THIS? WHAT HAVE WE EVER DONE TO THEM?
I SUGGEST WE GET AWAY FIRST, AND THEN PONDER THESE THINGS FROM A DISTANCE.
NO, I WANT TO FIND OUT NOW! WHAT ARE YOU AFTER? WHAT COULD YOU *POSSIBLY* WANT FROM US?
AH AHAH

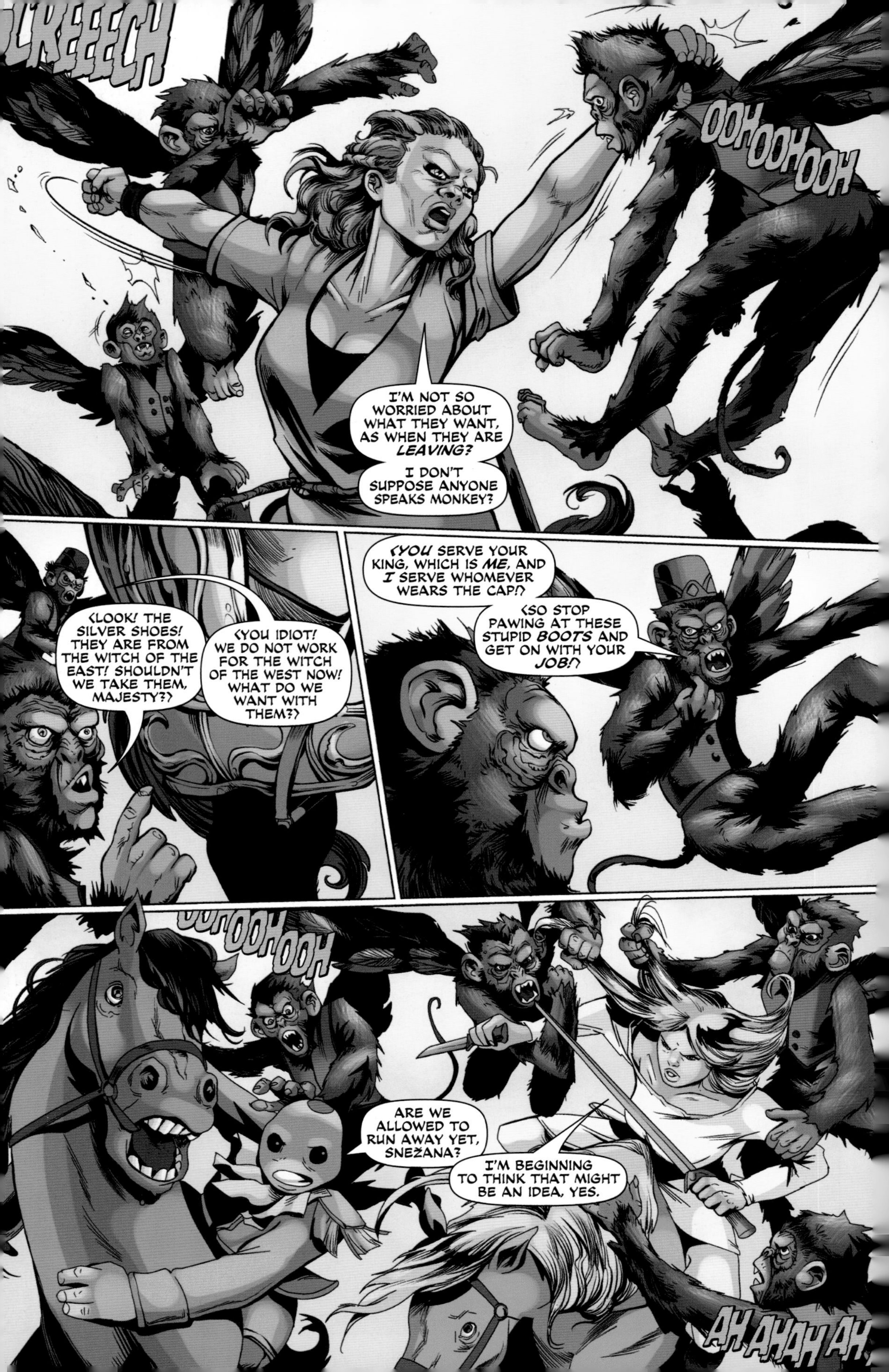
SKREEECH
OOHOOHOOH
I'M NOT SO WORRIED ABOUT WHAT THEY WANT, AS WHEN THEY ARE *LEAVING?*
I DON'T SUPPOSE ANYONE SPEAKS MONKEY?
‹LOOK! THE SILVER SHOES! THEY ARE FROM THE WITCH OF THE EAST! SHOULDN'T WE TAKE THEM, MAJESTY?›
‹YOU IDIOT! WE DO NOT WORK FOR THE WITCH OF THE WEST NOW! WHAT DO WE WANT WITH THEM?›
‹*YOU* SERVE YOUR KING, WHICH IS *ME*, AND *I* SERVE WHOMEVER WEARS THE CAP!›
‹SO STOP PAWING AT THESE STUPID *BOOTS* AND GET ON WITH YOUR *JOB!*›
OOHOOHOOH
ARE WE ALLOWED TO RUN AWAY YET, SNEŽANA?
I'M BEGINNING TO THINK THAT MIGHT BE AN IDEA, YES.
AH AH AH AH

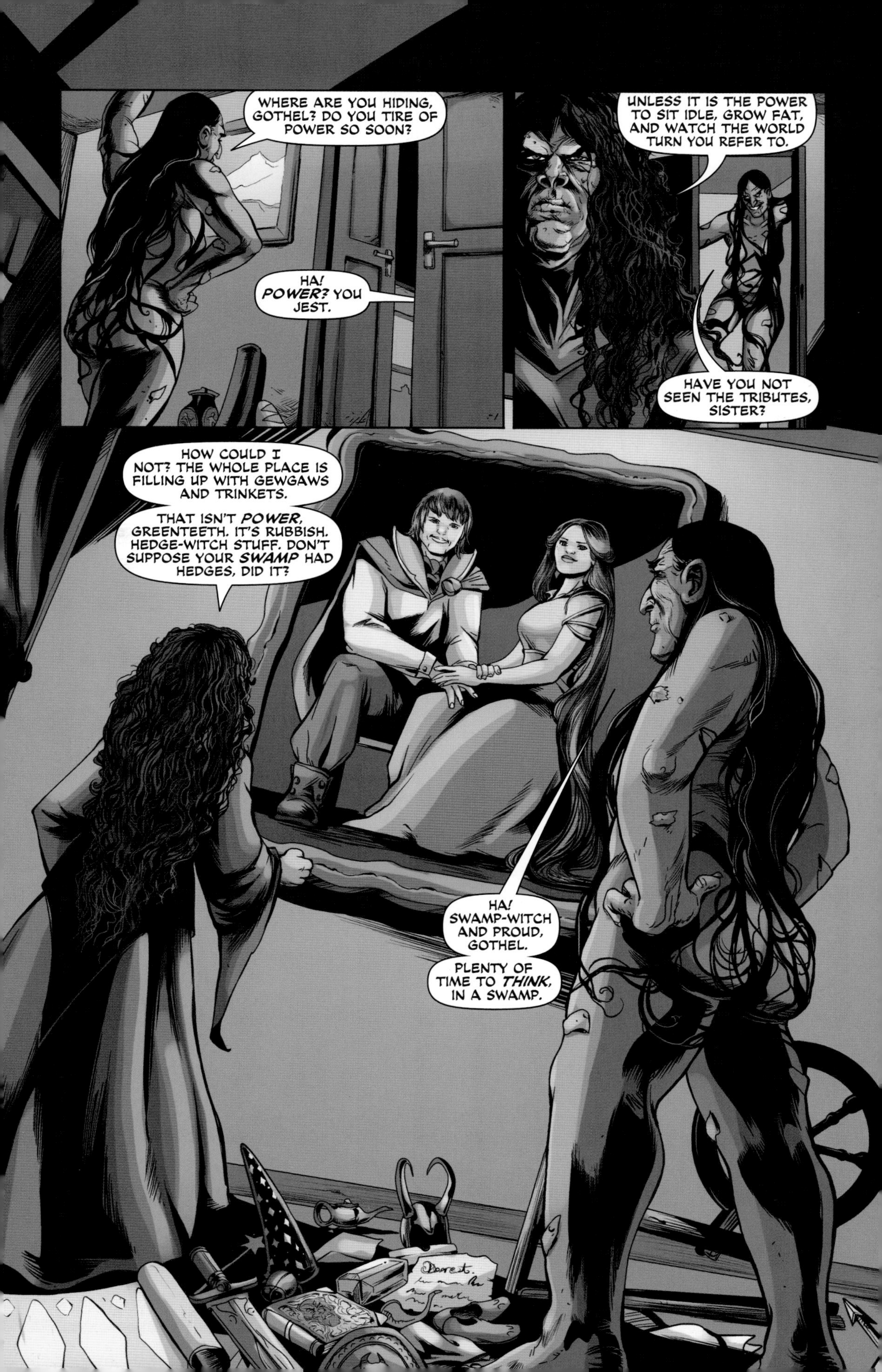
WHERE ARE YOU HIDING, GOTHEL? DO YOU TIRE OF POWER SO SOON?
HA! *POWER?* YOU JEST.
UNLESS IT IS THE POWER TO SIT IDLE, GROW FAT, AND WATCH THE WORLD TURN YOU REFER TO.
HAVE YOU NOT SEEN THE TRIBUTES, SISTER?
HOW COULD I NOT? THE WHOLE PLACE IS FILLING UP WITH GEWGAWS AND TRINKETS.
THAT ISN'T *POWER*, GREENTEETH. IT'S RUBBISH. HEDGE-WITCH STUFF. DON'T SUPPOSE YOUR *SWAMP* HAD HEDGES, DID IT?
HA! SWAMP-WITCH AND PROUD, GOTHEL.
PLENTY OF TIME TO *THINK*, IN A SWAMP.
Dearest.

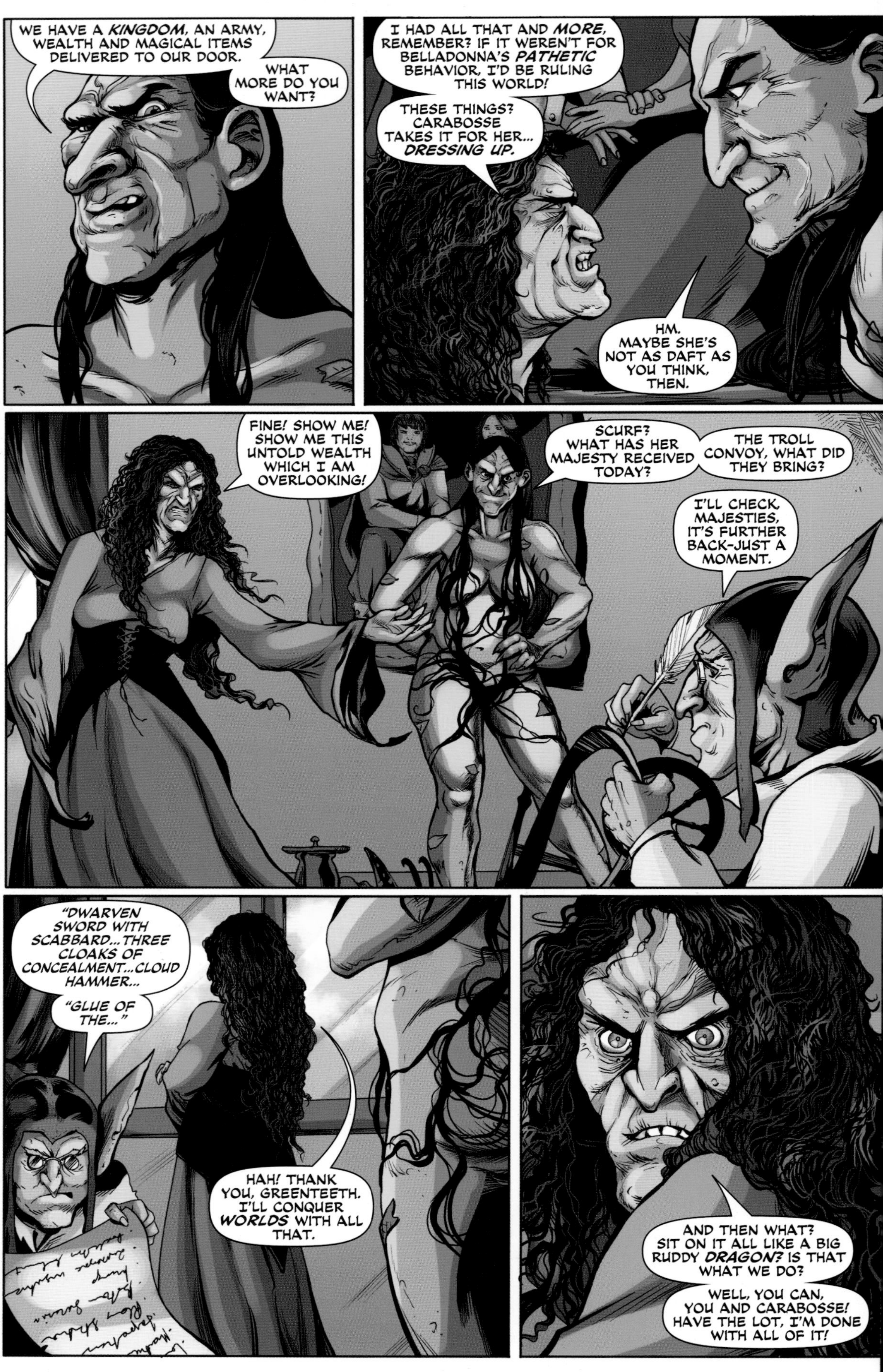
WE HAVE A KINGDOM, AN ARMY, WEALTH AND MAGICAL ITEMS DELIVERED TO OUR DOOR.
WHAT MORE DO YOU WANT?
I HAD ALL THAT AND MORE, REMEMBER? IF IT WEREN'T FOR BELLADONNA'S PATHETIC BEHAVIOR, I'D BE RULING THIS WORLD!
THESE THINGS? CARABOSSE TAKES IT FOR HER... DRESSING UP.
HM. MAYBE SHE'S NOT AS DAFT AS YOU THINK, THEN.
FINE! SHOW ME! SHOW ME THIS UNTOLD WEALTH WHICH I AM OVERLOOKING!
SCURF? WHAT HAS HER MAJESTY RECEIVED TODAY?
THE TROLL CONVOY, WHAT DID THEY BRING?
I'LL CHECK, MAJESTIES, IT'S FURTHER BACK-JUST A MOMENT.
"DWARVEN SWORD WITH SCABBARD...THREE CLOAKS OF CONCEALMENT...CLOUD HAMMER...
"GLUE OF THE..."
HAH! THANK YOU, GREENTEETH. I'LL CONQUER WORLDS WITH ALL THAT.
AND THEN WHAT? SIT ON IT ALL LIKE A BIG RUDDY DRAGON? IS THAT WHAT WE DO?
WELL, YOU CAN, YOU AND CARABOSSE! HAVE THE LOT, I'M DONE WITH ALL OF IT!

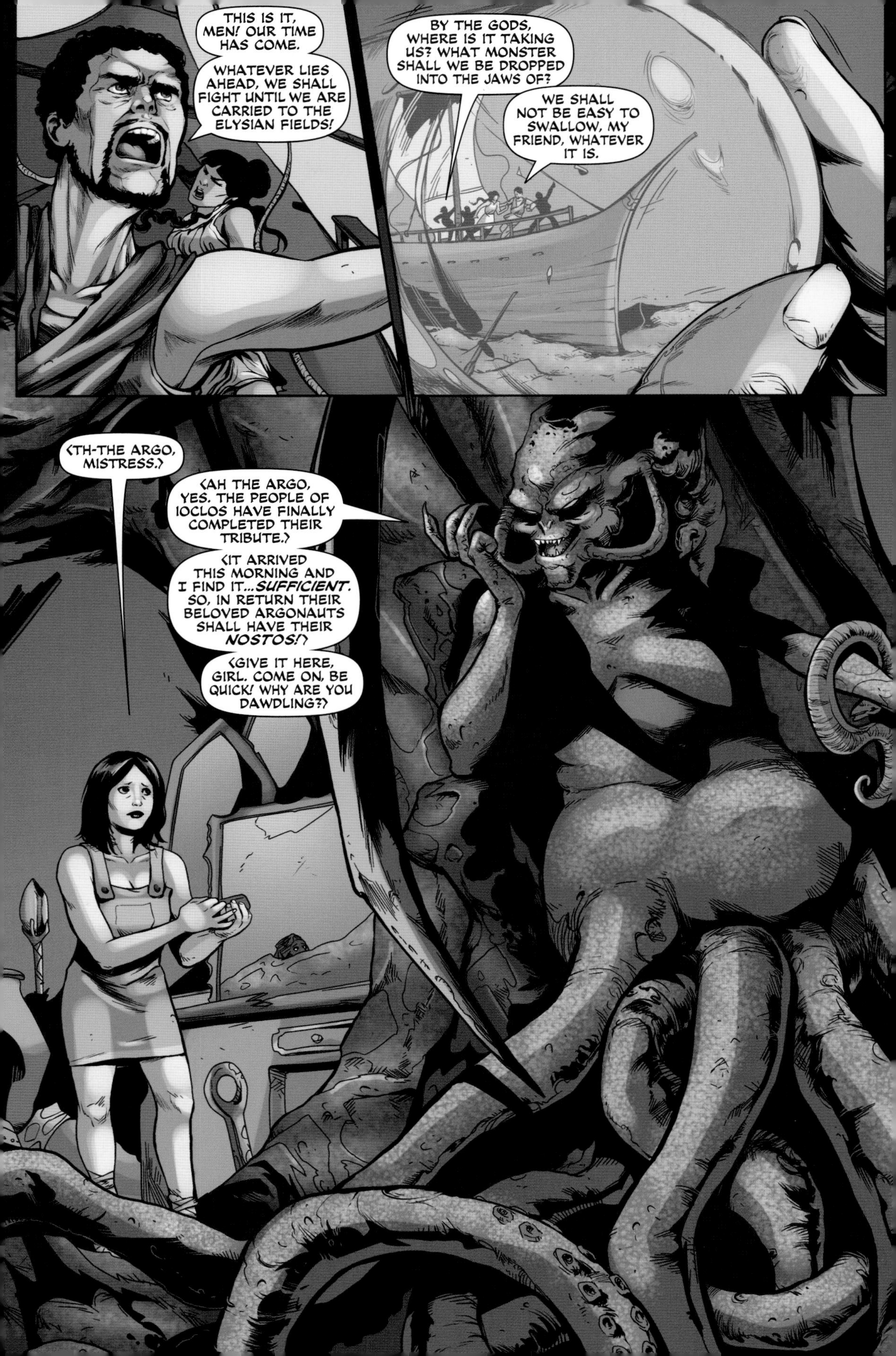
THIS IS IT, MEN! OUR TIME HAS COME.
WHATEVER LIES AHEAD, WE SHALL FIGHT UNTIL WE ARE CARRIED TO THE ELYSIAN FIELDS!
BY THE GODS, WHERE IS IT TAKING US? WHAT MONSTER SHALL WE BE DROPPED INTO THE JAWS OF?
WE SHALL NOT BE EASY TO SWALLOW, MY FRIEND, WHATEVER IT IS.
<TH-THE ARGO, MISTRESS.>
<AH THE ARGO, YES. THE PEOPLE OF IOCLOS HAVE FINALLY COMPLETED THEIR TRIBUTE.>
<IT ARRIVED THIS MORNING AND I FIND IT...*SUFFICIENT*. SO, IN RETURN THEIR BELOVED ARGONAUTS SHALL HAVE THEIR *NOSTOS!*>
<GIVE IT HERE, GIRL. COME ON, BE QUICK! WHY ARE YOU DAWDLING?>

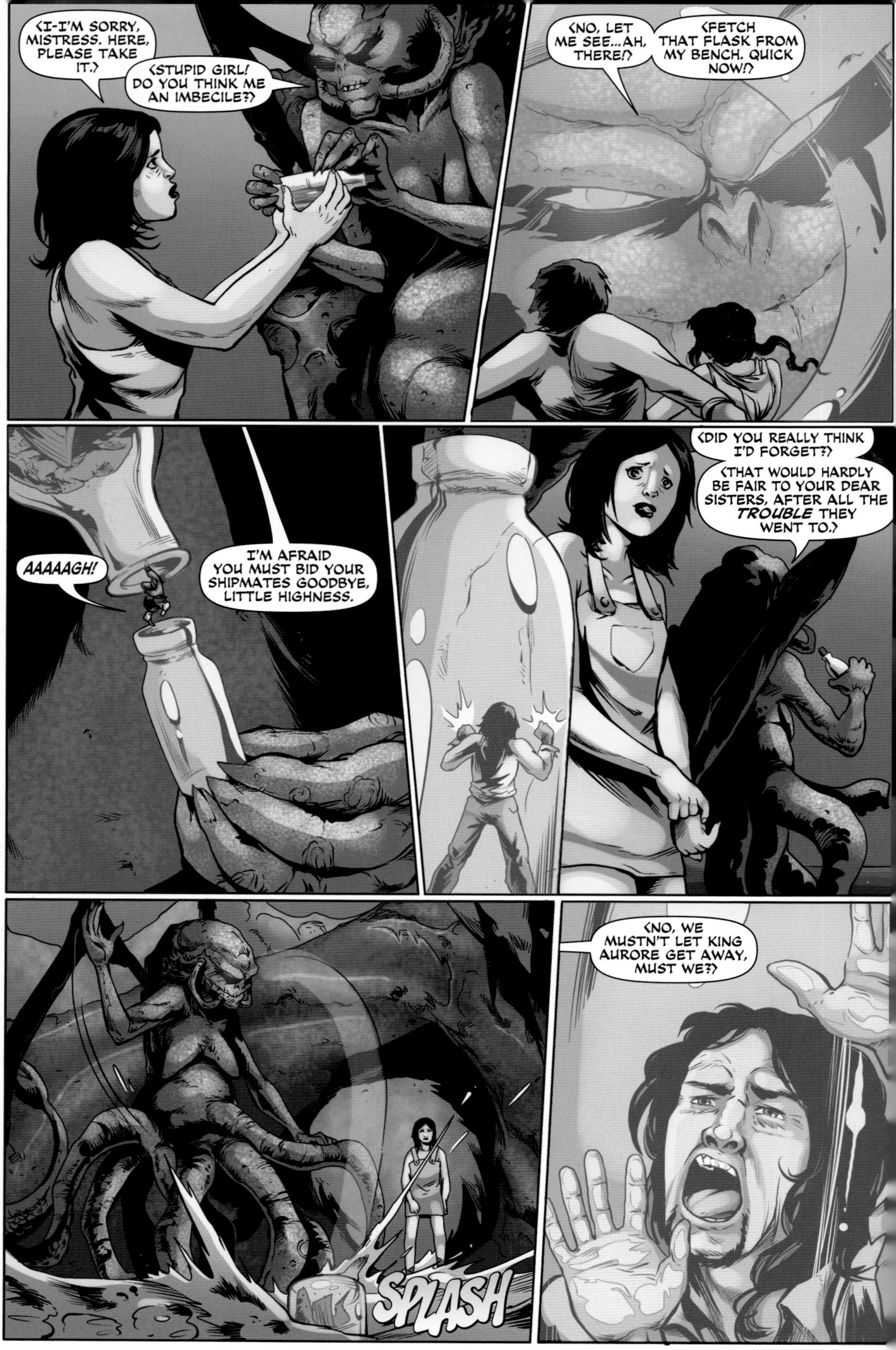

<I-I'M SORRY, MISTRESS. HERE, PLEASE TAKE IT.>
<STUPID GIRL! DO YOU THINK ME AN IMBECILE?>
<NO, LET ME SEE...AH, THERE!>
<FETCH THAT FLASK FROM MY BENCH. QUICK NOW!>
AAAAAGH!
I'M AFRAID YOU MUST BID YOUR SHIPMATES GOODBYE, LITTLE HIGHNESS.
<DID YOU REALLY THINK I'D FORGET?>
<THAT WOULD HARDLY BE FAIR TO YOUR DEAR SISTERS, AFTER ALL THE *TROUBLE* THEY WENT TO.>
SPLASH
<NO, WE MUSTN'T LET KING AURORE GET AWAY, MUST WE?>

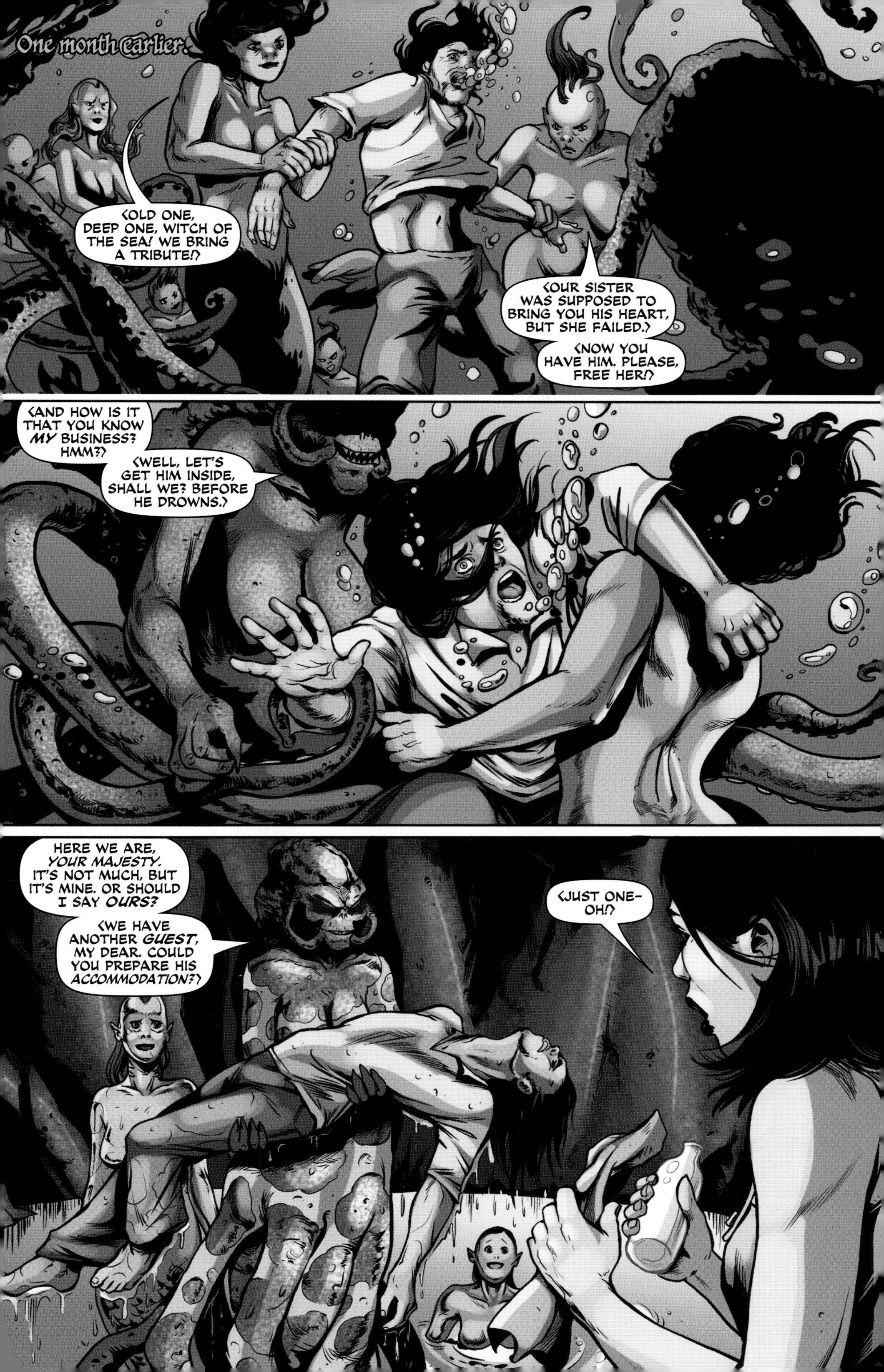
One month earlier.
<OLD ONE, DEEP ONE, WITCH OF THE SEA! WE BRING A TRIBUTE!>
<OUR SISTER WAS SUPPOSED TO BRING YOU HIS HEART, BUT SHE FAILED.>
<NOW YOU HAVE HIM. PLEASE, FREE HER!>
<AND HOW IS IT THAT YOU KNOW MY BUSINESS? HMM?>
<WELL, LET'S GET HIM INSIDE, SHALL WE? BEFORE HE DROWNS.>
HERE WE ARE, YOUR MAJESTY. IT'S NOT MUCH, BUT IT'S MINE. OR SHOULD I SAY OURS?
<WE HAVE ANOTHER GUEST, MY DEAR. COULD YOU PREPARE HIS ACCOMMODATION?>
<JUST ONE- OH!>

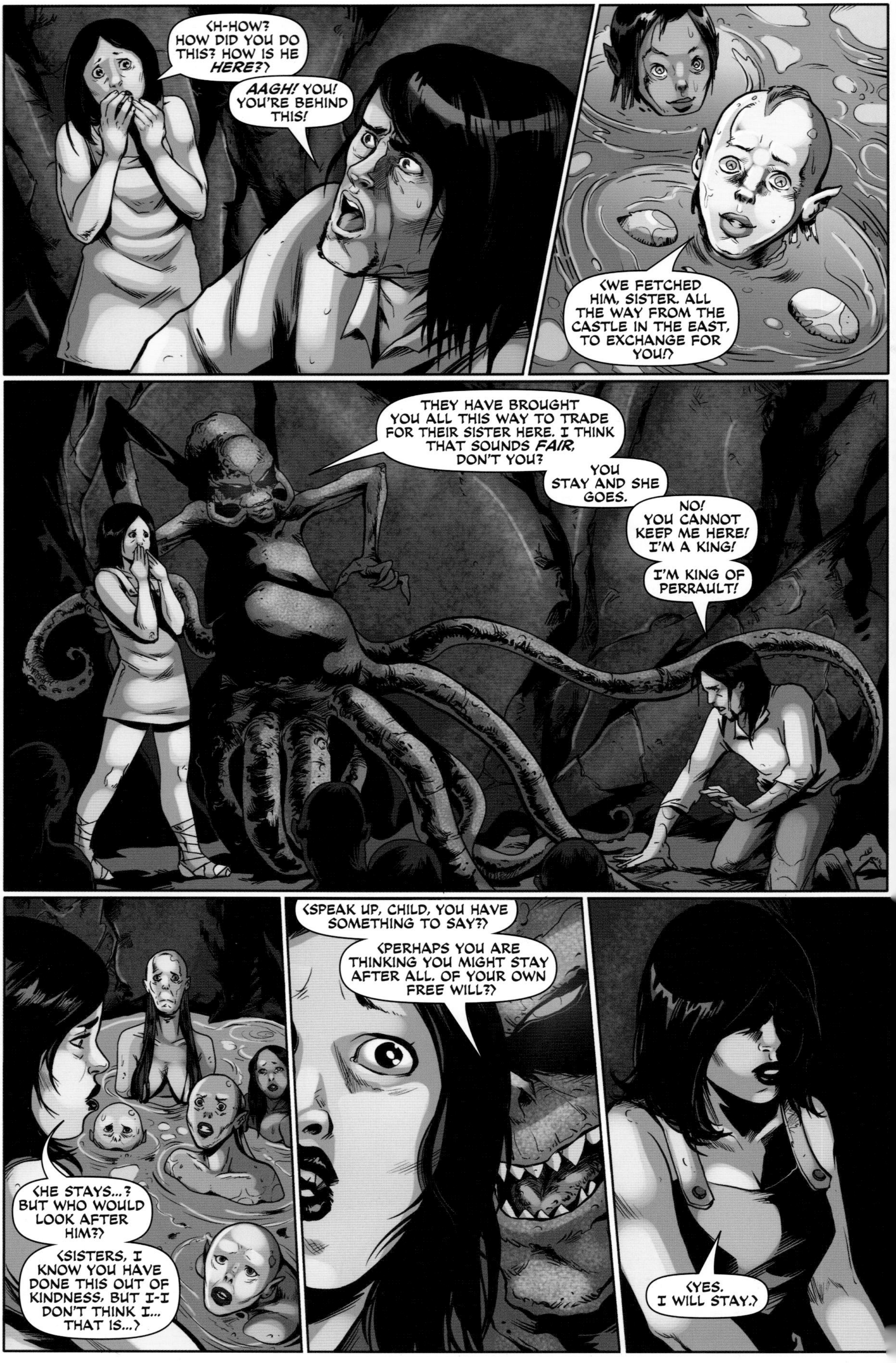
<H-HOW? HOW DID YOU DO THIS? HOW IS HE *HERE*?>
AAGH! YOU! YOU'RE BEHIND THIS!
<WE FETCHED HIM, SISTER. ALL THE WAY FROM THE CASTLE IN THE EAST, TO EXCHANGE FOR YOU!>
THEY HAVE BROUGHT YOU ALL THIS WAY TO TRADE FOR THEIR SISTER HERE. I THINK THAT SOUNDS *FAIR*, DON'T YOU?
YOU STAY AND SHE GOES.
NO! YOU CANNOT KEEP ME HERE! I'M A KING!
I'M KING OF PERRAULT!
<HE STAYS...? BUT WHO WOULD LOOK AFTER HIM?>
<SISTERS, I KNOW YOU HAVE DONE THIS OUT OF KINDNESS, BUT I-I DON'T THINK I... THAT IS...>
<SPEAK UP, CHILD, YOU HAVE SOMETHING TO SAY?>
<PERHAPS YOU ARE THINKING YOU MIGHT STAY AFTER ALL. OF YOUR OWN FREE WILL?>
<YES. I WILL STAY.>

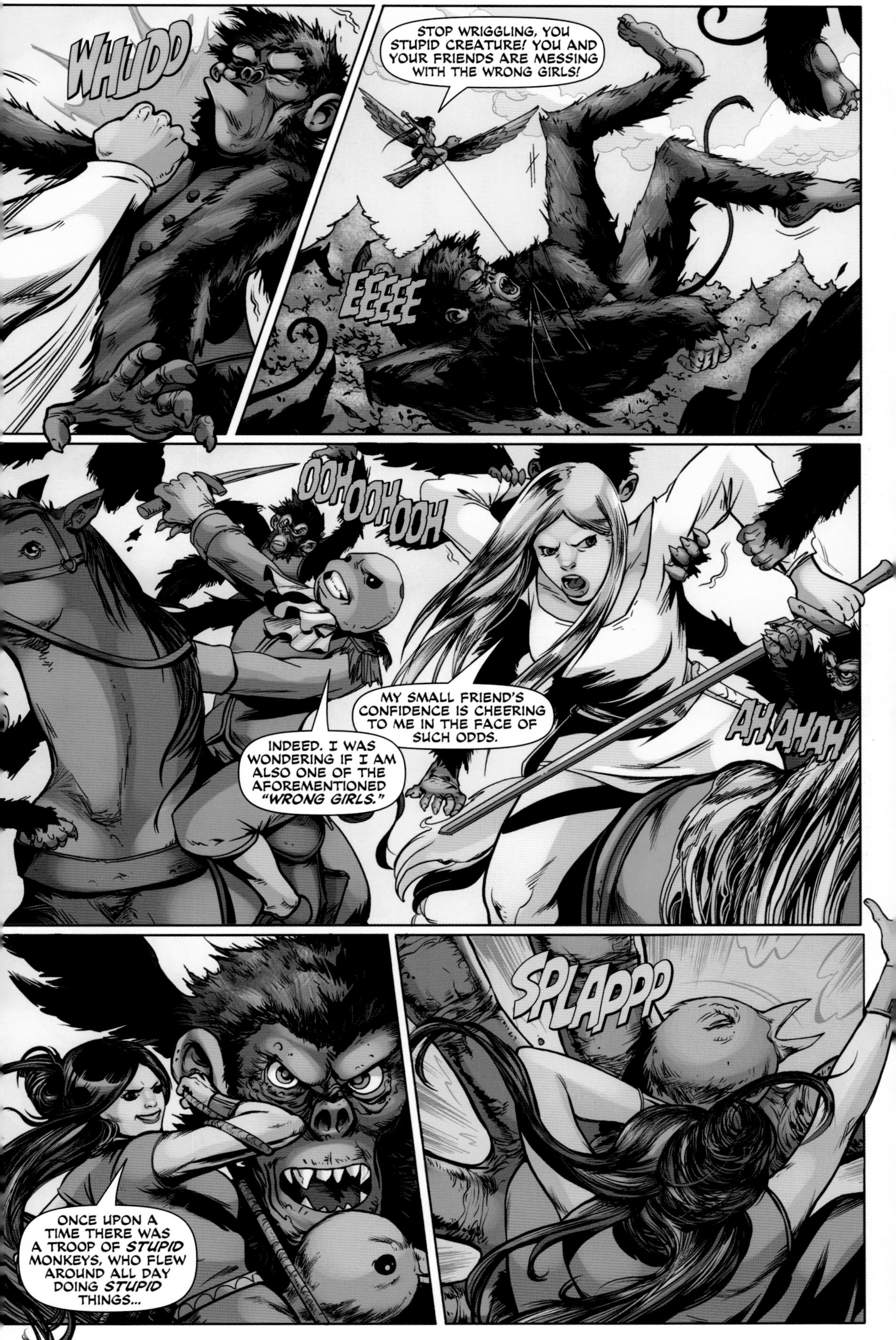
WHUDD
STOP WRIGGLING, YOU STUPID CREATURE! YOU AND YOUR FRIENDS ARE MESSING WITH THE WRONG GIRLS!
EEEEE
OOHOOHOOH
MY SMALL FRIEND'S CONFIDENCE IS CHEERING TO ME IN THE FACE OF SUCH ODDS.
INDEED. I WAS WONDERING IF I AM ALSO ONE OF THE AFOREMENTIONED "WRONG GIRLS."
AH AHAH
ONCE UPON A TIME THERE WAS A TROOP OF STUPID MONKEYS, WHO FLEW AROUND ALL DAY DOING STUPID THINGS...
SPLAPPP

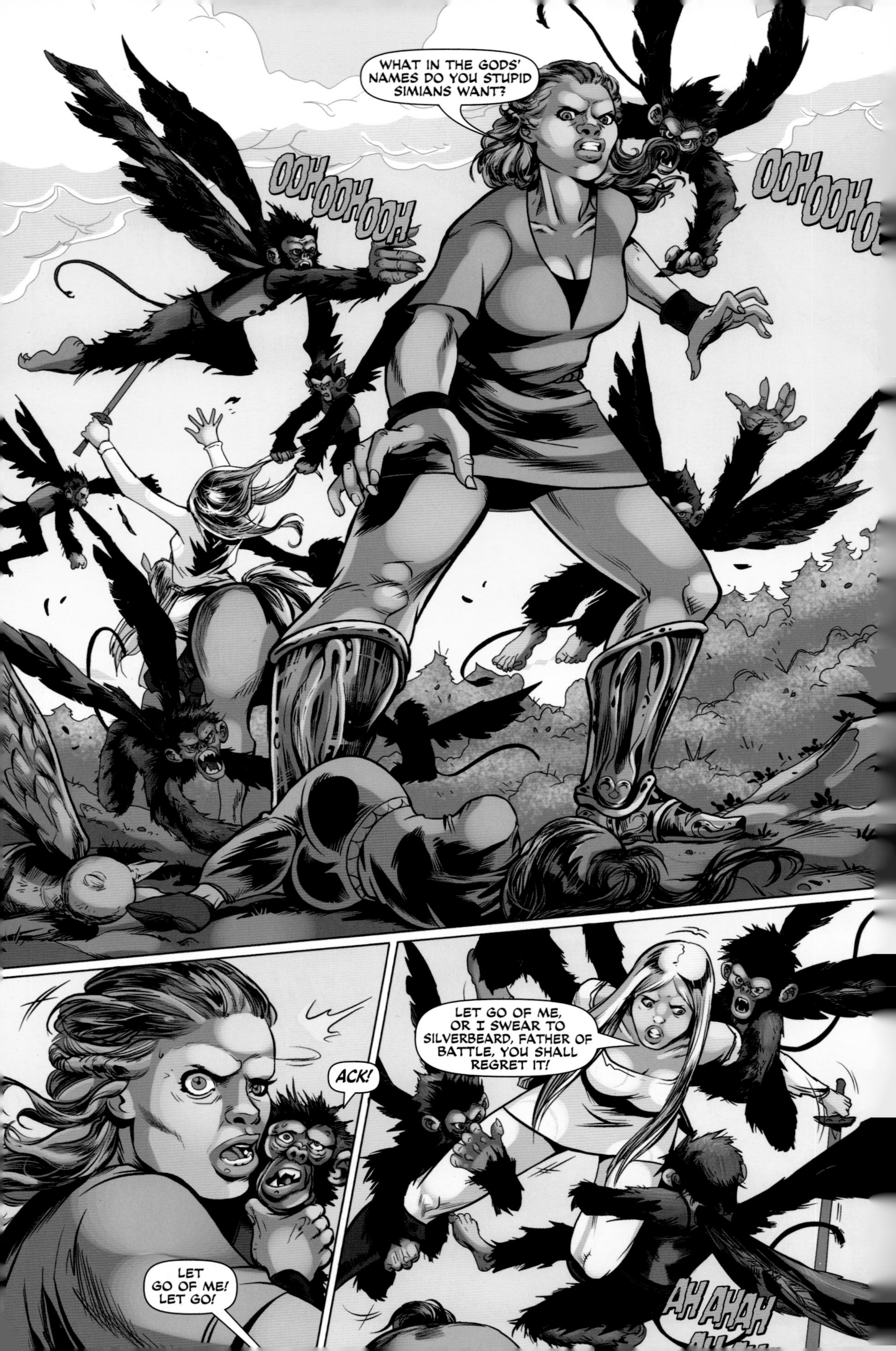
WHAT IN THE GODS' NAMES DO YOU STUPID SIMIANS WANT?
OOHOOHOOH
ACK!
LET GO OF ME! LET GO!
LET GO OF ME, OR I SWEAR TO SILVERBEARD, FATHER OF BATTLE, YOU SHALL REGRET IT!
AH AHAH

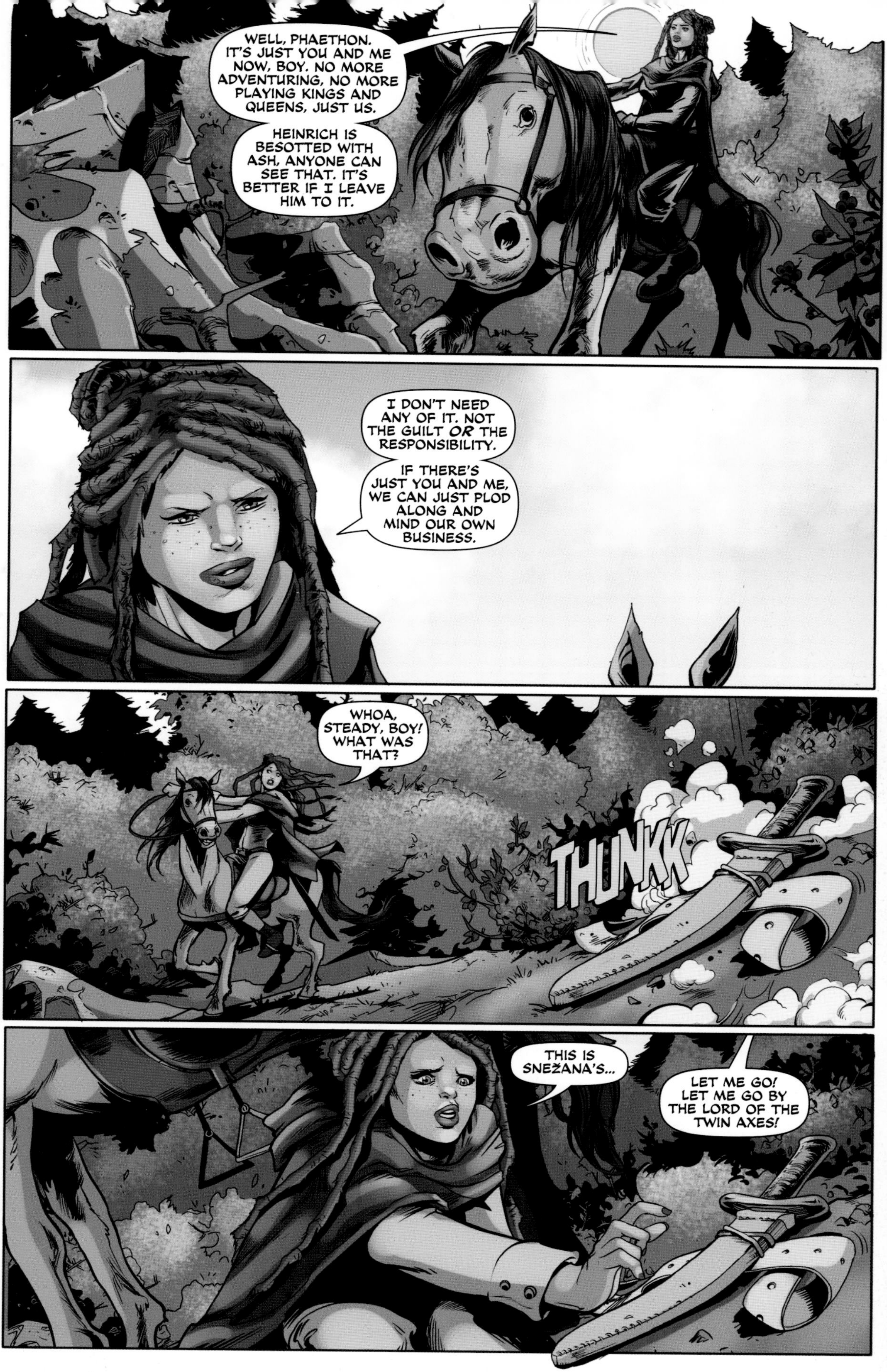
WELL, PHAETHON. IT'S JUST YOU AND ME NOW, BOY. NO MORE ADVENTURING, NO MORE PLAYING KINGS AND QUEENS, JUST US.
HEINRICH IS BESOTTED WITH ASH, ANYONE CAN SEE THAT. IT'S BETTER IF I LEAVE HIM TO IT.
I DON'T NEED ANY OF IT. NOT THE GUILT *OR* THE RESPONSIBILITY.
IF THERE'S JUST YOU AND ME, WE CAN JUST PLOD ALONG AND MIND OUR OWN BUSINESS.
WHOA, STEADY, BOY! WHAT WAS THAT?
THUNKK
THIS IS SNEŽANA'S...
LET ME GO! LET ME GO BY THE LORD OF THE TWIN AXES!

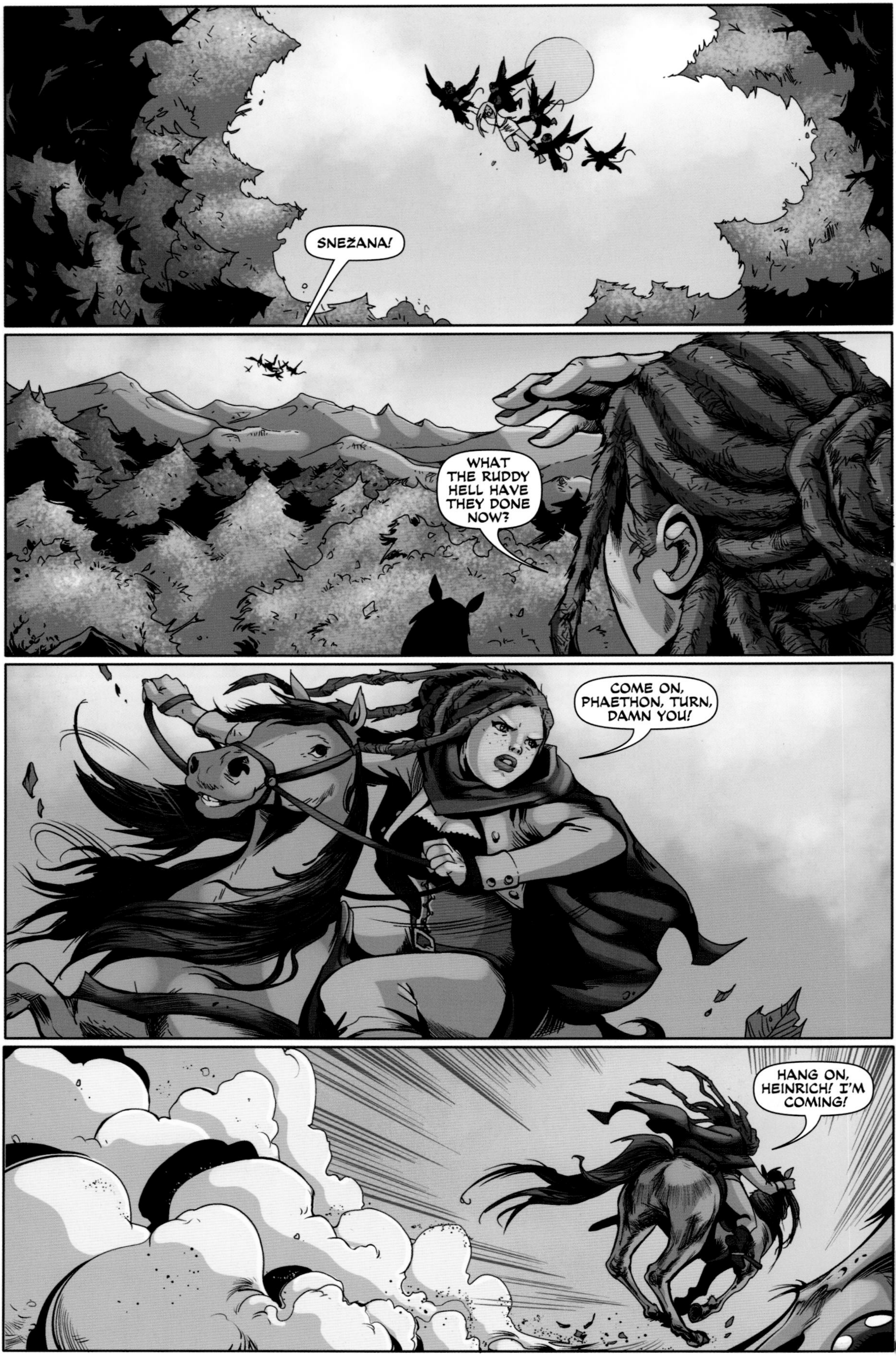
SNEŽANA!
WHAT THE RUDDY HELL HAVE THEY DONE NOW?
COME ON, PHAETHON, TURN, DAMN YOU!
HANG ON, HEINRICH! I'M COMING!

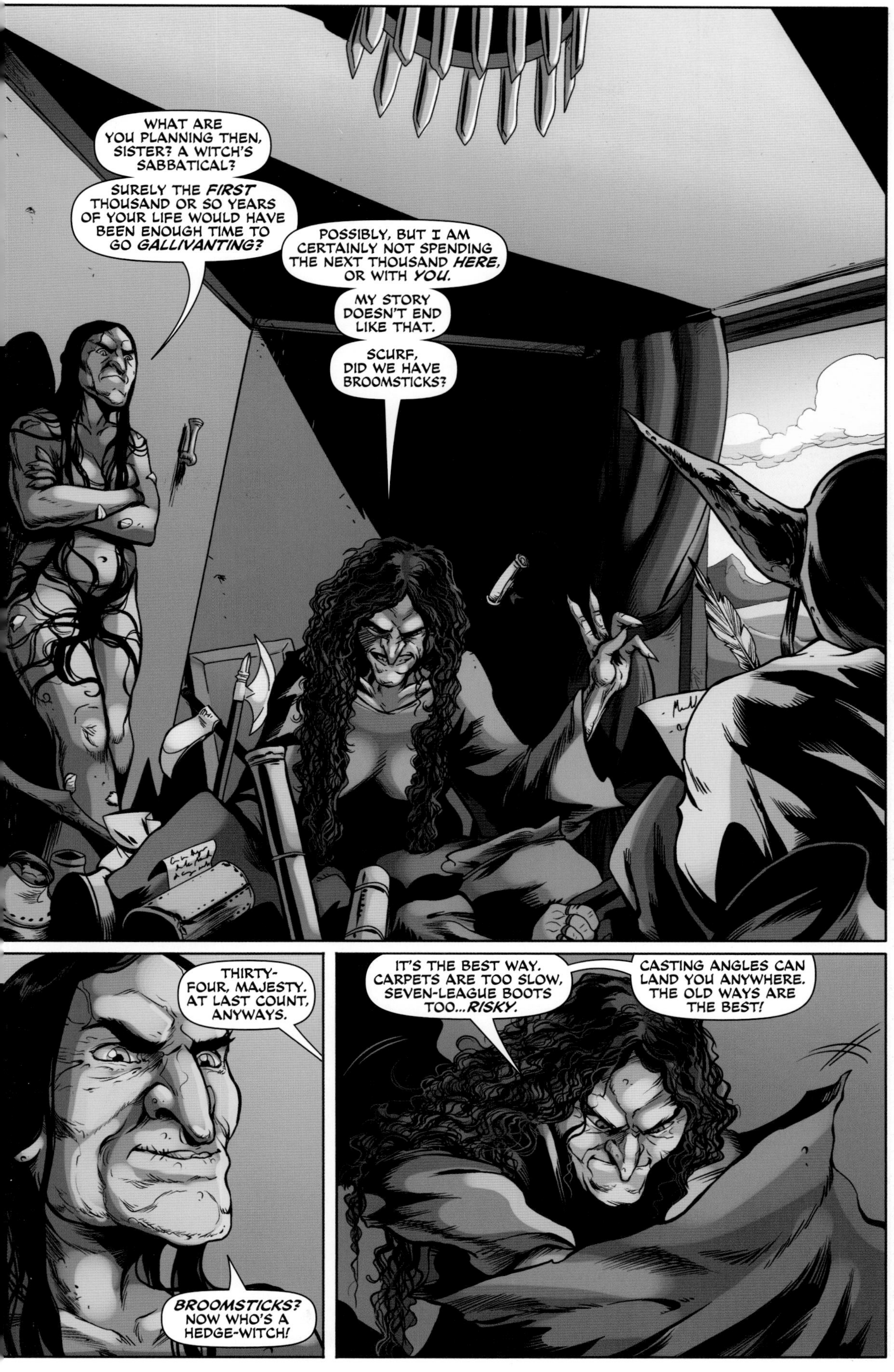
WHAT ARE YOU PLANNING THEN, SISTER? A WITCH'S SABBATICAL?
SURELY THE *FIRST* THOUSAND OR SO YEARS OF YOUR LIFE WOULD HAVE BEEN ENOUGH TIME TO GO *GALLIVANTING?*
POSSIBLY, BUT I AM CERTAINLY NOT SPENDING THE NEXT THOUSAND *HERE*, OR WITH *YOU.*
MY STORY DOESN'T END LIKE THAT.
SCURF, DID WE HAVE BROOMSTICKS?
THIRTY-FOUR, MAJESTY. AT LAST COUNT, ANYWAYS.
BROOMSTICKS? NOW WHO'S A HEDGE-WITCH!
IT'S THE BEST WAY. CARPETS ARE TOO SLOW, SEVEN-LEAGUE BOOTS TOO...*RISKY.*
CASTING ANGLES CAN LAND YOU ANYWHERE. THE OLD WAYS ARE THE BEST!

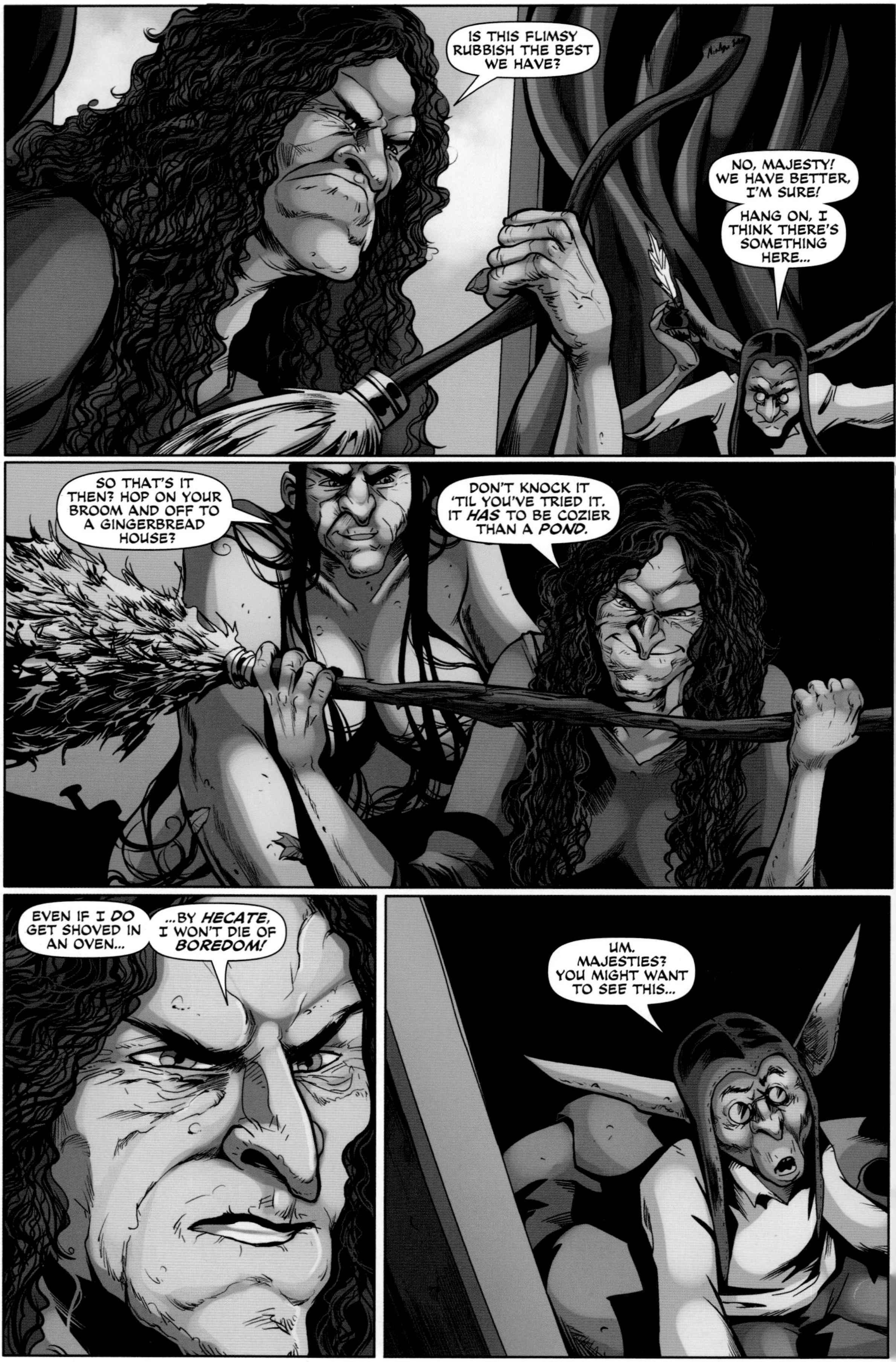
IS THIS FLIMSY RUBBISH THE BEST WE HAVE?
NO, MAJESTY! WE HAVE BETTER, I'M SURE!
HANG ON, I THINK THERE'S SOMETHING HERE...
SO THAT'S IT THEN? HOP ON YOUR BROOM AND OFF TO A GINGERBREAD HOUSE?
DON'T KNOCK IT 'TIL YOU'VE TRIED IT. IT *HAS* TO BE COZIER THAN A *POND.*
EVEN IF I *DO* GET SHOVED IN AN OVEN...
...BY *HECATE*, I WON'T DIE OF *BOREDOM!*
UM. MAJESTIES? YOU MIGHT WANT TO SEE THIS...

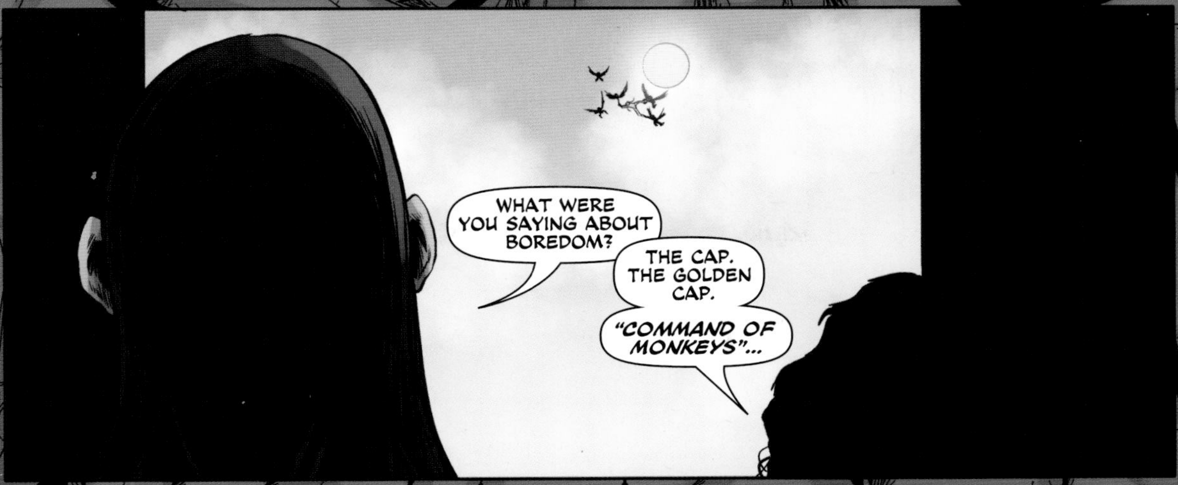
WHAT WERE YOU SAYING ABOUT BOREDOM?
THE CAP. THE GOLDEN CAP.
"COMMAND OF MONKEYS"...

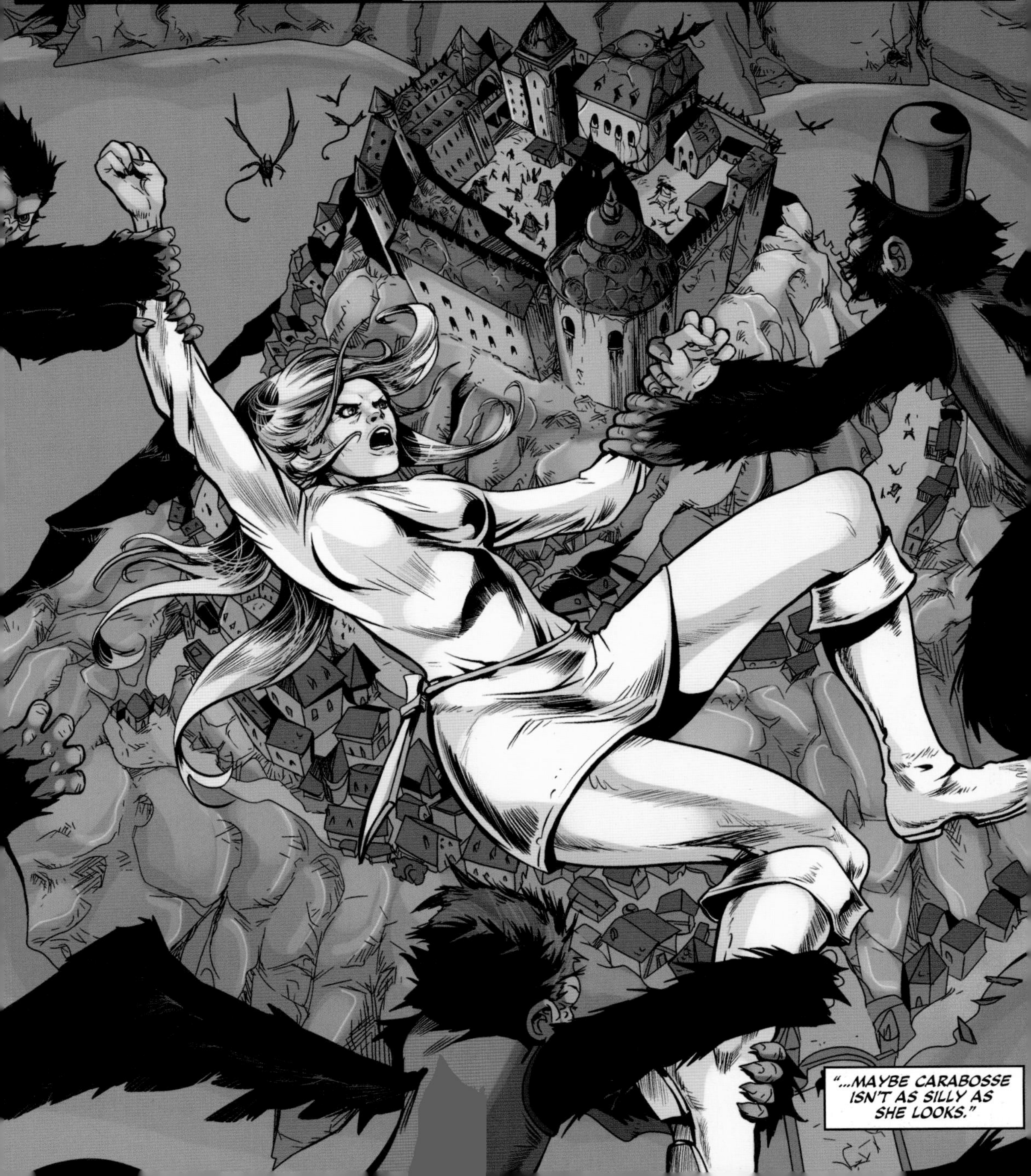
"...MAYBE CARABOSSE ISN'T AS SILLY AS SHE LOOKS."

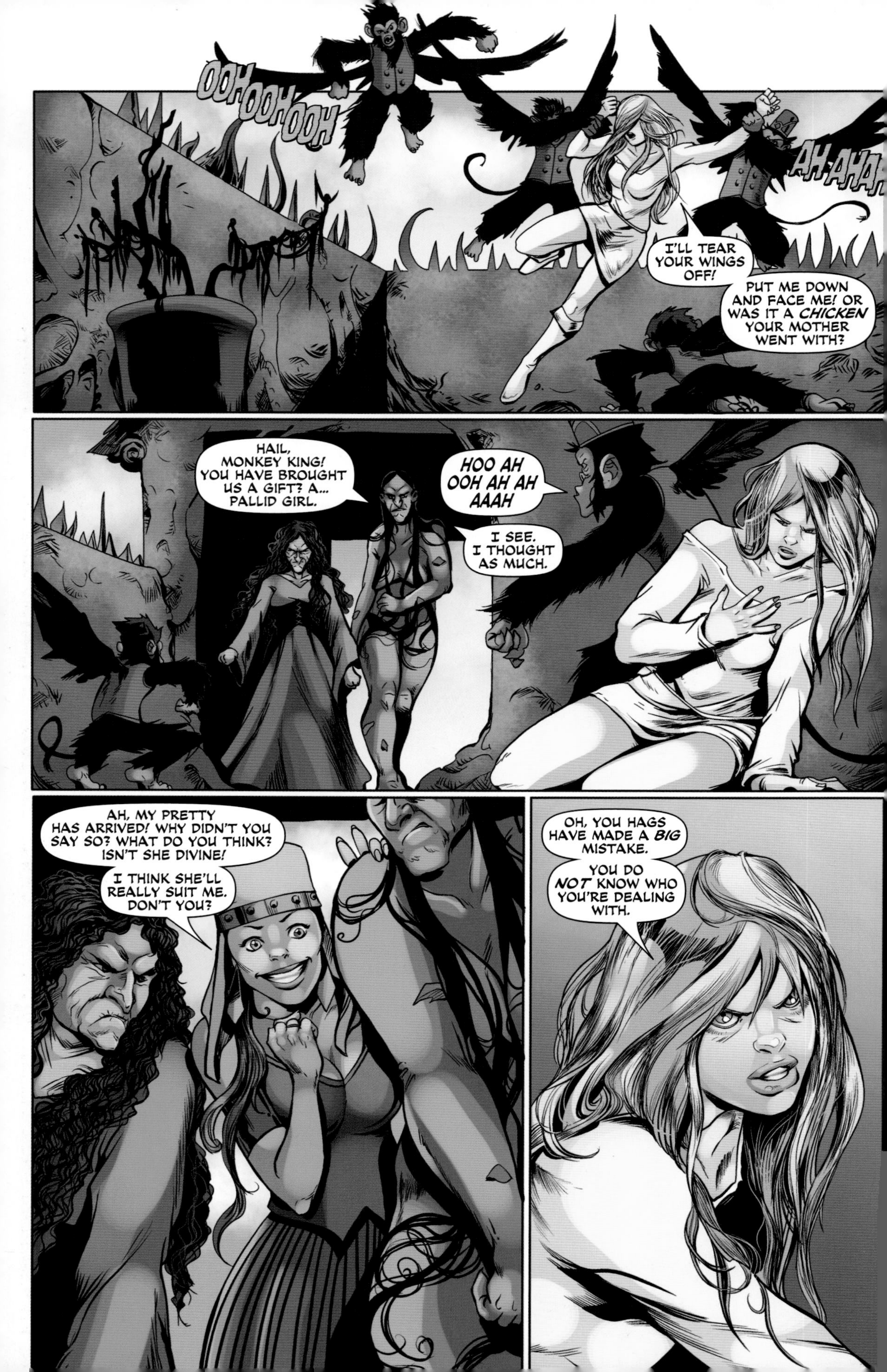
OOHOOHOOH
AH AHAH
I'LL TEAR YOUR WINGS OFF!
PUT ME DOWN AND FACE ME! OR WAS IT A *CHICKEN* YOUR MOTHER WENT WITH?
HAIL, MONKEY KING! YOU HAVE BROUGHT US A GIFT? A... PALLID GIRL.
HOO AH OOH AH AH AAAH
I SEE. I THOUGHT AS MUCH.
AH, MY PRETTY HAS ARRIVED! WHY DIDN'T YOU SAY SO? WHAT DO YOU THINK? ISN'T SHE DIVINE!
I THINK SHE'LL REALLY SUIT ME. DON'T YOU?
OH, YOU HAGS HAVE MADE A *BIG* MISTAKE.
YOU DO *NOT* KNOW WHO YOU'RE DEALING WITH.

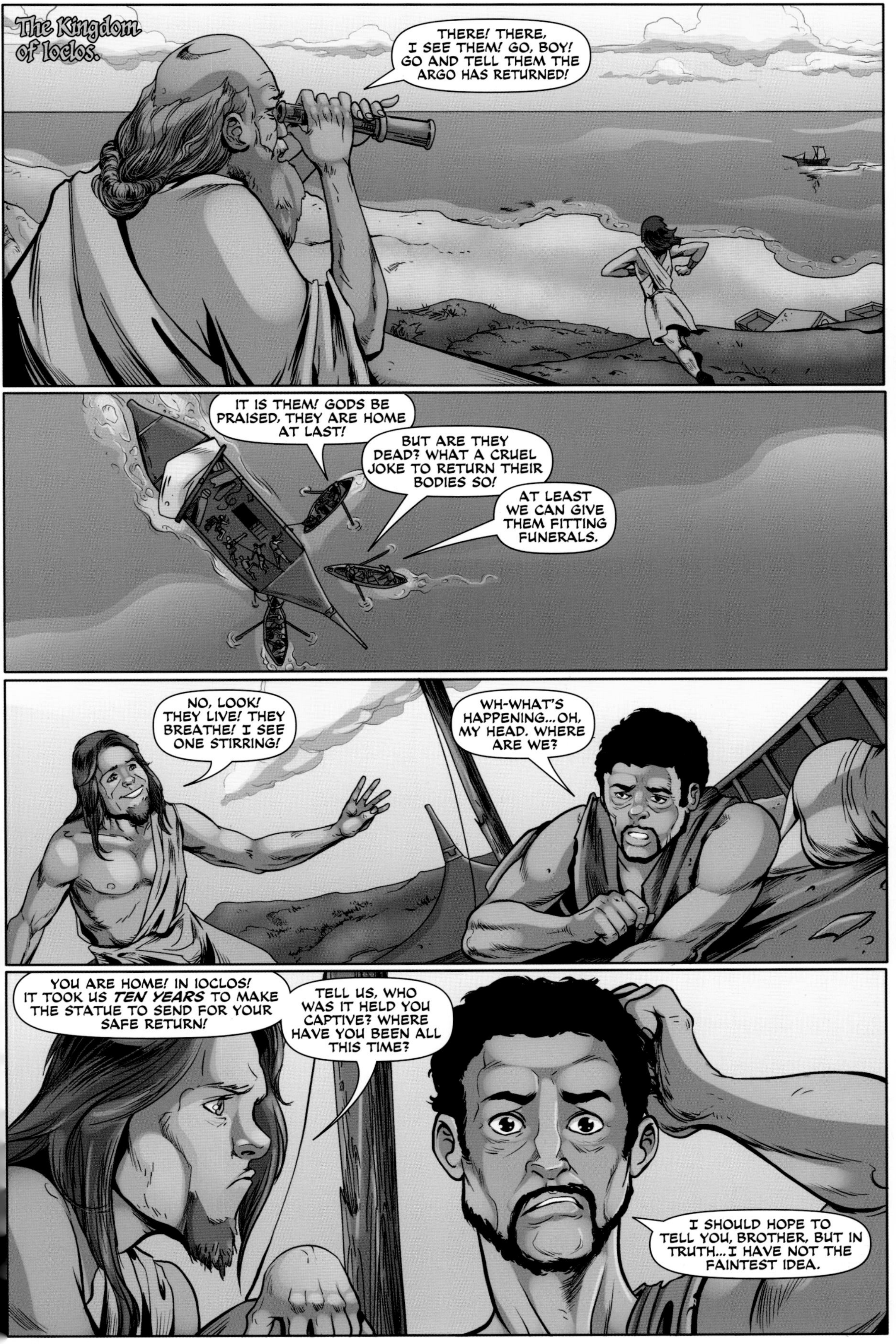
The Kingdom of Ioclos.
THERE! THERE, I SEE THEM! GO, BOY! GO AND TELL THEM THE ARGO HAS RETURNED!
IT IS THEM! GODS BE PRAISED, THEY ARE HOME AT LAST!
BUT ARE THEY DEAD? WHAT A CRUEL JOKE TO RETURN THEIR BODIES SO!
AT LEAST WE CAN GIVE THEM FITTING FUNERALS.
NO, LOOK! THEY LIVE! THEY BREATHE! I SEE ONE STIRRING!
WH-WHAT'S HAPPENING...OH, MY HEAD. WHERE ARE WE?
YOU ARE HOME! IN IOCLOS! IT TOOK US TEN YEARS TO MAKE THE STATUE TO SEND FOR YOUR SAFE RETURN!
TELL US, WHO WAS IT HELD YOU CAPTIVE? WHERE HAVE YOU BEEN ALL THIS TIME?
I SHOULD HOPE TO TELL YOU, BROTHER, BUT IN TRUTH...I HAVE NOT THE FAINTEST IDEA.

Chapter

13

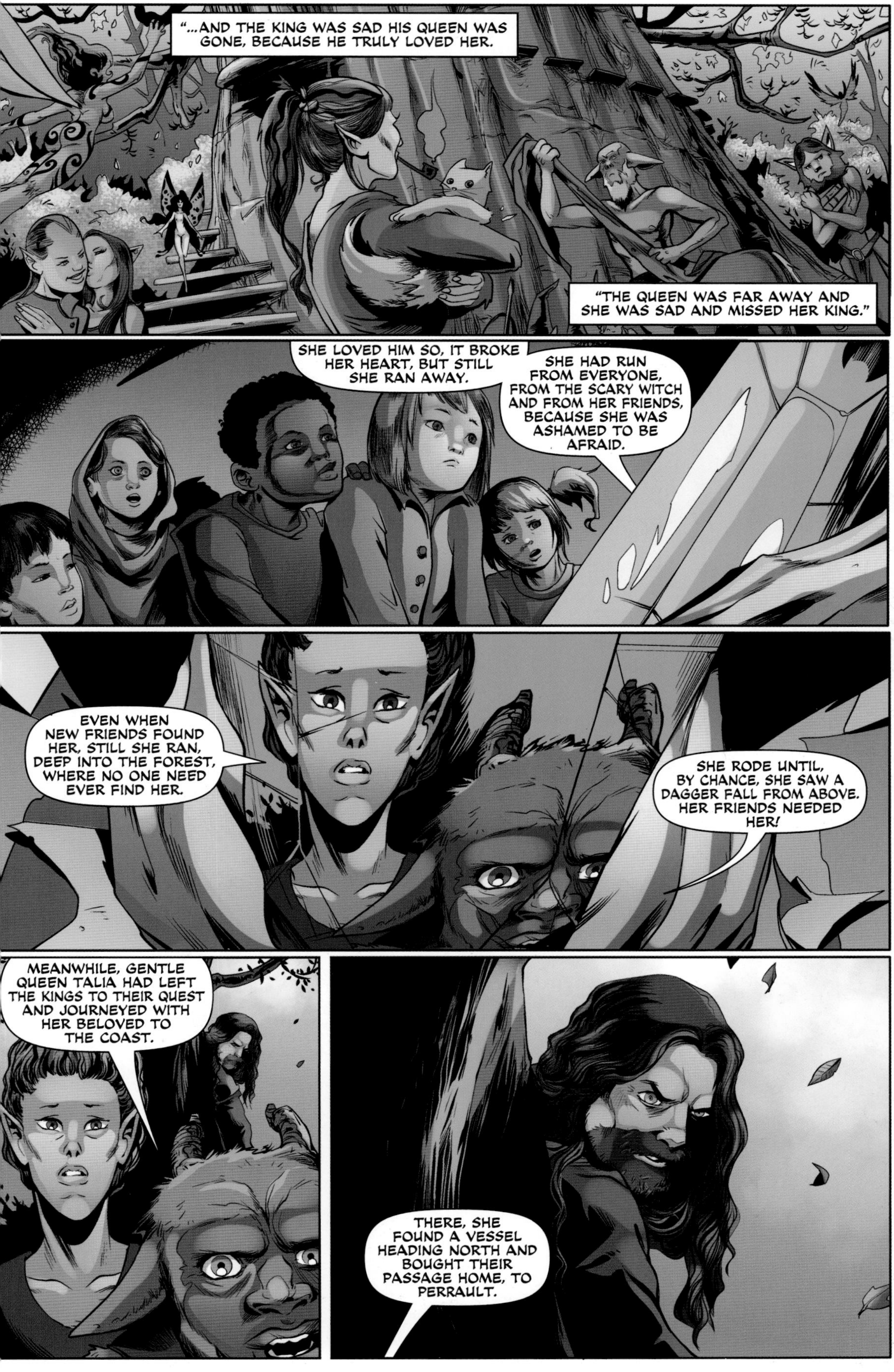
"...AND THE KING WAS SAD HIS QUEEN WAS GONE, BECAUSE HE TRULY LOVED HER.
"THE QUEEN WAS FAR AWAY AND SHE WAS SAD AND MISSED HER KING."
SHE LOVED HIM SO, IT BROKE HER HEART, BUT STILL SHE RAN AWAY.
SHE HAD RUN FROM EVERYONE, FROM THE SCARY WITCH AND FROM HER FRIENDS, BECAUSE SHE WAS ASHAMED TO BE AFRAID.
EVEN WHEN NEW FRIENDS FOUND HER, STILL SHE RAN, DEEP INTO THE FOREST, WHERE NO ONE NEED EVER FIND HER.
SHE RODE UNTIL, BY CHANCE, SHE SAW A DAGGER FALL FROM ABOVE. HER FRIENDS NEEDED HER!
MEANWHILE, GENTLE QUEEN TALIA HAD LEFT THE KINGS TO THEIR QUEST AND JOURNEYED WITH HER BELOVED TO THE COAST.
THERE, SHE FOUND A VESSEL HEADING NORTH AND BOUGHT THEIR PASSAGE HOME, TO PERRAULT.

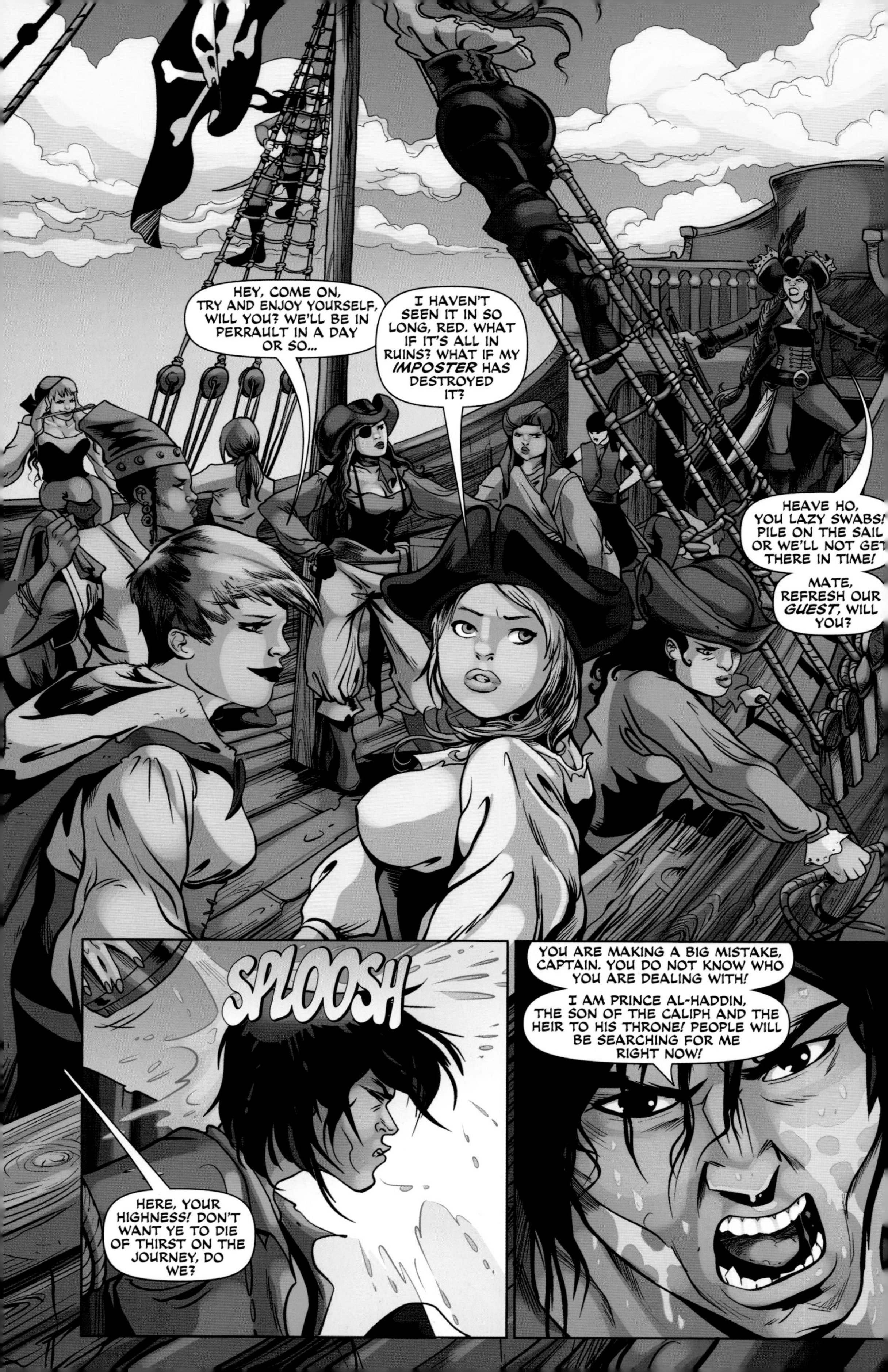
HEY, COME ON, TRY AND ENJOY YOURSELF, WILL YOU? WE'LL BE IN PERRAULT IN A DAY OR SO...
I HAVEN'T SEEN IT IN SO LONG, RED. WHAT IF IT'S ALL IN RUINS? WHAT IF MY *IMPOSTER* HAS DESTROYED IT?
HEAVE HO, YOU LAZY SWABS! PILE ON THE SAIL OR WE'LL NOT GET THERE IN TIME!
MATE, REFRESH OUR *GUEST*, WILL YOU?
SPLOOSH
HERE, YOUR HIGHNESS! DON'T WANT YE TO DIE OF THIRST ON THE JOURNEY, DO WE?
YOU ARE MAKING A BIG MISTAKE, CAPTAIN. YOU DO NOT KNOW WHO YOU ARE DEALING WITH!
I AM PRINCE AL-HADDIN, THE SON OF THE CALIPH AND THE HEIR TO HIS THRONE! PEOPLE WILL BE SEARCHING FOR ME RIGHT NOW!

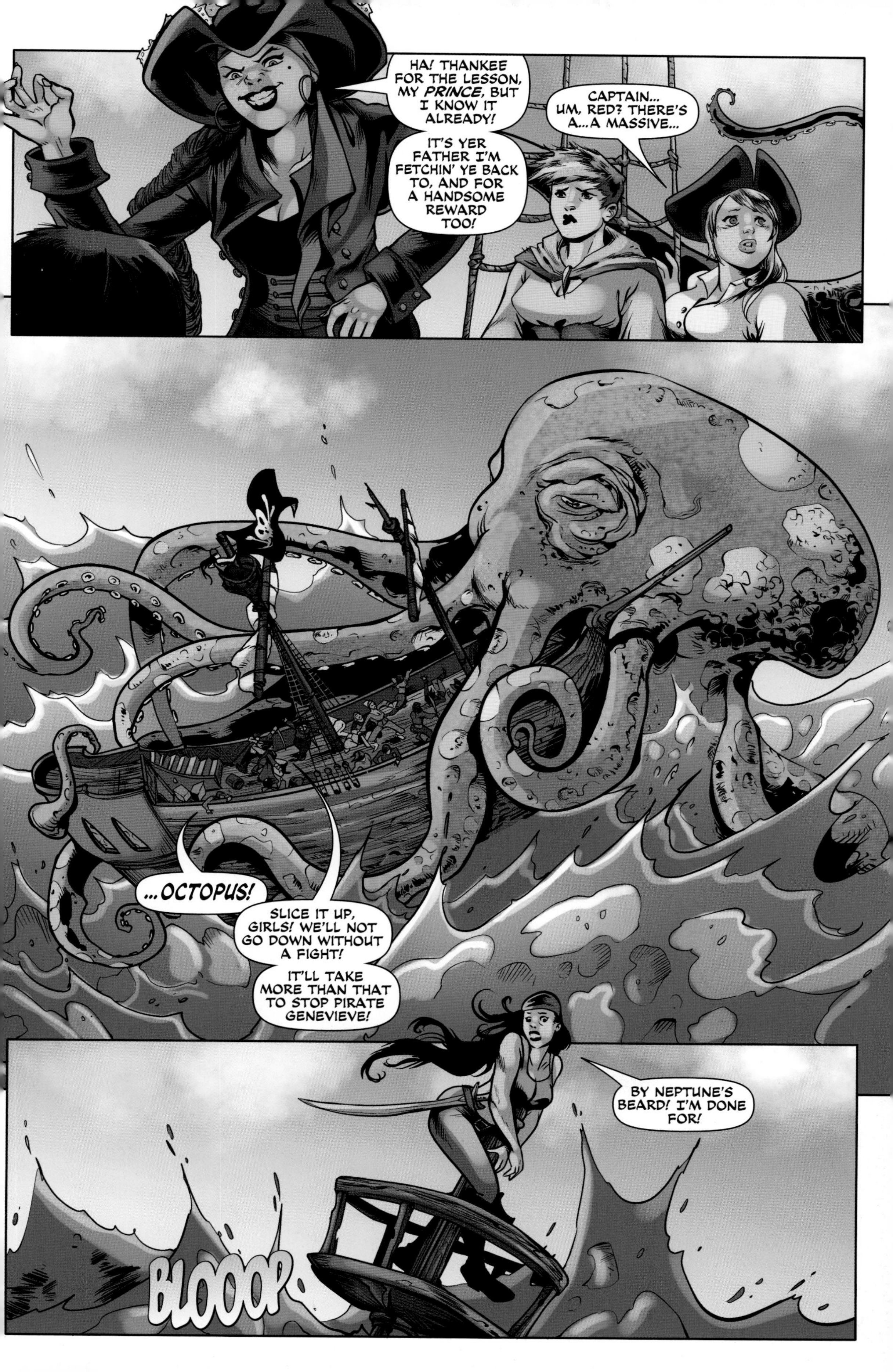
HA! THANKEE FOR THE LESSON, MY PRINCE, BUT I KNOW IT ALREADY!
IT'S YER FATHER I'M FETCHIN' YE BACK TO, AND FOR A HANDSOME REWARD TOO!
CAPTAIN... UM, RED? THERE'S A...A MASSIVE...
...OCTOPUS!
SLICE IT UP, GIRLS! WE'LL NOT GO DOWN WITHOUT A FIGHT!
IT'LL TAKE MORE THAN THAT TO STOP PIRATE GENEVIEVE!
BY NEPTUNE'S BEARD! I'M DONE FOR!
BLOOOP

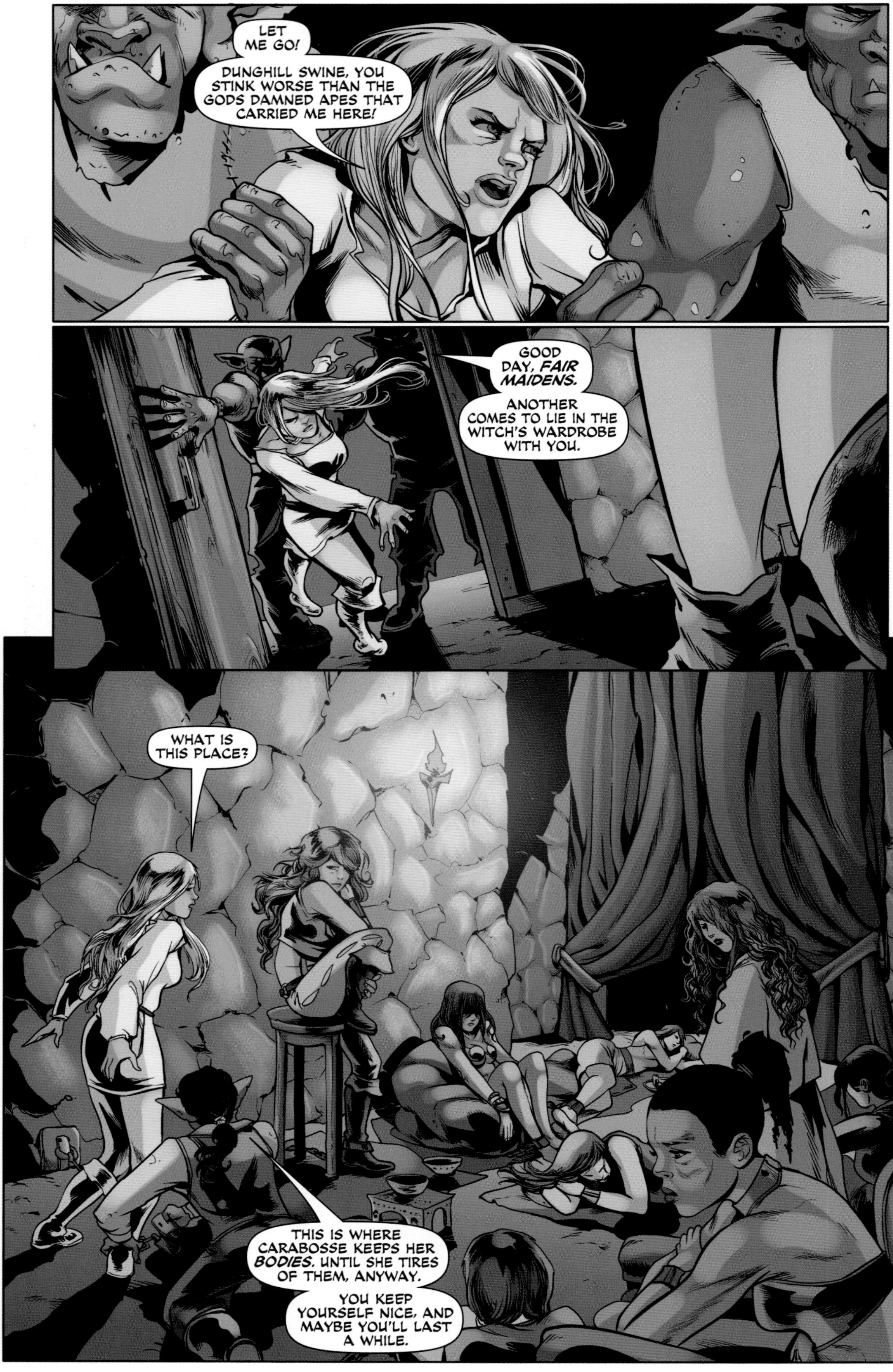
LET ME GO!
DUNGHILL SWINE, YOU STINK WORSE THAN THE GODS DAMNED APES THAT CARRIED ME HERE!
GOOD DAY, *FAIR MAIDENS.*
ANOTHER COMES TO LIE IN THE WITCH'S WARDROBE WITH YOU.
WHAT IS THIS PLACE?
THIS IS WHERE CARABOSSE KEEPS HER *BODIES*. UNTIL SHE TIRES OF THEM, ANYWAY.
YOU KEEP YOURSELF NICE, AND MAYBE YOU'LL LAST A WHILE.

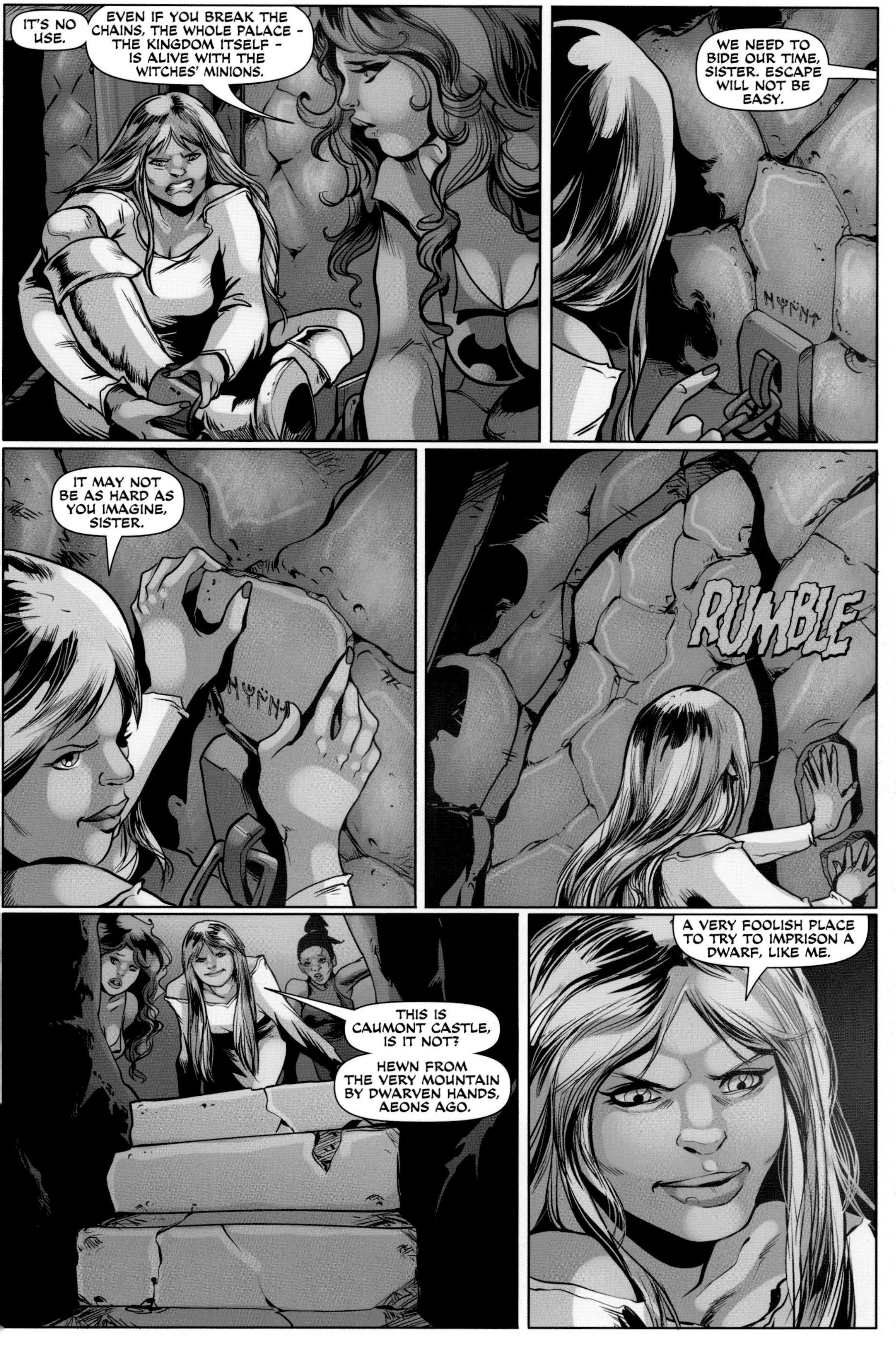
IT'S NO USE.
EVEN IF YOU BREAK THE CHAINS, THE WHOLE PALACE - THE KINGDOM ITSELF - IS ALIVE WITH THE WITCHES' MINIONS.
WE NEED TO BIDE OUR TIME, SISTER. ESCAPE WILL NOT BE EASY.
IT MAY NOT BE AS HARD AS YOU IMAGINE, SISTER.
RUMBLE
THIS IS CAUMONT CASTLE, IS IT NOT?
HEWN FROM THE VERY MOUNTAIN BY DWARVEN HANDS, AEONS AGO.
A VERY FOOLISH PLACE TO TRY TO IMPRISON A DWARF, LIKE ME.

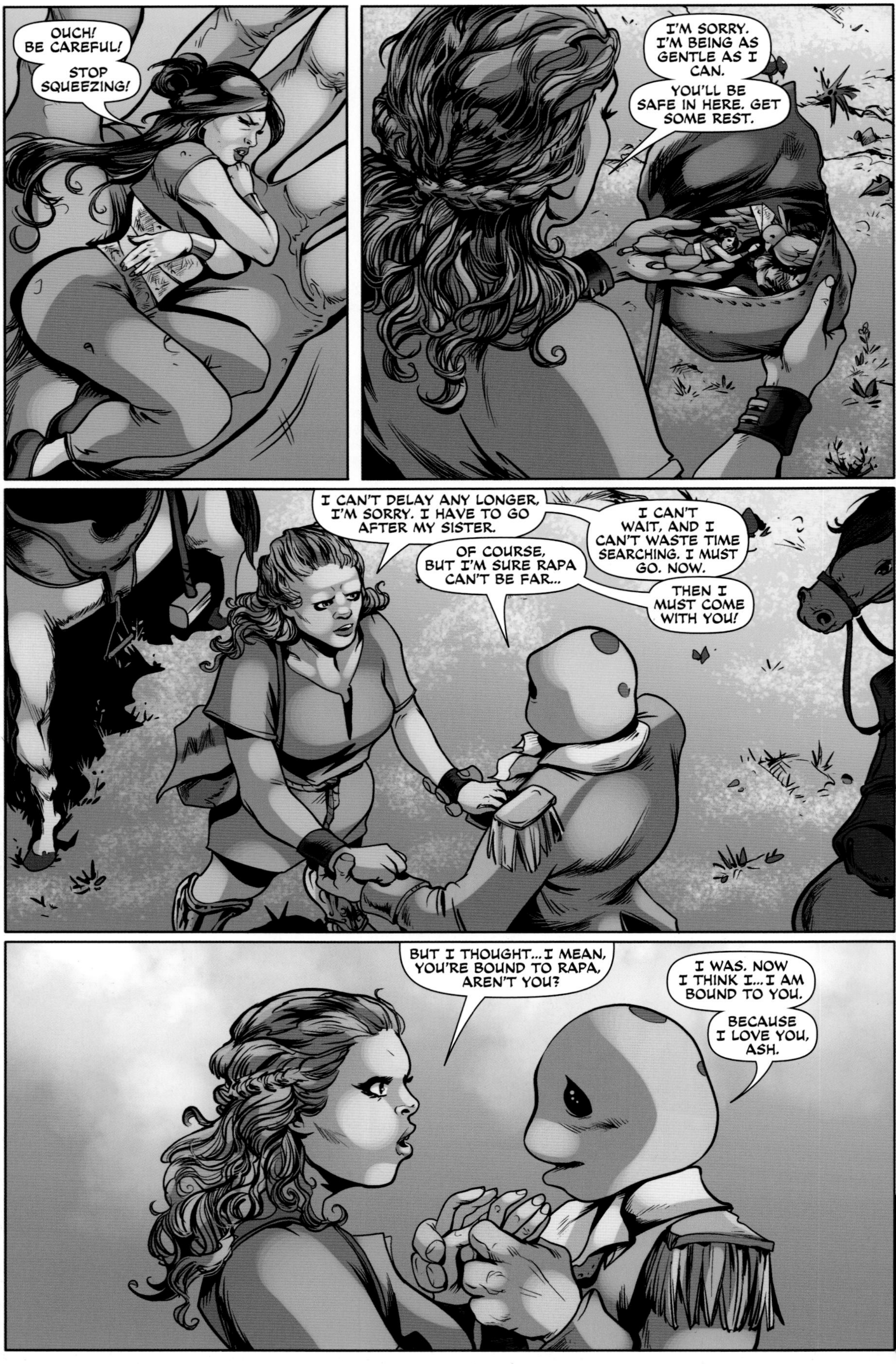
OUCH! BE CAREFUL!
STOP SQUEEZING!
I'M SORRY. I'M BEING AS GENTLE AS I CAN.
YOU'LL BE SAFE IN HERE. GET SOME REST.
I CAN'T DELAY ANY LONGER, I'M SORRY. I HAVE TO GO AFTER MY SISTER.
OF COURSE, BUT I'M SURE RAPA CAN'T BE FAR...
I CAN'T WAIT, AND I CAN'T WASTE TIME SEARCHING. I MUST GO. NOW.
THEN I MUST COME WITH YOU!
BUT I THOUGHT...I MEAN, YOU'RE BOUND TO RAPA, AREN'T YOU?
I WAS. NOW I THINK I...I AM BOUND TO YOU.
BECAUSE I LOVE YOU, ASH.

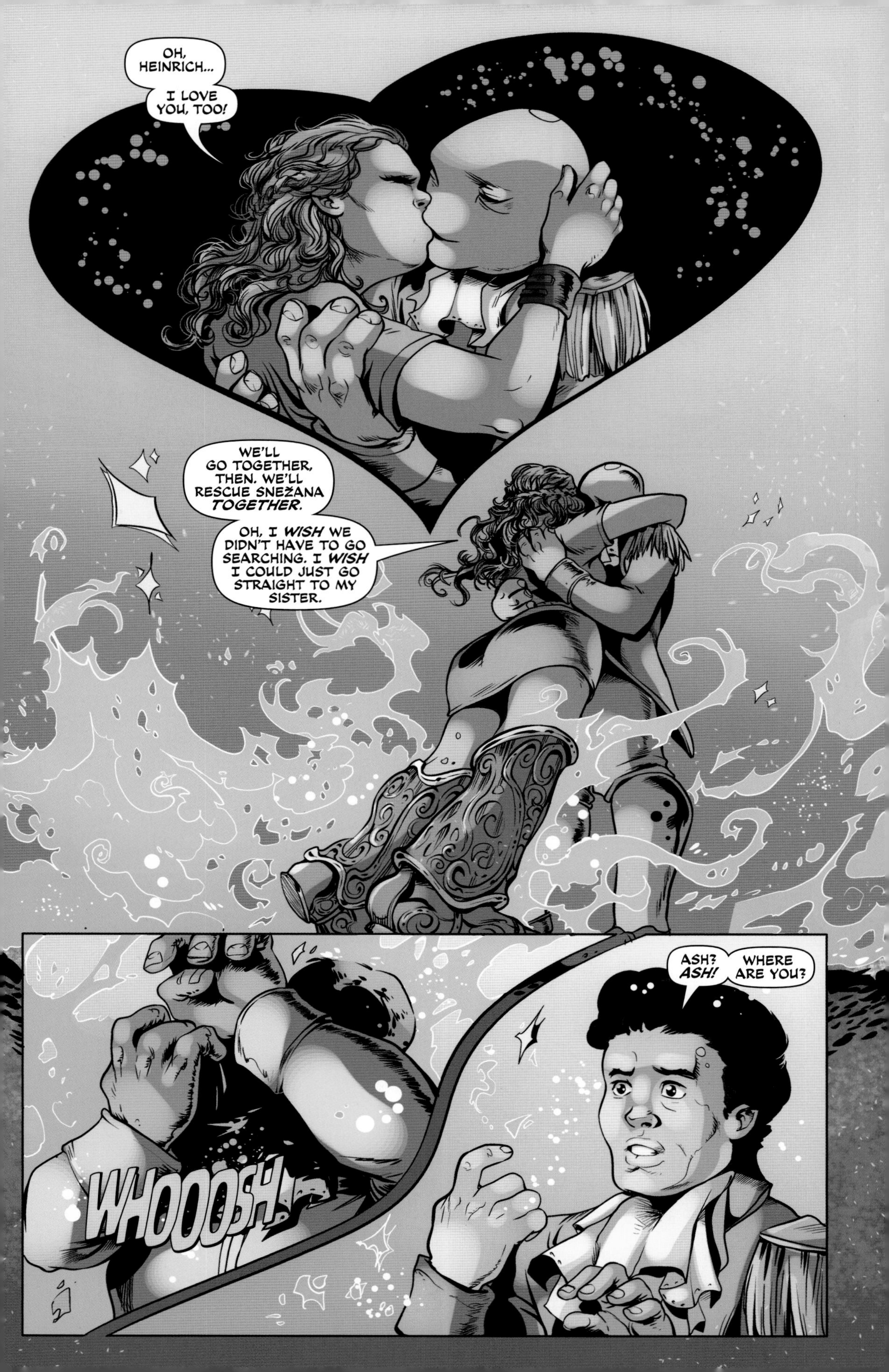
OH, HEINRICH...
I LOVE YOU, TOO!
WE'LL GO TOGETHER, THEN. WE'LL RESCUE SNEŽANA *TOGETHER*.
OH, I *WISH* WE DIDN'T HAVE TO GO SEARCHING. I *WISH* I COULD JUST GO STRAIGHT TO MY SISTER.
WHOOOSH!
ASH? *ASH!*
WHERE ARE YOU?

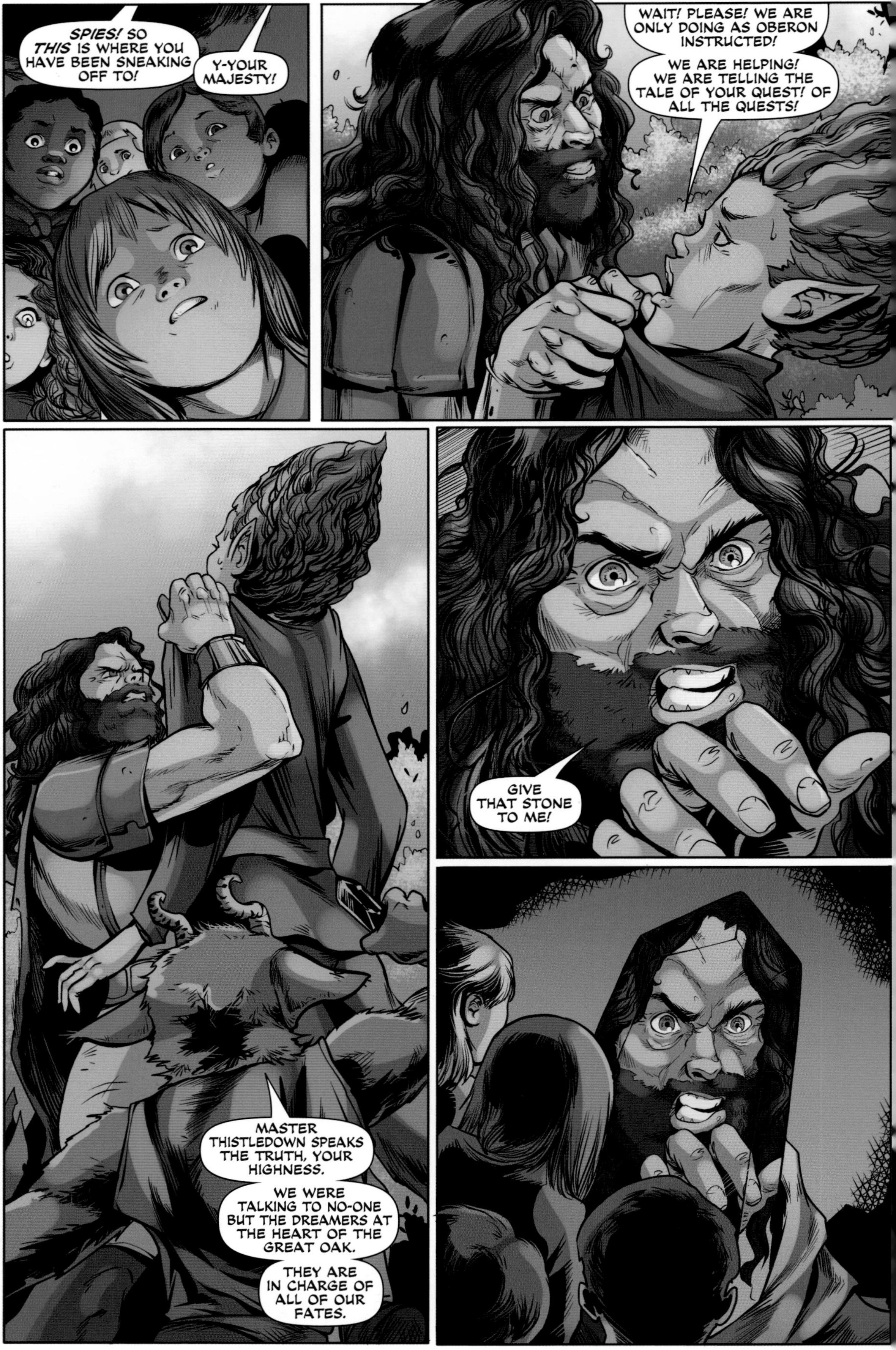
SPIES! SO THIS IS WHERE YOU HAVE BEEN SNEAKING OFF TO!
Y-YOUR MAJESTY!
WAIT! PLEASE! WE ARE ONLY DOING AS OBERON INSTRUCTED!
WE ARE HELPING! WE ARE TELLING THE TALE OF YOUR QUEST! OF ALL THE QUESTS!
MASTER THISTLEDOWN SPEAKS THE TRUTH, YOUR HIGHNESS.
WE WERE TALKING TO NO-ONE BUT THE DREAMERS AT THE HEART OF THE GREAT OAK.
THEY ARE IN CHARGE OF ALL OF OUR FATES.
GIVE THAT STONE TO ME!

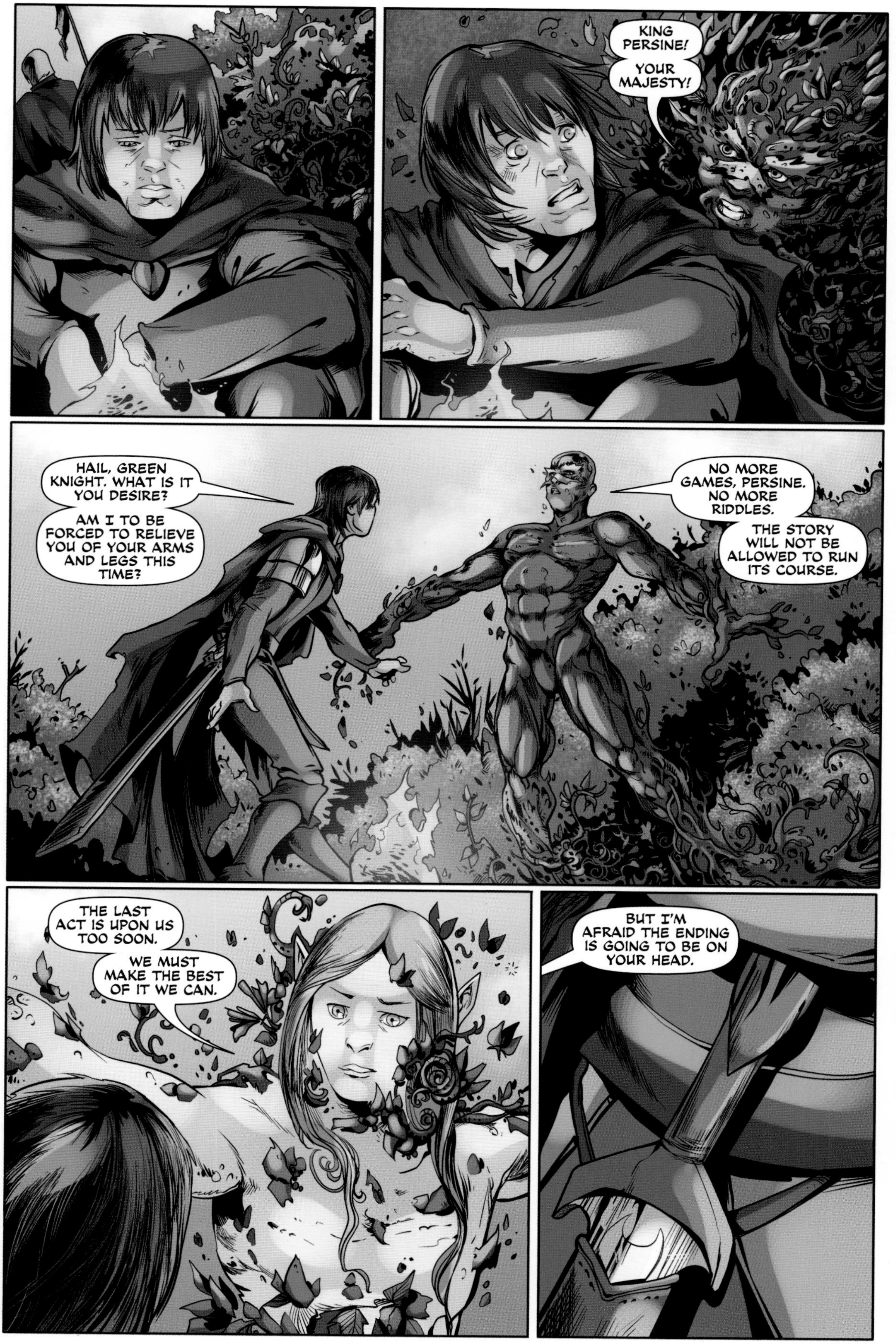
KING PERSINE!
YOUR MAJESTY!
HAIL, GREEN KNIGHT. WHAT IS IT YOU DESIRE?
AM I TO BE FORCED TO RELIEVE YOU OF YOUR ARMS AND LEGS THIS TIME?
NO MORE GAMES, PERSINE. NO MORE RIDDLES.
THE STORY WILL NOT BE ALLOWED TO RUN ITS COURSE.
THE LAST ACT IS UPON US TOO SOON.
WE MUST MAKE THE BEST OF IT WE CAN.
BUT I'M AFRAID THE ENDING IS GOING TO BE ON YOUR HEAD.

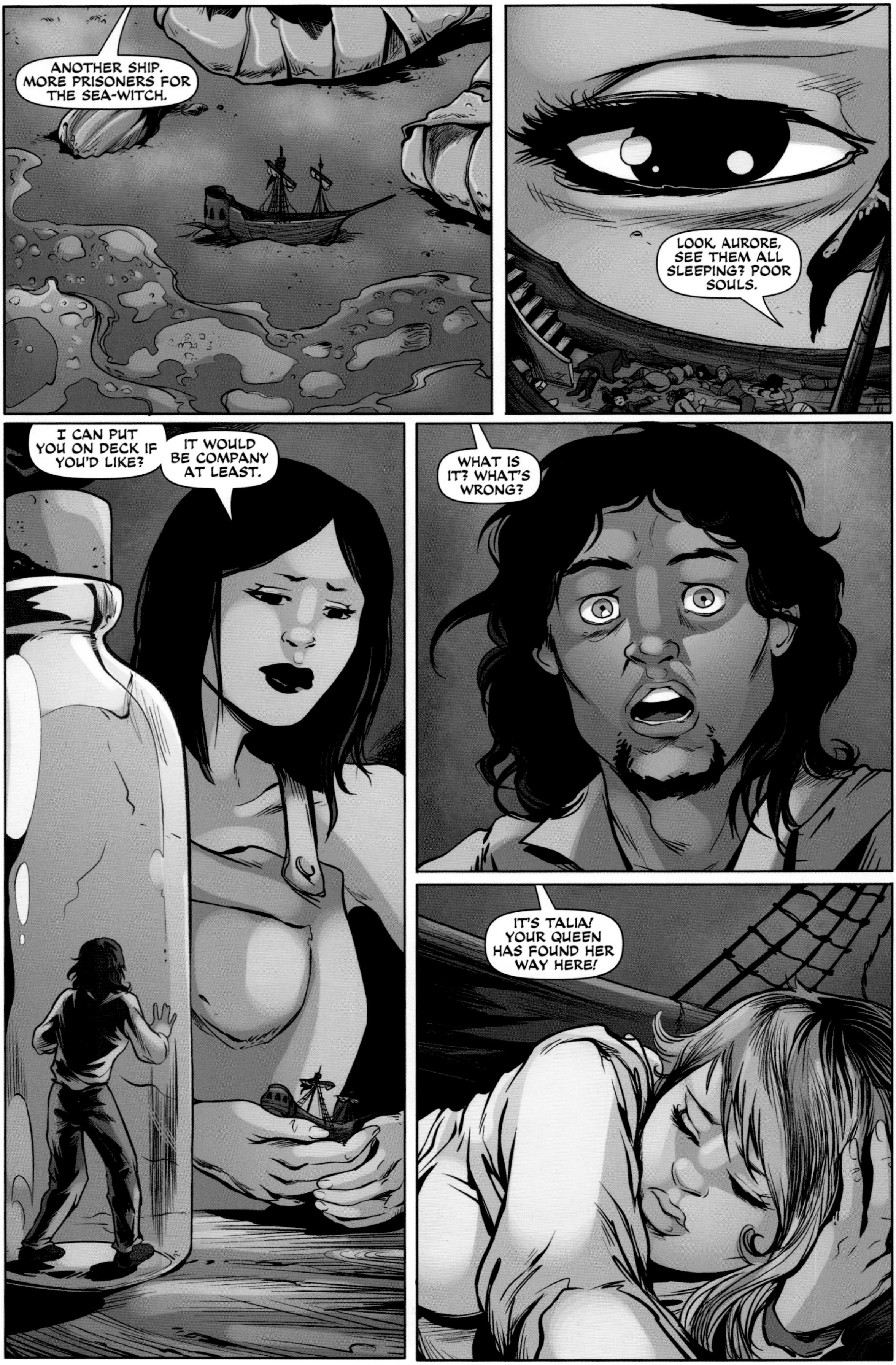
ANOTHER SHIP. MORE PRISONERS FOR THE SEA-WITCH.
LOOK, AURORE, SEE THEM ALL SLEEPING? POOR SOULS.
I CAN PUT YOU ON DECK IF YOU'D LIKE?
IT WOULD BE COMPANY AT LEAST.
WHAT IS IT? WHAT'S WRONG?
IT'S TALIA! YOUR QUEEN HAS FOUND HER WAY HERE!

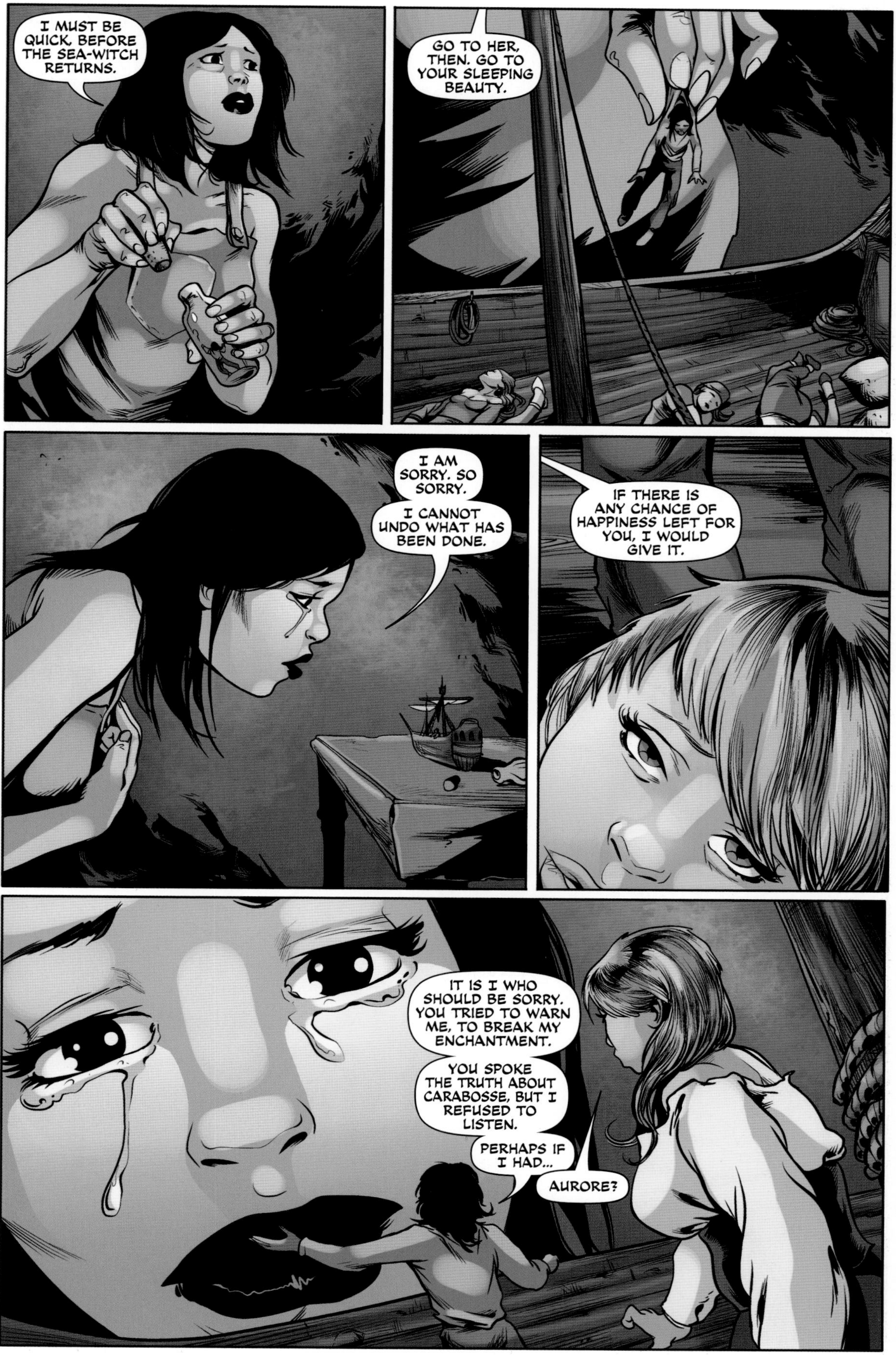
I MUST BE QUICK, BEFORE THE SEA-WITCH RETURNS.
GO TO HER, THEN. GO TO YOUR SLEEPING BEAUTY.
I AM SORRY. SO SORRY.
I CANNOT UNDO WHAT HAS BEEN DONE.
IF THERE IS ANY CHANCE OF HAPPINESS LEFT FOR YOU, I WOULD GIVE IT.
IT IS I WHO SHOULD BE SORRY. YOU TRIED TO WARN ME, TO BREAK MY ENCHANTMENT.
YOU SPOKE THE TRUTH ABOUT CARABOSSE, BUT I REFUSED TO LISTEN.
PERHAPS IF I HAD...
AURORE?

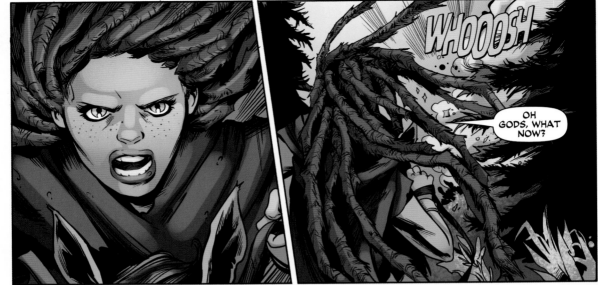

WHOOOSH

OH GODS, WHAT NOW?

HEY, YOU, WHAT WAS THAT FLASH?

ARE YOU HURT?

RAPA! I KNEW YOU'D COME BACK!

HEINRICH?

YOU'RE... YOU'RE NOT A FROG ANYMORE...?

I-I SAW SNEŽANA CARRIED OFF BY THOSE MONKEY-THINGS FROM THE FOREST...

DID THEY GET ASH AND TOMMELISE TOO?

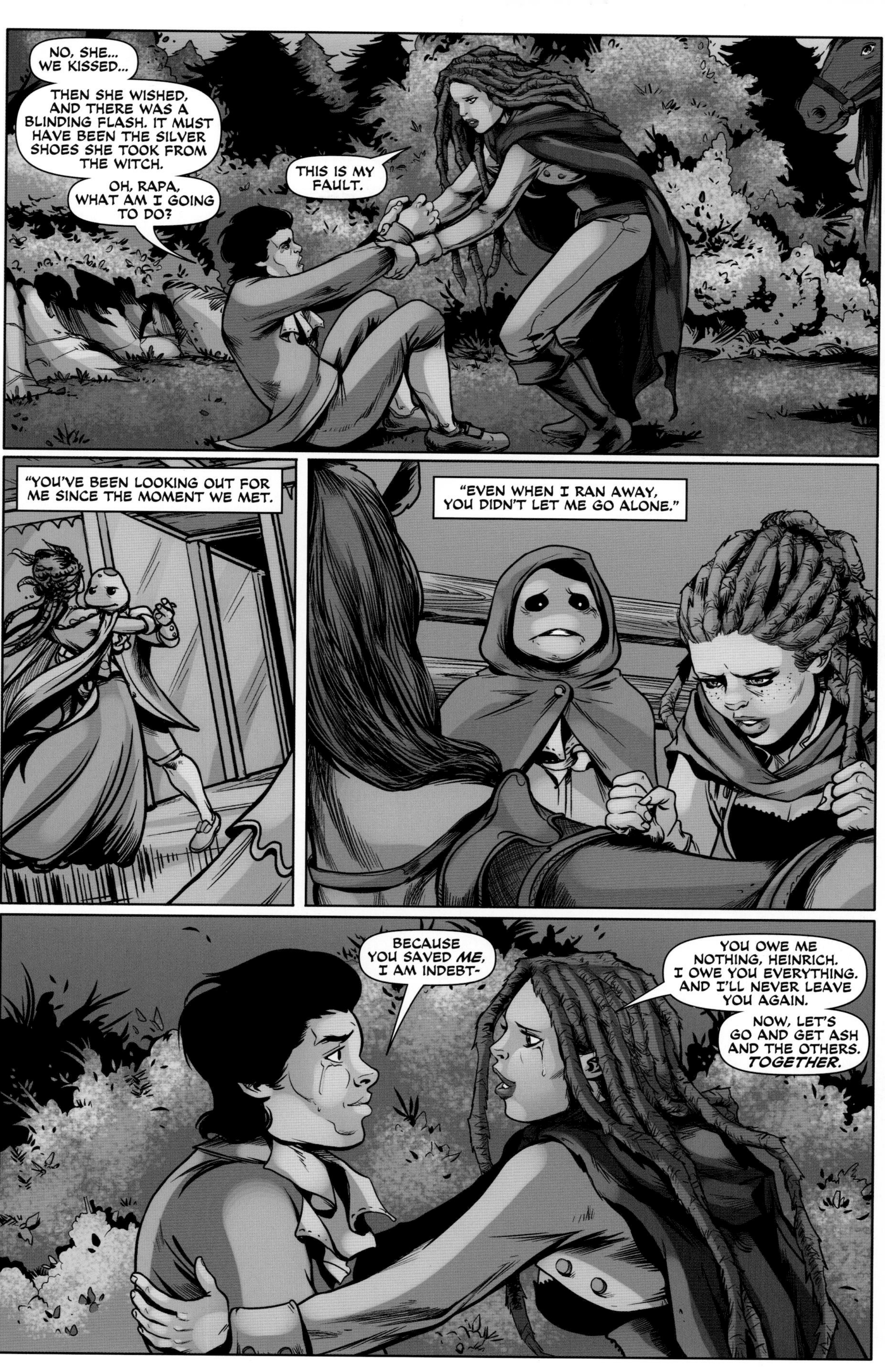
NO, SHE... WE KISSED...
THEN SHE WISHED, AND THERE WAS A BLINDING FLASH. IT MUST HAVE BEEN THE SILVER SHOES SHE TOOK FROM THE WITCH.
OH, RAPA, WHAT AM I GOING TO DO?
THIS IS MY FAULT.
"YOU'VE BEEN LOOKING OUT FOR ME SINCE THE MOMENT WE MET.
"EVEN WHEN I RAN AWAY, YOU DIDN'T LET ME GO ALONE."
BECAUSE YOU SAVED *ME*, I AM INDEBT-
YOU OWE ME NOTHING, HEINRICH. I OWE YOU EVERYTHING. AND I'LL NEVER LEAVE YOU AGAIN.
NOW, LET'S GO AND GET ASH AND THE OTHERS. ***TOGETHER.***

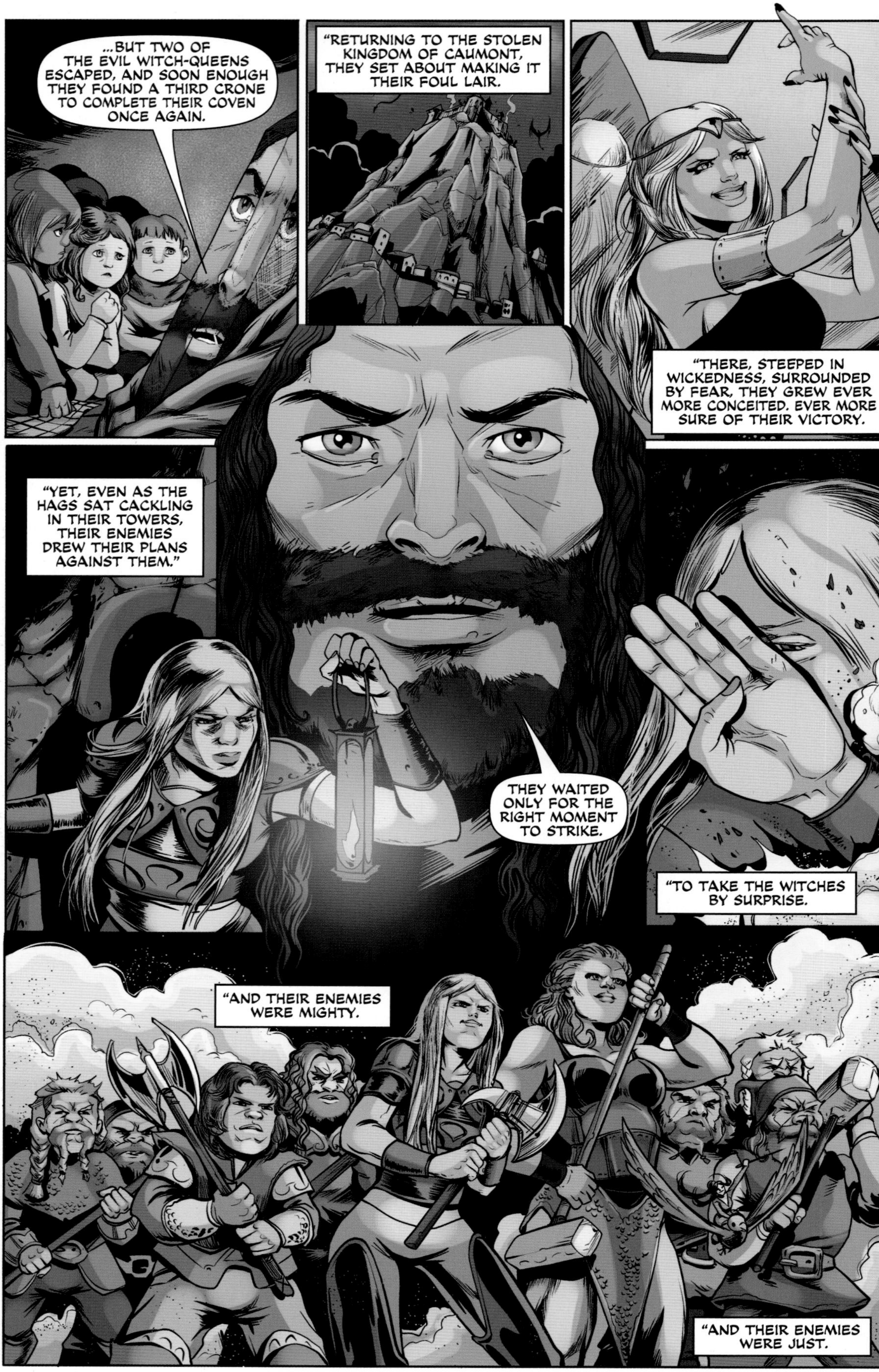
...BUT TWO OF THE EVIL WITCH-QUEENS ESCAPED, AND SOON ENOUGH THEY FOUND A THIRD CRONE TO COMPLETE THEIR COVEN ONCE AGAIN.
"RETURNING TO THE STOLEN KINGDOM OF CAUMONT, THEY SET ABOUT MAKING IT THEIR FOUL LAIR.
"THERE, STEEPED IN WICKEDNESS, SURROUNDED BY FEAR, THEY GREW EVER MORE CONCEITED. EVER MORE SURE OF THEIR VICTORY.
"YET, EVEN AS THE HAGS SAT CACKLING IN THEIR TOWERS, THEIR ENEMIES DREW THEIR PLANS AGAINST THEM."
THEY WAITED ONLY FOR THE RIGHT MOMENT TO STRIKE.
"TO TAKE THE WITCHES BY SURPRISE.
"AND THEIR ENEMIES WERE MIGHTY.
"AND THEIR ENEMIES WERE JUST.

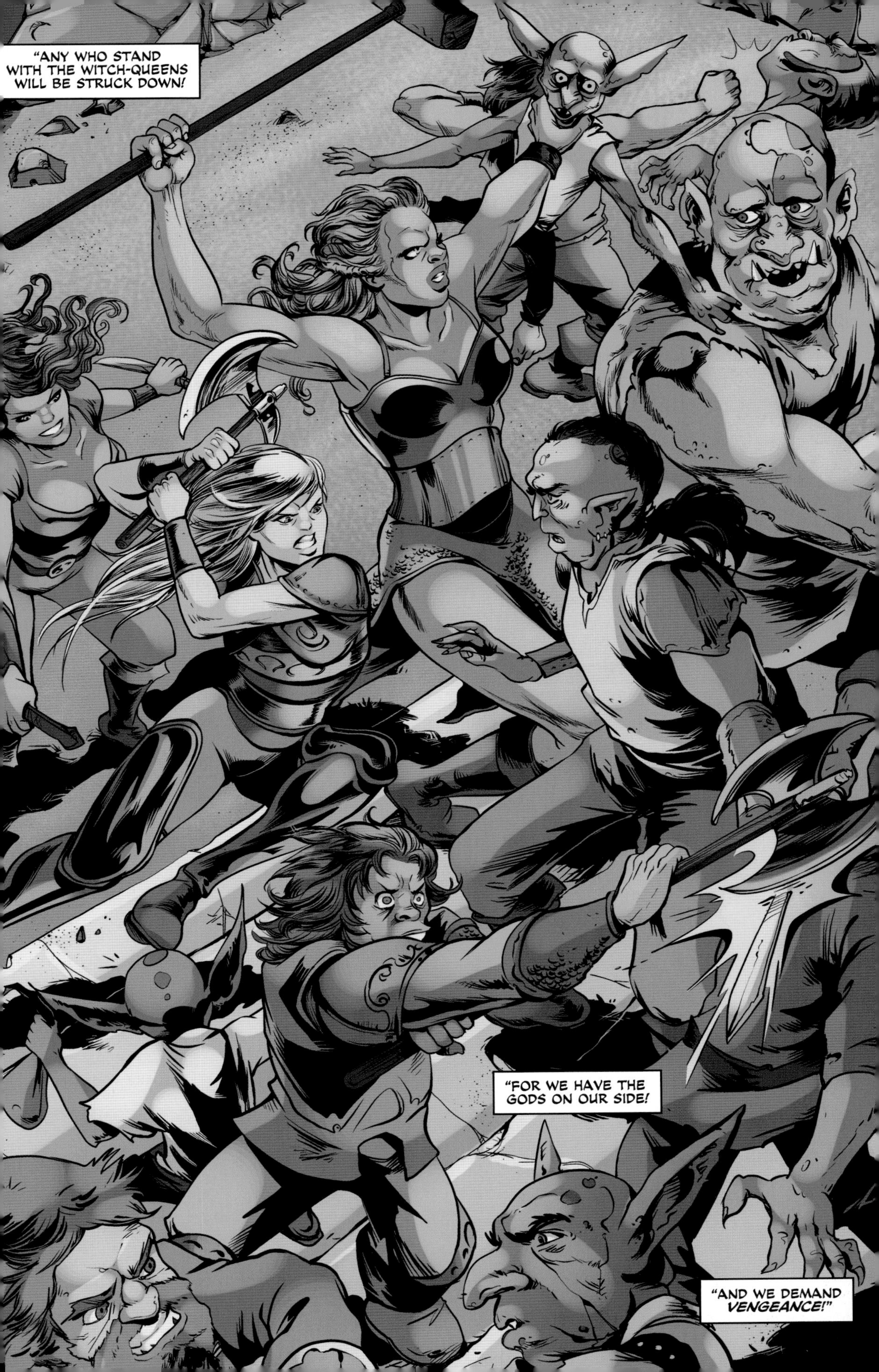
"ANY WHO STAND WITH THE WITCH-QUEENS WILL BE STRUCK DOWN!
"FOR WE HAVE THE GODS ON OUR SIDE!
"AND WE DEMAND *VENGEANCE!*"

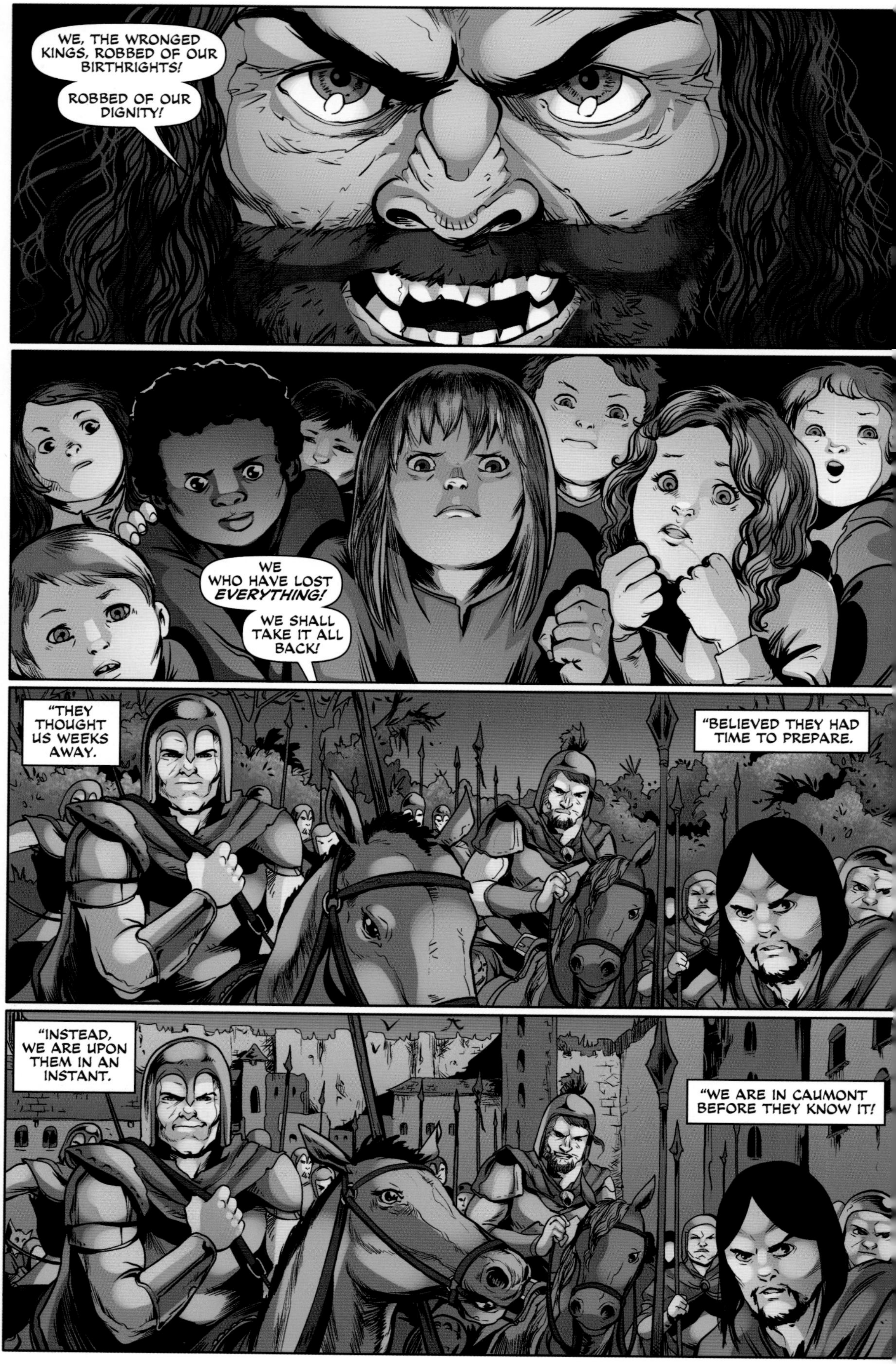
WE, THE WRONGED KINGS, ROBBED OF OUR BIRTHRIGHTS!
ROBBED OF OUR DIGNITY!
WE WHO HAVE LOST *EVERYTHING!*
WE SHALL TAKE IT ALL BACK!
"THEY THOUGHT US WEEKS AWAY.
"BELIEVED THEY HAD TIME TO PREPARE.
"INSTEAD, WE ARE UPON THEM IN AN INSTANT.
"WE ARE IN CAUMONT BEFORE THEY KNOW IT!

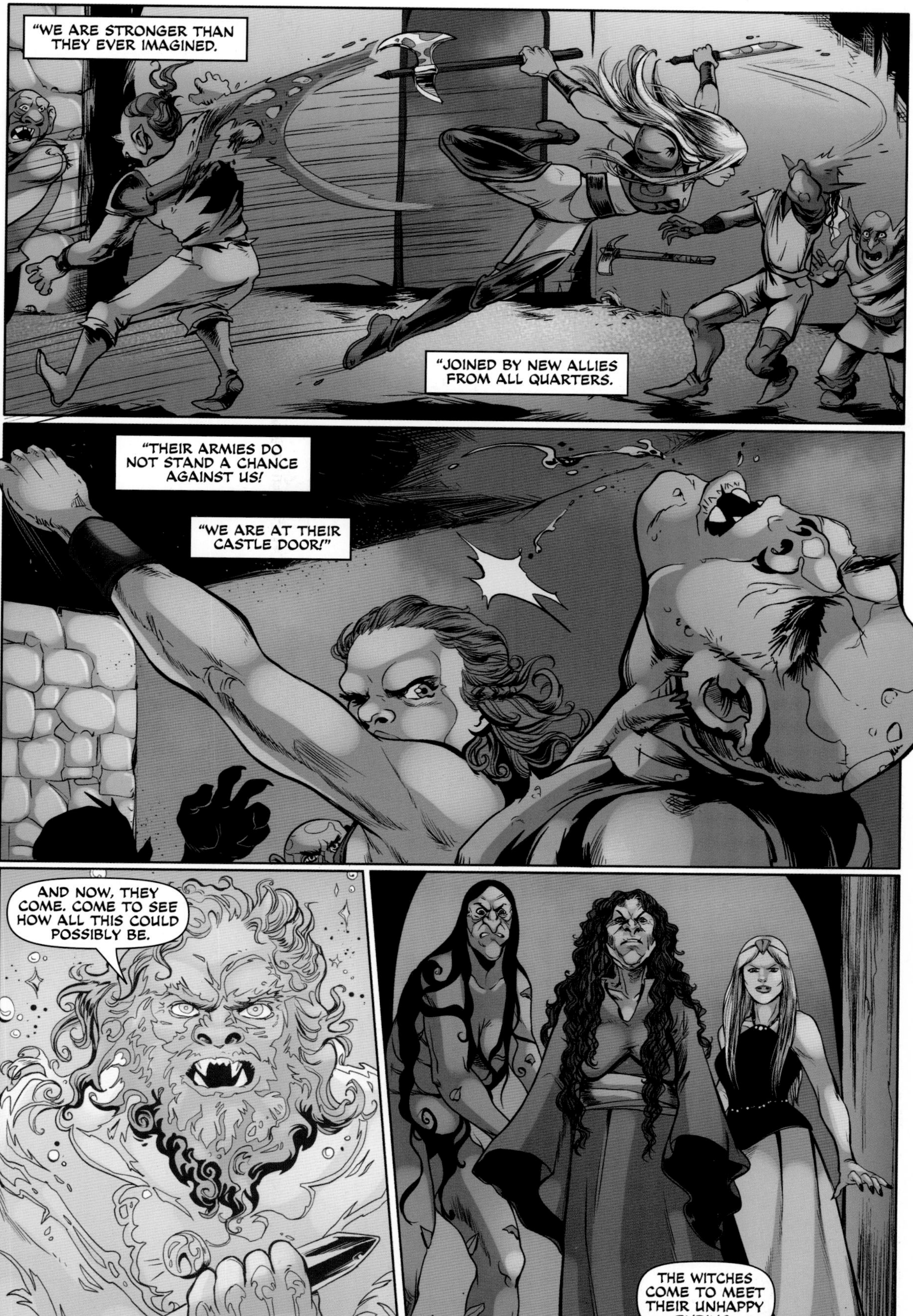
"WE ARE STRONGER THAN THEY EVER IMAGINED.
"JOINED BY NEW ALLIES FROM ALL QUARTERS.
"THEIR ARMIES DO NOT STAND A CHANCE AGAINST US!
"WE ARE AT THEIR CASTLE DOOR!"
AND NOW, THEY COME. COME TO SEE HOW ALL THIS COULD POSSIBLY BE.
THE WITCHES COME TO MEET THEIR UNHAPPY ENDING.

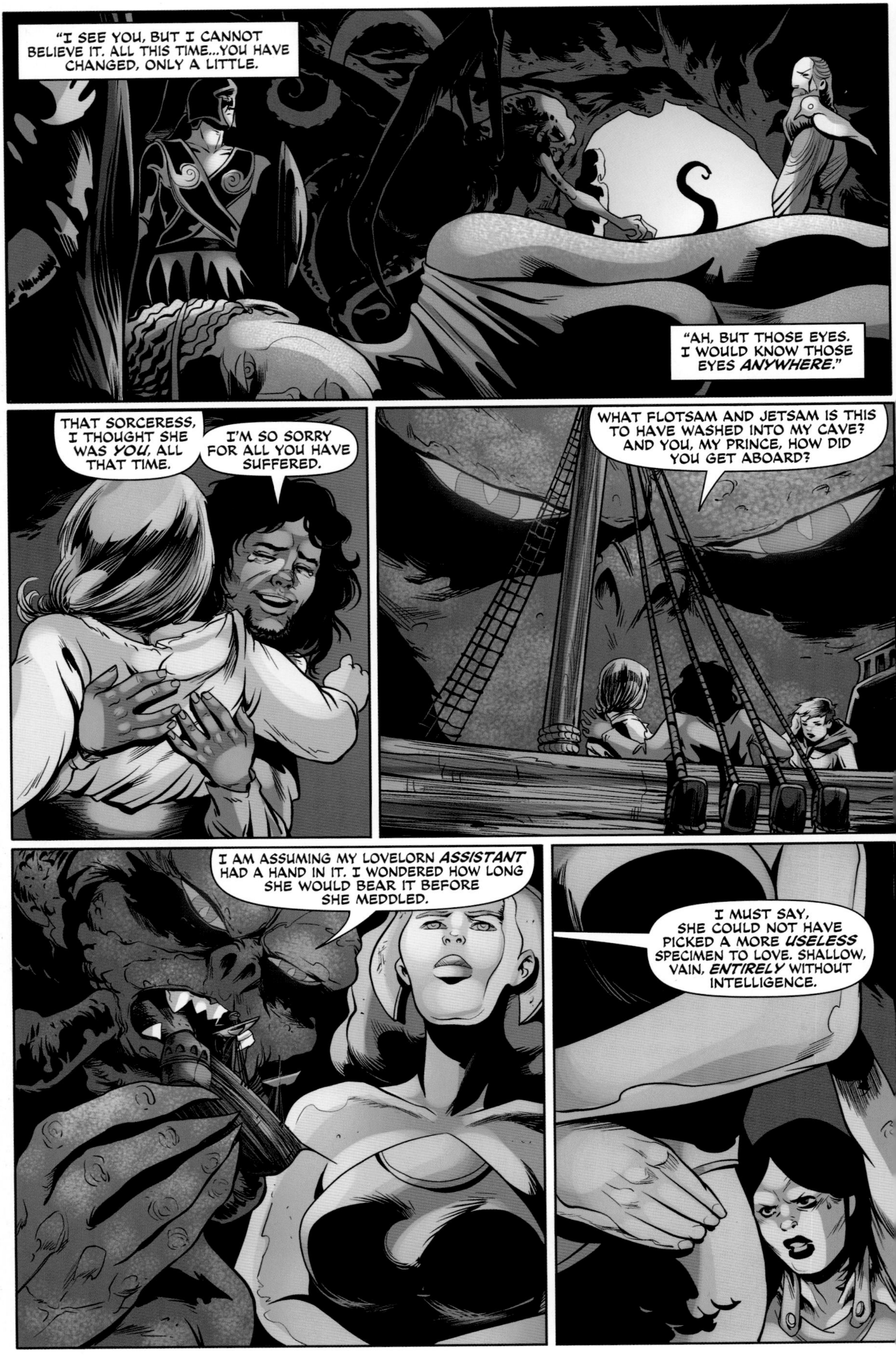
"I SEE YOU, BUT I CANNOT BELIEVE IT. ALL THIS TIME...YOU HAVE CHANGED, ONLY A LITTLE.
"AH, BUT THOSE EYES. I WOULD KNOW THOSE EYES *ANYWHERE*."
THAT SORCERESS, I THOUGHT SHE WAS *YOU*, ALL THAT TIME.
I'M SO SORRY FOR ALL YOU HAVE SUFFERED.
WHAT FLOTSAM AND JETSAM IS THIS TO HAVE WASHED INTO MY CAVE? AND YOU, MY PRINCE, HOW DID YOU GET ABOARD?
I AM ASSUMING MY LOVELORN *ASSISTANT* HAD A HAND IN IT. I WONDERED HOW LONG SHE WOULD BEAR IT BEFORE SHE MEDDLED.
I MUST SAY, SHE COULD NOT HAVE PICKED A MORE *USELESS* SPECIMEN TO LOVE. SHALLOW, VAIN, *ENTIRELY* WITHOUT INTELLIGENCE.

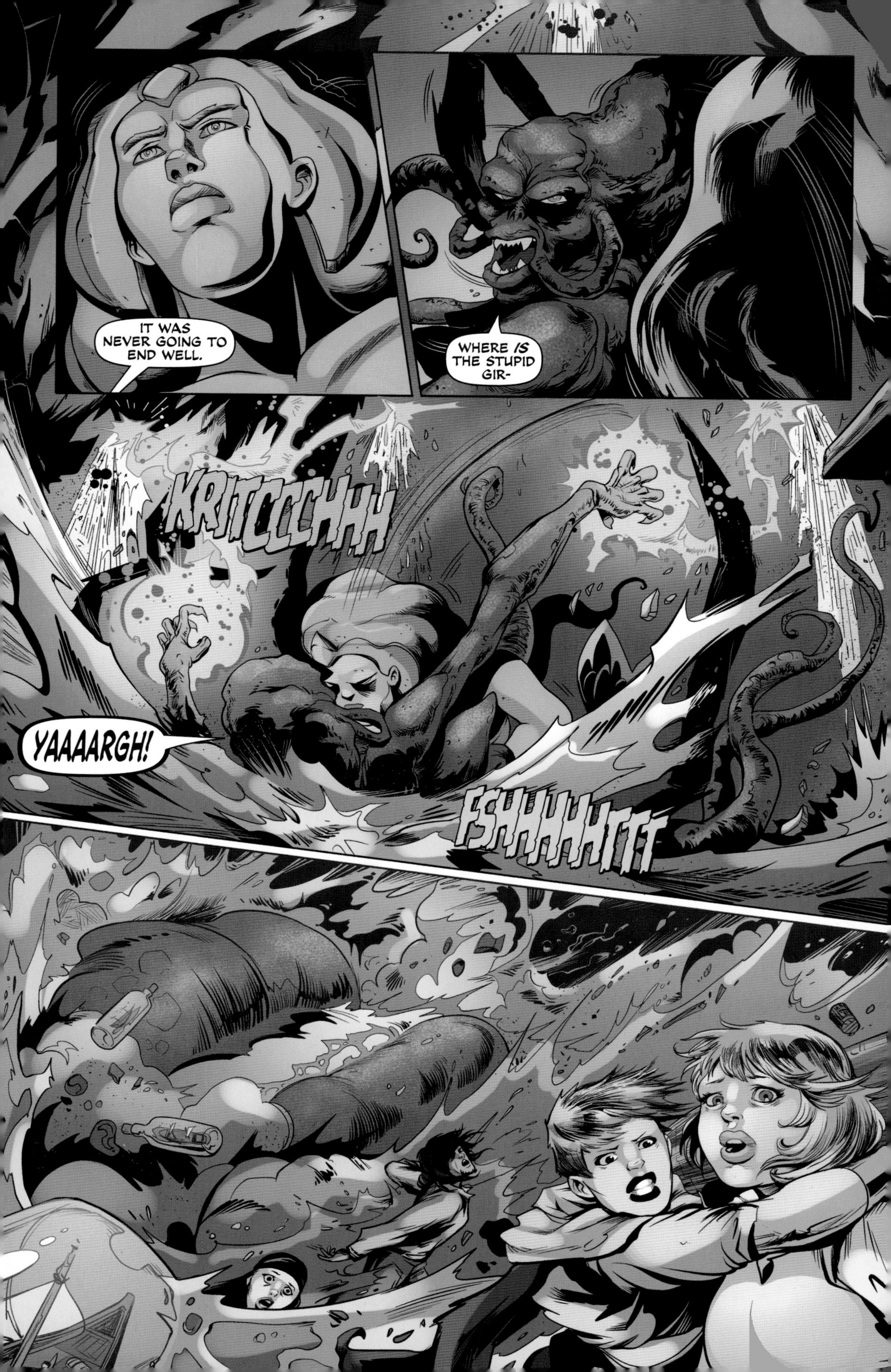
IT WAS NEVER GOING TO END WELL.
WHERE IS THE STUPID GIR-
KRITCCCHHH
YAAAARGH!
FSHHHHHTTT

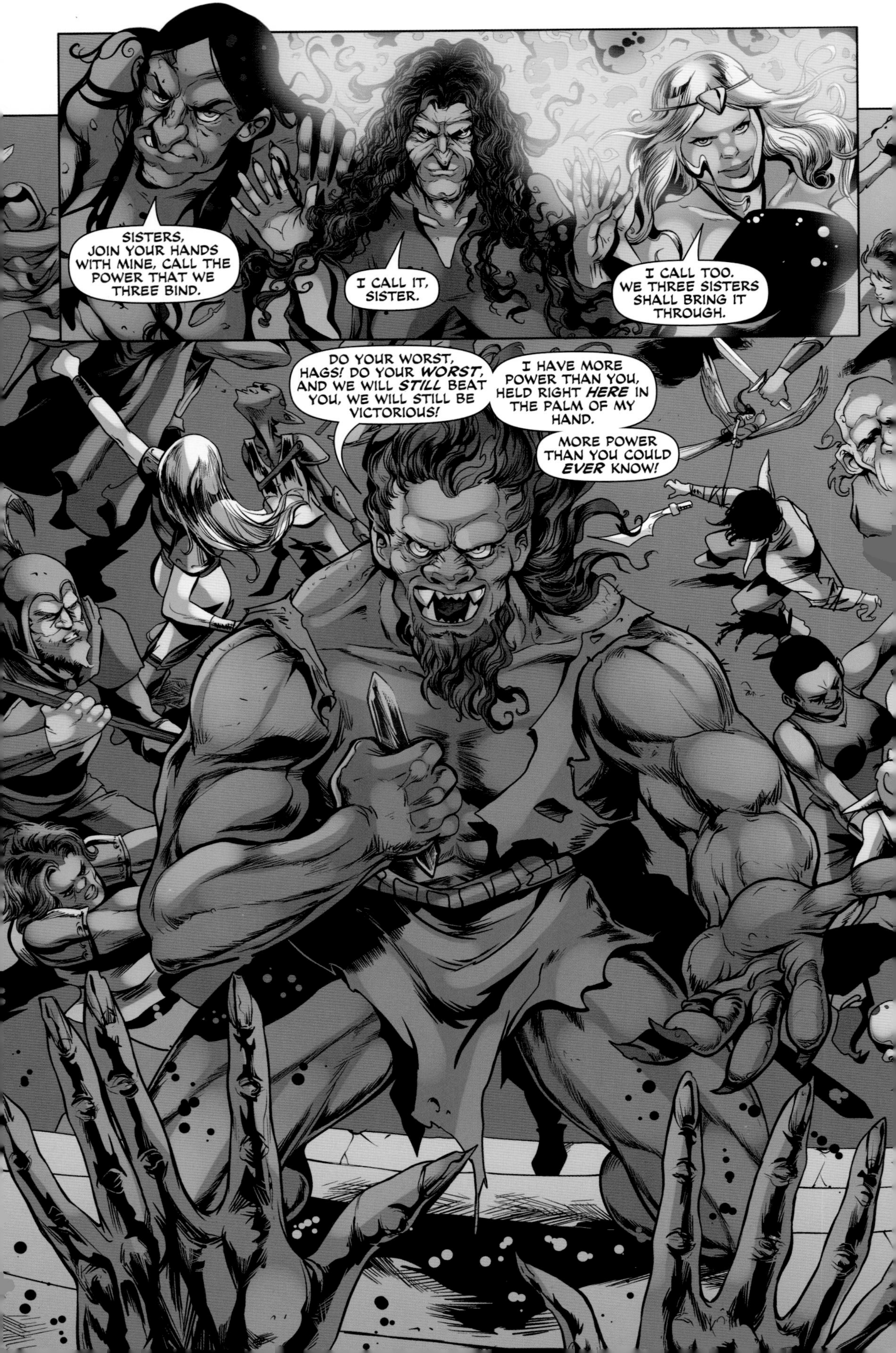
SISTERS, JOIN YOUR HANDS WITH MINE, CALL THE POWER THAT WE THREE BIND.
I CALL IT, SISTER.
I CALL TOO. WE THREE SISTERS SHALL BRING IT THROUGH.
DO YOUR WORST, HAGS! DO YOUR *WORST*, AND WE WILL *STILL* BEAT YOU, WE WILL STILL BE VICTORIOUS!
I HAVE MORE POWER THAN YOU, HELD RIGHT *HERE* IN THE PALM OF MY HAND.
MORE POWER THAN YOU COULD *EVER* KNOW!

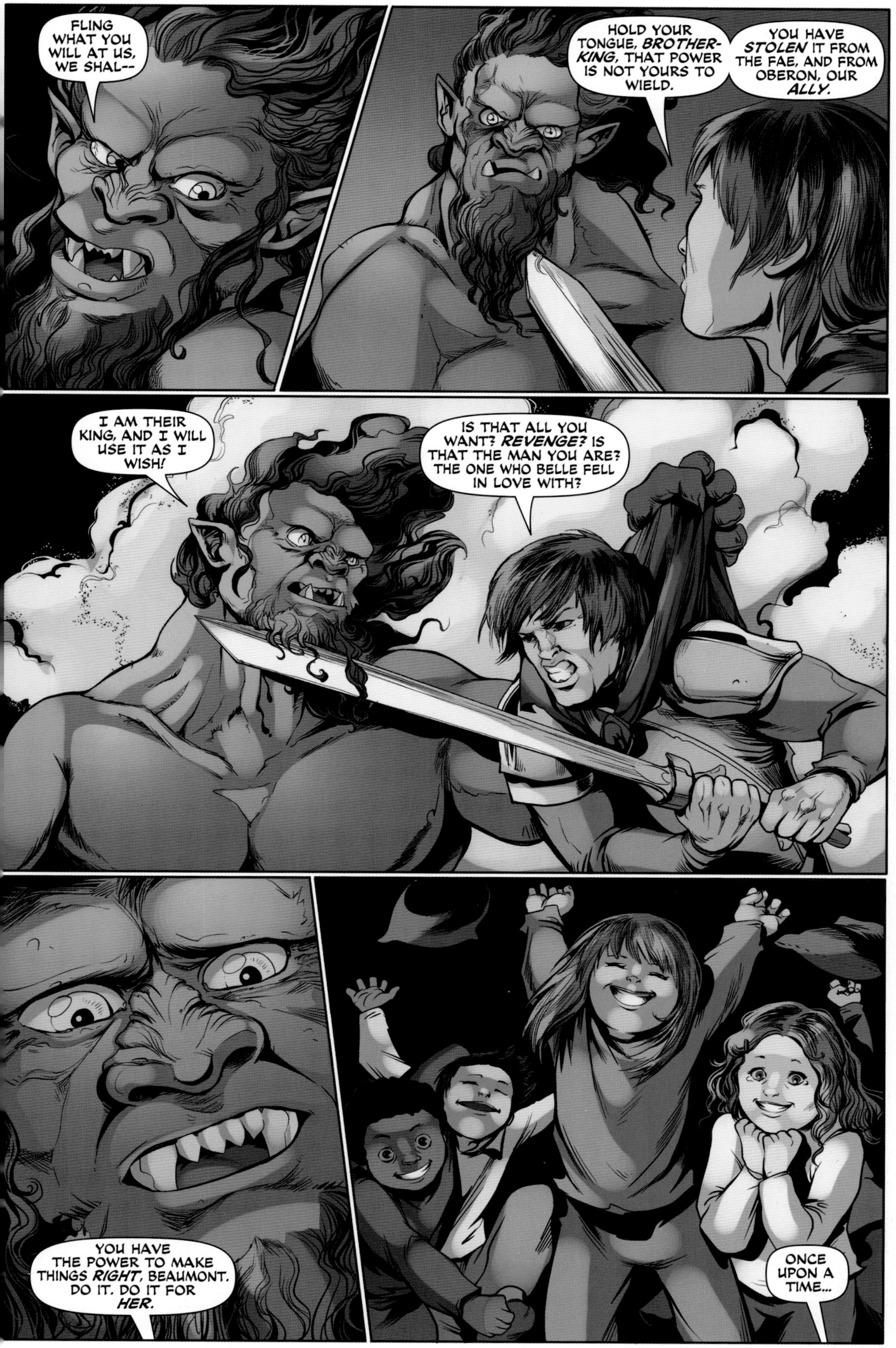
FLING WHAT YOU WILL AT US, WE SHAL--
HOLD YOUR TONGUE, *BROTHER-KING*, THAT POWER IS NOT YOURS TO WIELD.
YOU HAVE *STOLEN* IT FROM THE FAE, AND FROM OBERON, OUR *ALLY*.
I AM THEIR KING, AND I WILL USE IT AS I WISH!
IS THAT ALL YOU WANT? *REVENGE?* IS THAT THE MAN YOU ARE? THE ONE WHO BELLE FELL IN LOVE WITH?
YOU HAVE THE POWER TO MAKE THINGS *RIGHT*, BEAUMONT. DO IT. DO IT FOR *HER*.
ONCE UPON A TIME...

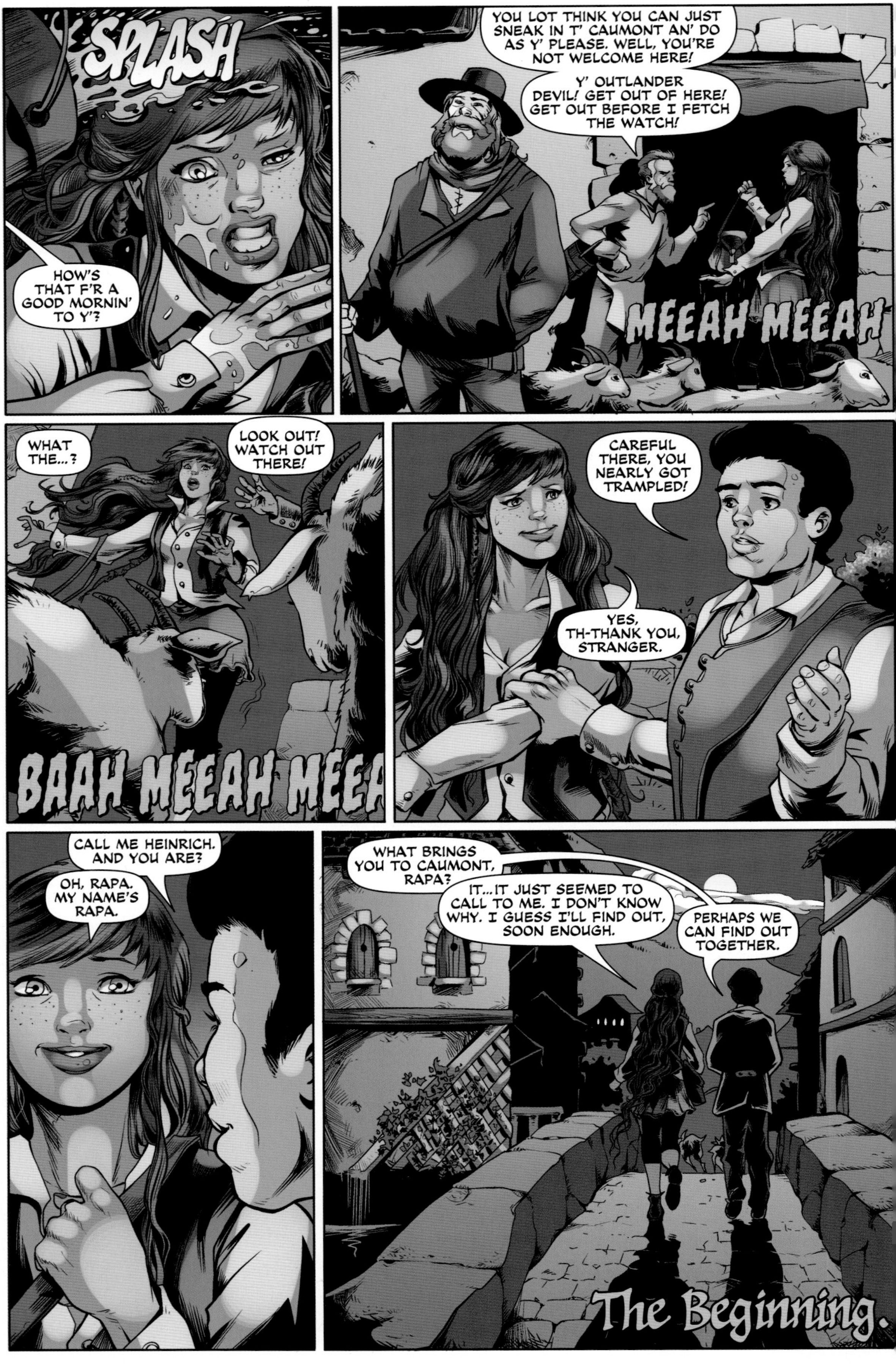
SPLASH
HOW'S THAT F'R A GOOD MORNIN' TO Y'?
YOU LOT THINK YOU CAN JUST SNEAK IN T' CAUMONT AN' DO AS Y' PLEASE. WELL, YOU'RE NOT WELCOME HERE!
Y' OUTLANDER DEVIL! GET OUT OF HERE! GET OUT BEFORE I FETCH THE WATCH!
MEEAH MEEAH
WHAT THE...?
LOOK OUT! WATCH OUT THERE!
BAAH MEEAH MEEA
CAREFUL THERE, YOU NEARLY GOT TRAMPLED!
YES, TH-THANK YOU, STRANGER.
CALL ME HEINRICH. AND YOU ARE?
OH, RAPA. MY NAME'S RAPA.
WHAT BRINGS YOU TO CAUMONT, RAPA?
IT...IT JUST SEEMED TO CALL TO ME. I DON'T KNOW WHY. I GUESS I'LL FIND OUT, SOON ENOUGH.
PERHAPS WE CAN FIND OUT TOGETHER.
The Beginning.

Giant Killer

one shot

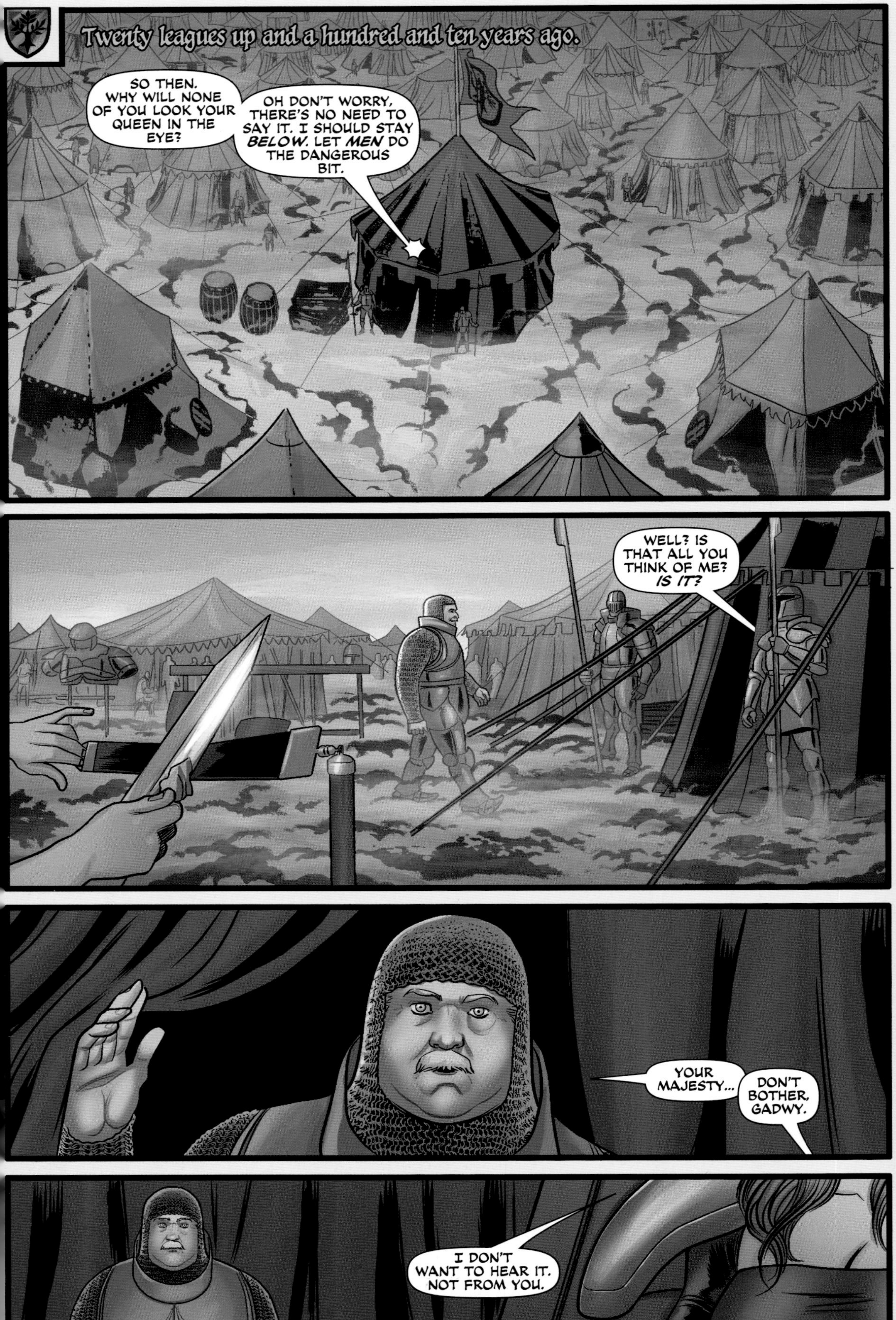
Twenty leagues up and a hundred and ten years ago.
SO THEN. WHY WILL NONE OF YOU LOOK YOUR QUEEN IN THE EYE?
OH DON'T WORRY, THERE'S NO NEED TO SAY IT. I SHOULD STAY *BELOW*. LET *MEN* DO THE DANGEROUS BIT.
WELL? IS THAT ALL YOU THINK OF ME? *IS IT?*
YOUR MAJESTY...
DON'T BOTHER, GADWY.
I DON'T WANT TO HEAR IT. NOT FROM YOU.

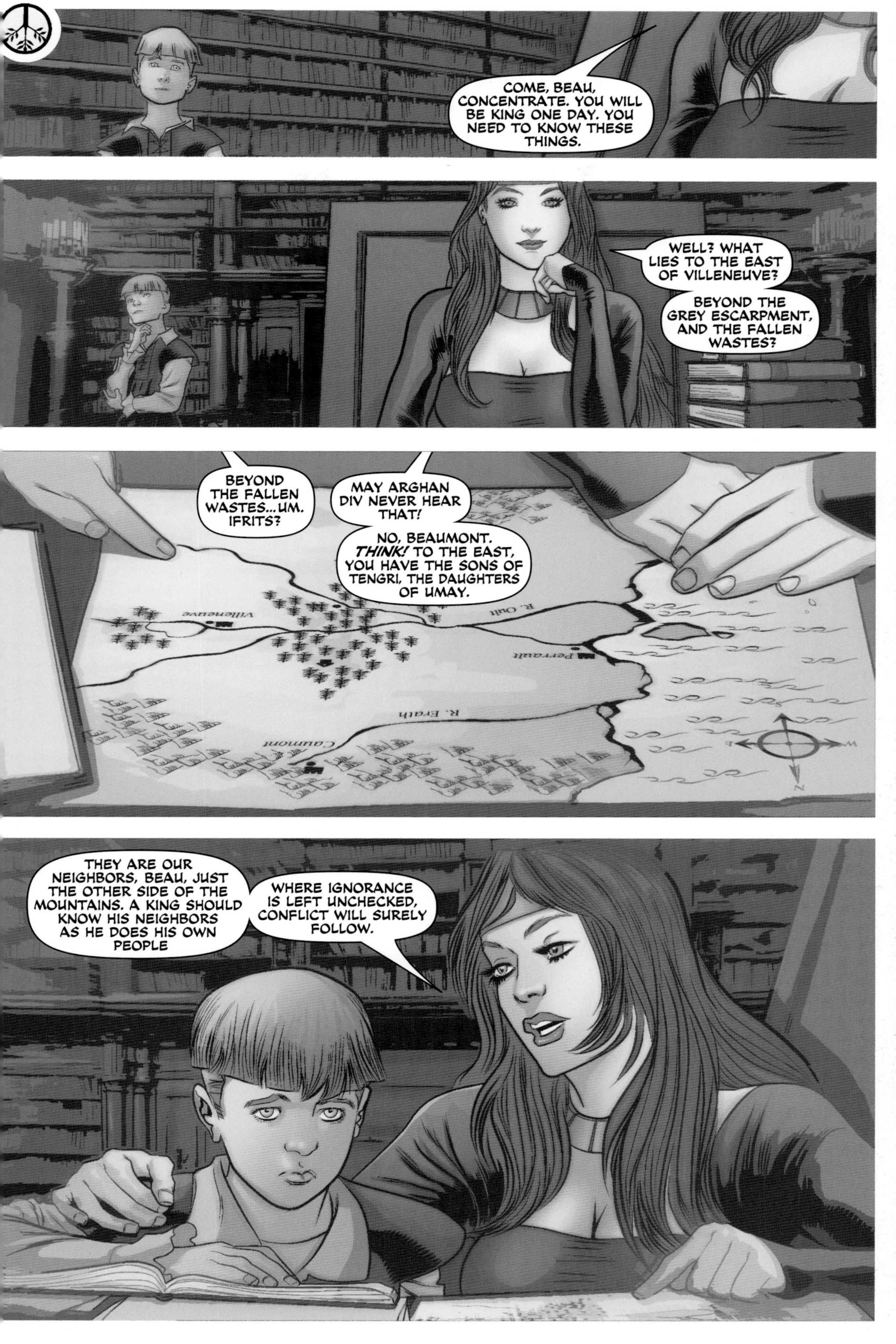
COME, BEAU, CONCENTRATE. YOU WILL BE KING ONE DAY. YOU NEED TO KNOW THESE THINGS.
WELL? WHAT LIES TO THE EAST OF VILLENEUVE?
BEYOND THE GREY ESCARPMENT, AND THE FALLEN WASTES?
BEYOND THE FALLEN WASTES...UM. IFRITS?
MAY ARGHAN DIV NEVER HEAR THAT!
NO, BEAUMONT. *THINK!* TO THE EAST, YOU HAVE THE SONS OF TENGRI, THE DAUGHTERS OF UMAY.
Villeneuve
Perrault
R. Erath
Caumont
THEY ARE OUR NEIGHBORS, BEAU, JUST THE OTHER SIDE OF THE MOUNTAINS. A KING SHOULD KNOW HIS NEIGHBORS AS HE DOES HIS OWN PEOPLE
WHERE IGNORANCE IS LEFT UNCHECKED, CONFLICT WILL SURELY FOLLOW.

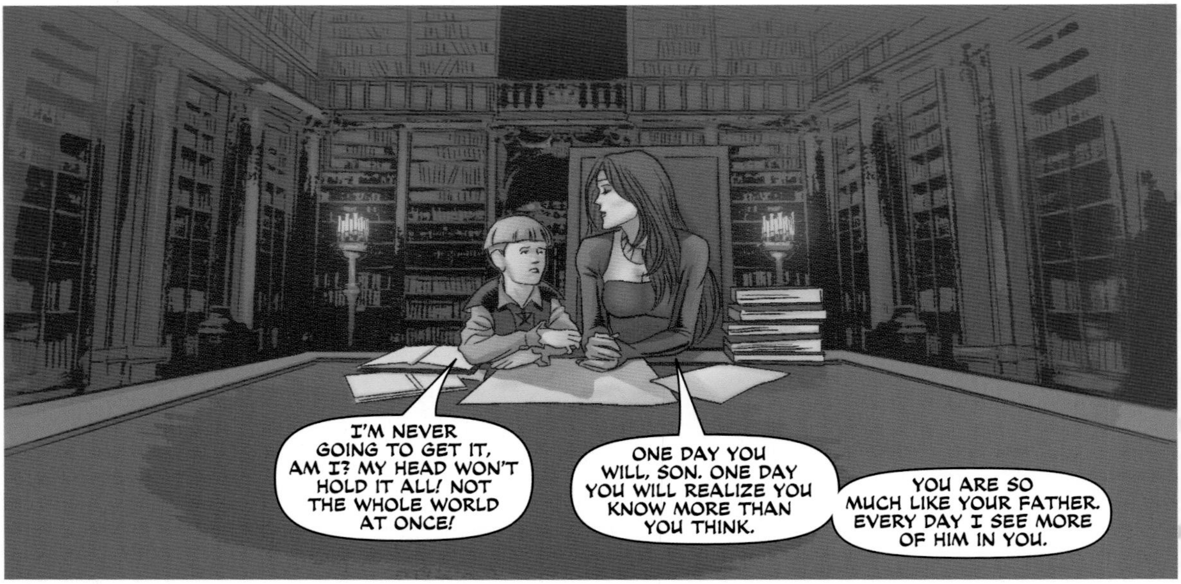
I'M NEVER GOING TO GET IT, AM I? MY HEAD WON'T HOLD IT ALL! NOT THE WHOLE WORLD AT ONCE!
ONE DAY YOU WILL, SON. ONE DAY YOU WILL REALIZE YOU KNOW MORE THAN YOU THINK.
YOU ARE SO MUCH LIKE YOUR FATHER. EVERY DAY I SEE MORE OF HIM IN YOU.

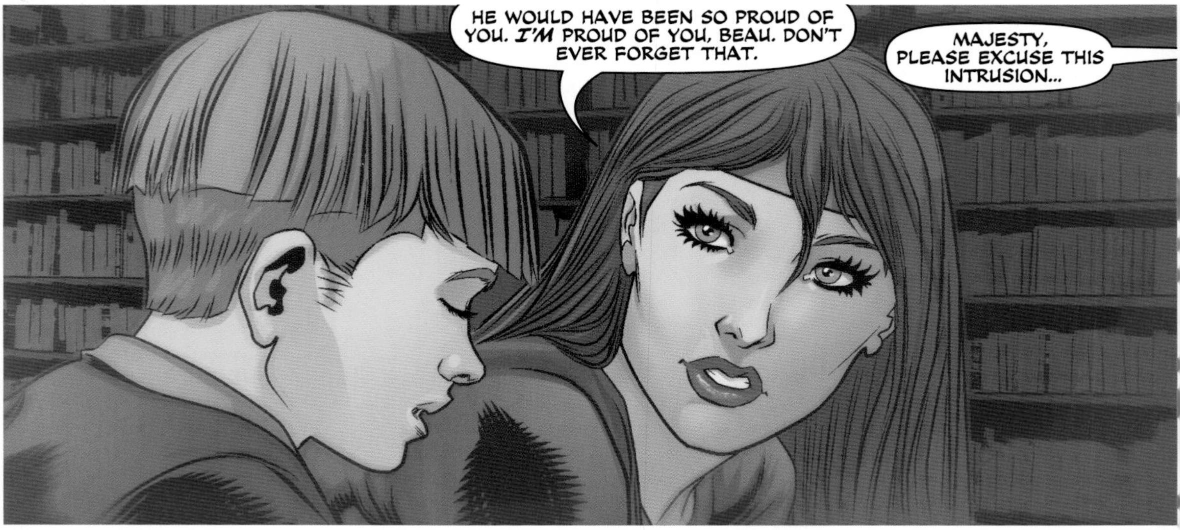
HE WOULD HAVE BEEN SO PROUD OF YOU. *I'M* PROUD OF YOU, BEAU. DON'T EVER FORGET THAT.
MAJESTY, PLEASE EXCUSE THIS INTRUSION...

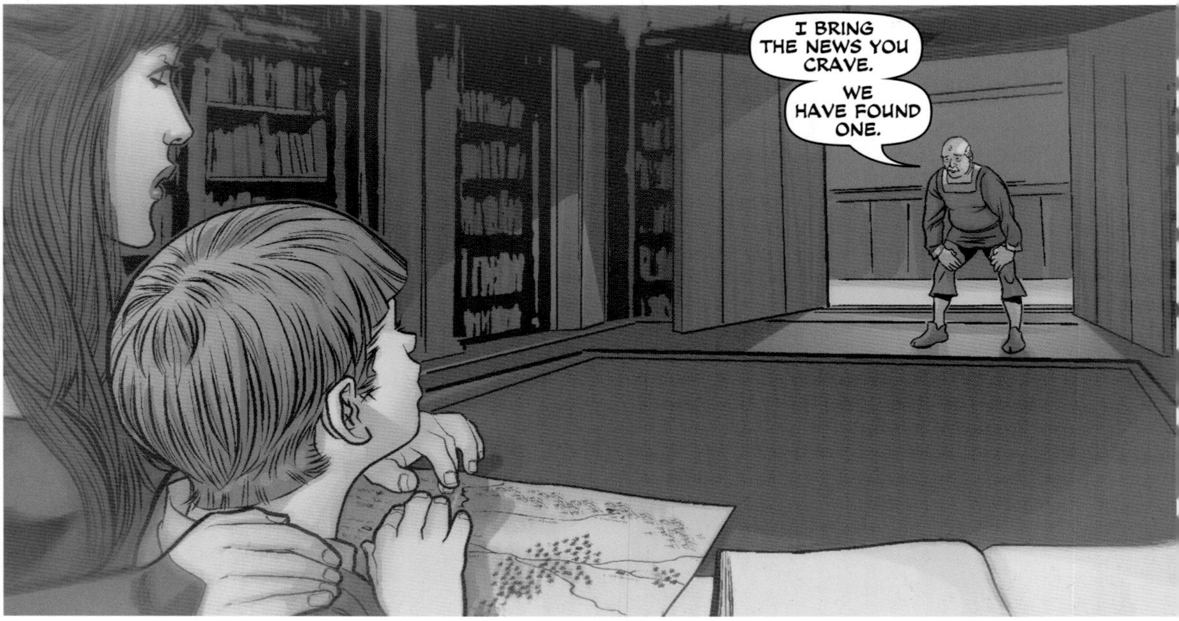
I BRING THE NEWS YOU CRAVE.
WE HAVE FOUND ONE.

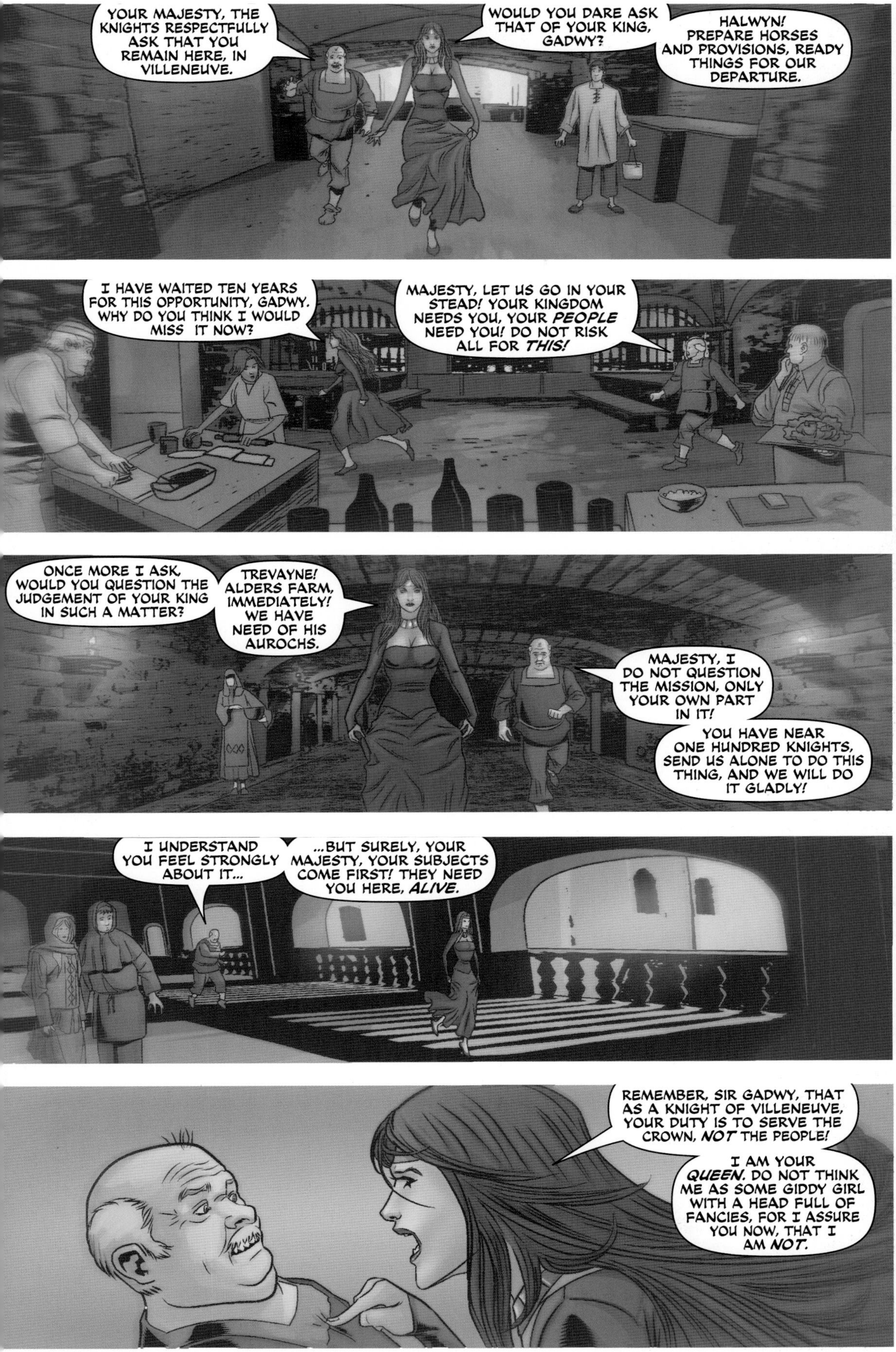
YOUR MAJESTY, THE KNIGHTS RESPECTFULLY ASK THAT YOU REMAIN HERE, IN VILLENEUVE.
WOULD YOU DARE ASK THAT OF YOUR KING, GADWY?
HALWYN! PREPARE HORSES AND PROVISIONS, READY THINGS FOR OUR DEPARTURE.
I HAVE WAITED TEN YEARS FOR THIS OPPORTUNITY, GADWY. WHY DO YOU THINK I WOULD MISS IT NOW?
MAJESTY, LET US GO IN YOUR STEAD! YOUR KINGDOM NEEDS YOU, YOUR *PEOPLE* NEED YOU! DO NOT RISK ALL FOR *THIS!*
ONCE MORE I ASK, WOULD YOU QUESTION THE JUDGEMENT OF YOUR KING IN SUCH A MATTER?
TREVAYNE! ALDERS FARM, IMMEDIATELY! WE HAVE NEED OF HIS AUROCHS.
MAJESTY, I DO NOT QUESTION THE MISSION, ONLY YOUR OWN PART IN IT!
YOU HAVE NEAR ONE HUNDRED KNIGHTS, SEND US ALONE TO DO THIS THING, AND WE WILL DO IT GLADLY!
I UNDERSTAND YOU FEEL STRONGLY ABOUT IT...
...BUT SURELY, YOUR MAJESTY, YOUR SUBJECTS COME FIRST! THEY NEED YOU HERE, *ALIVE.*
REMEMBER, SIR GADWY, THAT AS A KNIGHT OF VILLENEUVE, YOUR DUTY IS TO SERVE THE CROWN, *NOT* THE PEOPLE!
I AM YOUR *QUEEN.* DO NOT THINK ME AS SOME GIDDY GIRL WITH A HEAD FULL OF FANCIES, FOR I ASSURE YOU NOW, THAT I AM *NOT.*

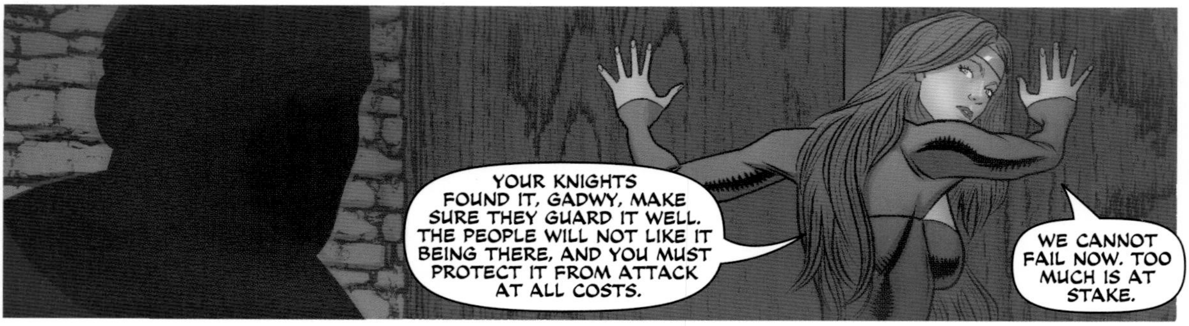
YOUR KNIGHTS FOUND IT, GADWY, MAKE SURE THEY GUARD IT WELL. THE PEOPLE WILL NOT LIKE IT BEING THERE, AND YOU MUST PROTECT IT FROM ATTACK AT ALL COSTS.
WE CANNOT FAIL NOW. TOO MUCH IS AT STAKE.
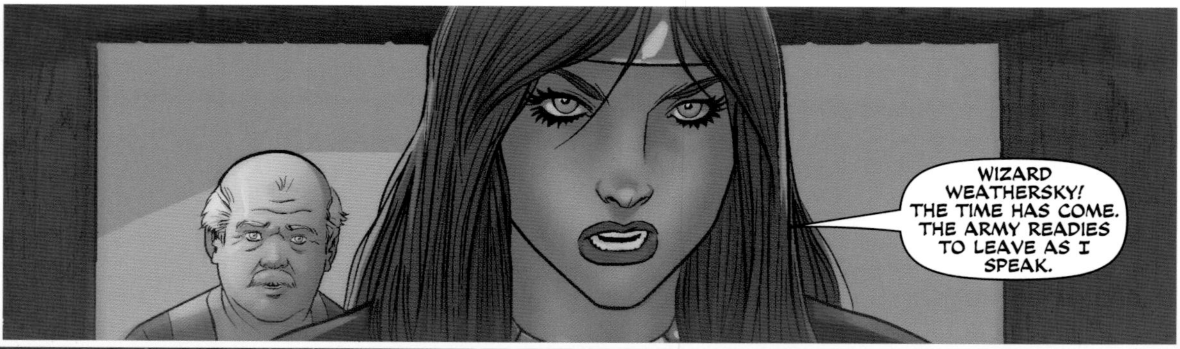
WIZARD WEATHERSKY! THE TIME HAS COME. THE ARMY READIES TO LEAVE AS I SPEAK.
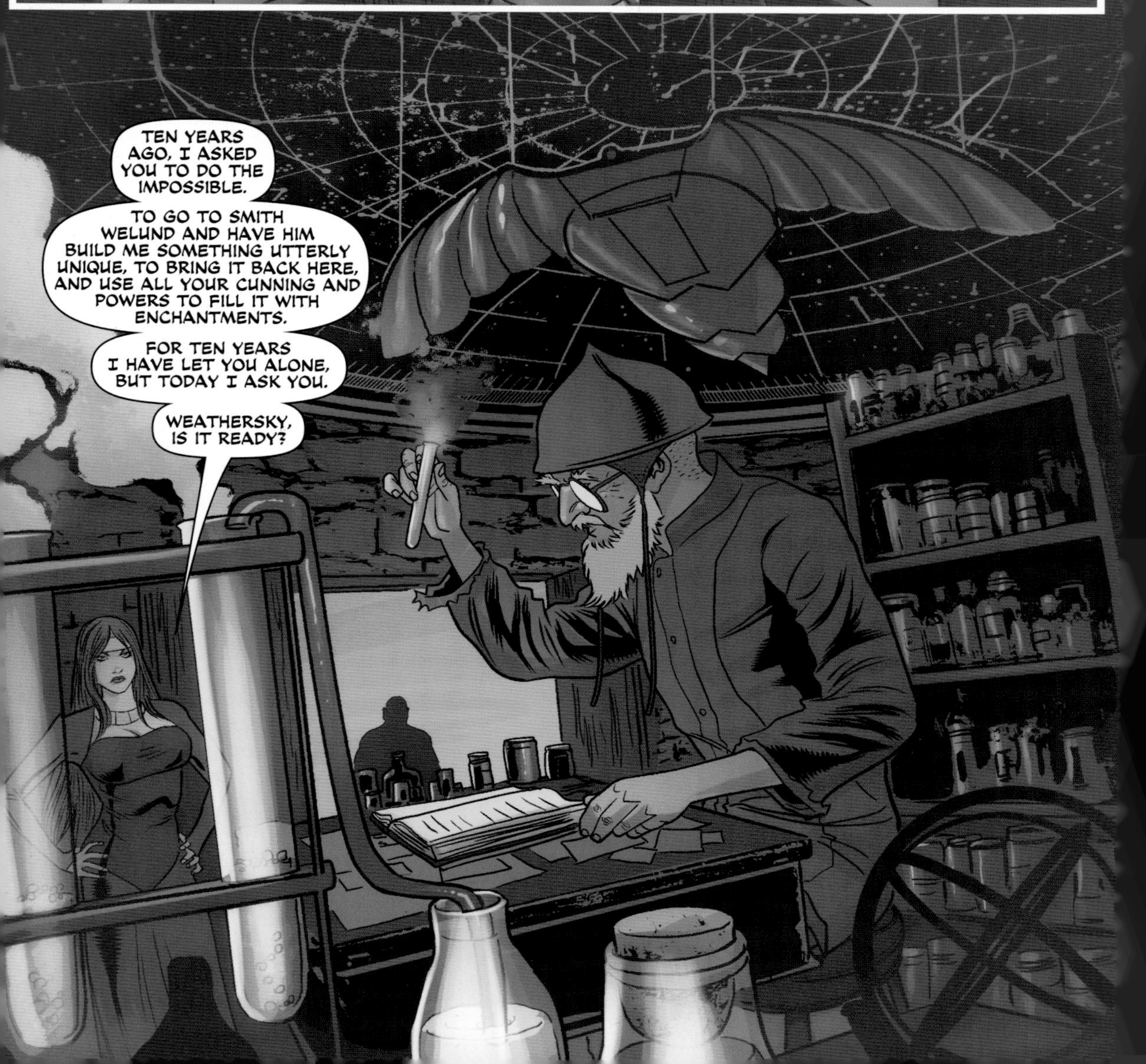
TEN YEARS AGO, I ASKED YOU TO DO THE IMPOSSIBLE.
TO GO TO SMITH WELUND AND HAVE HIM BUILD ME SOMETHING UTTERLY UNIQUE, TO BRING IT BACK HERE, AND USE ALL YOUR CUNNING AND POWERS TO FILL IT WITH ENCHANTMENTS.
FOR TEN YEARS I HAVE LET YOU ALONE, BUT TODAY I ASK YOU.
WEATHERSKY, IS IT READY?

READY YOURSELVES, MEN. WEATHERSKY SAYS WELUND'S WEAPONS WILL HOLD THE ENCHANTMENT FOR ONLY A FEW HOURS.
THIS IS OUR CHANCE, SO WE MUST TAKE IT.
I KNOW MANY OF YOU WOULD LIKE OUR QUEEN TO STAY BELOW, AND TO FIGHT IN HER PLACE.
BUT UNDERSTAND THIS: SHE IS DETERMINED TO SEE THIS THROUGH TO THE BITTER END.
TEN YEARS AGO, WE LOST A KING, BUT NOT A QUEEN. SHE HAS STAYED STRONG FOR *US*, ALL THOSE YEARS.
WE ARE STRONG AND RESOLUTE, AND WE SHALL STAND FIRM NO MATTER WHAT.
WE OWE IT TO OUR QUEEN.

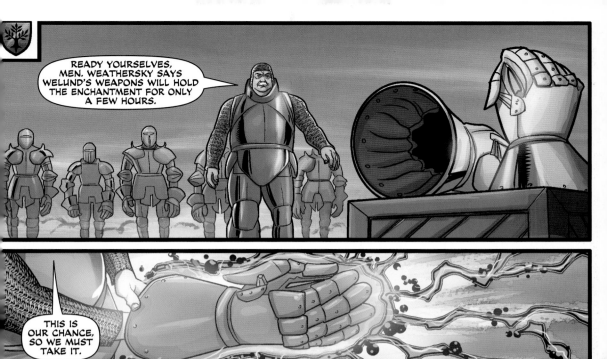

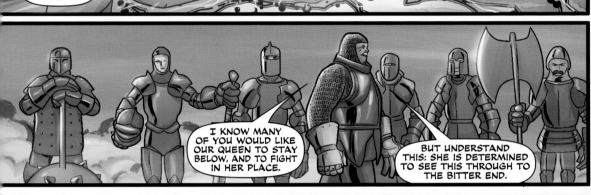

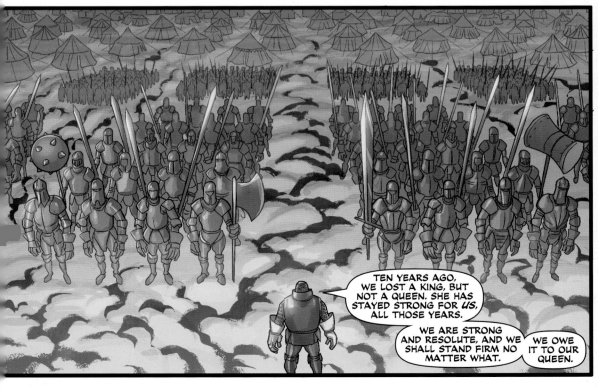

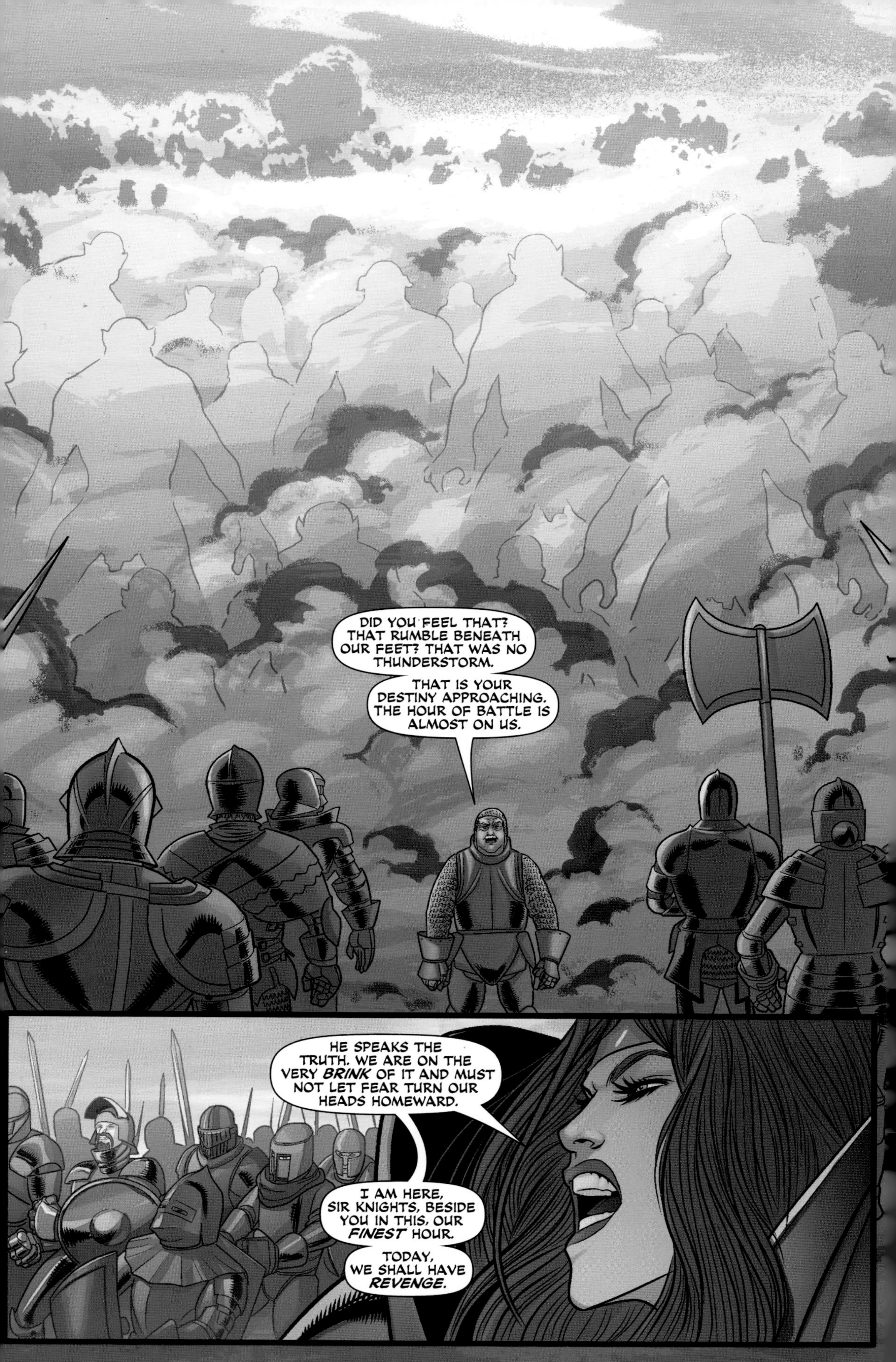
DID YOU FEEL THAT? THAT RUMBLE BENEATH OUR FEET? THAT WAS NO THUNDERSTORM.
THAT IS YOUR DESTINY APPROACHING. THE HOUR OF BATTLE IS ALMOST ON US.
HE SPEAKS THE TRUTH. WE ARE ON THE VERY *BRINK* OF IT AND MUST NOT LET FEAR TURN OUR HEADS HOMEWARD.
I AM HERE, SIR KNIGHTS, BESIDE YOU IN THIS, OUR *FINEST* HOUR.
TODAY, WE SHALL HAVE ***REVENGE.***

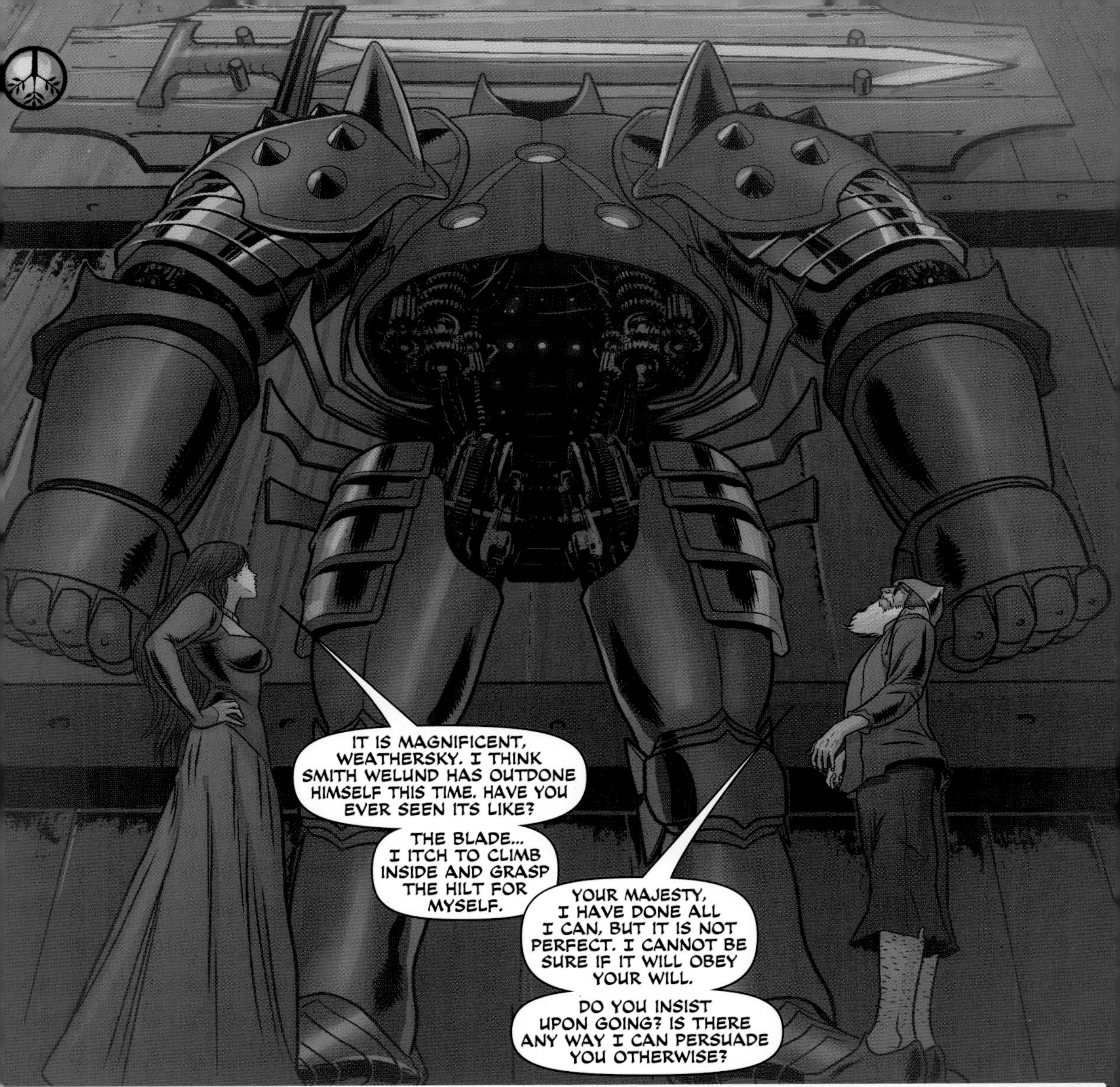
IT IS MAGNIFICENT, WEATHERSKY. I THINK SMITH WELUND HAS OUTDONE HIMSELF THIS TIME. HAVE YOU EVER SEEN ITS LIKE?
THE BLADE... I ITCH TO CLIMB INSIDE AND GRASP THE HILT FOR MYSELF.
YOUR MAJESTY, I HAVE DONE ALL I CAN, BUT IT IS NOT PERFECT. I CANNOT BE SURE IF IT WILL OBEY YOUR WILL.
DO YOU INSIST UPON GOING? IS THERE ANY WAY I CAN PERSUADE YOU OTHERWISE?
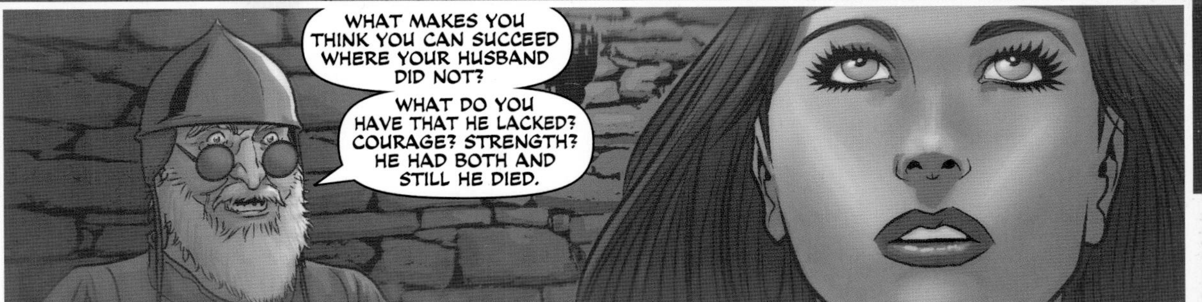
WHAT MAKES YOU THINK YOU CAN SUCCEED WHERE YOUR HUSBAND DID NOT?
WHAT DO YOU HAVE THAT HE LACKED? COURAGE? STRENGTH? HE HAD BOTH AND STILL HE DIED.
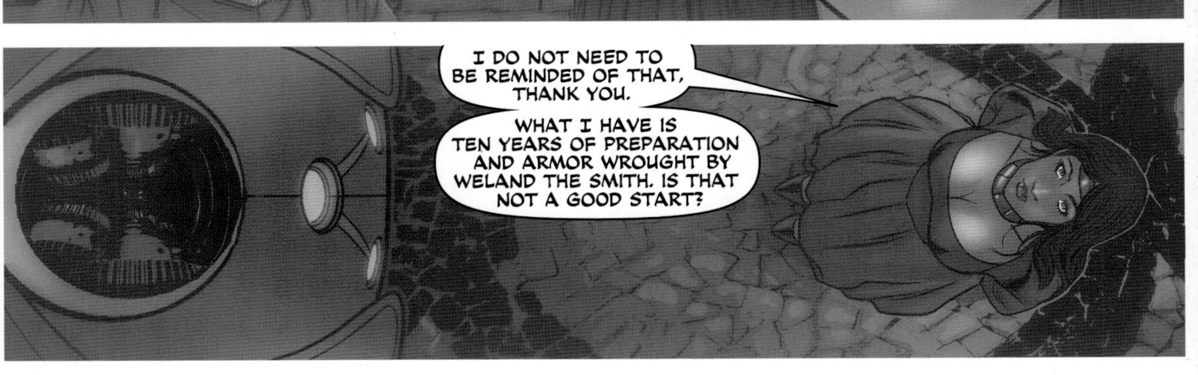
I DO NOT NEED TO BE REMINDED OF THAT, THANK YOU.
WHAT I HAVE IS TEN YEARS OF PREPARATION AND ARMOR WROUGHT BY WELAND THE SMITH. IS THAT NOT A GOOD START?

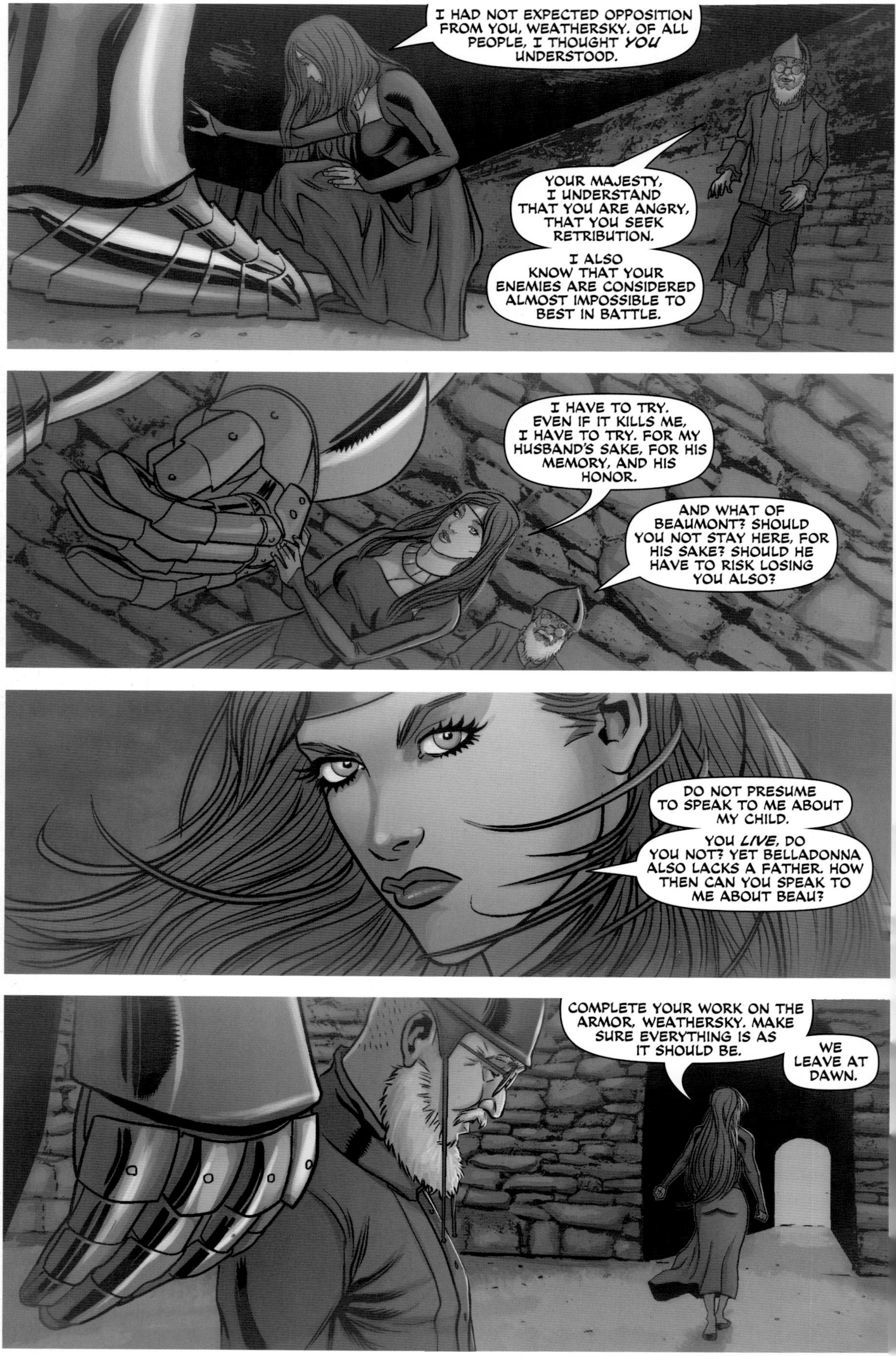
I HAD NOT EXPECTED OPPOSITION FROM YOU, WEATHERSKY. OF ALL PEOPLE, I THOUGHT *YOU* UNDERSTOOD.
YOUR MAJESTY, I UNDERSTAND THAT YOU ARE ANGRY, THAT YOU SEEK RETRIBUTION.
I ALSO KNOW THAT YOUR ENEMIES ARE CONSIDERED ALMOST IMPOSSIBLE TO BEST IN BATTLE.
I HAVE TO TRY. EVEN IF IT KILLS ME, I HAVE TO TRY. FOR MY HUSBAND'S SAKE, FOR HIS MEMORY, AND HIS HONOR.
AND WHAT OF BEAUMONT? SHOULD YOU NOT STAY HERE, FOR HIS SAKE? SHOULD HE HAVE TO RISK LOSING YOU ALSO?
DO NOT PRESUME TO SPEAK TO ME ABOUT MY CHILD.
YOU *LIVE*, DO YOU NOT? YET BELLADONNA ALSO LACKS A FATHER. HOW THEN CAN YOU SPEAK TO ME ABOUT BEAU?
COMPLETE YOUR WORK ON THE ARMOR, WEATHERSKY. MAKE SURE EVERYTHING IS AS IT SHOULD BE.
WE LEAVE AT DAWN.

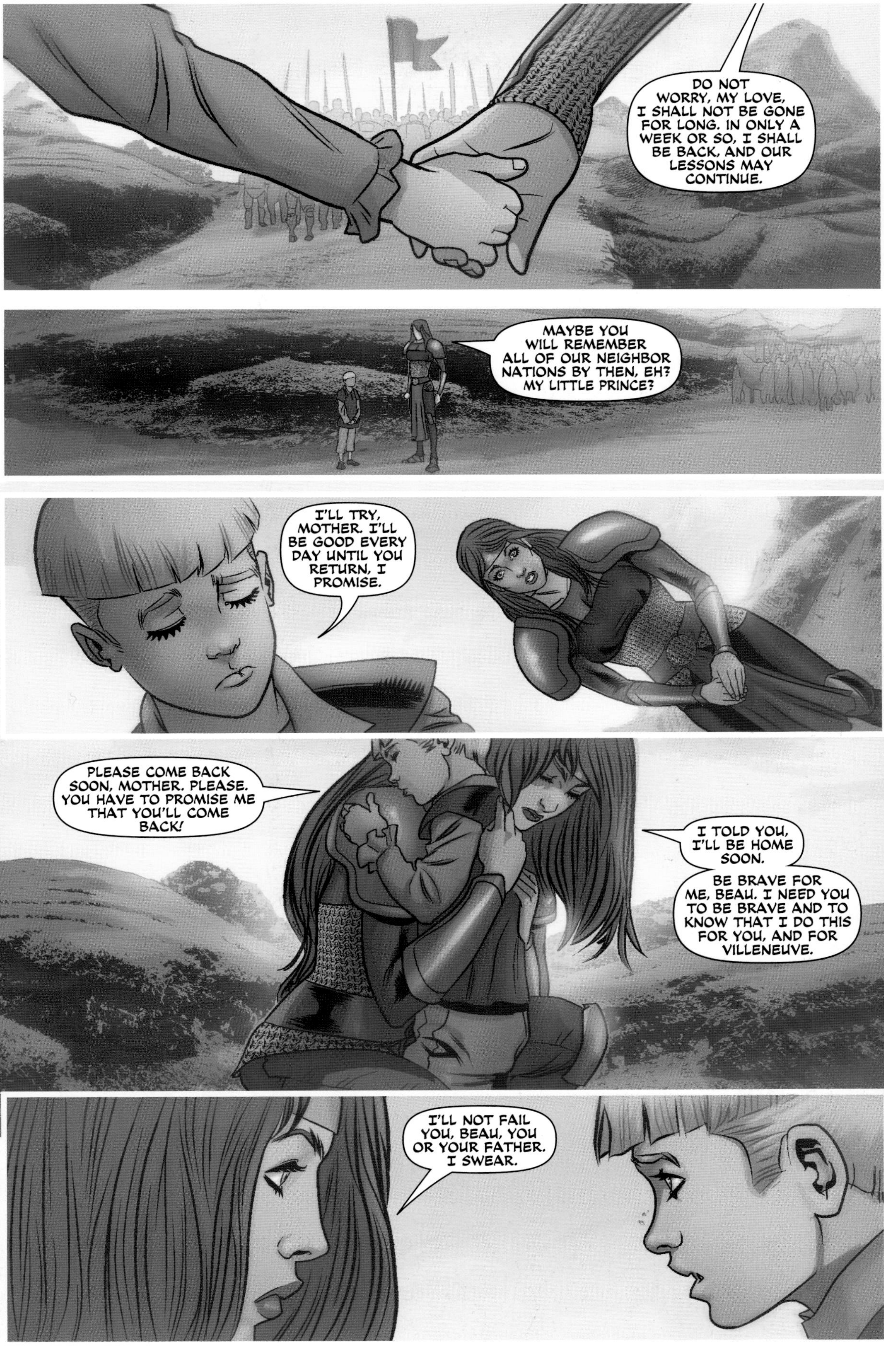
DO NOT WORRY, MY LOVE, I SHALL NOT BE GONE FOR LONG. IN ONLY A WEEK OR SO, I SHALL BE BACK, AND OUR LESSONS MAY CONTINUE.
MAYBE YOU WILL REMEMBER ALL OF OUR NEIGHBOR NATIONS BY THEN, EH? MY LITTLE PRINCE?
I'LL TRY, MOTHER. I'LL BE GOOD EVERY DAY UNTIL YOU RETURN, I PROMISE.
PLEASE COME BACK SOON, MOTHER. PLEASE. YOU HAVE TO PROMISE ME THAT YOU'LL COME BACK!
I TOLD YOU, I'LL BE HOME SOON.
BE BRAVE FOR ME, BEAU. I NEED YOU TO BE BRAVE AND TO KNOW THAT I DO THIS FOR YOU, AND FOR VILLENEUVE.
I'LL NOT FAIL YOU, BEAU, YOU OR YOUR FATHER. I SWEAR.

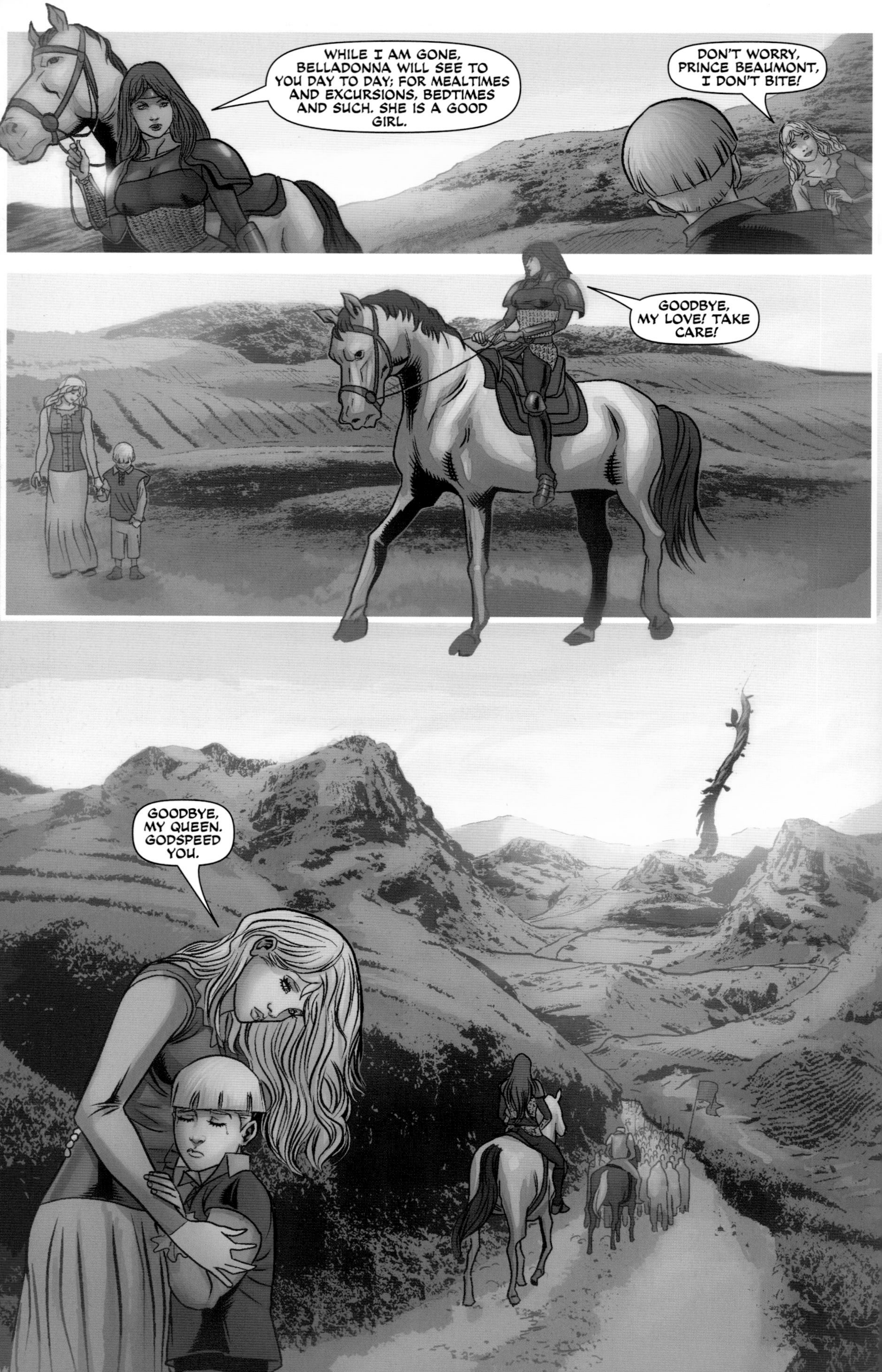
WHILE I AM GONE, BELLADONNA WILL SEE TO YOU DAY TO DAY; FOR MEALTIMES AND EXCURSIONS, BEDTIMES AND SUCH. SHE IS A GOOD GIRL.
DON'T WORRY, PRINCE BEAUMONT, I DON'T BITE!
GOODBYE, MY LOVE! TAKE CARE!
GOODBYE, MY QUEEN. GODSPEED YOU.

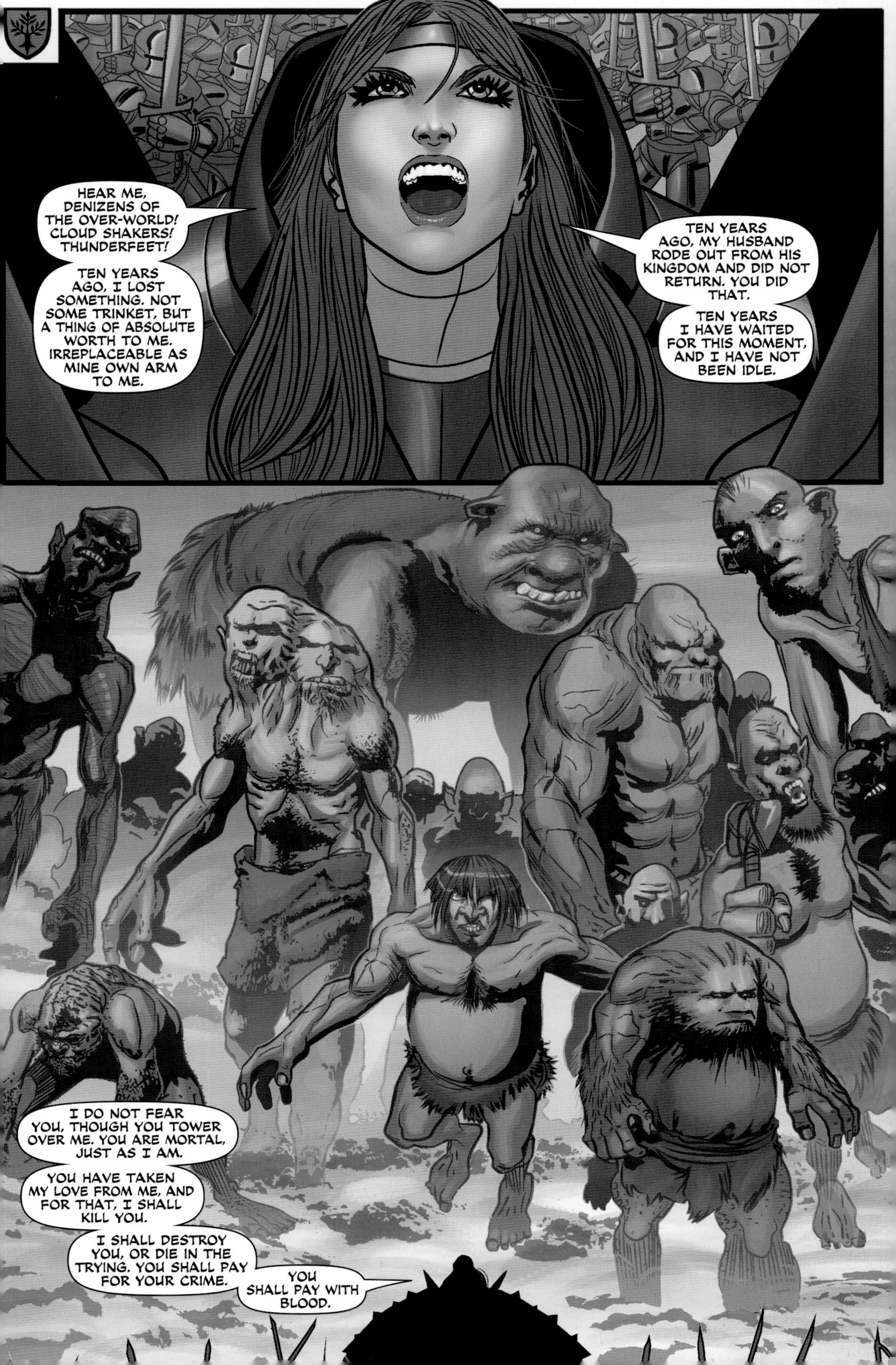
HEAR ME, DENIZENS OF THE OVER-WORLD! CLOUD SHAKERS! THUNDERFEET!
TEN YEARS AGO, I LOST SOMETHING. NOT SOME TRINKET, BUT A THING OF ABSOLUTE WORTH TO ME. IRREPLACEABLE AS MINE OWN ARM TO ME.
TEN YEARS AGO, MY HUSBAND RODE OUT FROM HIS KINGDOM AND DID NOT RETURN. YOU DID THAT.
TEN YEARS I HAVE WAITED FOR THIS MOMENT, AND I HAVE NOT BEEN IDLE.
I DO NOT FEAR YOU, THOUGH YOU TOWER OVER ME. YOU ARE MORTAL, JUST AS I AM.
YOU HAVE TAKEN MY LOVE FROM ME, AND FOR THAT, I SHALL KILL YOU.
I SHALL DESTROY YOU, OR DIE IN THE TRYING. YOU SHALL PAY FOR YOUR CRIME.
YOU SHALL PAY WITH BLOOD.

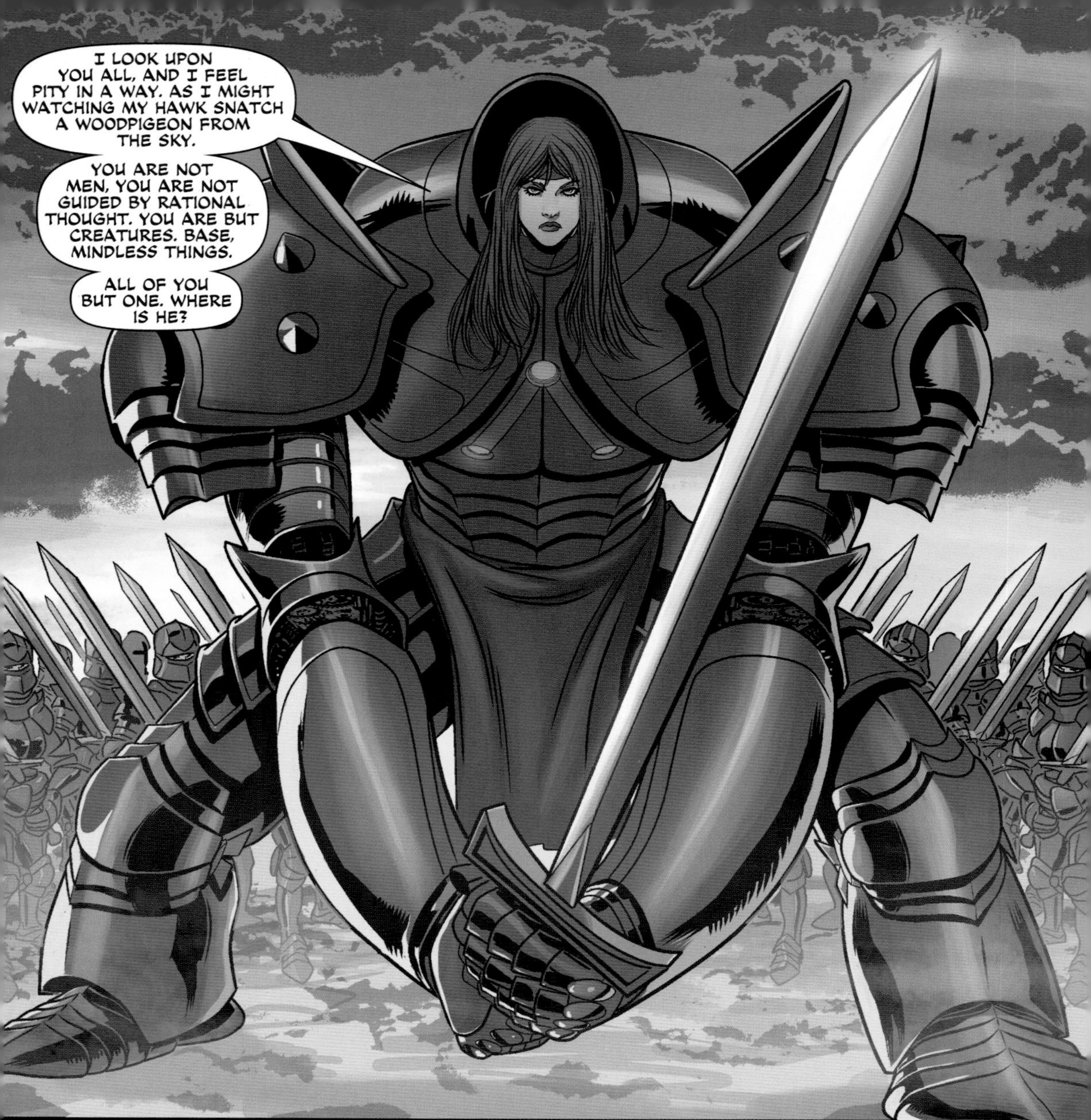
I LOOK UPON YOU ALL, AND I FEEL PITY IN A WAY. AS I MIGHT WATCHING MY HAWK SNATCH A WOODPIGEON FROM THE SKY.
YOU ARE NOT MEN, YOU ARE NOT GUIDED BY RATIONAL THOUGHT. YOU ARE BUT CREATURES. BASE, MINDLESS THINGS.
ALL OF YOU BUT ONE. WHERE IS HE?
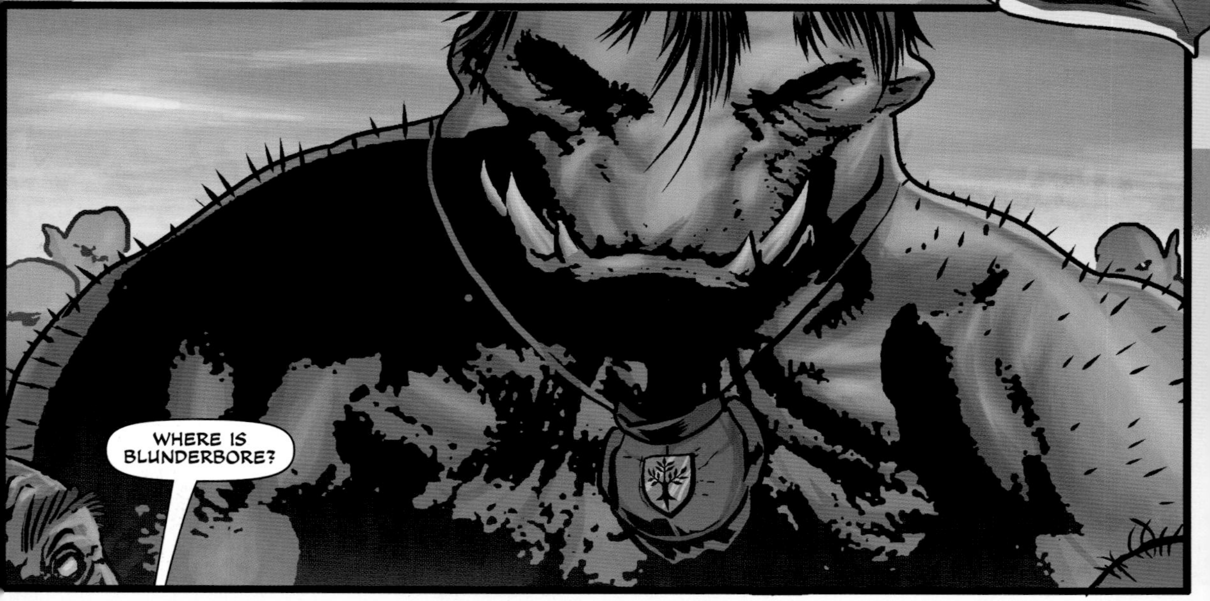
WHERE IS BLUNDERBORE?

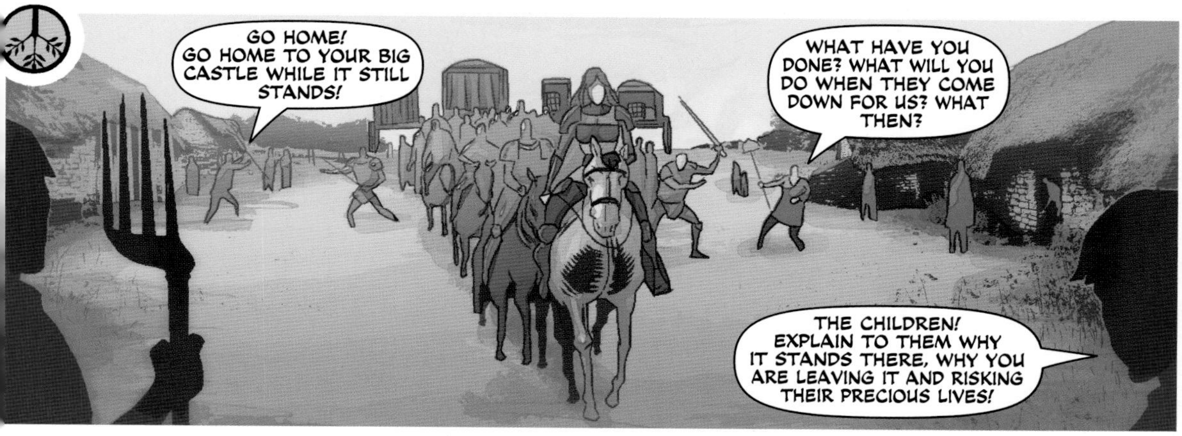
GO HOME! GO HOME TO YOUR BIG CASTLE WHILE IT STILL STANDS!
WHAT HAVE YOU DONE? WHAT WILL YOU DO WHEN THEY COME DOWN FOR US? WHAT THEN?
THE CHILDREN! EXPLAIN TO THEM WHY IT STANDS THERE, WHY YOU ARE LEAVING IT AND RISKING THEIR PRECIOUS LIVES!

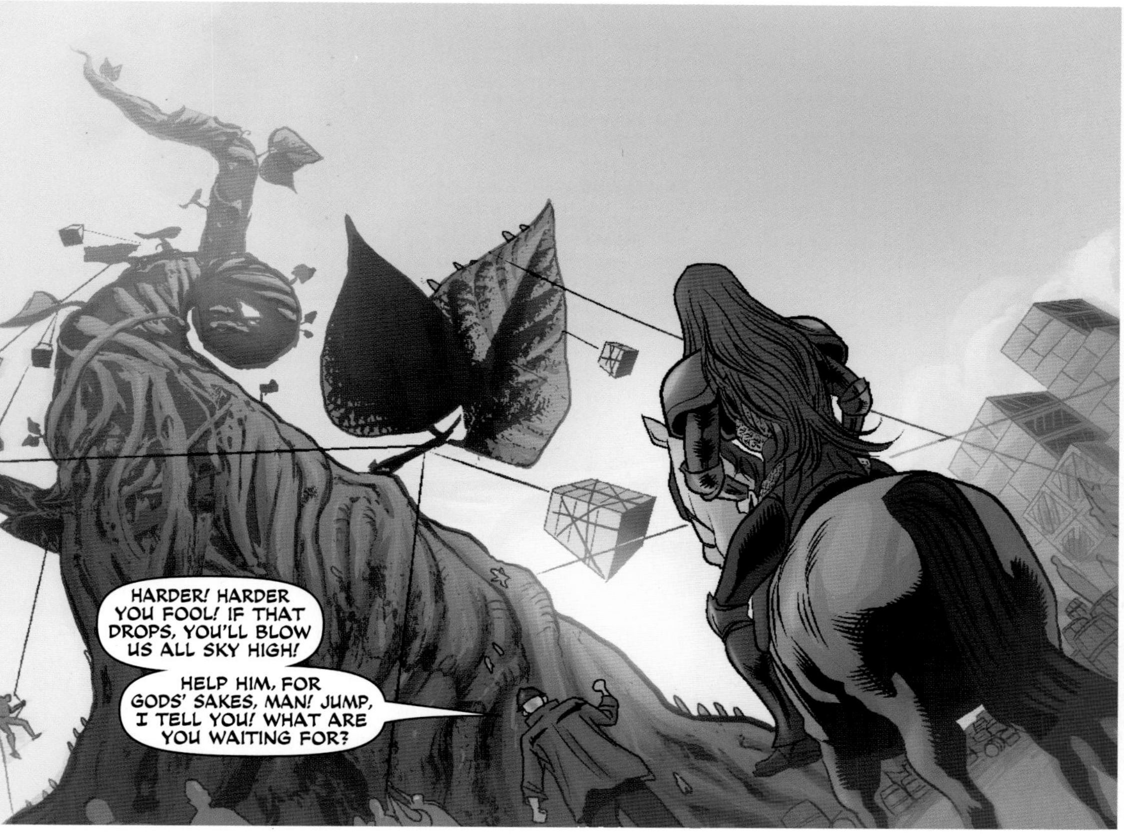
HARDER! HARDER YOU FOOL! IF THAT DROPS, YOU'LL BLOW US ALL SKY HIGH!
HELP HIM, FOR GODS' SAKES, MAN! JUMP, I TELL YOU! WHAT ARE YOU WAITING FOR?

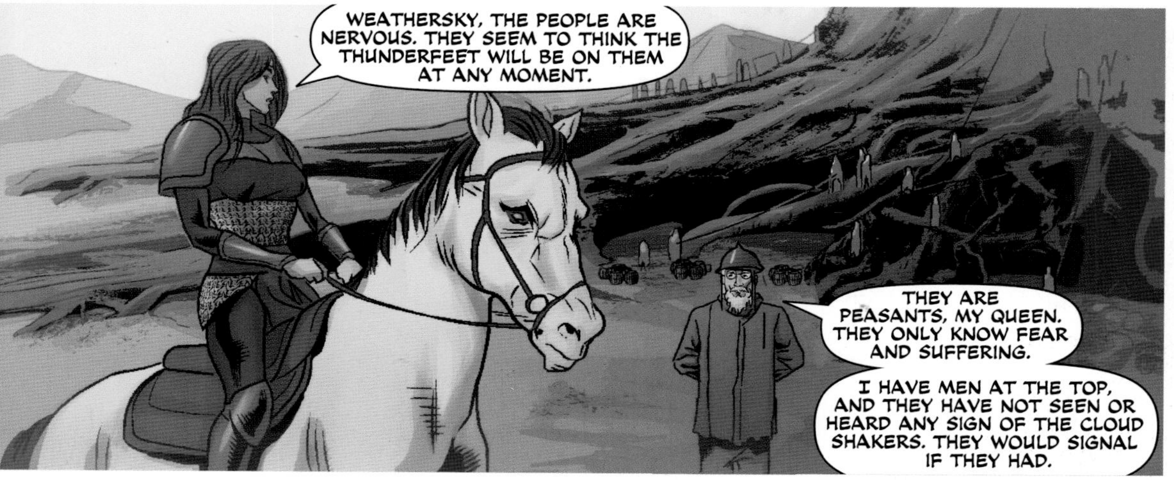
WEATHERSKY, THE PEOPLE ARE NERVOUS. THEY SEEM TO THINK THE THUNDERFEET WILL BE ON THEM AT ANY MOMENT.
THEY ARE PEASANTS, MY QUEEN. THEY ONLY KNOW FEAR AND SUFFERING.
I HAVE MEN AT THE TOP, AND THEY HAVE NOT SEEN OR HEARD ANY SIGN OF THE CLOUD SHAKERS. THEY WOULD SIGNAL IF THEY HAD.

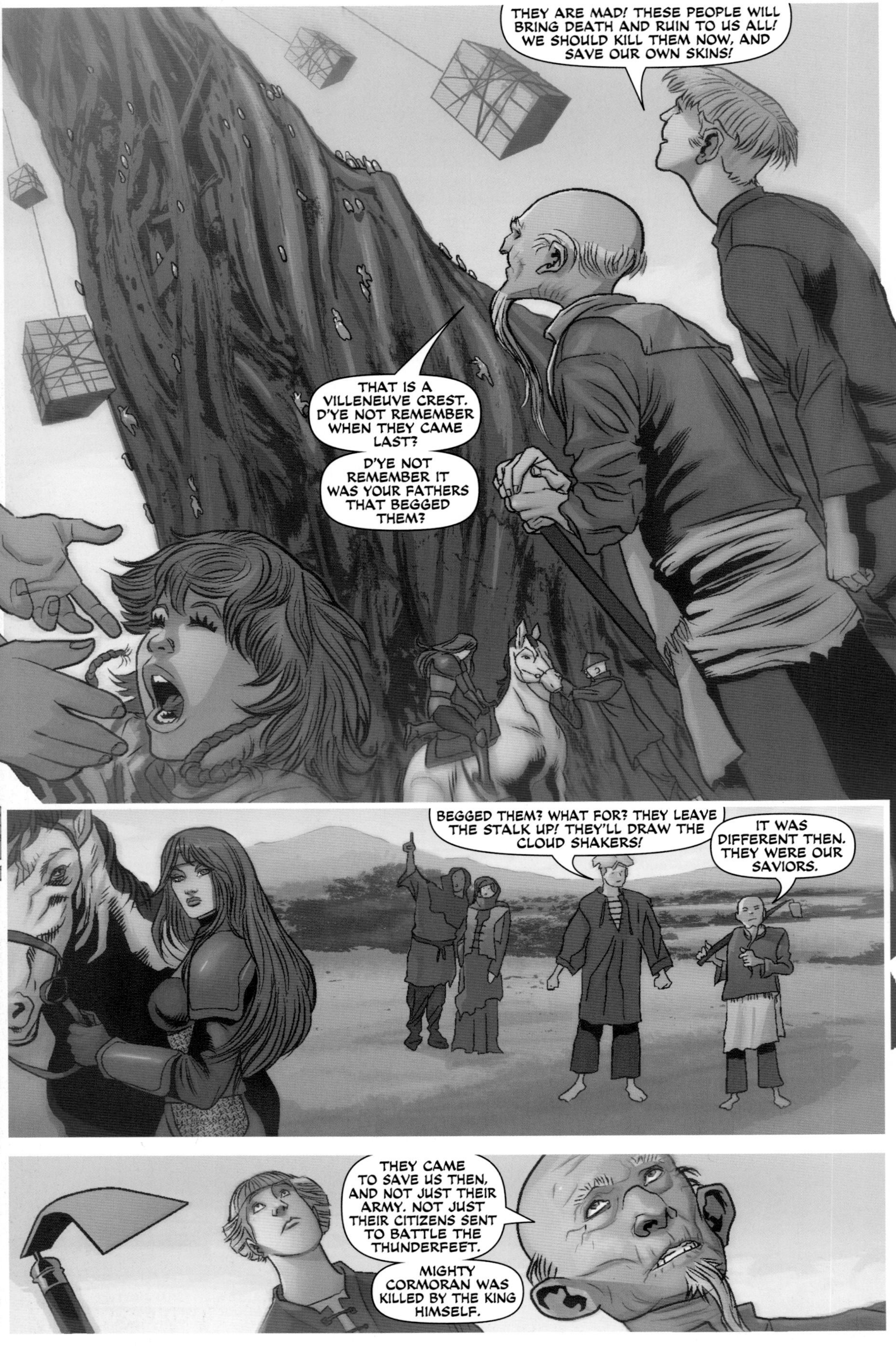
THEY ARE MAD! THESE PEOPLE WILL BRING DEATH AND RUIN TO US ALL! WE SHOULD KILL THEM NOW, AND SAVE OUR OWN SKINS!
THAT IS A VILLENEUVE CREST. D'YE NOT REMEMBER WHEN THEY CAME LAST?
D'YE NOT REMEMBER IT WAS YOUR FATHERS THAT BEGGED THEM?
BEGGED THEM? WHAT FOR? THEY LEAVE THE STALK UP! THEY'LL DRAW THE CLOUD SHAKERS!
IT WAS DIFFERENT THEN. THEY WERE OUR SAVIORS.
THEY CAME TO SAVE US THEN, AND NOT JUST THEIR ARMY. NOT JUST THEIR CITIZENS SENT TO BATTLE THE THUNDERFEET.
MIGHTY CORMORAN WAS KILLED BY THE KING HIMSELF.

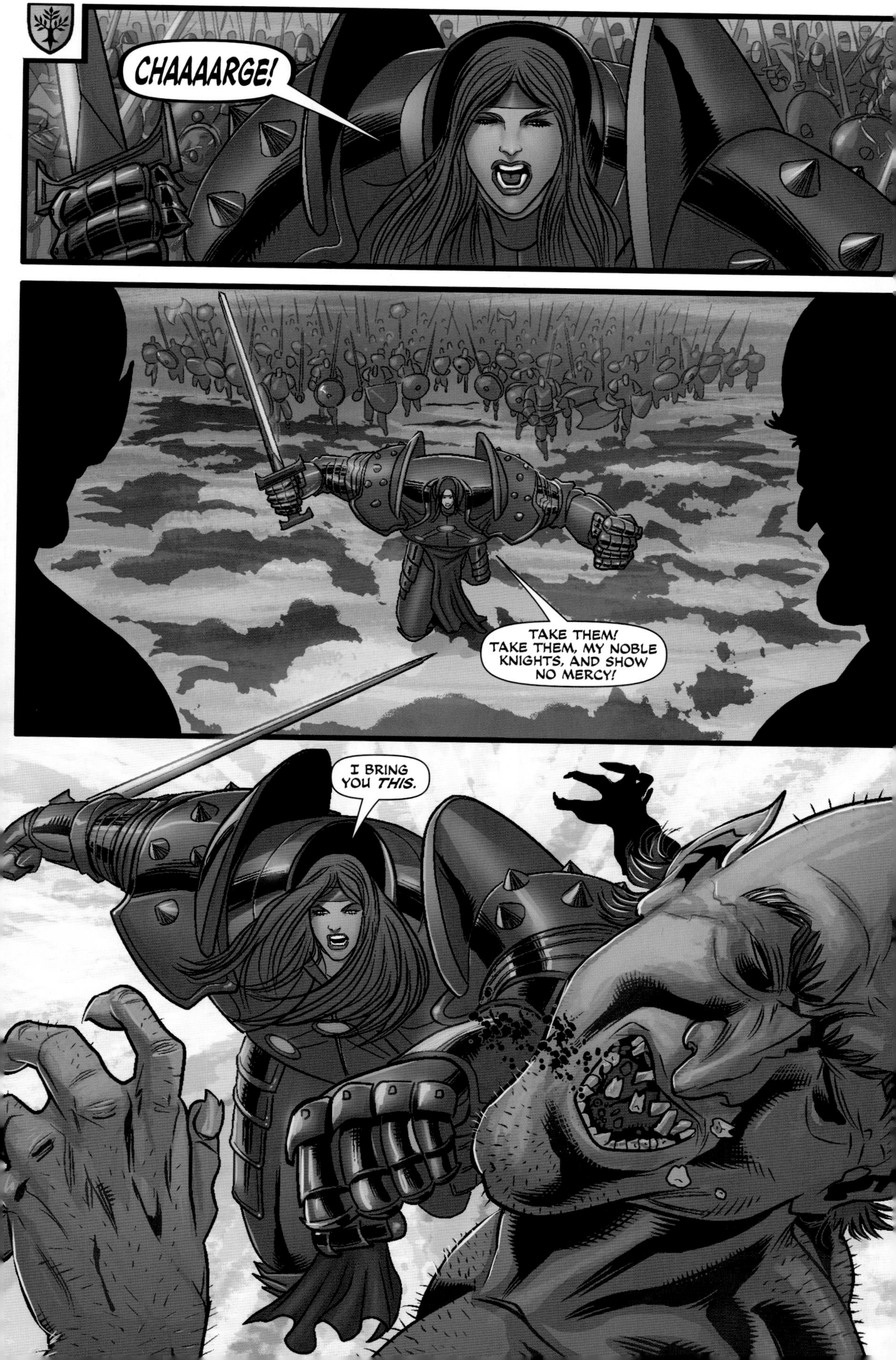
CHAAAARGE!
TAKE THEM! TAKE THEM, MY NOBLE KNIGHTS, AND SHOW NO MERCY!
I BRING YOU *THIS*.

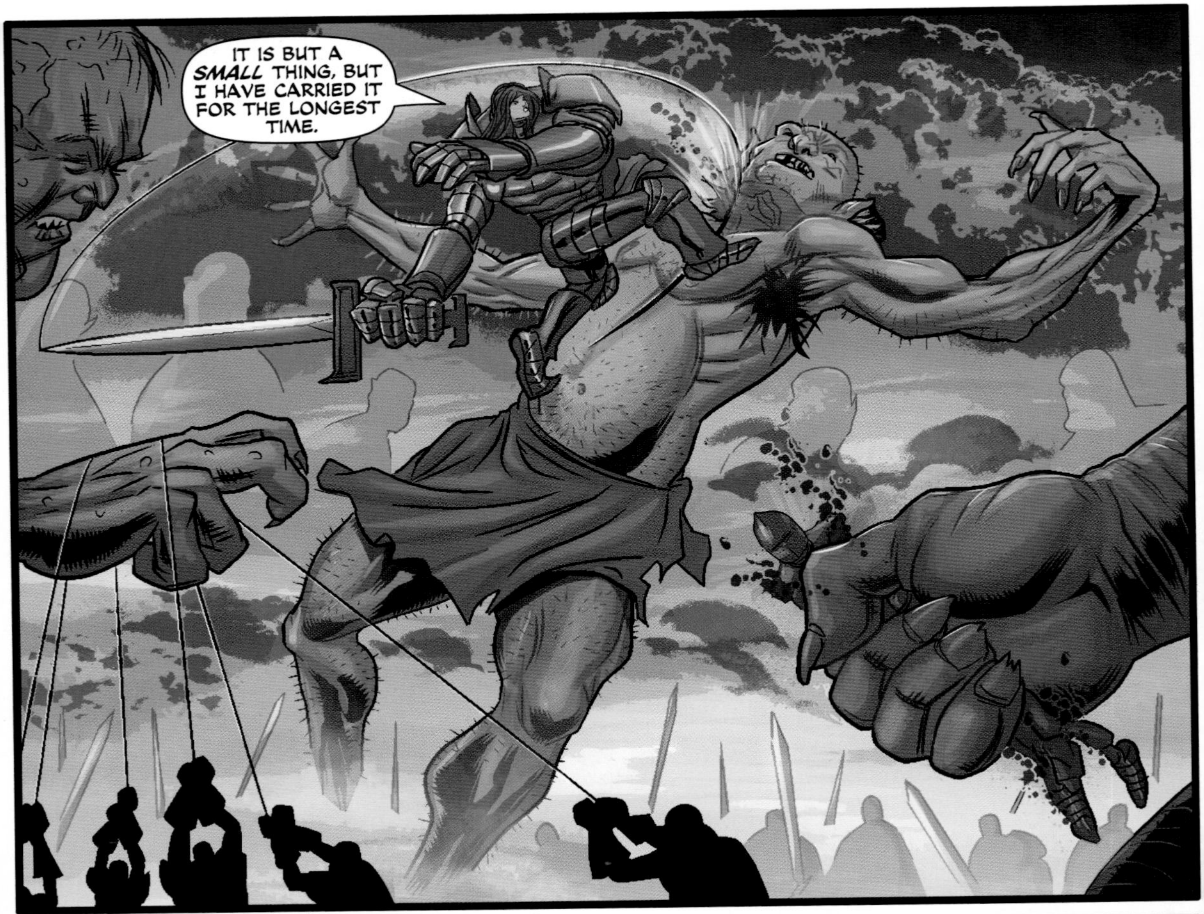
IT IS BUT A *SMALL* THING, BUT I HAVE CARRIED IT FOR THE LONGEST TIME.
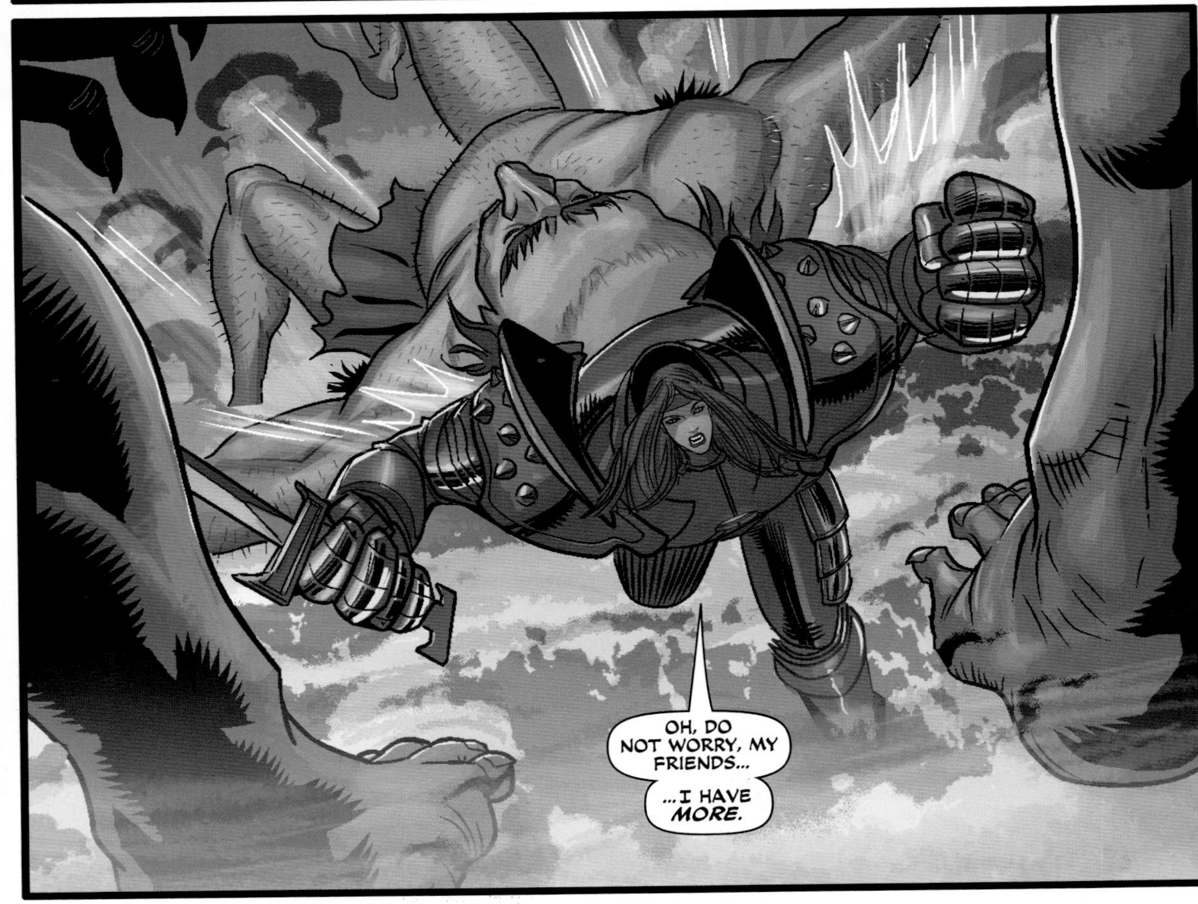
OH, DO NOT WORRY, MY FRIENDS...
...I HAVE *MORE*.

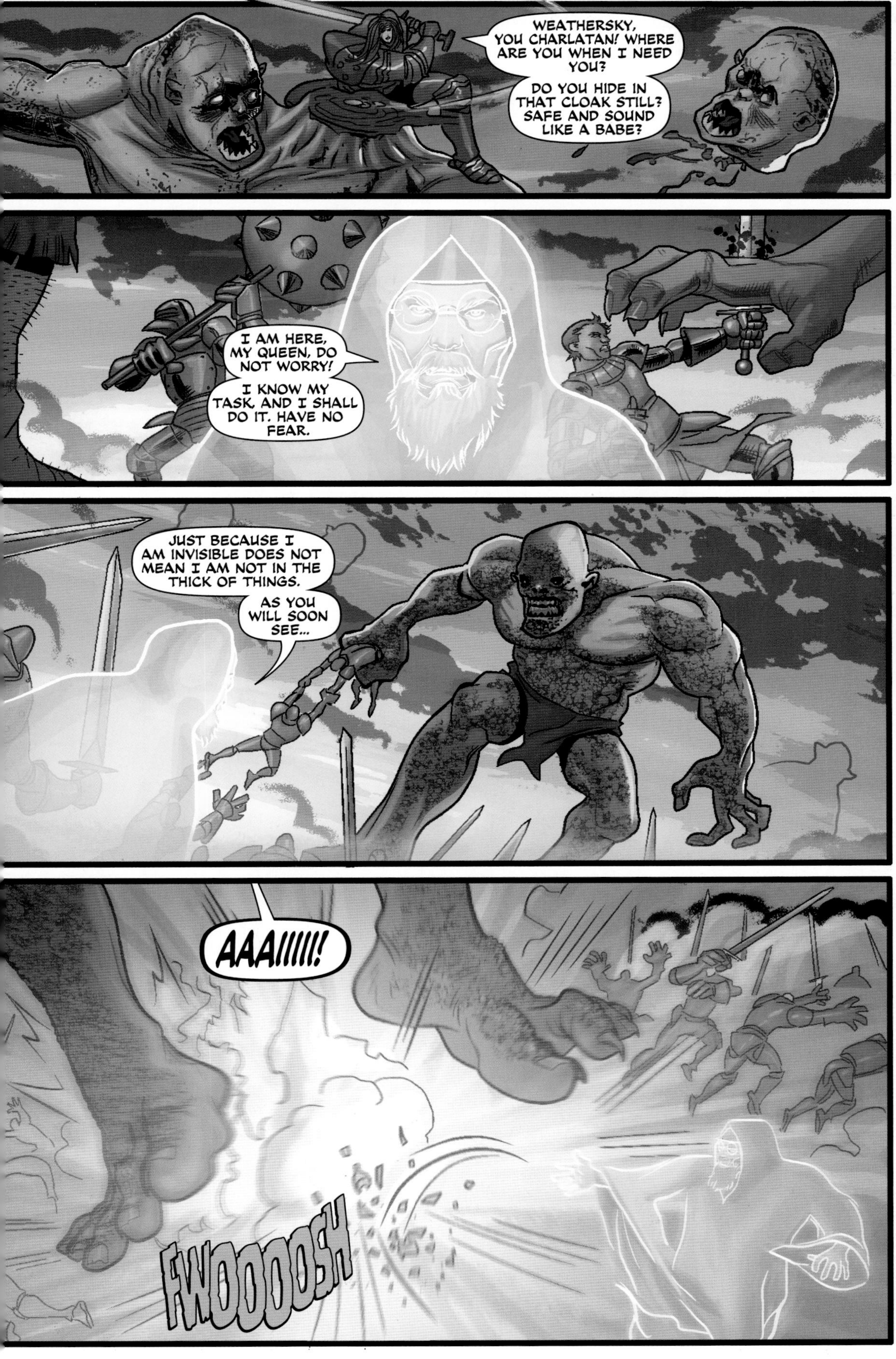
WEATHERSKY, YOU CHARLATAN! WHERE ARE YOU WHEN I NEED YOU?
DO YOU HIDE IN THAT CLOAK STILL? SAFE AND SOUND LIKE A BABE?
I AM HERE, MY QUEEN, DO NOT WORRY!
I KNOW MY TASK, AND I SHALL DO IT. HAVE NO FEAR.
JUST BECAUSE I AM INVISIBLE DOES NOT MEAN I AM NOT IN THE THICK OF THINGS.
AS YOU WILL SOON SEE...
AAAIIIII!
FWOOOOSH

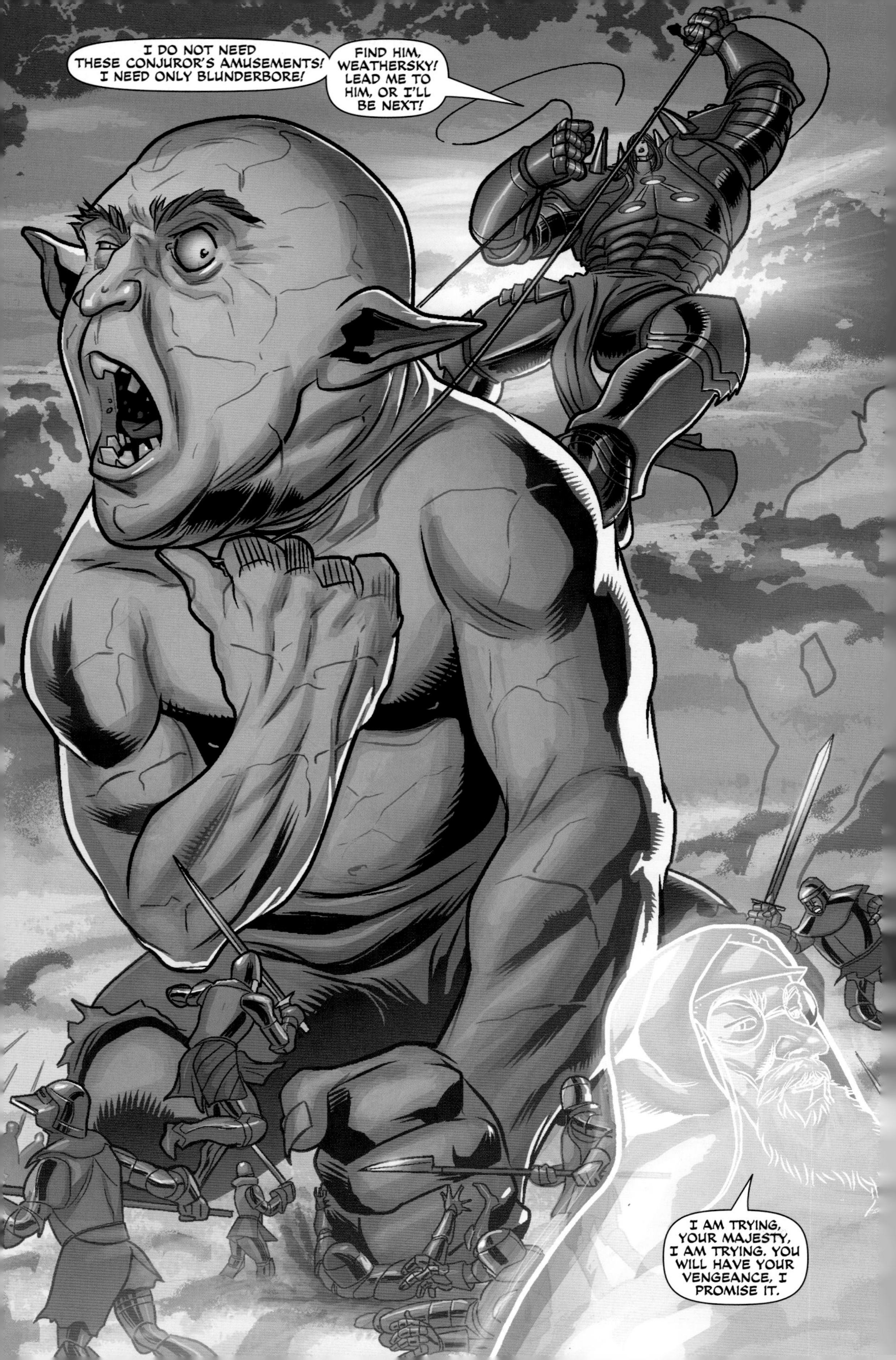

I DO NOT NEED THESE CONJUROR'S AMUSEMENTS! I NEED ONLY BLUNDERBORE!
FIND HIM, WEATHERSKY! LEAD ME TO HIM, OR I'LL BE NEXT!
I AM TRYING, YOUR MAJESTY, I AM TRYING. YOU WILL HAVE YOUR VENGEANCE, I PROMISE IT.

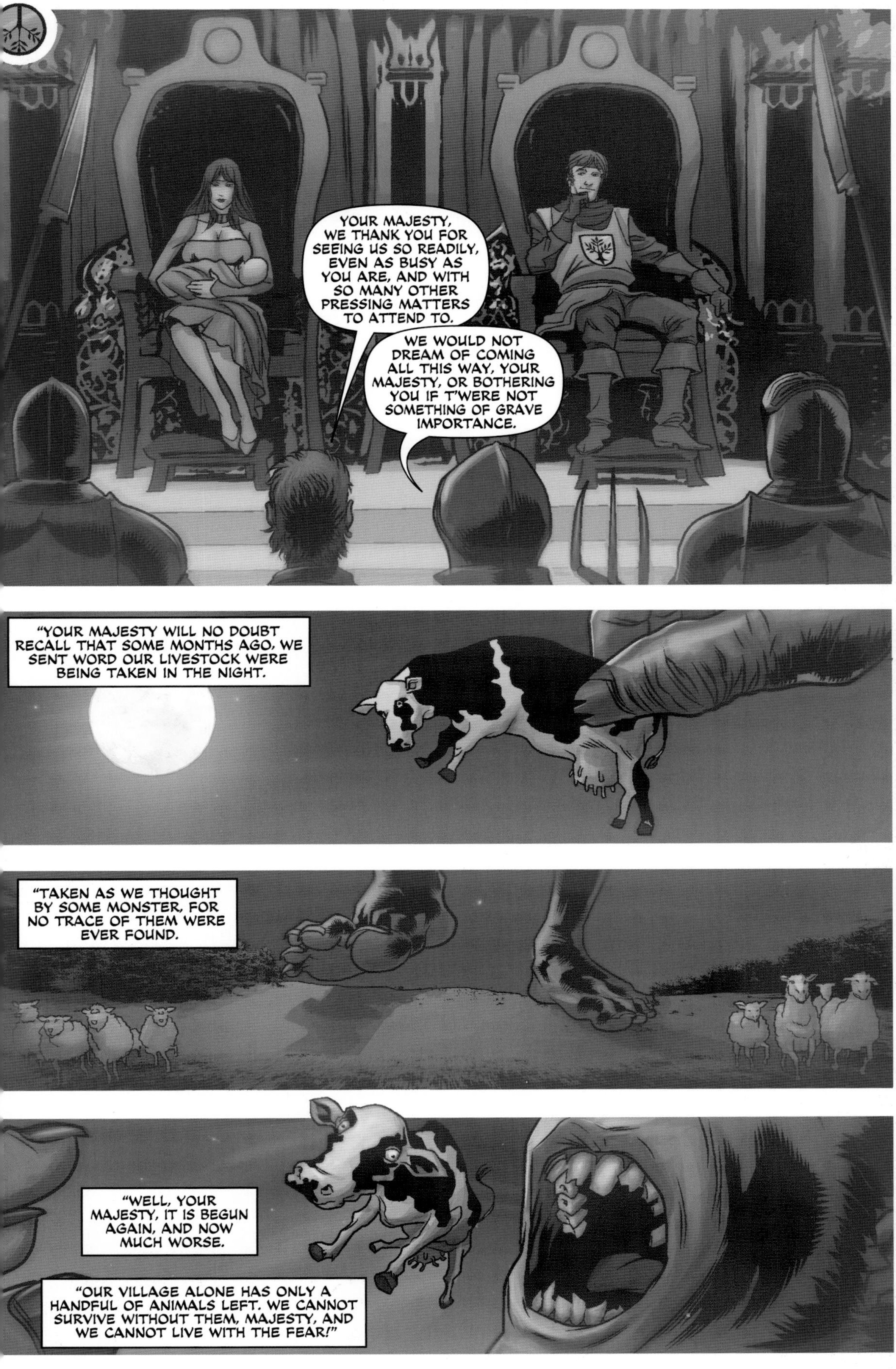
YOUR MAJESTY, WE THANK YOU FOR SEEING US SO READILY, EVEN AS BUSY AS YOU ARE, AND WITH SO MANY OTHER PRESSING MATTERS TO ATTEND TO.
WE WOULD NOT DREAM OF COMING ALL THIS WAY, YOUR MAJESTY, OR BOTHERING YOU IF T'WERE NOT SOMETHING OF GRAVE IMPORTANCE.
"YOUR MAJESTY WILL NO DOUBT RECALL THAT SOME MONTHS AGO, WE SENT WORD OUR LIVESTOCK WERE BEING TAKEN IN THE NIGHT.
"TAKEN AS WE THOUGHT BY SOME MONSTER, FOR NO TRACE OF THEM WERE EVER FOUND.
"WELL, YOUR MAJESTY, IT IS BEGUN AGAIN, AND NOW MUCH WORSE.
"OUR VILLAGE ALONE HAS ONLY A HANDFUL OF ANIMALS LEFT. WE CANNOT SURVIVE WITHOUT THEM, MAJESTY, AND WE CANNOT LIVE WITH THE FEAR!"

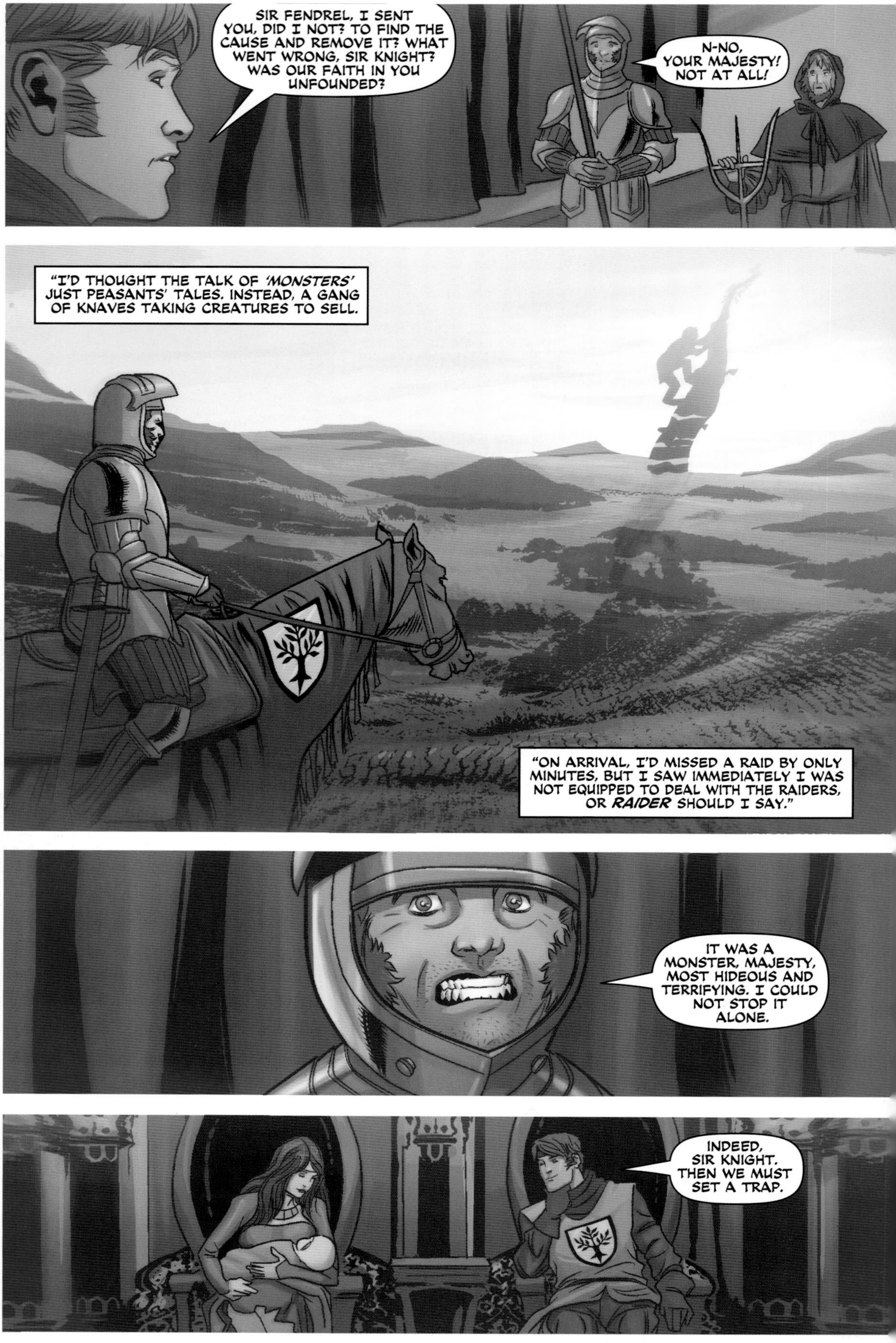
SIR FENDREL, I SENT YOU, DID I NOT? TO FIND THE CAUSE AND REMOVE IT? WHAT WENT WRONG, SIR KNIGHT? WAS OUR FAITH IN YOU UNFOUNDED?
N-NO, YOUR MAJESTY! NOT AT ALL!
"I'D THOUGHT THE TALK OF *'MONSTERS'* JUST PEASANTS' TALES. INSTEAD, A GANG OF KNAVES TAKING CREATURES TO SELL.
"ON ARRIVAL, I'D MISSED A RAID BY ONLY MINUTES, BUT I SAW IMMEDIATELY I WAS NOT EQUIPPED TO DEAL WITH THE RAIDERS, OR ***RAIDER*** SHOULD I SAY."
IT WAS A MONSTER, MAJESTY, MOST HIDEOUS AND TERRIFYING. I COULD NOT STOP IT ALONE.
INDEED, SIR KNIGHT. THEN WE MUST SET A TRAP.

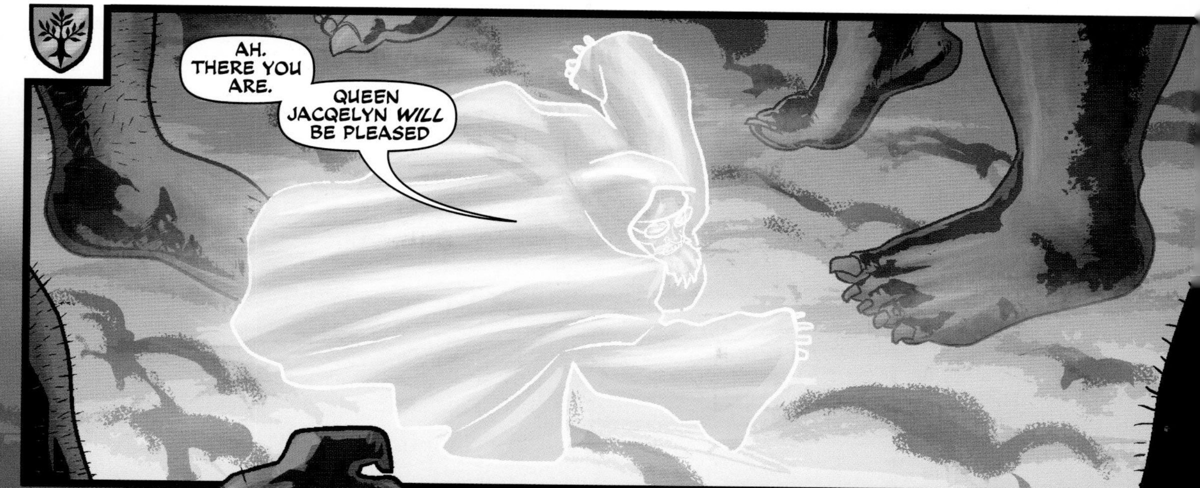
AH. THERE YOU ARE.
QUEEN JACQELYN *WILL* BE PLEASED
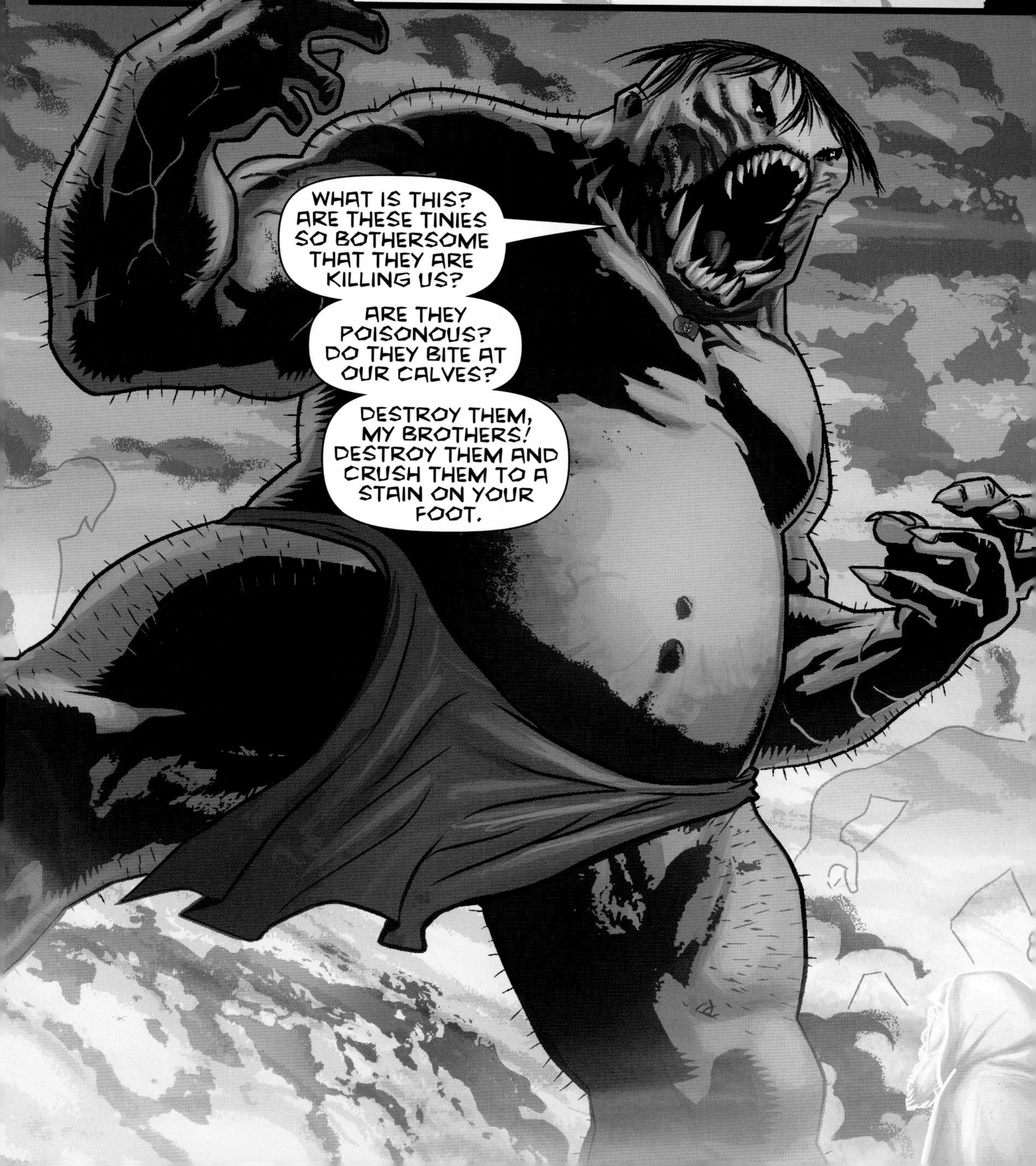
WHAT IS THIS? ARE THESE TINIES SO BOTHERSOME THAT THEY ARE KILLING US?
ARE THEY POISONOUS? DO THEY BITE AT OUR CALVES?
DESTROY THEM, MY BROTHERS! DESTROY THEM AND CRUSH THEM TO A STAIN ON YOUR FOOT.

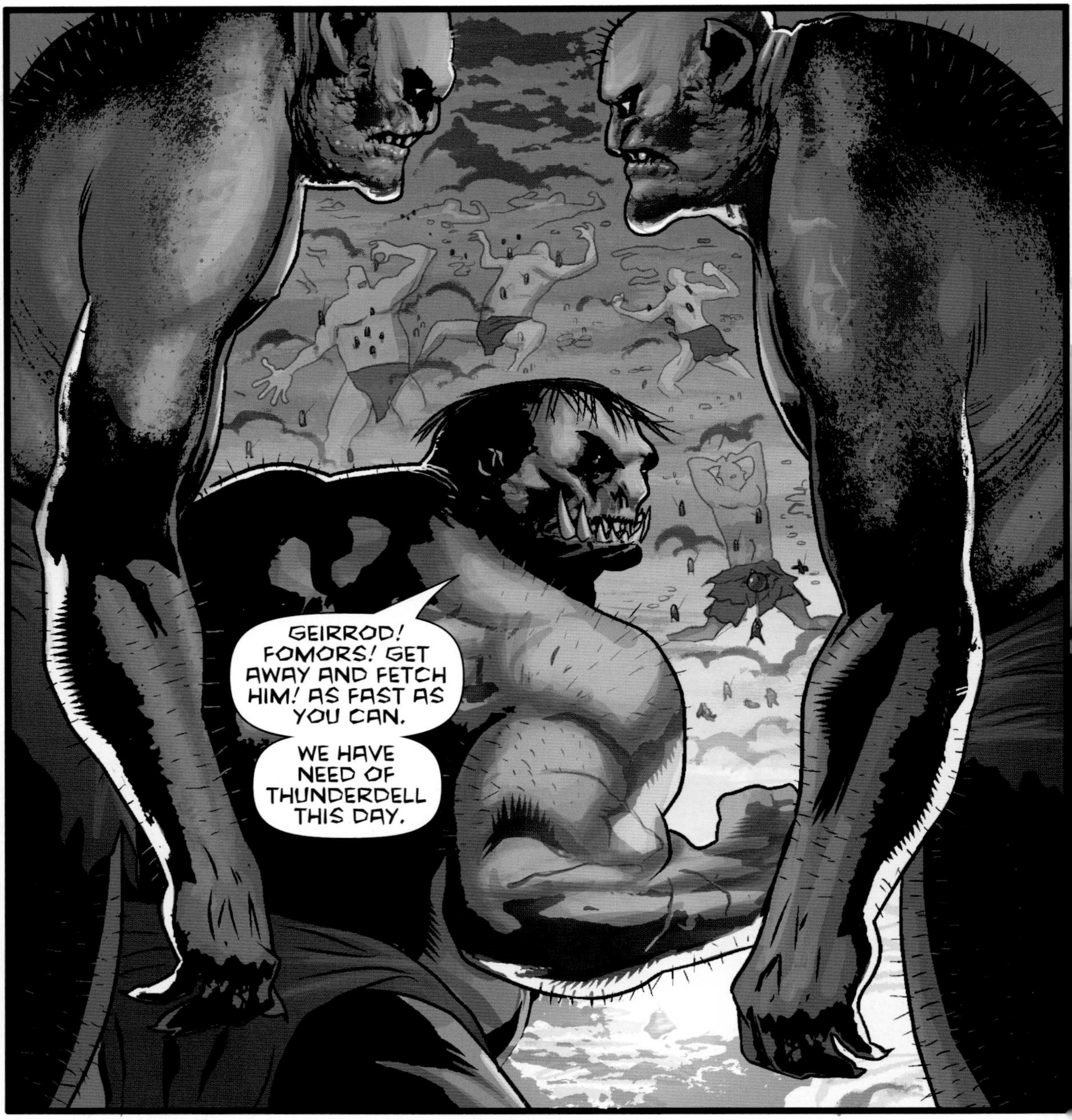
GEIRROD! FOMORS! GET AWAY AND FETCH HIM! AS FAST AS YOU CAN.
WE HAVE NEED OF THUNDERDELL THIS DAY.
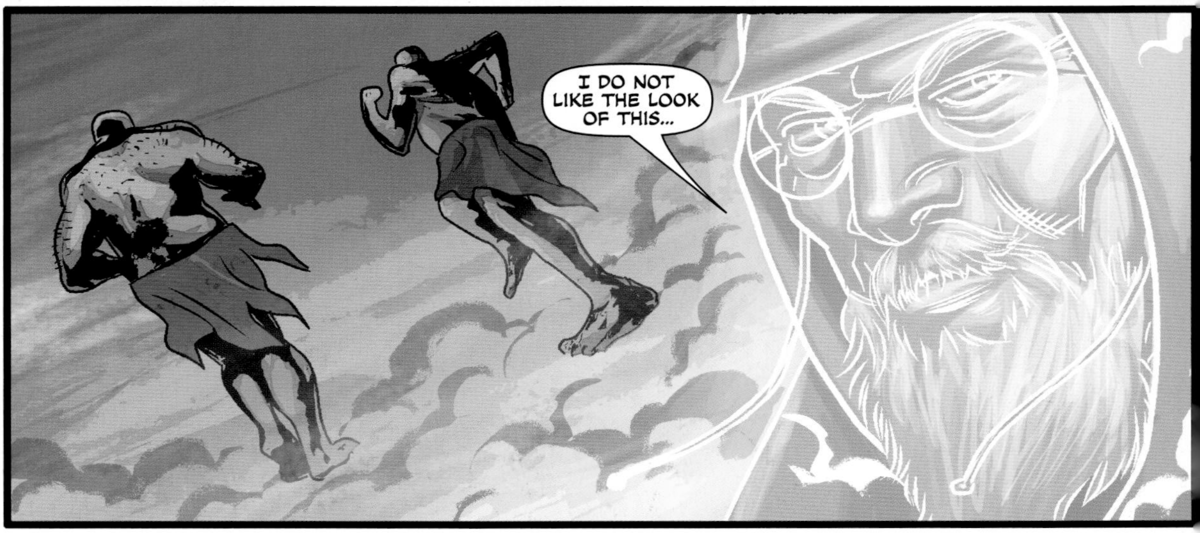
I DO NOT LIKE THE LOOK OF THIS...

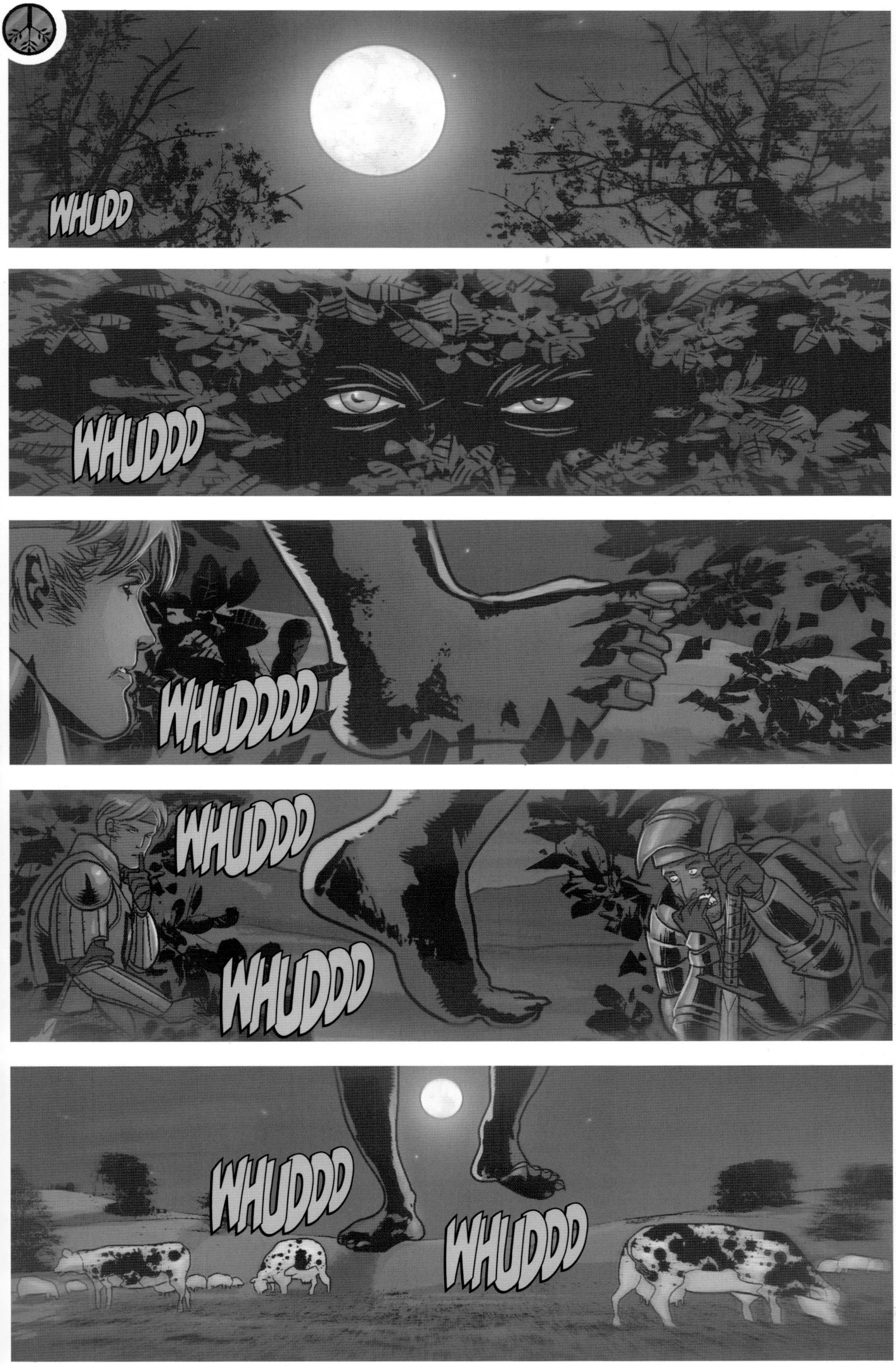
WHUDD
WHUDDD
WHUDDDD
WHUDDD
WHUDDD
WHUDDD
WHUDDD

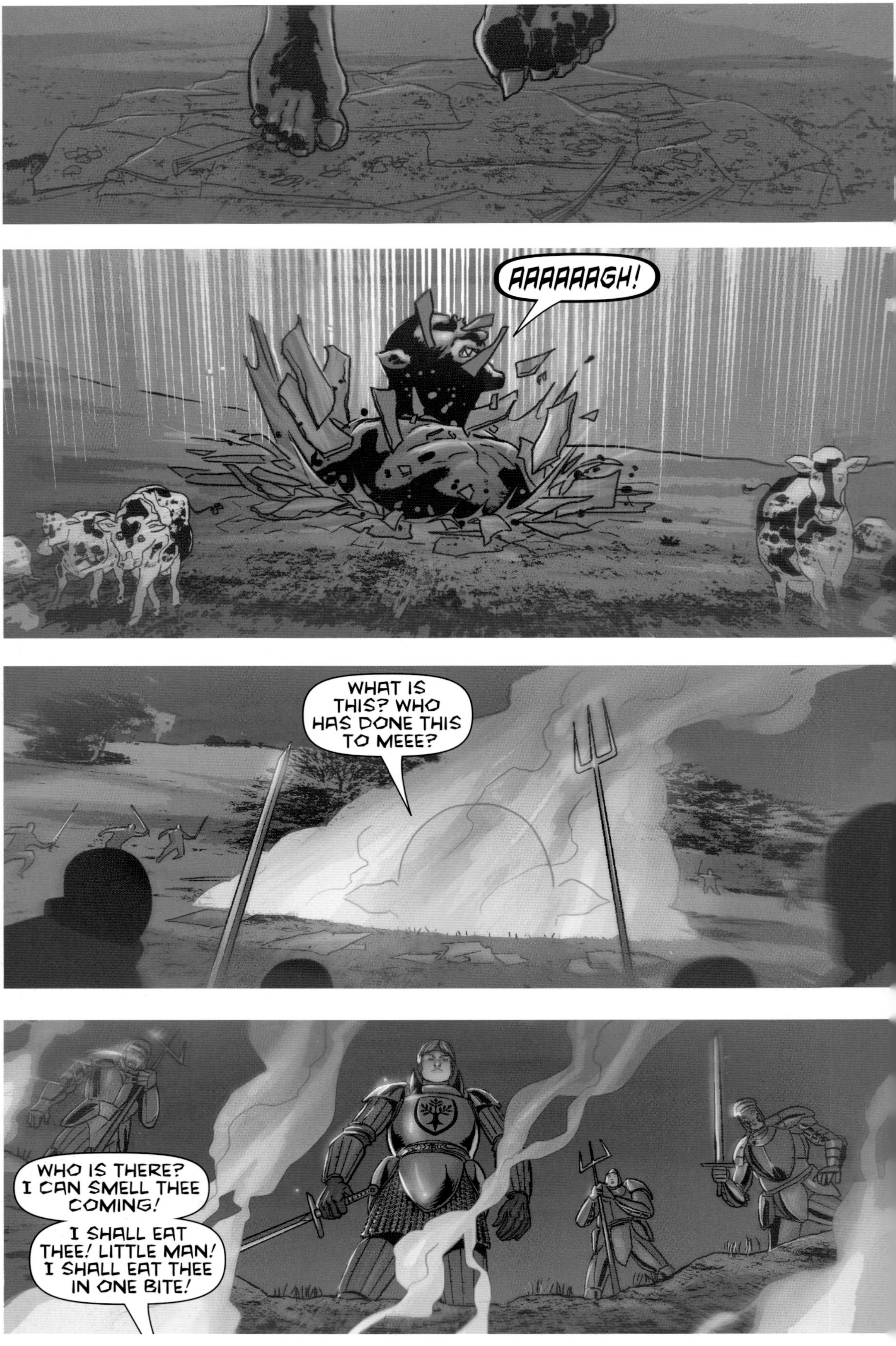
AAAAAAAGH!
WHAT IS THIS? WHO HAS DONE THIS TO MEEE?
WHO IS THERE? I CAN SMELL THEE COMING!
I SHALL EAT THEE! LITTLE MAN! I SHALL EAT THEE IN ONE BITE!

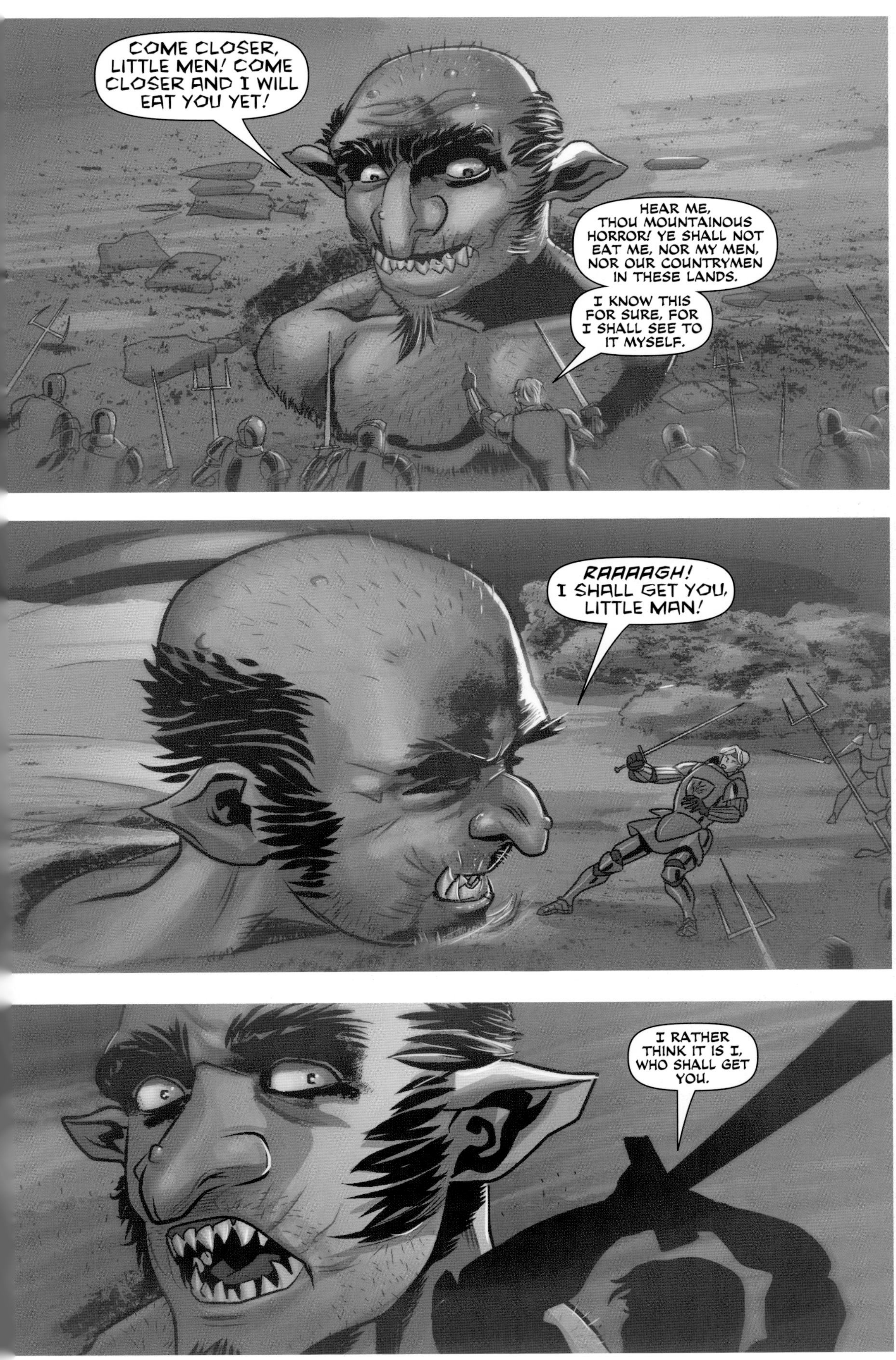
COME CLOSER, LITTLE MEN! COME CLOSER AND I WILL EAT YOU YET!
HEAR ME, THOU MOUNTAINOUS HORROR! YE SHALL NOT EAT ME, NOR MY MEN, NOR OUR COUNTRYMEN IN THESE LANDS.
I KNOW THIS FOR SURE, FOR I SHALL SEE TO IT MYSELF.
RAAAAGH! I SHALL GET YOU, LITTLE MAN!
I RATHER THINK IT IS I, WHO SHALL GET YOU.

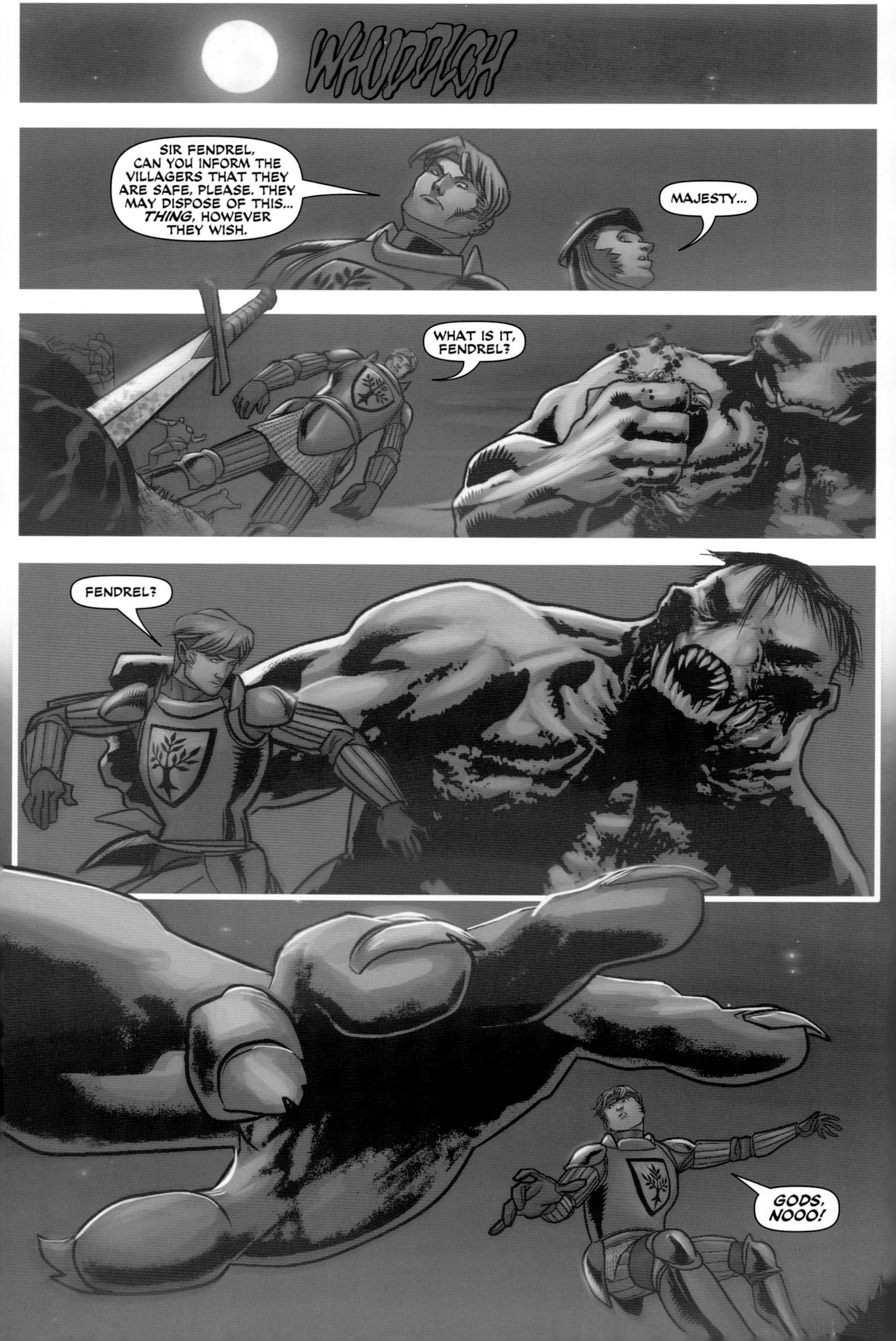
WHUDDLCH
SIR FENDREL, CAN YOU INFORM THE VILLAGERS THAT THEY ARE SAFE, PLEASE. THEY MAY DISPOSE OF THIS... *THING*, HOWEVER THEY WISH.
MAJESTY...
WHAT IS IT, FENDREL?
FENDREL?
GODS, NOOO!

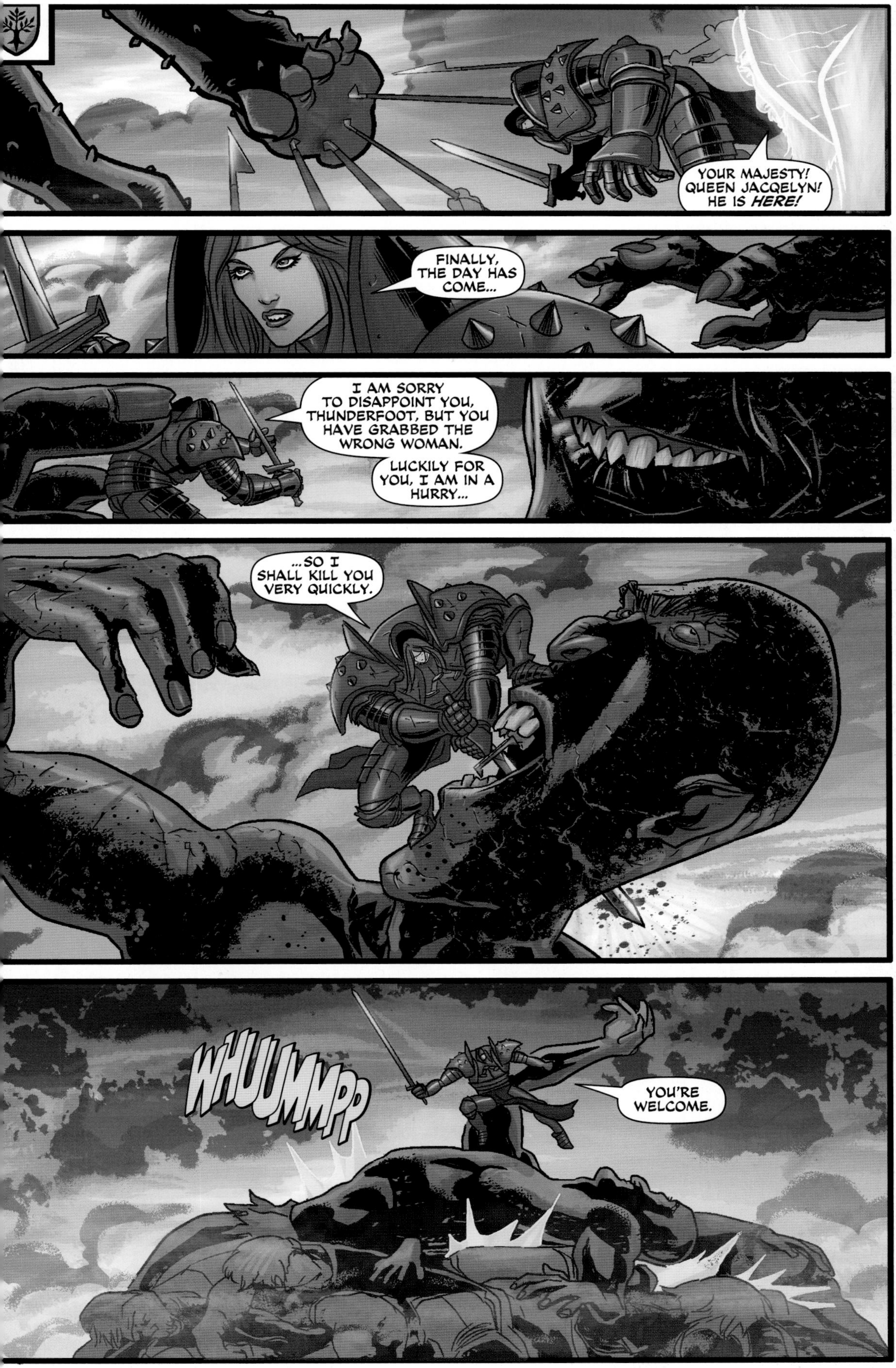
YOUR MAJESTY! QUEEN JACQELYN! HE IS *HERE!*
FINALLY, THE DAY HAS COME...
I AM SORRY TO DISAPPOINT YOU, THUNDERFOOT, BUT YOU HAVE GRABBED THE WRONG WOMAN.
LUCKILY FOR YOU, I AM IN A HURRY...
...SO I SHALL KILL YOU VERY QUICKLY.
WHUUMMPP
YOU'RE WELCOME.

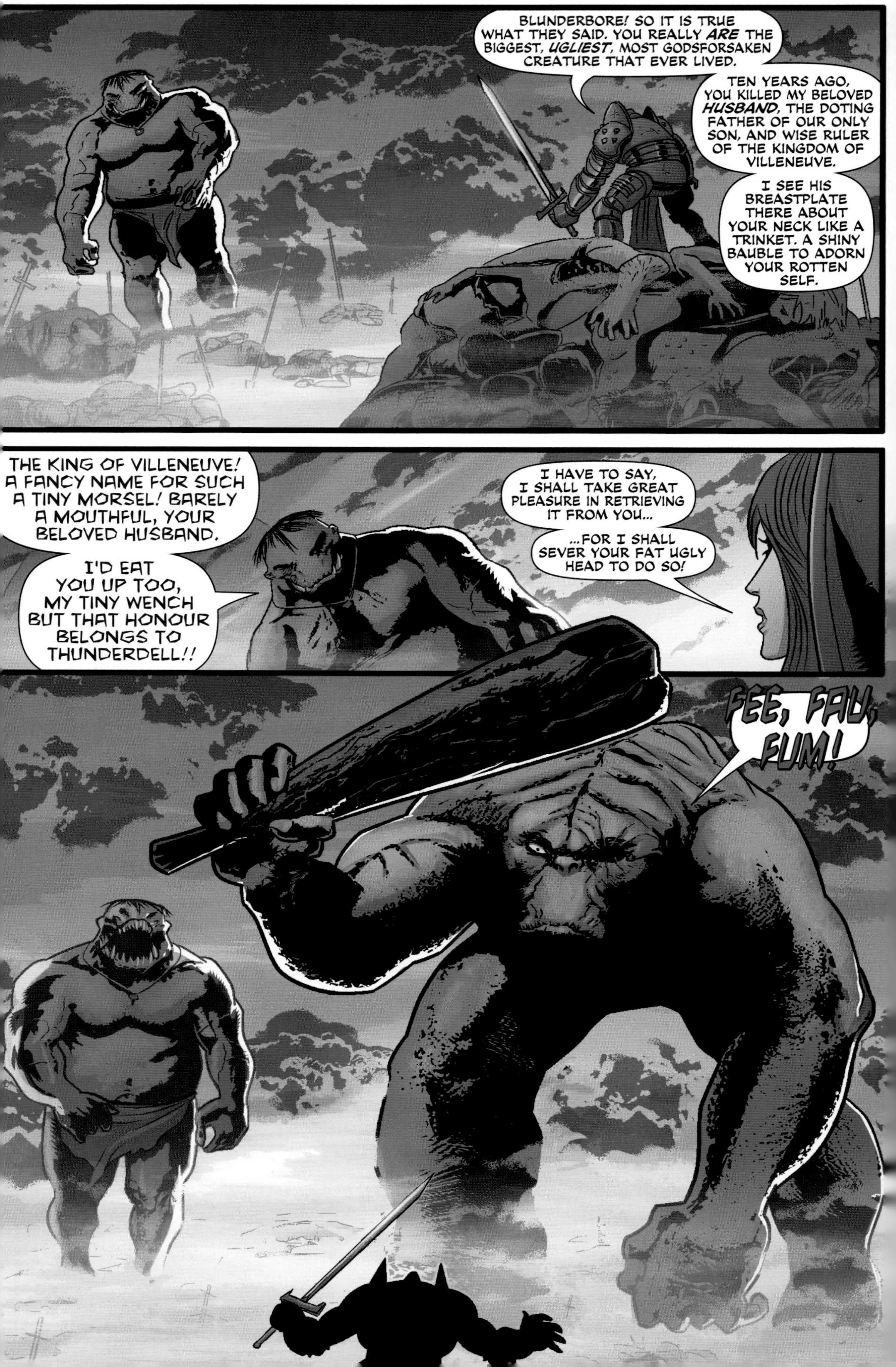
BLUNDERBORE! SO IT IS TRUE WHAT THEY SAID. YOU REALLY *ARE* THE BIGGEST, *UGLIEST*, MOST GODSFORSAKEN CREATURE THAT EVER LIVED.
TEN YEARS AGO, YOU KILLED MY BELOVED *HUSBAND*, THE DOTING FATHER OF OUR ONLY SON, AND WISE RULER OF THE KINGDOM OF VILLENEUVE.
I SEE HIS BREASTPLATE THERE ABOUT YOUR NECK LIKE A TRINKET. A SHINY BAUBLE TO ADORN YOUR ROTTEN SELF.
THE KING OF VILLENEUVE! A FANCY NAME FOR SUCH A TINY MORSEL! BARELY A MOUTHFUL, YOUR BELOVED HUSBAND.
I'D EAT YOU UP TOO, MY TINY WENCH BUT THAT HONOUR BELONGS TO THUNDERDELL!!
I HAVE TO SAY, I SHALL TAKE GREAT PLEASURE IN RETRIEVING IT FROM YOU...
...FOR I SHALL SEVER YOUR FAT UGLY HEAD TO DO SO!
FEE, FAU, FUM!

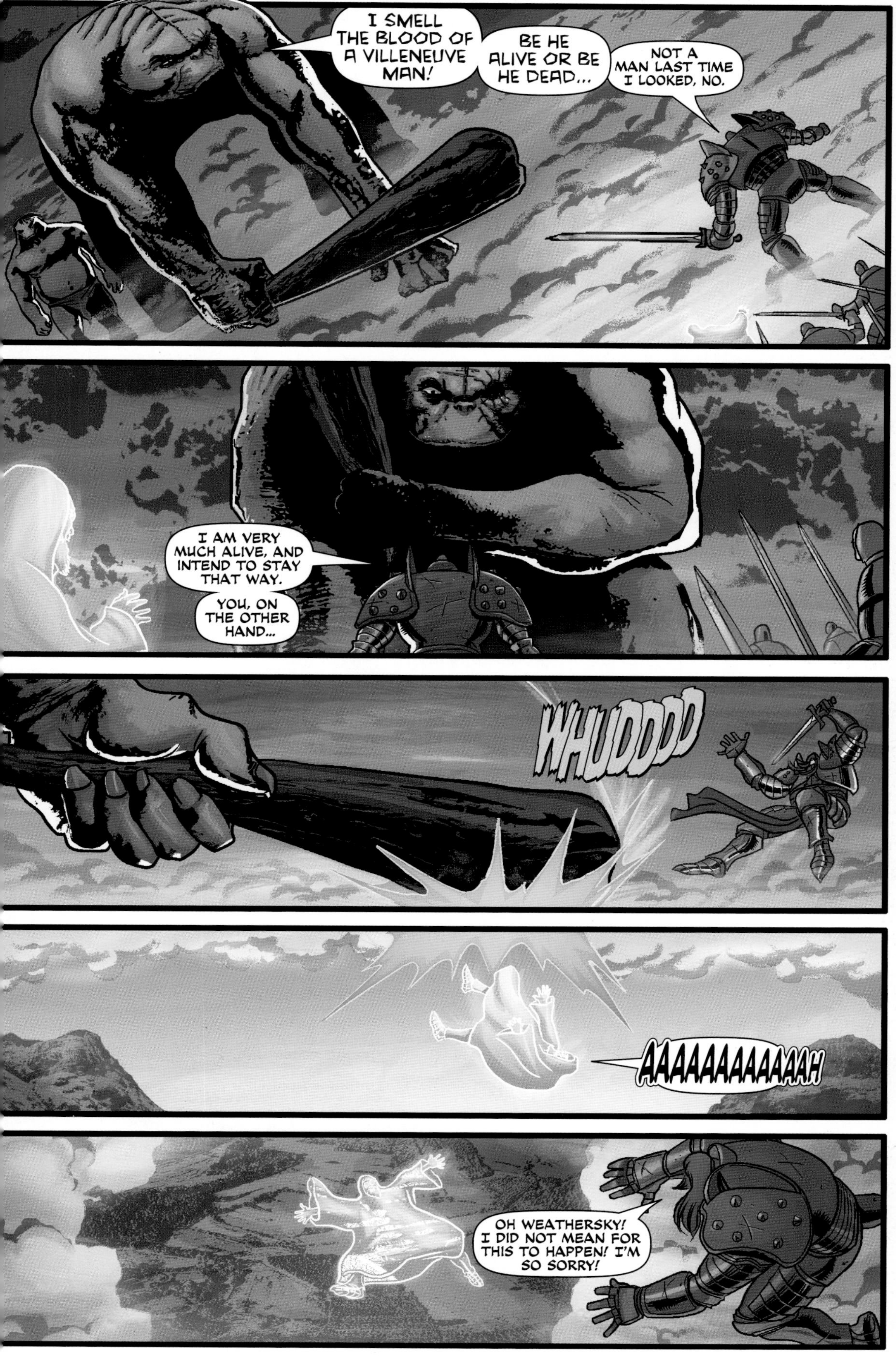
I SMELL THE BLOOD OF A VILLENEUVE MAN!
BE HE ALIVE OR BE HE DEAD...
NOT A MAN LAST TIME I LOOKED, NO.
I AM VERY MUCH ALIVE, AND INTEND TO STAY THAT WAY.
YOU, ON THE OTHER HAND...
WHUDDDD
AAAAAAAAAAAH
OH WEATHERSKY! I DID NOT MEAN FOR THIS TO HAPPEN! I'M SO SORRY!

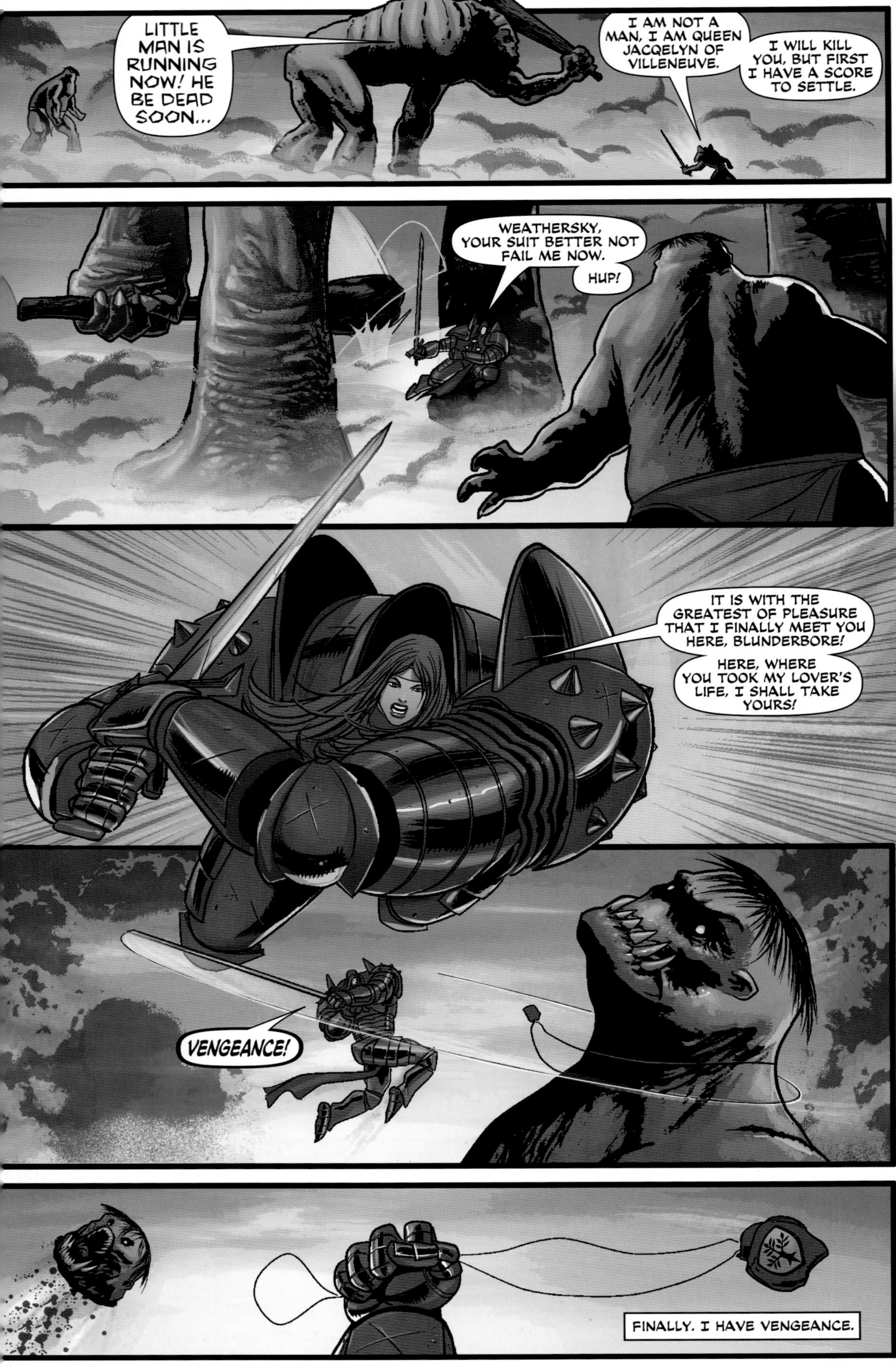
LITTLE MAN IS RUNNING NOW! HE BE DEAD SOON...
I AM NOT A MAN, I AM QUEEN JACQELYN OF VILLENEUVE.
I WILL KILL YOU, BUT FIRST I HAVE A SCORE TO SETTLE.
WEATHERSKY, YOUR SUIT BETTER NOT FAIL ME NOW.
HUP!
IT IS WITH THE GREATEST OF PLEASURE THAT I FINALLY MEET YOU HERE, BLUNDERBORE!
HERE, WHERE YOU TOOK MY LOVER'S LIFE, I SHALL TAKE YOURS!
VENGEANCE!
FINALLY. I HAVE VENGEANCE.

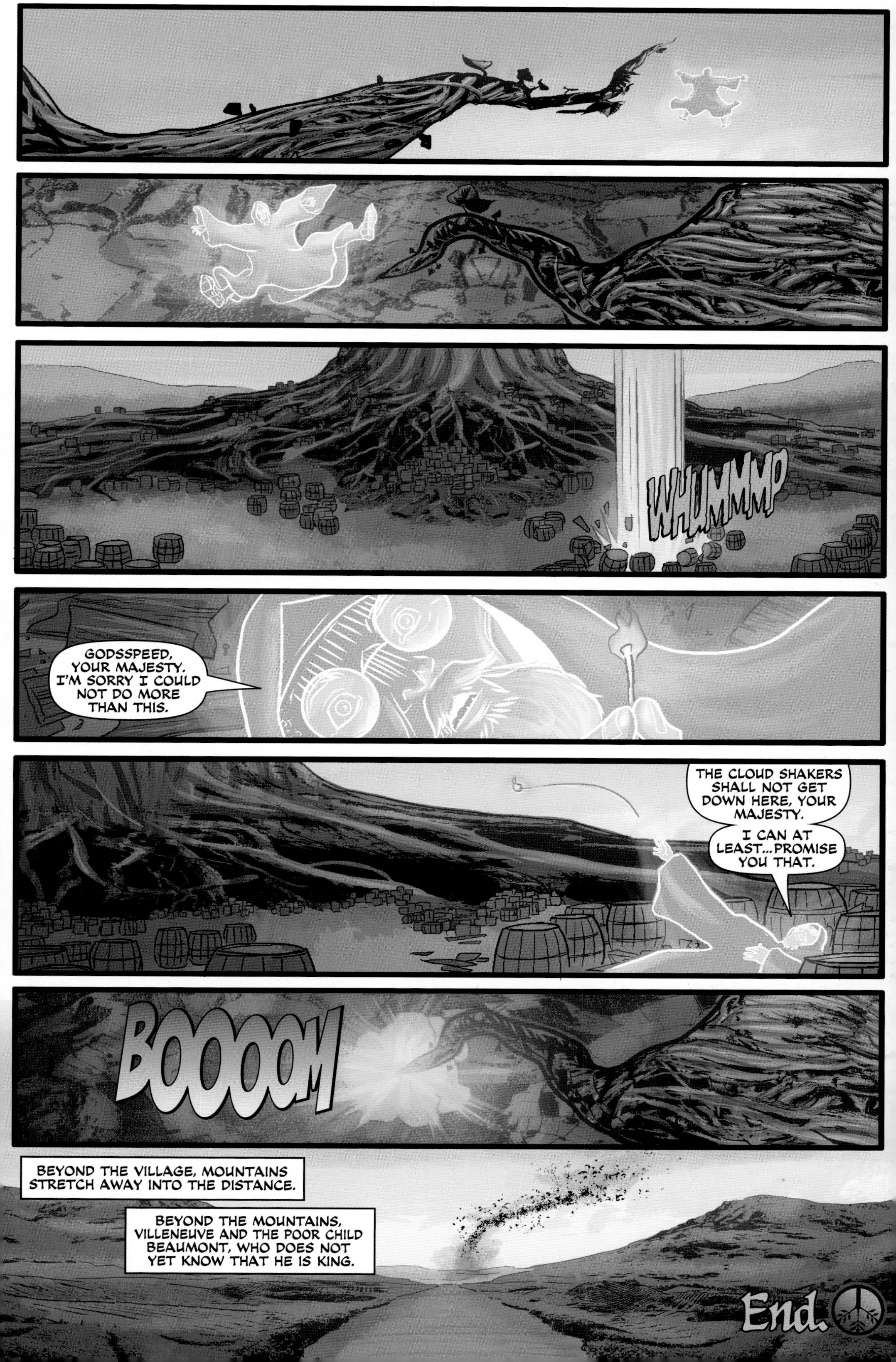
WHUMMMP
GODSSPEED, YOUR MAJESTY. I'M SORRY I COULD NOT DO MORE THAN THIS.
THE CLOUD SHAKERS SHALL NOT GET DOWN HERE, YOUR MAJESTY.
I CAN AT LEAST...PROMISE YOU THAT.
BOOOOM
BEYOND THE VILLAGE, MOUNTAINS STRETCH AWAY INTO THE DISTANCE.
BEYOND THE MOUNTAINS, VILLENEUVE AND THE POOR CHILD BEAUMONT, WHO DOES NOT YET KNOW THAT HE IS KING.
End.

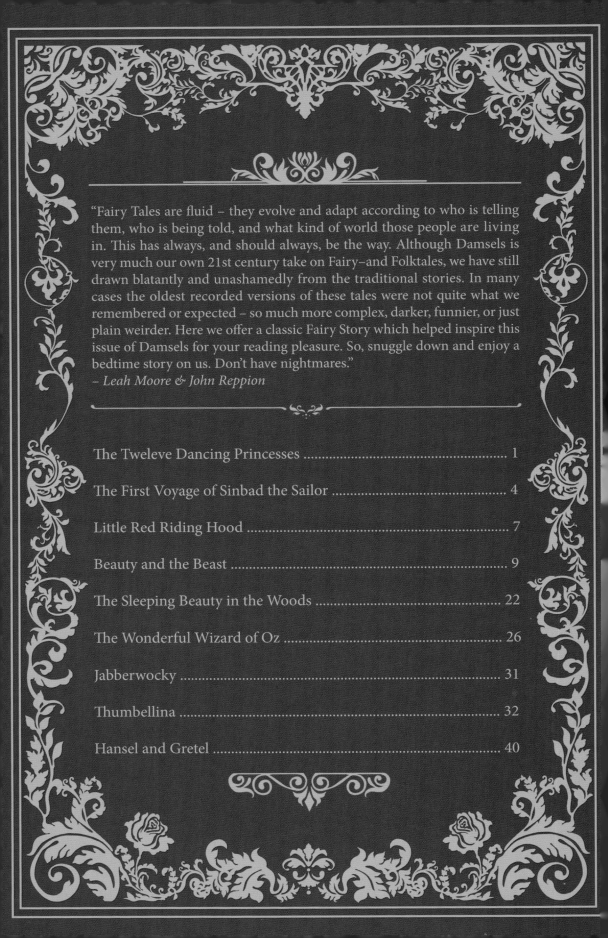

"Fairy Tales are fluid – they evolve and adapt according to who is telling them, who is being told, and what kind of world those people are living in. This has always, and should always, be the way. Although Damsels is very much our own 21st century take on Fairy–and Folktales, we have still drawn blatantly and unashamedly from the traditional stories. In many cases the oldest recorded versions of these tales were not quite what we remembered or expected – so much more complex, darker, funnier, or just plain weirder. Here we offer a classic Fairy Story which helped inspire this issue of Damsels for your reading pleasure. So, snuggle down and enjoy a bedtime story on us. Don't have nightmares."
– *Leah Moore & John Reppion*

The Twelve Dancing Princesses

by The Brothers Grimm

There was a king who had twelve beautiful daughters. They slept in twelve beds all in one room; and when they went to bed, the doors were shut and locked up; but every morning their shoes were found to be quite worn through as if they had been danced in all night; and yet nobody could find out how it happened, or where they had been.

Then the king made it known to all the land, that if any person could discover the secret, and find out where it was that the princesses danced in the night, he should have the one he liked best for his wife, and should be king after his death; but whoever tried and did not succeed, after three days and nights, should be put to death.

A king's son soon came. He was well entertained, and in the evening was taken to the chamber next to the one where the princesses lay in their twelve beds. There he was to sit and watch where they went to dance; and, in order that nothing might pass without his hearing it, the door of his chamber was left open. But the king's son soon fell asleep; and when he awoke in the morning he found that the princesses had all been dancing, for the soles of their shoes were full of holes. The same thing happened the second and third night: so the king ordered his head to be cut off. After him came several others; but they had all the same luck, and all lost their lives in the same manner.

Now it chanced that an old soldier, who had been wounded in battle and could fight no longer, passed through the country where this king reigned: and as he was travelling through a wood, he met an old woman, who asked him where he was going. 'I hardly know where I am going, or what I had better do,' said the soldier; 'but I think I should like very well to find out where it is that the princesses dance, and then in time I might be a king.' 'Well,' said the old dame, 'that is no very hard task: only take care not to drink any of the wine which one of the princesses will bring to you in the evening; and as soon as she leaves you pretend to be fast asleep.'

Then she gave him a cloak, and said, 'As soon as you put that on you will become invisible, and you will then be able to follow the princesses wherever they go.' When the soldier heard all this good counsel, he determined to try his luck: so he went to the king, and said he was willing to undertake the task.

He was as well received as the others had been, and the king ordered fine royal robes to be given him; and when the evening came he was led to the outer chamber. Just

as he was going to lie down, the eldest of the princesses brought him a cup of wine; but the soldier threw it all away secretly, taking care not to drink a drop. Then he laid himself down on his bed, and in a little while began to snore very loud as if he was fast asleep. When the twelve princesses heard this they laughed heartily; and the eldest said, 'This fellow too might have done a wiser thing than lose his life in this way!' Then they rose up and opened their drawers and boxes, and took out all their fine clothes, and dressed themselves at the glass, and skipped about as if they were eager to begin dancing. But the youngest said, 'I don't know how it is, while you are so happy I feel very uneasy; I am sure some mischance will befall us.' 'You simpleton,' said the eldest, 'you are always afraid; have you forgotten how many kings' sons have already watched in vain? And as for this soldier, even if I had not given him his sleeping draught, he would have slept soundly enough.'

When they were all ready, they went and looked at the soldier; but he snored on, and did not stir hand or foot: so they thought they were quite safe; and the eldest went up to her own bed and clapped her hands, and the bed sank into the floor and a trap-door flew open. The soldier saw them going down through the trap-door one after another, the eldest leading the way; and thinking he had no time to lose, he jumped up, put on the cloak which the old woman had given him, and followed them; but in the middle of the stairs he trod on the gown of the youngest princess, and she cried out to her sisters, 'All is not right; someone took hold of my gown.' 'You silly creature!' said the eldest, 'it is nothing but a nail in the wall.' Then down they all went, and at the bottom they found themselves in a most delightful grove of trees; and the leaves were all of silver, and glittered and sparkled beautifully. The soldier wished to take away some token of the place; so he broke off a little branch, and there came a loud noise from the tree. Then the youngest daughter said again, 'I am sure all is not right—did not you hear that noise? That never happened before.' But the eldest said, 'It is only our princes, who are shouting for joy at our approach.'

Then they came to another grove of trees, where all the leaves were of gold; and afterwards to a third, where the leaves were all glittering diamonds. And the soldier broke a branch from each; and every time there was a loud noise, which made the youngest sister tremble with fear; but the eldest still said, it was only the princes, who were crying for joy. So they went on till they came to a great lake; and at the side of the lake there lay twelve little boats with twelve handsome princes in them, who seemed to be waiting there for the princesses.

One of the princesses went into each boat, and the soldier stepped into the same boat with the youngest. As they were rowing over the lake, the prince who was in the boat with the youngest princess and the soldier said, 'I do not know why it is, but though I am rowing with all my might we do not get on so fast as usual, and I am quite tired: the boat seems very heavy today.' 'It is only the heat of the weather,' said the princess: 'I feel it very warm too.'

On the other side of the lake stood a fine illuminated castle, from which came the merry music of horns and trumpets. There they all landed, and went into the castle, and each prince danced with his princess; and the soldier, who was all the time invisible, danced with them too; and when any of the princesses had a cup of wine set by her, he drank it all up, so that when she put the cup to her mouth it was empty. At this, too, the youngest sister was terribly frightened, but the eldest always silenced her. They danced on till three o'clock in the morning, and then all their shoes were worn out, so that they were obliged to leave off. The princes rowed them back again over the lake (but this time the soldier placed himself in the boat with the eldest princess); and on the opposite shore they took leave of each other, the princesses promising to come again the next night.

When they came to the stairs, the soldier ran on before the princesses, and laid himself down; and as the twelve sisters slowly came up very much tired, they heard him snoring in his bed; so they said, 'Now all is quite safe'; then they undressed themselves, put away their fine clothes, pulled off their shoes, and went to bed. In the morning the soldier said nothing about what had happened, but determined to see more of this strange adventure, and went again the second and third night; and every thing happened just as before; the princesses danced each time till their shoes were worn to pieces, and then returned home. However, on the third night the soldier carried away one of the golden cups as a token of where he had been.

As soon as the time came when he was to declare the secret, he was taken before the king with the three branches and the golden cup; and the twelve princesses stood listening behind the door to hear what he would say. And when the king asked him. 'Where do my twelve daughters dance at night?' he answered, 'With twelve princes in a castle under ground.' And then he told the king all that had happened, and showed him the three branches and the golden cup which he had brought with him. Then the king called for the princesses, and asked them whether what the soldier said was true: and when they saw that they were discovered, and that it was of no use to deny what had happened, they confessed it all. And the king asked the soldier which of them he would choose for his wife; and he answered, 'I am not very young, so I will have the eldest.'—And they were married that very day, and the soldier was chosen to be the king's heir.

The End

The First Voyage of Sinbad the Sailor

from "Fairy Tales from the Arabian Nights"

My father left me a considerable estate, the best part of which I spent in riotous living during my youth; but I perceived my error, and reflected that riches were perishable, and quickly consumed by such ill managers as myself. I further considered that by my irregular way of living I had wretchedly misspent my time which is the most valuable thing in the world. Struck with those reflections, I collected the remains of my furniture, and sold all my patrimony by public auction to the highest bidder. Then I entered into a contract with some merchants, who traded by sea: I took the advice of such as I thought most capable to give it me; and resolving to improve what money I had, I went to Balsora and embarked with several merchants on board a ship which we jointly fitted out.

We set sail, and steered our course towards the East Indies, through the Persian Gulf, which is formed by the coasts of Arabia Felix on the right, and by those of Persia on the left, and, according to common opinion, is seventy leagues across at the broadest part. The eastern sea, as well as that of the Indies, is very spacious: it is bounded on one side by the coasts of Abyssinia, and is 4,500 leagues in length to the isles of Vakvak. At first I was troubled with sea-sickness, but speedily recovered my health, and was not afterwards troubled with that disease.

In our voyage we touched at several islands, where we sold or exchanged our goods. One day, whilst under sail, we were becalmed near a little island, almost even with the surface of the water, which resembled a green meadow. The captain ordered his sails to be furled, and permitted such persons as had a mind to do so to land upon the island, amongst whom I was one.

But while we were diverting ourselves with eating and drinking, and recovering ourselves from the fatigue of the sea, the island on a sudden trembled, and shook us terribly.

They perceived the trembling of the island on board the ship, and called us to re-embark speedily, or we should all be lost, for what we took for an island was only the back of a whale. The nimblest got into the sloop, others betook themselves to swimming; but for my part I was still upon the back of the whale when he dived into the sea, and had time only to catch hold of a piece of wood that we had brought out of the ship to make a fire. Meanwhile, the captain, having received those on board who were in the sloop, and taken up some of those that swam, resolved to use the favourable gale that had just risen, and hoisting his sails, pursued his voyage, so that it was impossible for me to regain the ship.

Thus was I exposed to the mercy of the waves, and struggled for my life all the rest of the day and the following night. Next morning I found my strength gone, and despaired of saving my life, when happily a wave threw me against an island. The bank was high and rugged, so that I could scarcely have got up had it not been for some roots of trees, which fortune seemed to have preserved in this place for my safety. Being got up, I lay down upon the ground half dead until the sun appeared; then, though I was very feeble, both by reason of my hard labour and want of food, I crept along to look for some herbs fit to eat, and had the good luck not only to find some, but likewise a spring of excellent water, which contributed much to restore me. After this I advanced farther into the island, and came at last into a fine plain, where I perceived a horse feeding at a great distance. I went towards him, between hope and fear, not knowing whether I was going to lose my life or save it. Presently I heard the voice of a man from under ground, who immediately appeared to me, and asked who I was. I gave him an account of my adventure; after which, taking me by the hand, he led me into a cave, where there were several other people, no less amazed to see me than I was to see them.

I ate some victuals which they offered me, and then asked them what they did in such a desert place. They answered that they were grooms belonging to King Mihrage, sovereign of the island, and that every year they brought thither the king's horses. They added that they were to get home to-morrow, and had I been one day later I must have perished, because the inhabited part of the island was at a great distance, and it would have been impossible for me to have got thither without a guide.

Next morning they returned with their horses to the capital of the island, took me with them, and presented me to King Mihrage. He asked me who I was, and by what adventure I came into his dominions? And, after I had satisfied him he told me he was much concerned for my misfortune, and at the same time ordered that I should want for nothing, which his officers were so generous and careful as to see exactly fulfilled.

Being a merchant, I frequented the society of men of my own profession, and particularly inquired for those who were strangers, if perhaps I might hear any news from Bagdad, or find an opportunity to return thither, for King Mihrage's capital was situated on the edge of the sea, and had a fine harbour, where ships arrived daily from the different quarters of the world. I frequented also the society of the learned Indians, and took delight in hearing them discourse; but withal I took care to make my court regularly to the king, and conversed with the governors and petty kings, his tributaries, that were about him. They asked me a thousand questions about my country, and I, being willing to inform myself as to their laws and customs, asked them everything which I thought worth knowing.

There belonged to this king an island named Cassel. They assured me that every night a noise of drums was heard there, whence the mariners fancied that it was the residence of Degial. I had a great mind to see this wonderful place, and on my way thither saw fishes of one hundred and two hundred cubits long, that occasion more fear than hurt, for they are so timid that they will fly at the rattling of two sticks or boards. I saw likewise other fishes, about a cubit in length, that had heads like owls.

As I was one day at the port after my return, a ship arrived, and as soon as she cast anchor, they began to unload her, and the merchants on board ordered their goods to be carried into the warehouse. As I cast my eye upon some bales, and looked at the name, I found my own, and perceived the bales to be the same that I had embarked at Balsora. I also knew the captain; but being persuaded that he believed me to be drowned, I went and asked him whose bales they were. He replied: 'They belonged to a merchant of Bagdad, called Sinbad, who came to sea with us; but one day, being near an island, as we thought, he went ashore with several other passengers upon this supposed island, which was only a monstrous whale that lay asleep upon the surface of the water; but as soon as he felt the heat of the fire they had kindled on his back to dress some victuals he began to move, and dived under water: most of the persons who were upon him perished, and among them unfortunate Sinbad. Those bales belonged to him, and I am resolved to trade with them until I meet with some of his family, to whom I may return the profit.'

'Captain,' said I, 'I am that Sinbad whom you thought to be dead, and those bales are mine.'

When the captain heard me speak thus, 'O heaven,' said he, 'whom can we ever trust now-a-days? There is no faith left among men. I saw Sinbad perish with my own eyes, and the passengers on board saw it as well as I, and yet you tell me you are that Sinbad. What impudence is this! To look at you, one would take you to be a man of honesty, and yet you tell a horrible falsehood, in order to possess yourself of what does not belong to you.'

'Have patience, captain,' replied I; 'do me the favour to hear what I have to say.'

'Very well,' said he, 'speak; I am ready to hear you.' Then I told him how I escaped, and by what adventure I met with the grooms of King Mihrage, who brought me to his court.

He was soon persuaded that I was no cheat, for there came people from his ship who knew me, paid me great compliments, and expressed much joy to see me alive. At last he knew me himself, and embracing me, 'Heaven be praised,' said he, 'for your happy escape; I cannot enough express my joy for it: there are your goods; take and do with them what you will.' I thanked him, acknowledged his honesty, and in return offered him part of my goods as a present, which he generously refused.

I took out what was most valuable in my bales, and presented it to King Mihrage, who, knowing my misfortune, asked me how I came by such rarities. I acquainted him with the whole story. He was mightily pleased at my good luck, accepted my present, and gave me one much more considerable in return. Upon this I took leave of him, and went aboard the same ship, after I had exchanged my goods for the commodities of that country. I carried with me wood of aloes, sandal, camphor, nutmegs, cloves, pepper, and ginger. We passed by several islands, and at last arrived at Balsora, from whence I came to this city, with the value of one hundred thousand sequins. My family and I received one another with transports of sincere friendship. I bought slaves and fine lands, and built me a great house. And thus I settled myself, resolving to forget the miseries I had suffered, and to enjoy the pleasures of life.

The End

Little Red Riding Hood

Once upon a time there lived in a certain village a little country girl, the prettiest creature who was ever seen. Her mother was excessively fond of her; and her grandmother doted on her still more. This good woman had a little red riding hood made for her. It suited the girl so extremely well that everybody called her Little Red Riding Hood.

One day her mother, having made some cakes, said to her, "Go, my dear, and see how your grandmother is doing, for I hear she has been very ill. Take her a cake, and this little pot of butter."

Little Red Riding Hood set out immediately to go to her grandmother, who lived in another village.

As she was going through the wood, she met with a wolf, who had a very great mind to eat her up, but he dared not, because of some woodcutters working nearby in the forest. He asked her where she was going. The poor child, who did not know that it was dangerous to stay and talk to a wolf, said to him, "I am going to see my grandmother and carry her a cake and a little pot of butter from my mother."

"Does she live far off?" said the wolf.

"Oh I say," answered Little Red Riding Hood; "it is beyond that mill you see there, at the first house in the village."

"Well," said the wolf, "and I'll go and see her too. I'll go this way and go you that, and we shall see who will be there first."

The wolf ran as fast as he could, taking the shortest path, and the little girl took a roundabout way, entertaining herself by gathering nuts, running after butterflies, and gathering bouquets of little flowers. It was not long before the wolf arrived at the old woman's house. He knocked at the door: tap, tap.

"Who's there?"

"Your grandchild, Little Red Riding Hood," replied the wolf, counterfeiting her voice; "who has brought you a cake and a little pot of butter sent you by mother."

The good grandmother, who was in bed, because she was somewhat ill, cried

out, "Pull the bobbin, and the latch will go up."

The wolf pulled the bobbin, and the door opened, and then he immediately fell upon the good woman and ate her up in a moment, for it been more than three days since he had eaten. He then shut the door and got into the grandmother's bed, expecting Little Red Riding Hood, who came some time afterwards and knocked at the door: tap, tap.

"Who's there?"

Little Red Riding Hood, hearing the big voice of the wolf, was at first afraid; but believing her grandmother had a cold and was hoarse, answered, "It is your grandchild Little Red Riding Hood, who has brought you a cake and a little pot of butter mother sends you."

The wolf cried out to her, softening his voice as much as he could, "Pull the bobbin, and the latch will go up."

Little Red Riding Hood pulled the bobbin, and the door opened.

The wolf, seeing her come in, said to her, hiding himself under the bedclothes, "Put the cake and the little pot of butter upon the stool, and come get into bed with me."

Little Red Riding Hood took off her clothes and got into bed. She was greatly amazed to see how her grandmother looked in her nightclothes, and said to her, "Grandmother, what big arms you have!"

"All the better to hug you with, my dear."

"Grandmother, what big legs you have!"

"All the better to run with, my child."

"Grandmother, what big ears you have!"

"All the better to hear with, my child."

"Grandmother, what big eyes you have!"

"All the better to see with, my child."

"Grandmother, what big teeth you have got!"

"All the better to eat you up with."

And, saying these words, this wicked wolf fell upon Little Red Riding Hood, and ate her all up.

The End

Beauty and the Beast

by Gabrielle-Suzanne Barbot de Villeneuve

Once on a time, in a very far-off country, there lived a merchant who had been so fortunate in all his undertakings that he was enormously rich. As he had, however, six sons and six daughters, he found that his money was not too much to let them all have everything they fancied, as they were accustomed to do.

But one day a most unexpected misfortune befell them. Their house caught fire and was speedily burnt to the ground, with all the splendid furniture, books, pictures, gold, silver, and precious goods it contained; and this was only the beginning of their troubles. Their father, who had till this moment prospered in all ways, suddenly lost every ship he had on the sea, either by dint of pirates, shipwreck, or fire. Then he heard that his clerks in distant countries, whom he trusted entirely, had proved unfaithful; and at last, from great wealth he fell into the direst poverty.

All that he had left was a little house in a desolate place, at least a hundred leagues from the town in which he had lived, and to this he was forced to retreat with his children, who were in despair at the idea of leading such a different life. Indeed, the daughters at first hoped that their friends, who had been so numerous while they were rich, would insist on their staying in their houses now they no longer possessed one. But they soon found that they were left alone, and that their former friends even attributed their misfortunes to their own extravagance, and showed no intention of offering them any help. So nothing was left for them but to take their departure to the cottage, which stood in the midst of a dark forest, and seemed to be the most dismal place on the face of the earth. As they were too poor to have any servants, the girls had to work hard, like peasants, and the sons, for their part, cultivated the fields to earn their living. Roughly clothed, and living in the simplest way, the girls regretted unceasingly the luxuries and amusements of their former life; only the youngest tried to be brave and cheerful. She had been as sad as anyone when misfortune overtook her father, but, soon recovering her natural gaiety, she set to work to make the best of things, to amuse her father and brothers as well as she could, and to try to persuade her sisters to join her in dancing and singing. But they would do nothing of the sort, and, because she was not as doleful as themselves, they declared that this miserable life was all she was fit for. But she was really far prettier and cleverer than they were; indeed, she was so lovely that she was always called Bella. After two years, when they were all beginning to get used to their new life, something happened to disturb their tranquillity. Their father received the news that one of his ships, which he had believed to be lost, had come safely into port with a rich cargo. All the sons and daughters at once thought that their poverty was at an end, and wanted to set out directly for the town; but their father, who was more prudent, begged them to wait a little,

9

and though it was harvest time, and he could ill be spared, determined to go himself first, to make inquiries. Only the youngest daughter had any doubt but that they would soon again be as rich as they were before, or at least rich enough to live comfortably in some town where they would find amusement and gay companions once more. So they all loaded their father with commissions for jewels and dresses which it would have taken a fortune to buy; only Bella, feeling sure that it was of no use, didn't ask for anything. Her father, noticing her silence, said: "And what shall I bring for you, Bella?"

"The only thing I wish for is to see you come home safely," she answered.

But this only vexed her sisters, who fancied she was blaming them for having asked for such costly things. Her father, however, was pleased, but as he thought that at her age she certainly ought to like pretty presents, he told her to choose something.

"Well, dear father," she said, "as you insist on it, I beg that you'll bring me a rose. I haven't seen one since we came here, and I love them so much."

So the merchant set out and reached the town as quickly as possible, only to find that his former companions, believing him to be dead, had divided between them the goods which the ship had brought; and after six months of trouble and expense he found himself as poor as when he started, having been able to recover only just enough to pay the cost of his journey. To make matters worse, he was obliged to leave the town in the most terrible weather, so that by the time he was within a few leagues of his home he was almost exhausted with cold and fatigue. Though he knew it would take some hours to get through the forest, he was so anxious to be at his journey's end that he resolved to go on; but night overtook him, and the deep snow and bitter frost made it impossible for his horse to carry him any further. Not a house was to be seen; the only shelter he could get was the hollow trunk of a great tree, and there he crouched all the night, which seemed to him the longest he had ever known. In spite of his weariness, the howling of the wolves kept him awake. When at last the day broke he was not much better off, for the falling snow had covered up every path, and he didn't know which way to turn.

At length he made out some sort of track, and though at the beginning it was so rough and slippery that he fell down more than once, it presently became easier, and led him into an avenue of trees which ended in a splendid castle. It seemed to the merchant very strange that no snow had fallen in the avenue, which was entirely composed of orange trees, covered with flowers and fruit. When he reached the first court of the castle, he saw before him a flight of agate steps, and went up them, passing through several splendidly furnished rooms. The pleasant warmth of the air revived him, and he felt very hungry; but there seemed to be nobody in all this vast and splendid castle whom he could ask to give him something to eat. Deep silence reigned everywhere, and at last, tired of roaming through empty rooms and galleries, he stopped in a room smaller than the rest, where a fire was burning and a couch was drawn up closely to it. Thinking that this must be prepared for someone who was expected, he sat down to wait till he should come, and very soon fell into a sweet sleep.

When his extreme hunger wakened him after several hours, he was still alone; but a little table, on which was a good dinner, had been drawn up close to him, and as he had eaten nothing for twenty-four hours, he lost no time in beginning his meal, hoping that he might soon have the opportunity of thanking his considerate entertainer, whomever it might be. But no one appeared, and even after another long sleep, from which he awoke completely refreshed, there was no sign of anybody, though a fresh meal of dainty cakes and fruit was prepared on the little table at his elbow. Being naturally timid, the silence began to terrify him, and he resolved to search once more through all the rooms; but it was of no use. Not even a servant was to be seen; there was no sign of life in the castle! He began to wonder what he should do, and to amuse himself by pretending that all the treasures he saw were his own, and considering how he would divide them among his children. Then he went down into the garden, and though it was winter everywhere else, here the sun shone, and the birds sang, and the flowers bloomed, and the air was soft and sweet. The merchant, in ecstacies with all he saw and heard, said to himself:

"All this must be meant for me. I'll go this minute and bring my children to share all these delights."

In spite of being so cold and weary when he reached the castle, he had taken his horse to the stable and fed it. Now he thought he would saddle it for his homeward journey, and he turned down the path which led to the stable. This path had a hedge of roses on each side of it, and the merchant thought he had never seen or smelt such exquisite flowers. They reminded him of his promise to Bella, and he stopped and had just gathered one to take to her when he was startled by a strange noise behind him. Turning round, he saw a frightful Beast, which seemed to be very angry and said, in a terrible voice:

"Who told you that you might gather my roses? Wasn't it enough that I allowed you to be in my castle and was kind to you? This is the way you show your gratitude, by stealing my flowers! But your insolence shall not go unpunished." The merchant, terrified by these furious words, dropped the fatal rose, and throwing himself on his knees, cried: "Pardon me, noble sir. I'm truly grateful to you for your hospitality which was so magnificent that I couldn't imagine that you would be offended by my taking such a little thing as a rose." But the rich beast's anger was not lessened by this speech.

"You're very ready with excuses and flattery," he cried, "But that won't save you from the death you deserve."

"Alas!" thought the merchant, "if my daughter could only know what danger her rose has brought me into!"

And in despair he began to tell the rich beast all his misfortunes, and the reason of his journey, not forgetting to mention Bella s request.

"A king's ransom would hardly have procured all that my other daughters asked." He said. "But I thought that I might at least take Bella her rose. I beg you to forgive me, for you see I meant no harm."

The rich beast considered for a moment, and then he said, in a less furious tone:

"I'll forgive you on one condition—that you'll give me one of your daughters."
"Ah!" cried the merchant, "if I were cruel enough to buy my own life at the expense of one of my children's, what excuse could I invent to bring her here?"

"No excuse would be necessary," answered the rich beast. "If she comes at all she must come willingly. On no other condition will I have her. See if any one of them is courageous enough, and loves you well enough to come and save your life. You seem to be an honest man, so I'll trust you to go home. I give you a month to see if any of your daughters will come back with you and stay here, to let you go free. If none of them are willing, you must come alone, after bidding them good-bye forever, for then you'll belong to me. And don't imagine that you can hide from me, for if you fail to keep your word I'll come and fetch you!" added the beast, grimly.

The merchant accepted this proposal, though he didn't really think any of his daughters could be persuaded to come. He promised to return at the time appointed, and then, anxious to escape from the presence of the rich beast, asked permission to set off at once. But the beast answered that he couldn't go till next day.

"Then, you'll find a horse ready for you," he said. "Now go and eat your supper, and await my orders."

The poor merchant, more dead than alive, went back to his room, where the most delicious supper was already served on the little table which was drawn up before a blazing fire. But he was too terrified to eat, and only tasted a few of the dishes, for fear the beast should be angry if he didn't obey his orders. When he had finished, he heard a great noise in the next room, which he knew meant that the beast was coming. As he could do nothing to escape his visit, the only thing that remained was to seem as little afraid as possible; so when the beast appeared and asked roughly if he had supped well, the merchant answered humbly that he had, thanks to his host's kindness. Then the beast warned him to remember their agreement, and to prepare his daughter exactly for what she had to expect.

"Don't get up tomorrow," he added, "till you see the sun and hear a golden bell ring. Then you'll find your breakfast waiting for you here, and the horse you are to ride will be ready in the courtyard. He'll also bring you back again when you come with your daughter a month from now. Farewell. Take a rose to Bella, and remember your promise!"

The merchant was only too glad when the beast went away, and though he couldn't sleep for sadness, he lay down till the sun rose. Then, after a hasty breakfast, he went to gather Bella's rose, and mounted his horse, which carried him off so swiftly that in an instant he had lost sight of the castle. He was still wrapped in gloomy thoughts when it stopped before the door of the cottage.

His sons and daughters, who had been very uneasy at his long absence, rushed to meet him, eager to know the result of his journey, which, seeing him mounted on a splendid horse and wrapped in a rich mantle, they supposed to be favourable. He hid the truth from them at first, only saying sadly to Bella as he gave her the rose:

"Here is what you asked me to bring you; you little know what it has cost."

But this excited their curiosity so greatly that presently he told them his adventures from beginning to end, and then they were all very unhappy. The girls lamented loudly over their lost hopes, and the sons declared that their father shouldn't return to this terrible castle, and began to make plans for killing the rich beast if it should come to fetch him. But he reminded them that he had promised to go back. The girls were very angry with Bella, and said it was all her faul; that if she had asked for something sensible this would never have happened, and complained bitterly that they should have to suffer for her folly.

Poor Bella, much distressed, said to them:

"I have, indeed, caused this misfortune, but I assure you I did it innocently. Who could have guessed that to ask for a rose in the middle of summer would cause so much misery? But as I did the mischief it's only just that I should suffer for it. I'll therefore go back with my father to keep his promise."

At first nobody would hear of this arrangement, and her father and brothers, who loved her dearly, declared that nothing should make them let her go; but Bella was firm. As the time drew near, she divided all her little possessions between her sisters, and said good-bye to everything she loved, and when the fatal day came she encouraged and cheered her father as they mounted together the horse which had brought him back. It seemed to fly rather than gallop, but so smoothly that Bella was not frightened; indeed, she would have enjoyed the journey if she had not feared what might happen to her at the end of it. Her father still tried to persuade her to go back, but in vain. While they were talking the night fell, and then, to their great surprise, wonderful coloured lights began to shine in all directions, and splendid fireworks blazed out before them; all the forest was illuminated by them, and even felt pleasantly warm, though it had been bitterly cold before. This lasted till they reached the avenue of orange trees, where statues were holding flaming torches; when they got nearer to the castle they saw that it was illuminated from the roof to the ground, and music sounded softly from the courtyard. "The rich beast must be very hungry," said Bella, trying to laugh, "if he makes all this rejoicing over the arrival of his prey."

In spite of her anxiety, she couldn't help admiring all the wonderful things she saw.

The horse stopped at the foot of the flight of steps leading to the terrace, and when they had dismounted, her father led her to the little room he had been in before, where they found a splendid fire burning, and the table daintily spread with a delicious supper.

The merchant knew that this was meant for them, and Bella, who was rather less frightened now that she had passed through so many rooms and seen nothing of the rich beast, was quite willing to begin, for her long ride had made her very hungry. But they had hardly finished their meal when the noise of the beast's footsteps were heard approaching, and Bella clung to her father in terror, which became all the greater when she saw how frightened he was. But when the beast really appeared, though she trembled at the sight of him, she made a great effort to hide her terror, and saluted him respectfully.

This evidently pleased the rich beast. After looking at her, he said, in a tone that might have struck terror into the boldest heart, though he didn't seem to be angry:

"Good-evening, old man. Good-evening, Bella."

The merchant was too terrified to reply, but Bella answered sweetly: "Good-evening, Beast."

"Have you come willingly?" asked the beast. "Will you be content to stay here when your father goes away?"

Bella answered bravely that she was quite prepared to stay.

"I'm pleased with you," said the rich beast. "As you have come of your own accord, you may stay. As for you, old man," he added, turning to the merchant, "at sunrise tomorrow you'll take your departure. When the bell rings, get up quickly and eat your breakfast, and you'll find the same horse waiting to take you home; but remember that you must never expect to see my castle again."

Then turning to Bella, he said:

"Take your father into the next room, and help him to choose everything you think your brothers and sisters would like to have. You'll find two travelling-trunks there; fill them as full as you can. It's only just that you should send them something very precious as a remembrance of yourself."

Then he went away, after saying, "Good-bye, Bella; good-bye, old man"; and though Bella was beginning to think with great dismay of her father's departure, she was afraid to disobey the rich beast's orders. They went into the next room, which had shelves and cupboards all round it, and they were greatly surprised at the riches it contained. There were splendid dresses fit for a queen, with all the ornaments that were to be worn with them; and when Bella opened the cupboards she was quite dazzled by the gorgeous jewels that lay in heaps upon every shelf. After choosing a vast quantity, which she divided between her sisters—for she had made a heap of the wonderful dresses for each of them—she opened the last chest, which was full of gold.

"I think, father," she said, "that, as the gold will be more useful to you, we had better take out the other things again, and fill the trunks with it." So they did this; but the more they put in, the more room there seemed to be, and at last they put back all the jewels and dresses they had taken out, and Bella even added as many more of the jewels as she could carry at once; and then the trunks were not too full, but they were so heavy that an elephant couldn't have carried them!

"The rich beast was mocking us," cried the merchant; "he must have pretended to give us all these things, knowing that I couldn't carry them away."

"Let's wait and see," answered Bella. "I can't believe that he meant to deceive us. All we can do is to fasten them up and leave them ready."

So they did this and returned to the little room, where, to their astonishment, they found breakfast ready. The merchant ate his with a good appetite, as the rich beast's generosity made him believe that he might perhaps venture to come back soon and see Bella. But she felt sure that her father was leaving her forever, so she was very sad when the bell rang sharply for the second time, and warned them that the time had come for them to part. They went down into the courtyard, where two horses were waiting: one loaded with the two trunks, the other for him to ride. They were pawing the ground in their impatience to start, and the merchant was forced to bid Bella a hasty farewell; as soon as he was mounted he went off at such a pace that she lost sight of him in an instant. Then Bella began to cry, and wandered sadly back to her own room. But she soon found that she was very sleepy, and as she had nothing better to do she lay down and instantly fell asleep. She dreamed that she was walking by a brook bordered with trees, and lamenting her sad fate, when a young prince, handsomer than anyone she had ever seen, and with a voice that went straight to her heart, came to her and said, "Ah, Bella! you're not so unfortunate as you suppose. Here you'll be rewarded for all you have suffered elsewhere. Your every wish shall be gratified. Only try to find me out, no matter how I may be disguised, as I love you dearly, and in making me happy you'll find your own happiness. Be as true-hearted as you are beautiful, and we shall have nothing left to wish for."

"What can I do, prince, to make you happy?" asked Bella.

"Only be grateful," he answered, "and don't trust too much to your eyes. And, above all, don't desert me till you have saved me from my cruel misery."

After this she thought she found herself in a room with a stately and beautiful lady, who said to her:

"Dear Bella, try not to regret all you have left behind you, for you're destined to a better fate. Only don't let yourself be deceived by appearances."

Bella found her dreams so interesting that she was in no hurry to wake, but presently the clock roused her by calling her name softly twelve times. She got up and found her dressing-table set out with everything she could possibly want; and when her toilet was finished she found dinner was waiting in the room next to hers. But dinner does not take very long when you're all by yourself, and very soon she sat down cozily in the corner of a sofa, and began to think about the charming prince she had seen in her dream.

"He said I could make him happy," said Bella to herself.

"It seems, then, that this horrible Beast keeps him a prisoner. How can I set him free? I wonder why they both told me not to trust to appearances? I don't understand it. But, after all, it was only a dream, so why should I trouble myself about it? I had better go and find something to do to amuse myself."

So she got up and began to explore some of the many rooms of the castle.

The first she entered was lined with mirrors, and Bella saw herself reflected on every side, and thought she had never seen such a charming room. A bracelet which was hanging from a chandelier caught her eye, and on taking it down she was greatly surprised to find that it held a portrait of her unknown admirer, just as she had seen him in her dream. With great delight she slipped the bracelet on her arm, and went on into a gallery of pictures, where she soon found a portrait of the same handsome prince, as large as life, and so well painted that as she studied it he seemed to smile kindly at her. Tearing herself away from the portrait at last, she passed through into a room which contained every musical instrument under the sun, and here she amused herself for a long while in trying some of them, and singing till she was tired. The next room was a library, and she saw everything she had ever wanted to read, as well as everything she had read, and it seemed to her that a whole lifetime wouldn't be enough to even read the names of the books, there were so many. By this time it was growing dusk, and wax candles in diamond and ruby candlesticks were beginning to light themselves in every room.

Bella found her supper served just at the time she preferred to have it, but she didn't see anyone or hear a sound, and though her father had warned her that she would be alone, she began to find it rather dull.

Presently she heard the rich beast coming, and wondered tremblingly if he meant to eat her up now.

However, he didn't seem at all ferocious, and only said gruffly:

"Good-evening, Bella." She answered cheerfully and managed to conceal her terror. Then the rich beast asked her how she had been amusing herself, and she told him all the rooms she had seen.

He asked if she thought she could be happy in his castle; and Bella answered that everything was so beautiful that she would be very hard to please if she couldn't be happy. And after about an hour's talk Bella began to think that the rich beast was not nearly so terrible as she had first supposed. He got up to leave her, and asked in his gruff voice:

"Do you love me, Bella? Will you marry me?"

"Oh! what shall I say?" cried Bella, for she was afraid to make the rich beast angry by refusing.

"Say 'yes' or 'no' without fear," he replied.

"Oh! no, Beast," said Bella hastily.

"Since you won't, good-night, Bella," he said.

And she answered, "Good-night, Beast," very glad to find that her refusal had not provoked him. After he was gone she was very soon in bed and asleep, and dreaming of her unknown prince. She thought he came and said to her:

"Ah, Bella! why are you so unkind to me? I fear I'm fated to be unhappy for many a long day still."

And then her dreams changed, but the charming prince figured in them all. When morning came her first thought was to look at the portrait, and see if it was really like him, and she found that it certainly was.

This morning she decided to amuse herself in the garden, for the sun shone, and all the fountains were playing; but she was astonished to find that every place was familiar to her, and presently she came to the brook where the myrtle trees were growing where she had first met the prince in her dream, and that made her think more than ever that he must be kept a prisoner by the rich beast. When she was tired she went back to the castle, and found a new room full of materials for every kind of work—ribbons to make into bows, and silks to work into flowers. Then there was an aviary full of rare birds, which were so tame that they flew to Bella as soon as they saw her, and perched on her shoulders and her head.

"Pretty little creatures," she said, "how I wish that your cage was nearer to my room, that I might often hear you sing!"

So saying, she opened a door, and found, to her delight, that it led into her own room, though she had thought it was quite in the other side of the castle.

There were more birds in a room farther on, parrots and cockatoos that could talk, and they greeted Bella by name; indeed, she found them so entertaining that she took one or two back to her room, and they talked to her while she was at supper; after which the rich beast paid her his usual visit, and asked her the same questions as before, and then with a gruff "good-night" he took his departure, and Bella went to bed to dream of her mysterious prince.

The days passed swiftly in different amusements, and after a while Bella found out another strange thing in the castle, which often pleased her when she was tired of being alone. There was one room which she had not noticed particularly; it was empty, except that under each of the windows stood a very comfortable chair; and the first time she had looked out of the window it had seemed to her that a black curtain prevented her from seeing anything outside. But the second time she went into the room, happening to be tired, she sat down in one of the chairs, when instantly the curtain was rolled aside, and a most amusing pantomime was acted before her; there were dances, and coloured lights, and music, and pretty dresses, and it was all so gay that Bella was in ecstacies. After that she tried the other seven windows in turn, and there was some new and surprising entertainment to be seen from each of them, so that Bella never could feel lonely any more. Every evening after supper the beast came to see her, and always before saying good-night asked her in his terrible voice:

"Bella, will you marry me?"

And it seemed to Bella, now she understood him better, that when she said, "No, Beast," he went away quite sad. But her happy dreams of the handsome young prince soon made her forget the poor Beast, and the only thing that at all disturbed her was to be constantly told to distrust appearances, to let her heart guide her, and not her eyes, and many other equally perplexing things, which, consider as she would, she couldn't understand.

This went on for a long time, till at last, happy as she was, Bella began to long for the sight of her father and her brothers and sisters; and one night, seeing her look very sad, the rich beast asked her what was the matter. Bella had quite ceased to be afraid of him. Now she knew that he was really gentle in spite of his ferocious looks and his dreadful voice. She answered that she was longing to see her home once more. On hearing this the rich beast seemed sadly distressed, and cried miserably:

"Ah! Bella, have you the heart to desert an unhappy Beast like this? What more do you want to make you happy? Is it because you hate me that you want to escape?"
"No, dear Beast," answered Bella softly, "I don't hate you, and I should be very sorry never to see you any more, but I long to see my father again. Only let me go for two months, and

I promise to come back to you and stay for the rest of my life."

The rich beast, who had been sighing dolefully while she spoke, now replied:

"I can't refuse you anything you ask, even though it should cost me my life. Take the four boxes you'll find in the room next to your own, and fill them with everything you wish to take with you. But remember your promise and come back when the two months are over, or you may have cause to repent it, for if you don't come in good time you'll find your faithful Beast dead. You won't need any chariot to bring you back. Only say good-bye to all your brothers and sisters the night before you come away, and when you have gone to bed turn this ring round on your finger and say firmly: 'I wish to go back to my castle and see my Beast again.' Good-night, Bella. Fear nothing, sleep peacefully, and before long you shall see your father once more."

As soon as Bella was alone she hastened to fill the boxes with all the rare and precious things she saw about her, and only when she was tired of heaping things into them did they seem to be full.

Then she went to bed, but could hardly sleep for joy. And when at last she did begin to dream of her beloved prince she was grieved to see him stretched on a grassy bank, sad and weary, and hardly like himself.

"What's the matter?" she cried.

He looked at her reproachfully, and said:

"How can you ask me, cruel one? Are you not leaving me to my death perhaps?"

"Ah! don't be so sorrowful," cried Bella; "I'm only going to assure my father that I'm safe and happy. I've promised the rich beast faithfully that I'll come back, and he would die of grief if I didn't keep my word!"

"What would that matter to you?" said the prince "Surely you wouldn't care?"

"Indeed, I should be ungrateful if I didn't care for such a kind Beast," cried Bella indignantly. "I would die to save him from pain. I assure you it's not his fault that he is so ugly."

Just then a strange sound woke her—someone was speaking not very far away; and opening her eyes she found herself in a room she had never seen before, which was certainly not nearly so splendid as those she was used to in the rich beast's castle. Where could she be? She got up and dressed hastily, and then saw that the boxes she had packed the night before were all in the room.

While she was wondering by what magic the rich beast had transported the boxes and herself to this strange place she suddenly heard her father's voice, and rushed out and greeted him joyfully. Her brothers and sisters were all astonished at her appearance, as they had never expected to see her again, and there was no end to the questions they asked her. She had also much to hear about what had happened to them while she was away, and of her father's journey home. But when they heard that she had only come to be with them for a short time, and then must go back to the beast's castle forever, they lamented loudly. Then Bella asked her father what he thought could be the meaning of her strange dreams, and why the prince constantly begged her not to trust to appearances. After much consideration, he answered: "You tell me yourself that the rich beast, frightful as he is, loves you dearly, and deserves your love and gratitude for his gentleness and kindness; I think the prince must mean you to understand that you ought to reward him by doing as he wishes you to, in spite of his ugliness."

Bella couldn't help seeing that this seemed very probable; still, when she thought of her dear prince who was so handsome, she didn't feel at all inclined to marry the beast. At any rate, for two months she need not decide, but could enjoy herself with her sisters. But though they were rich now, and lived in town again, and had plenty of acquaintances, Bella found that nothing amused her very much; and she often thought of the castle, where she was so happy, especially as, at home, she never once dreamed of her dear prince, and she felt quite sad without him.

Her sisters seemed to have become quite used to being without her, and found her rather in the way, so she wouldn't have been sorry when the two months were over, but for her father and brothers, who begged her to stay, and seemed so grieved at the thought of her departure that she had not the courage to say good-bye to them. Every day when she got up she meant to say it at night, and when night came she put it off again, till at last she had a dismal dream which helped her to make up her mind. She dreamed she was wandering on a lonely path in the castle gardens, when she heard groans which seemed to come from some bushes hiding the entrance of a cave. Running quickly to see what could be the matter, she found the beast stretched out on his side, apparently dying. He reproached her faintly with being the cause of his distress, and at the same moment a stately lady appeared, and said very gravely:

"Ah! Bella, you're only just in time to save his life. See what happens when people don't keep their promises! If you had delayed one day more, you would have found him dead."

Bella was so terrified by this dream that the next morning she announced her intention of going back at once, and that very night she said good-bye to her father and all her brothers and sisters, and as soon as she was in bed she turned her ring round on her finger, and said firmly, "I wish to go back to my castle and see my Beast again," as she had been told to do.

Then she fell asleep instantly, and only woke up to hear the clock saying "Bella, Bella" twelve times in its musical voice, which told her at once that she was really in the castle once more. Everything was just as before, and her birds were so glad to see her! But Bella thought she had never known such a long day, for she was so anxious to see the beast again that she felt as if suppertime would never come.

But when it did come and no Beast appeared she was really frightened; so, after listening and waiting for a long time, she ran down into the garden to search for him. Up and down the paths and avenues ran poor Bella, calling him in vain, for no one answered, and not a trace of him could she find; till at last, quite tired, she stopped for a minute's rest, and saw that she was standing opposite the shady path she had seen in her dream. She rushed down it, and, sure enough, there was the cave, and in it lay the beast—asleep, as Bella thought. Quite glad to have found him, she ran up and stroked his head, but, to her horror, he didn't move or open his eyes.

"Oh! he is dead; and it's all my fault," said Bella, crying bitterly.

But then, looking at him again, she fancied he still breathed and, hastily fetching some water from the nearest fountain, she sprinkled it over his face. To her great delight, he began to revive.

"Oh! Beast, how you frightened me!" she cried. "I never knew how much I loved you till just now, when I feared I was too late to save your life."

"Can you really love such an ugly creature as I am?" asked the beast faintly. "Ah! Bella, you only came just in time. I was dying because I thought you had forgotten your promise. But go back now and rest, I shall see you again by and by."

Bella, who had half expected that he would be angry with her, was reassured by his gentle voice, and went back to the castle, where supper was awaiting her; and afterward the rich beast came in as usual, and talked about the time she had spent with her father, asking if she had enjoyed herself, and if they had all been very glad to see her.

Bella answered politely, and quite enjoyed telling him all that had happened to her. And when at last the time came for him to go, and he asked, as he had so often asked before, "Bella, will you marry me?" She answered softly, "Yes, dear Beast."

As she spoke a blaze of light sprang up before the windows of the castle; fireworks crackled and guns banged, and across the avenue of orange trees, in letters all made of fireflies, was written: "Long live the prince and his Bride."

Turning to ask the beast what it could all mean, Bella found that he had disappeared, and in his place stood her long-loved prince! At the same moment the wheels of a chariot were heard on the terrace, and two ladies entered the room. One of them Bella recognized as the stately lady she had seen in her dreams; the other was also so grand and queenly that Bella hardly knew which to greet first.

But the one she already knew said to her companion:

"Well, queen, this is Bella, who has had the courage to rescue your son from the terrible enchantment. They love one another, and only your consent to their marriage is wanting to make them perfectly happy."

"I consent with all my heart," cried the queen. "How can I ever thank you enough, charming girl, for having restored my dear son to his natural form?"

And then she tenderly embraced Bella and the prince, who had meanwhile been greeting the fairy and receiving her congratulations.

"Now," said the fairy to Bella, "I suppose you would like me to send for all your brothers and sisters to dance at your wedding?"

And so she did, and the marriage was celebrated the very next day with the utmost splendour, and Bella and the prince lived happily ever after.

The End

The Sleeping Beauty in the Woods

by Charles Perrault

Once there was a king and a queen who had no children. They were so sad that they had no children, that their sadness cannot be expressed. They went to all the waters of the world; made vows and pilgrimages. They tried everything, but to no end. Until, at last, the queen had a daughter.

There was a very fine christening, and the princess had for her godmothers all the fairies they could find in the whole kingdom (of which there were seven), so that each one might give her a gift, as was the custom for fairies in those days. By this means, the princess might have all the perfections imaginable.

After the christening ceremonies were over, the company returned to the king's palace where a great feast was prepared for the fairies. Placed before each of them was a magnificent case of gold, wherein there was a spoon, knife, and fork, all of pure gold, set with diamonds and rubies. But, as they were all sitting down at the meal, they saw a very old fairy come into the Hall, whom had not been invited, because it had been over fifty years since she had been seen out of her tow, and so it was believed that she was either dead or under an evil enchantment.

The king ordered for her a case, but could not furnish her with a gold case like the others, because only seven had been commissioned for the seven fairies. The old fairy fancied she was slighted and muttered some threats between her teeth. One of the young fairies who sat by her overheard her grumbling and, guessing that she might give the little princess an unlucky gift, went, as soon as they rose from table, and hid herself behind the hangings so that she might speak last and repair the evil which the old fairy might intend.

Meanwhile, all the fairies began to give their gift to the princess. The youngest gave her the gift of beauty, that she should might be the most beautiful person in the world; the next, that she should have the wit of an angel; the third, that she should have grace in everything that she did; the fourth, that she should dance perfectly; the fifth, that she should sing like an nightingale; and the sixth, that she should play all kinds of music to the utmost perfection.

The old fairy's turn came next. With a head shaking more with spite than age, she said that the princess should have her hand pierced with a spindle and die of the wound. This terrible gift made the whole palace tremble, and everyone began to cry.

At this very instant, the young fairy came out from behind the hangings and spoke these words aloud:

"Assure yourselves, O King and Queen, that your daughter shall not die of this disaster. It is true, I do not have the power to undo entirely what my elder has done. The princess shall indeed pierce her hand with a spindle; but, instead of dying, she shall fall into a deep sleep that shall last a hundreds years, at the end of which a king's son shall come and awaken her."

The king, to avoid the misfortune foretold by the old fairy, immediately called for a proclamation to be made, whereby everybody was forbidden--on pain of death--to spin with a distaff and spindle, or to have so much as any spindles in their houses.

Fifteen or sixteen years later, on a day when the king and queen were in a far corner of the vast palace, the young and beautiful princess amused herself by running up and down the corridors, going from one apartment to another, until she came into a little room at the top of a tower, where a good old woman, alone, was spinning with her wheel, for she had never heard of the king's law against spindles.

"What are you doing there, good woman?" the princess asked.

"I am spinning, my child," said the old woman, who did not know who the princess was.

"Ha!" said the princess, "this is very pretty. How do you do it? Give it to me, that I may see if I can do the same."

Now, whether it was because she was too hasty, or somewhat clumsy, or because the old fairy had ordained it, but no sooner had the princess taken the spindle, she pierced her hand and swooned.

The good old woman, not knowing what to do, cried out for help. People came rushing from all over the palace, and they came in great numbers. When they saw the princess lying in a profound sleep on the floor, they threw cold water on her face, they unlaced her clothes, struck her on the palms of her hands, and rubbed her temples with smelling salts, but nothing could be done to wake the princess.

Now the king, who came up at the noise, when he saw his sleeping daughter, recalled to himself the prediction of the fairies. He called for the princess to be carried into the finest apartment in the palace and to be laid upon a bed embroidered with silver and gold.

If you had seen her, one might have mistaken her for a little angel, for she was still so very beautiful and her slumber had not diminished her complexion one bit: her cheeks were carnation and her lips were coral; indeed, her eyes were shut, but she breathed softly, which satisfied those about her that she was not dead. The king commanded that they not disturb her and let her sleep quietly until her hour of waking came.

Now, when this occurred, the good fairy, who had saved her life by condemning her to sleep a hundred years, was in the kingdom of Matakin, twelve thousand leagues away. However, she was quickly informed by a little dwarf who had the Boots of Seven Leagues, boots with which he could tread over seven leagues of ground in one stride. The fairy came immediately, and she arrived, about an hour after, in a fiery chariot drawn by dragons.

The king helped the fairy out of the chariot. She approved everything the king had done for the princess but, as she had very great foresight, she thought that when the princess awoke, she might not know what to do with herself, being all alone in this old palace. So, the fairy touched everyone in the palace with her wand (except, of course, the king and queen)—governesses, maids of honor, ladies of the bedchamber, gentlemen, officers, stewards, cooks, undercooks, scullions, guards with their beefeaters, pages, and footmen—likewise, she touched all the horses in the stables, the great dogs in the outward court, and pretty little Mopsey, the princess's pet spaniel, which lay by her on the bed. Immediately, upon her touching them, they all fell asleep so that they might not awake before their mistress, and so they might be ready to wait upon her when she wanted them. The very spits at the fire, as full as they could hold of partridges and pheasants, also fell asleep. All this was done in a moment, as fairies do not tarry in doing their business.

And now, the king and queen kissed their dear child without waking her, and went out of the palace to set forth a new proclamation that nobody should dare to come near it. This, however, was unnecessary, for in a quarter of an hour's time, there grew up all about the park such a vast number of trees, great and small, bushes and brambles, twining one within another, that neither man nor beast could pass through. They grew so high that nothing could be seen except the very tops of the towers of the palace. Nobody doubted, but this displayed an extraordinary sample of the fairy's art: that the princess, while sleeping, might have nothing to fear from any curious people.

When a hundreds were gone, the son of the then reigning king, who was of another lineage than the sleeping princess, who was hunting on that side of the country asked what towers these were, which he saw in the middle of a great thick wood.

Everyone answered according to the stories they had heard. Some said that it was a ruinous old castle, haunted by spirits. Others claimed that all the sorcerers and witches of the country kept their Sabbath or night's meeting in those halls. The common opinion was that an ogre lived there, and that he carried thither all the little children he could catch, so that he may eat them up at his leisure, without anybody being able to follow him, as he was the only one with the power to pass through the wood.

The prince was a uncertain of which story he should believe, when a very good countryman said to him, "May it please your royal highness, it is now about fifty years since I head from my father, who heard from my grandfather, that there was in this castle a princess—the most beautiful ever seen—who was cursed to sleep there a hundred years, and should be awakened by a king's son, for whom she was reserved."

The young prince was all on fire at these words, believing—without weighing the matter—that he could put an end to this rare adventure and, pushed by love and honor, resolved that moment to look into it.

Just as he had advanced toward the wood, all the great trees, bushes, and brambles gave way to let him pass through. He walked up to the castle which he saw at the end of a large avenue. To his surprise, he saw that none of his people could follow him, because the trees closed up once again behind him. He did not cease from his task, however, for a young and amorous prince is always valiant.

He came into a space outside court where everything he saw might have frozen the most fearless person with horror. There reigned all over a most frightful silence and the image of death showed itself everywhere: there was nothing to be seen by stretched-out bodies of men and animals, all appearing to be dead. However, he knew by their ruby faces and pimpled noses that they were only sleeping, and in their goblets still remained some drops of wine, so it was clear they had fallen asleep in their cups.

He then crossed a court paved with marble, went up the stairs and came into the guard chamber, where guards were standing in their ranks, with their muskets upon their shoulders, and snoring as loud as they could. After that, he went through several rooms full of gentlemen and ladies, all asleep, some standing, others sitting. At last, he came into a chamber all gilded with gold, where he saw upon a bed, the curtains of which were open, the finest sight he ever beheld: a princess, who appeared to be about fifteen or sixteen years of age, and whose bright and resplendent beauty was quite heavenly. He approached with trembling admiration and fell down before her upon his knees.

At that moment, the enchantment came to an end, and the princess awakened and looked on him with tender eyes. "Is it you, my prince?" said she to him, "You have waited a long while."

The prince, charmed by these words, and much more with the manner in which they were spoken, knew not how to show his joy and gratitude. He assured her that he loved her more than he loved himself—more than anyone or anything in the whole world. Their conversation made little sense, as they wept more than they spoke, and what was said was with little eloquence, but a great deal of love. He was more at a loss than she, but we need not wonder as to why: she had time to think on what to say to him, for it is very probable (though history mentions nothing of it) that the good fairy had given her many agreeable dreams during her long sleep. In short, they talked for hours, and yet they said not half what they had to say.

In the meanwhile, the whole palace awaked, and as all of them were not in love, they were all desperately hungry, having not eaten for a hundred years. The chief lady of honor, being very impatient, told the princess that supper was served. The prince helped the princess rise. She was entirely dressed, and very magnificently, but his royal highness took care not to tell the princess that she was dressed akin his great-grandmother, as the fashion had changed much in a hundred years. Nevertheless, she looked not a bit less charming or beautiful.

They went into the great hall of mirrors, where they supped and were served by the princess's officers. The violinists and hautboys played old tunes, which were very excellent despite it being over a hundred years since they last played. After supper, without wasting any time, the lord almoner married them in the chapel of the castle.

The End

The Wonderful Wizard of Oz

by L. Frank Baum

CHAPTER 2

THE COUNCIL WITH THE MUNCHKINS

She was awakened by a shock, so sudden and severe that if Dorothy had not been lying on the soft bed she might have been hurt. As it was, the jar made her catch her breath and wonder what had happened; and Toto put his cold little nose into her face and whined dismally. Dorothy sat up and noticed that the house was not moving; nor was it dark, for the bright sunshine came in at the window, flooding the little room. She sprang from her bed and with Toto at her heels ran and opened the door.

The little girl gave a cry of amazement and looked about her, her eyes growing bigger and bigger at the wonderful sights she saw.

The cyclone had set the house down very gently--for a cyclone--in the midst of a country of marvelous beauty. There were lovely patches of greensward all about, with stately trees bearing rich and luscious fruits. Banks of gorgeous flowers were on every hand, and birds with rare and brilliant plumage sang and fluttered in the trees and bushes. A little way off was a small brook, rushing and sparkling along between green banks, and murmuring in a voice very grateful to a little girl who had lived so long on the dry, gray prairies.

While she stood looking eagerly at the strange and beautiful sights, she noticed coming toward her a group of the queerest people she had ever seen. They were not as big as the grown folk she had always been used to; but neither were they very small. In fact, they seemed about as tall as Dorothy, who was a well-grown child for her age, although they were, so far as looks go, many years older.

Three were men and one a woman, and all were oddly dressed. They wore round hats that rose to a small point a foot above their heads, with little bells around the brims that tinkled sweetly as they moved. The hats of the men were blue; the little woman's hat was white, and she wore a white gown that hung in pleats from her shoulders. Over it were sprinkled little stars that glistened in the sun like diamonds. The men were dressed in blue, of the same shade as their hats, and wore well-polished boots with a deep roll of blue at the tops. The men, Dorothy thought, were about as old as Uncle Henry, for two

of them had beards. But the little woman was doubtless much older. Her face was covered with wrinkles, her hair was nearly white, and she walked rather stiffly.

When these people drew near the house where Dorothy was standing in the doorway, they paused and whispered among themselves, as if afraid to come farther. But the little old woman walked up to Dorothy, made a low bow and said, in a sweet voice:

"You are welcome, most noble Sorceress, to the land of the Munchkins. We are so grateful to you for having killed the Wicked Witch of the East, and for setting our people free from bondage."

Dorothy listened to this speech with wonder. What could the little woman possibly mean by calling her a sorceress, and saying she had killed the Wicked Witch of the East? Dorothy was an innocent, harmless little girl, who had been carried by a cyclone many miles from home; and she had never killed anything in all her life.

But the little woman evidently expected her to answer; so Dorothy said, with hesitation, "You are very kind, but there must be some mistake. I have not killed anything."

"Your house did, anyway," replied the little old woman, with a laugh, "and that is the same thing. See!" she continued, pointing to the corner of the house. "There are her two feet, still sticking out from under a block of wood."

Dorothy looked, and gave a little cry of fright. There, indeed, just under the corner of the great beam the house rested on, two feet were sticking out, shod in silver shoes with pointed toes.

"Oh, dear! Oh, dear!" cried Dorothy, clasping her hands together in dismay. "The house must have fallen on her. Whatever shall we do?"

"There is nothing to be done," said the little woman calmly.

"But who was she?" asked Dorothy.

"She was the Wicked Witch of the East, as I said," answered the little woman. "She has held all the Munchkins in bondage for many years, making them slave for her night and day. Now they are all set free, and are grateful to you for the favor."

"Who are the Munchkins?" inquired Dorothy.

"They are the people who live in this land of the East where the Wicked Witch ruled."

"Are you a Munchkin?" asked Dorothy.

"No, but I am their friend, although I live in the land of the North. When they saw the Witch of the East was dead the Munchkins sent a swift messenger to me, and I came at once. I am the Witch of the North."

"Oh, gracious!" cried Dorothy. "Are you a real witch?"

"Yes, indeed," answered the little woman. "But I am a good witch, and the people love me. I am not as powerful as the Wicked Witch was who ruled here, or I should have set the people free myself."

"But I thought all witches were wicked," said the girl, who was half frightened at facing a real witch.

"Oh, no, that is a great mistake. There were only four witches in all the Land of Oz, and two of them, those who live in the North and the South, are good witches. I know this is true, for I am one of them myself, and cannot be mistaken. Those who dwelt in the East and the West were, indeed, wicked witches; but now that you have killed one of them, there is but one Wicked Witch in all the Land of Oz--the one who lives in the West."

"But," said Dorothy, after a moment's thought, "Aunt Em has told me that the witches were all dead--years and years ago."

"Who is Aunt Em?" inquired the little old woman.

"She is my aunt who lives in Kansas, where I came from."

The Witch of the North seemed to think for a time, with her head bowed and her eyes upon the ground. Then she looked up and said, "I do not know where Kansas is, for I have never heard that country mentioned before. But tell me, is it a civilized country?"

"Oh, yes," replied Dorothy.

"Then that accounts for it. In the civilized countries I believe there are no witches left, nor wizards, nor sorceresses, nor magicians. But, you see, the Land of Oz has never been civilized, for we are cut off from all the rest of the world. Therefore we still have witches and wizards amongst us."

"Who are the wizards?" asked Dorothy.

"Oz himself is the Great Wizard," answered the Witch, sinking her voice to a whisper. "He is more powerful than all the rest of us together. He lives in the City of Emeralds."

Dorothy was going to ask another question, but just then the Munchkins, who had been standing silently by, gave a loud shout and pointed to the corner of the house where the Wicked Witch had been lying.

"What is it?" asked the little old woman, and looked, and began to laugh. The feet of the dead Witch had disappeared entirely, and nothing was left but the silver shoes.

"She was so old," explained the Witch of the North, "that she dried up quickly in the sun. That is the end of her. But the silver shoes are yours, and you shall have them to wear." She reached down and picked up the shoes, and after shaking the dust out of them handed them to Dorothy.

"The Witch of the East was proud of those silver shoes," said one of the Munchkins, "and there is some charm connected with them; but what it is we never knew."

Dorothy carried the shoes into the house and placed them on the table. Then she came out again to the Munchkins and said:

"I am anxious to get back to my aunt and uncle, for I am sure they will worry about me. Can you help me find my way?"

The Munchkins and the Witch first looked at one another, and then at Dorothy, and then shook their heads.

"At the East, not far from here," said one, "there is a great desert, and none could live to cross it."

"It is the same at the South," said another, "for I have been there and seen it. The South is the country of the Quadlings."

"I am told," said the third man, "that it is the same at the West. And that country, where the Winkies live, is ruled by the Wicked Witch of the West, who would make you her slave if you passed her way."

"The North is my home," said the old lady, "and at its edge is the same great desert that surrounds this Land of Oz. I'm afraid, my dear, you will have to live with us."

Dorothy began to sob at this, for she felt lonely among all these strange people. Her tears seemed to grieve the kind-hearted Munchkins, for they immediately took out their handkerchiefs and began to weep also. As for the little old woman, she took off her cap and balanced the point on the end of her nose, while she counted "One, two, three" in a solemn voice. At once the cap changed to a slate, on which was written in big, white chalk marks:

"LET DOROTHY GO TO THE CITY OF EMERALDS"

The little old woman took the slate from her nose, and having read the words on it, asked, "Is your name Dorothy, my dear?"

"Yes," answered the child, looking up and drying her tears.

"Then you must go to the City of Emeralds. Perhaps Oz will help you."

"Where is this city?" asked Dorothy.

"It is exactly in the center of the country, and is ruled by Oz, the Great Wizard I told you of."

"Is he a good man?" inquired the girl anxiously.

"He is a good Wizard. Whether he is a man or not I cannot tell, for I have never seen him."

"How can I get there?" asked Dorothy.

"You must walk. It is a long journey, through a country that is sometimes pleasant and sometimes dark and terrible. However, I will use all the magic arts I know of to keep you from harm."

"Won't you go with me?" pleaded the girl, who had begun to look upon the little old woman as her only friend.

"No, I cannot do that," she replied, "but I will give you my kiss, and no one will dare injure a person who has been kissed by the Witch of the North."

She came close to Dorothy and kissed her gently on the forehead. Where her lips touched the girl they left a round, shining mark, as Dorothy found out soon after.

"The road to the City of Emeralds is paved with yellow brick," said the Witch, "so you cannot miss it. When you get to Oz do not be afraid of him, but tell your story and ask him to help you. Good-bye, my dear."

The three Munchkins bowed low to her and wished her a pleasant journey, after which they walked away through the trees. The Witch gave Dorothy a friendly little nod, whirled around on her left heel three times, and straightway disappeared, much to the surprise of little Toto, who barked after her loudly enough when she had gone, because he had been afraid even to growl while she stood by.

But Dorothy, knowing her to be a witch, had expected her to disappear in just that way, and was not surprised in the least.

The End

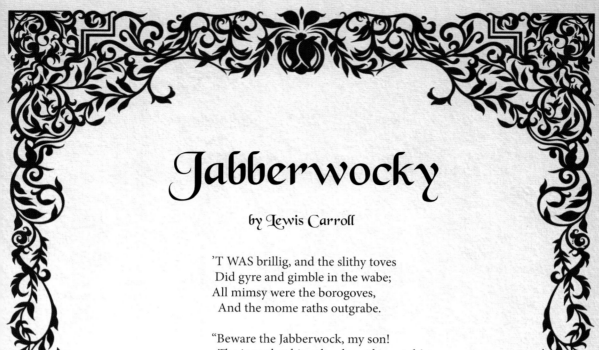

Jabberwocky

by Lewis Carroll

'T WAS brillig, and the slithy toves
  Did gyre and gimble in the wabe;
All mimsy were the borogoves,
  And the mome raths outgrabe.

"Beware the Jabberwock, my son!
  The jaws that bite, the claws that catch!
Beware the Jubjub bird, and shun
  The frumious Bandersnatch!"

He took his vorpal sword in hand:
  Long time the manxome foe he sought—
So rested he by the Tumtum tree,
  And stood awhile in thought.

And as in uffish thought he stood,
  The Jabberwock, with eyes of flame,
Came whiffling through the tulgey wood,
  And burbled as it came!

One, two! One, two! And through and through
  The vorpal blade went snicker-snack!
He left it dead, and with its head
  He went galumphing back.

"And hast thou slain the Jabberwock?
  Come to my arms, my beamish boy!
O frabjous day! Callooh! Callay!"
  He chortled in his joy.

'T was brillig, and the slithy toves
  Did gyre and gimble in the wabe;
All mimsy were the borogoves,
  And the mome raths outgrabe.

Thumbelina

by Hans Christian Anderson

There was once a woman who wanted to have quite a tiny, little child, but she did not know where to get one from. So one day she went to an old Witch and said to her: 'I should so much like to have a tiny, little child; can you tell me where I can get one?'

'Oh, we have just got one ready!' said the Witch. 'Here is a barley-corn for you, but it's not the kind the farmer sows in his field, or feeds the cocks and hens with, I can tell you. Put it in a flower-pot, and then you will see something happen.'

'Oh, thank you!' said the woman, and gave the Witch a shilling, for that was what it cost. Then she went home and planted the barley-corn; immediately there grew out of it a large and beautiful flower, which looked like a tulip, but the petals were tightly closed as if it were still only a bud.

'What a beautiful flower!' exclaimed the woman, and she kissed the red and yellow petals; but as she kissed them the flower burst open. It was a real tulip, such as one can see any day; but in the middle of the blossom, on the green velvety petals, sat a little girl, quite tiny, trim, and pretty. She was scarcely half a thumb in height; so they called her Thumbelina. An elegant polished walnut-shell served Thumbelina as a cradle, the blue petals of a violet were her mattress, and a rose-leaf her coverlid. There she lay at night, but in the day-time she used to play about on the table; here the woman had put a bowl, surrounded by a ring of flowers, with their stalks in water, in the middle of which floated a great tulip pedal, and on this Thumbelina sat, and sailed from one side of the bowl to the other, rowing herself with two white horse-hairs for oars. It was such a pretty sight! She could sing, too, with a voice more soft and sweet than had ever been heard before.

One night, when she was lying in her pretty little bed, an old toad crept in through a broken pane in the window. She was very ugly, clumsy, and clammy; she hopped on to the table where Thumbelina lay asleep under the red rose-leaf.

'This would make a beautiful wife for my son,' said the toad, taking up the walnut-shell, with Thumbelina inside, and hopping with it through the window into the garden.

There flowed a great wide stream, with slippery and marshy banks; here the toad lived with her son. Ugh! how ugly and clammy he was, just like his mother! 'Croak, croak, croak!' was all he could say when he saw the pretty little girl in the walnut-shell.

'Don't talk so load, or you'll wake her,' said the old toad. 'She might escape us

even now; she is as light as a feather. We will put her at once on a broad water-lily leaf in the stream. That will be quite an island for her; she is so small and light. She can't run away from us there, whilst we are preparing the guest-chamber under the marsh where she shall live.'

Outside in the brook grew many water-lilies, with broad green leaves, which looked as if they were swimming about on the water.

The leaf farthest away was the largest, and to this the old toad swam with Thumbelina in her walnut-shell.

The tiny Thumbelina woke up very early in the morning, and when she saw where she was she began to cry bitterly; for on every side of the great green leaf was water, and she could not get to the land.

The old toad was down under the marsh, decorating her room with rushes and yellow marigold leaves, to make it very grand for her new daughter-in-law; then she swam out with her ugly son to the leaf where Thumbelina lay. She wanted to fetch the pretty cradle to put it into her room before Thumbelina herself came there. The old toad bowed low in the water before her, and said: 'Here is my son; you shall marry him, and live in great magnificence down under the marsh.'

'Croak, croak, croak!' was all that the son could say. Then they took the neat little cradle and swam away with it; but Thumbelina sat alone on the great green leaf and wept, for she did not want to live with the clammy toad, or marry her ugly son. The little fishes swimming about under the water had seen the toad quite plainly, and heard what she had said; so they put up their heads to see the little girl. When they saw her, they thought her so pretty that they were very sorry she should go down with the ugly toad to live. No; that must not happen. They assembled in the water round the green stalk which supported the leaf on which she was sitting, and nibbled the stem in two. Away floated the leaf down the stream, bearing Thumbelina far beyond the reach of the toad.

On she sailed past several towns, and the little birds sitting in the bushes saw her, and sang, 'What a pretty little girl!' The leaf floated farther and farther away; thus Thumbelina left her native land.

A beautiful little white butterfly fluttered above her, and at last settled on the leaf. Thumbelina pleased him, and she, too, was delighted, for now the toads could not reach her, and it was so beautiful where she was travelling; the sun shone on the water and made it sparkle like the brightest silver. She took off her sash, and tied one end round the butterfly; the other end she fastened to the leaf, so that now it glided along with her faster than ever.

A great cockchafer came flying past; he caught sight of Thumbelina, and in a moment had put his arms round her slender waist, and had flown off with her to a tree. The green leaf floated away down the stream, and the butterfly with it, for he was fastened to the leaf and could not get loose from it. Oh, dear! how terrified poor little Thumbelina was when the cockchafer flew off with her to the tree! But she was especially distressed on the beautiful white butterfly's account, as she had tied him fast, so that if he could not get away he must starve to death. But the cockchafer did not trouble himself about that; he sat down with her on a large green leaf, gave her the honey out of the flowers to eat, and told her that she was very pretty, although she wasn't in the least like a cockchafer. Later on, all the other cockchafers who lived in the same tree came to pay calls; they examined Thumbelina closely, and remarked, 'Why, she has only two legs! How very miserable!'

'She has no feelers!' cried another.

'How ugly she is!' said all the lady chafers—and yet Thumbelina was really very pretty.

The cockchafer who had stolen her knew this very well; but when he heard all the ladies saying she was ugly, he began to think so too, and would not keep her; she might go wherever she liked. So he flew down from the tree with her and put her on a daisy. There she sat and wept, because she was so ugly that the cockchafer would have nothing to do with her; and yet she was the most beautiful creature imaginable, so soft and delicate, like the loveliest rose-leaf.

The whole summer poor little Thumbelina lived alone in the great wood. She plaited a bed for herself of blades of grass, and hung it up under a clover-leaf, so that she was protected from the rain; she gathered honey from the flowers for food, and drank the dew on the leaves every morning. Thus the summer and autumn passed, but then came winter—the long, cold winter. All the birds who had sung so sweetly about her had flown away; the trees shed their leaves, the flowers died; the great clover-leaf under which she had lived curled up, and nothing remained of it but the withered stalk. She was terribly cold, for her clothes were ragged, and she herself was so small and thin. Poor little Thumbelina! she would surely be frozen to death. It began to snow, and every snow-flake that fell on her was to her as a whole shovelful thrown on one of us, for we are so big, and she was only an inch high. She wrapt herself round in a dead leaf, but it was torn in the middle and gave her no warmth; she was trembling with cold.

Just outside the wood where she was now living lay a great corn-field. But the corn had been gone a long time; only the dry, bare stubble was left standing in the frozen ground. This made a forest for her to wander about in. All at once she came across the door of a field-mouse, who had a little hole under a corn-stalk. There the mouse lived warm and snug, with a store-room full of corn, a splendid kitchen and dining-room. Poor little Thumbelina went up to the door and begged for a little piece of barley, for she had not had anything to eat for the last two days.

'Poor little creature!' said the field-mouse, for she was a kind-hearted old thing at the bottom. 'Come into my warm room and have some dinner with me.'

As Thumbelina pleased her, she said: 'As far as I am concerned you may spend the winter with me; but you must keep my room clean and tidy, and tell me stories, for I like that very much.'

And Thumbelina did all that the kind old field-mouse asked, and did it remarkably well too.

'Now I am expecting a visitor,' said the field-mouse; 'my neighbour comes to call on me once a week. He is in better circumstances than I am, has great, big rooms, and wears a fine black-velvet coat. If you could only marry him, you would be well provided for. But he is blind. You must tell him all the prettiest stories you know.'

But Thumbelina did not trouble her head about him, for he was only a mole. He came and paid them a visit in his black-velvet coat.

'He is so rich and so accomplished,' the field-mouse told her.

'His house is twenty times larger than mine; he possesses great knowledge, but he cannot bear the sun and the beautiful flowers, and speaks slightingly of them, for he has never seen them.'

Thumbelina had to sing to him, so she sang 'Lady-bird, lady-bird, fly away home!' and other songs so prettily that the mole fell in love with her; but he did not say anything, he was a very cautious man. A short time before he had dug a long passage through the ground from his own house to that of his neighbour; in this he gave the field-mouse and Thumbelina permission to walk as often as they liked. But he begged them not to be afraid of the dead bird that lay in the passage: it was a real bird with beak and feathers, and must have died a little time ago, and now laid buried just where he had made his tunnel. The mole took a piece of rotten wood in his mouth, for that glows like fire in the dark, and went in front, lighting them through the long dark passage. When they came to the place where the dead bird lay, the mole put his broad nose against the ceiling and pushed a hole through, so that the daylight could shine down. In the middle of the path lay a dead swallow, his pretty wings pressed close to his sides, his claws and head drawn under his feathers; the poor bird had evidently died of cold. Thumbelina was very sorry, for she was very fond of all little birds; they had sung and twittered so beautifully to her all through the summer. But the mole kicked him with his bandy legs and said:

'Now he can't sing any more! It must be very miserable to be a little bird! I'm thankful that none of my little children are; birds always starve in winter.'

'Yes, you speak like a sensible man,' said the field-mouse. 'What has a bird, in spite of all his singing, in the winter-time? He must starve and freeze, and that must be very pleasant for him, I must say!'

Thumbelina did not say anything; but when the other two had passed on she bent down to the bird, brushed aside the feathers from his head, and kissed his closed eyes gently. 'Perhaps it was he that sang to me so prettily in the summer,' she thought. 'How much pleasure he did give me, dear little bird!'

The mole closed up the hole again which let in the light, and then escorted the ladies home. But Thumbelina could not sleep that night; so she got out of bed, and plaited a great big blanket of straw, and carried it off, and spread it over the dead bird, and piled upon it thistle-down as soft as cotton-wool, which she had found in the field-mouse's room, so that the poor little thing should lie warmly buried.

'Farewell, pretty little bird!' she said. 'Farewell, and thank you for your beautiful songs in the summer, when the trees were green, and the sun shone down warmly on us!' Then she laid her head against the bird's heart. But the bird was not dead: he had been frozen, but now that she had warmed him, he was coming to life again.

In autumn the swallows fly away to foreign lands; but there are some who are late in starting, and then they get so cold that they drop down as if dead, and the snow comes and covers them over.

Thumbelina trembled, she was so frightened; for the bird was very large in comparison with herself—only an inch high. But she took courage, piled up the down more closely over the poor swallow, fetched her own coverlid and laid it over his head.

Next night she crept out again to him. There he was alive, but very weak; he could only open his eyes for a moment and look at Thumbelina, who was standing in front of him with a piece of rotten wood in her hand, for she had no other lantern.

'Thank you, pretty little child!' said the swallow to her. 'I am so beautifully warm! Soon I shall regain my strength, and then I shall be able to fly out again into the warm sunshine.'

'Oh!' she said, 'it is very cold outside; it is snowing and freezing! stay in your warm bed; I will take care of you!'

Then she brought him water in a petal, which he drank, after which he related to her how he had torn one of his wings on a bramble, so that he could not fly as fast as the other swallows, who had flown far away to warmer lands. So at last he had dropped down exhausted, and then he could remember no more. The whole winter he remained down there, and Thumbelina looked after him and nursed him tenderly. Neither the mole nor the field-mouse learnt anything of this, for they could not bear the poor swallow.

When the spring came, and the sun warmed the earth again, the swallow said farewell to Thumbelina, who opened the hole in the roof for him which the mole had made. The sun shone brightly down upon her, and the swallow asked her if she would go with him; she could sit upon his back. Thumbelina wanted very much to fly far away into the green wood, but she knew that the old field-mouse would be sad if she ran away. 'No, I mustn't come!' she said.

'Farewell, dear good little girl!' said the swallow, and flew off into the sunshine. Thumbelina gazed after him with the tears standing in her eyes, for she was very fond of the swallow.

'Tweet, tweet!' sang the bird, and flew into the green wood. Thumbelina was very unhappy. She was not allowed to go out into the warm sunshine. The corn which had been sowed in the field over the field-mouse's home grew up high into the air, and made a thick forest for the poor little girl, who was only an inch high.

'Now you are to be a bride, Thumbelina!' said the field-mouse, 'for our neighbour has proposed for you! What a piece of fortune for a poor child like you! Now you must set to work at your linen for your dowry, for nothing must be lacking if you are to become the wife of our neighbour, the mole!'

Thumbelina had to spin all day long, and every evening the mole visited her, and told her that when the summer was over the sun would not shine so hot; now it was burning the earth as hard as a stone. Yes, when the summer had passed, they would keep the wedding.

But she was not at all pleased about it, for she did not like the stupid mole. Every morning when the sun was rising, and every evening when it was setting, she would steal out of the house-door, and when the breeze parted the ears of corn so that she could see the blue sky through them, she thought how bright and beautiful it must be outside, and longed to see her dear swallow again. But he never came; no doubt he had flown away far into the great green wood.

By the autumn Thumbelina had finished the dowry.

'In four weeks you will be married!' said the field-mouse; 'don't be obstinate, or I shall bite you with my sharp white teeth! You will get a fine husband! The King himself has not such a velvet coat. His store-room and cellar are full, and you should be thankful for that.'

Well, the wedding-day arrived. The mole had come to fetch Thumbelina to live with him deep down under the ground, never to come out into the warm sun again, for that was what he didn't like. The poor little girl was very sad; for now she must say good-bye to the beautiful sun.

'Farewell, bright sun!' she cried, stretching out her arms towards it, and taking another step outside the house; for now the corn had been reaped, and only the dry stubble was left standing. 'Farewell, farewell!' she said, and put her arms round a little red flower that grew there. 'Give my love to the dear swallow when you see him!'

'Tweet, tweet!' sounded in her ear all at once. She looked up. There was the swallow flying past! As soon as he saw Thumbelina, he was very glad. She told him how unwilling she was to marry the ugly mole, as then she had to live underground where the sun never shone, and she could not help bursting into tears.

'The cold winter is coming now,' said the swallow. 'I must fly away to warmer lands: will you come with me? You can sit on my back, and we will fly far away from the ugly mole and his dark house, over the mountains, to the warm countries where the sun shines more brightly than here, where it is always summer, and there are always beautiful flowers. Do come with me, dear little Thumbelina, who saved my life when I lay frozen in the dark tunnel!'

'Yes, I will go with you,' said Thumbelina, and got on the swallow's back, with her feet on one of his outstretched wings. Up he flew into the air, over woods and seas, over the great mountains where the snow is always lying. And if she was cold she crept under his warm feathers, only keeping her little head out to admire all the beautiful things in the world beneath. At last they came to warm lands; there the sun was brighter, the sky seemed twice as high, and in the hedges hung the finest green and purple grapes; in the woods grew oranges and lemons: the air was scented with myrtle and mint, and on the roads were pretty little children running about and playing with great gorgeous butterflies. But the swallow flew on farther, and it became more and more beautiful. Under the most splendid green trees besides a blue lake stood a glittering white-marble castle. Vines hung about the high pillars; there were many swallows' nests, and in one of these lived the swallow who was carrying Thumbelina.

'Here is my house!' said he. 'But it won't do for you to live with me; I am not tidy enough to please you. Find a home for yourself in one of the lovely flowers that grow down there; now I will set you down, and you can do whatever you like.'

'That will be splendid!' said she, clapping her little hands.

There lay a great white marble column which had fallen to the ground and broken into three pieces, but between these grew the most beautiful white flowers. The swallow flew down with Thumbelina, and set her upon one of the broad leaves. But there, to her astonishment, she found a tiny little man sitting in the middle of the flower, as white and transparent as if he were made of glass; he had the prettiest golden crown on his head, and the most beautiful wings on his shoulders; he himself was no bigger than Thumbelina. He was the spirit of the flower. In each blossom there dwelt a tiny man or woman; but this one was the King over the others.

'How handsome he is!' whispered Thumbelina to the swallow.

The little Prince was very much frightened at the swallow, for in comparison with one so tiny as himself he seemed a giant. But when he saw Thumbelina, he was delighted, for she was the most beautiful girl he had ever seen. So he took his golden crown from off his head and put it on hers, asking her her name, and if she would be his wife, and then she would be Queen of all the flowers. Yes! he was a different kind of husband to the son of the toad and the mole with the black-velvet coat. So she said 'Yes' to the noble Prince. And out of each flower came a lady and gentleman, each so tiny and pretty that it was a pleasure to see them. Each brought Thumbelina a present, but the best of all was a beautiful pair of wings which were fastened on to her back, and now she too could fly from flower to flower. They all wished her joy, and the swallow sat above in his nest and sang the wedding march, and that he did as well as he could; but he was sad, because he was very fond of Thumbelina and did not want to be separated from her.

'You shall not be called Thumbelina!' said the spirit of the flower to her; 'that is an ugly name, and you are much too pretty for that. We will call you May Blossom.'

'Farewell, farewell!' said the little swallow with a heavy heart, and flew away to farther lands, far, far away, right back to Denmark. There he had a little nest above a window, where his wife lived, who can tell fairy-stories. 'Tweet, tweet!' he sang to her. And that is the way we learnt the whole story.

The End

Hansel and Gretel

Hard by a great forest dwelt a poor wood-cutter with his wife and his two children. The boy was called Hansel and the girl Gretel. He had little to bite and to break, and once when great dearth fell on the land, he could no longer procure even daily bread. Now when he thought over this by night in his bed, and tossed about in his anxiety, he groaned and said to his wife: 'What is to become of us? How are we to feed our poor children, when we no longer have anything even for ourselves?' 'I'll tell you what, husband,' answered the woman, 'early tomorrow morning we will take the children out into the forest to where it is the thickest; there we will light a fire for them, and give each of them one more piece of bread, and then we will go to our work and leave them alone. They will not find the way home again, and we shall be rid of them.' 'No, wife,' said the man, 'I will not do that; how can I bear to leave my children alone in the forest?—the wild animals would soon come and tear them to pieces.' 'O, you fool!' said she, 'then we must all four die of hunger, you may as well plane the planks for our coffins,' and she left him no peace until he consented. 'But I feel very sorry for the poor children, all the same,' said the man.

The two children had also not been able to sleep for hunger, and had heard what their stepmother had said to their father. Gretel wept bitter tears, and said to Hansel: 'Now all is over with us.' 'Be quiet, Gretel,' said Hansel, 'do not distress yourself, I will soon find a way to help us.' And when the old folks had fallen asleep, he got up, put on his little coat, opened the door below, and crept outside. The moon shone brightly, and the white pebbles which lay in front of the house glittered like real silver pennies. Hansel stooped and stuffed the little pocket of his coat with as many as he could get in. Then he went back and said to Gretel: 'Be comforted, dear little sister, and sleep in peace, God will not forsake us,' and he lay down again in his bed. When day dawned, but before the sun had risen, the woman came and awoke the two children, saying: 'Get up, you sluggards! we are going into the forest to fetch wood.' She gave each a little piece of bread, and said: 'There is something for your dinner, but do not eat it up before then, for you will get nothing else.' Gretel took the bread under her apron, as Hansel had the pebbles in his pocket. Then they all set out together on the way to the forest. When they had walked a short time, Hansel stood still and peeped back at the house, and did so again and again. His father said: 'Hansel, what are you looking at there and staying behind for? Pay attention, and do not forget how to use your legs.' 'Ah, father,' said Hansel, 'I am looking at my little white cat, which is sitting up on the roof, and wants to say goodbye to me.' The wife said: 'Fool, that is not your little cat, that is the morning sun which is shining on the chimneys.' Hansel, however, had not been looking back at the cat, but had been constantly throwing one of the white pebble-stones out of his pocket on the road.

When they had reached the middle of the forest, the father said: 'Now, children,

pile up some wood, and I will light a fire that you may not be cold.' Hansel and Gretel gathered brushwood together, as high as a little hill. The brushwood was lighted, and when the flames were burning very high, the woman said: 'Now, children, lay yourselves down by the fire and rest, we will go into the forest and cut some wood. When we have done, we will come back and fetch you away.'

Hansel and Gretel sat by the fire, and when noon came, each ate a little piece of bread, and as they heard the strokes of the wood-axe they believed that their father was near. It was not the axe, however, but a branch which he had fastened to a withered tree which the wind was blowing backwards and forwards. And as they had been sitting such a long time, their eyes closed with fatigue, and they fell fast asleep. When at last they awoke, it was already dark night. Gretel began to cry and said: 'How are we to get out of the forest now?' But Hansel comforted her and said: 'Just wait a little, until the moon has risen, and then we will soon find the way.' And when the full moon had risen, Hansel took his little sister by the hand, and followed the pebbles which shone like newly-coined silver pieces, and showed them the way.

They walked the whole night long, and by break of day came once more to their father's house. They knocked at the door, and when the woman opened it and saw that it was Hansel and Gretel, she said: 'You naughty children, why have you slept so long in the forest?—we thought you were never coming back at all!' The father, however, rejoiced, for it had cut him to the heart to leave them behind alone.

Not long afterwards, there was once more great dearth throughout the land, and the children heard their mother saying at night to their father: 'Everything is eaten again, we have one half loaf left, and that is the end. The children must go, we will take them farther into the wood, so that they will not find their way out again; there is no other means of saving ourselves!' The man's heart was heavy, and he thought: 'It would be better for you to share the last mouthful with your children.' The woman, however, would listen to nothing that he had to say, but scolded and reproached him. He who says A must say B, likewise, and as he had yielded the first time, he had to do so a second time also.

The children, however, were still awake and had heard the conversation. When the old folks were asleep, Hansel again got up, and wanted to go out and pick up pebbles as he had done before, but the woman had locked the door, and Hansel could not get out. Nevertheless he comforted his little sister, and said: 'Do not cry, Gretel, go to sleep quietly, the good God will help us.'

Early in the morning came the woman, and took the children out of their beds. Their piece of bread was given to them, but it was still smaller than the time before. On the way into the forest Hansel crumbled his in his pocket, and often stood still and threw a morsel on the ground. 'Hansel, why do you stop and look round?' said the father, 'go on.' 'I am looking back at my little pigeon which is sitting on the roof, and wants to say goodbye to me,' answered Hansel. 'Fool!' said the woman, 'that is not your little pigeon, that is the morning sun that is shining on the chimney.' Hansel, however little by little, threw all the crumbs on the path.

The woman led the children still deeper into the forest, where they had never in their lives been before. Then a great fire was again made, and the mother said: 'Just sit there, you children, and when you are tired you may sleep a little; we are going into the forest to cut wood, and in the evening when we are done, we will come and fetch you away.' When it was noon, Gretel shared her piece of bread with Hansel, who had scattered his by the way. Then they fell asleep and evening passed, but no one came to the poor children. They did not awake until it was dark night, and Hansel comforted his little sister and said: 'Just wait, Gretel, until the moon rises, and then we shall see the crumbs of bread which I have strewn about, they will show us our way home again.' When the moon came they set out, but they found no crumbs, for the many thousands of birds which fly about in the woods and fields had picked them all up. Hansel said to Gretel: 'We shall soon find the way,' but they did not find it. They walked the whole night and all the next day too from morning till evening, but they did not get out of the forest, and were very hungry, for they had nothing to eat but two or three berries, which grew on the ground. And as they were so weary that their legs would carry them no longer, they lay down beneath a tree and fell asleep.

It was now three mornings since they had left their father's house. They began to walk again, but they always came deeper into the forest, and if help did not come soon, they must die of hunger and weariness. When it was mid-day, they saw a beautiful snow-white bird sitting on a bough, which sang so delightfully that they stood still and listened to it. And when its song was over, it spread its wings and flew away before them, and they followed it until they reached a little house, on the roof of which it alighted; and when they approached the little house they saw that it was built of bread and covered with cakes, but that the windows were of clear sugar. 'We will set to work on that,' said Hansel, 'and have a good meal. I will eat a bit of the roof, and you Gretel, can eat some of the window, it will taste sweet.' Hansel reached up above, and broke off a little of the roof to try how it tasted, and Gretel leant against the window and nibbled at the panes. Then a soft voice cried from the parlour:

'Nibble, nibble, gnaw,
Who is nibbling at my little house?'
The children answered:
The wind, the wind,
The heaven-born wind,'

and went on eating without disturbing themselves. Hansel, who liked the taste of the roof, tore down a great piece of it, and Gretel pushed out the whole of one round window-pane, sat down, and enjoyed herself with it. Suddenly the door opened, and a woman as old as the hills, who supported herself on crutches, came creeping out. Hansel and Gretel were so terribly frightened that they let fall what they had in their hands. The old woman, however, nodded her head, and said: 'Oh, you dear children, who has brought you here? do come in, and stay with me. No harm shall happen to you.' She took them both by the hand, and led them into her little house. Then good food was set before them, milk and pancakes, with sugar, apples, and nuts. Afterwards two pretty little beds were covered with clean white linen, and Hansel and Gretel lay down in them, and thought they were in heaven.

The old woman had only pretended to be so kind; she was in reality a wicked witch, who lay in wait for children, and had only built the little house of bread in order to entice them there. When a child fell into her power, she killed it, cooked and ate it, and that was a feast day with her. Witches have red eyes, and cannot see far, but they have a keen scent like the beasts, and are aware when human beings draw near. When Hansel and Gretel came into her neighbourhood, she laughed with malice, and said mockingly: 'I have them, they shall not escape me again!' Early in the morning before the children were awake, she was already up, and when she saw both of them sleeping and looking so pretty, with their plump and rosy cheeks she muttered to herself: 'That will be a dainty mouthful!' Then she seized Hansel with her shrivelled hand, carried him into a little stable, and locked him in behind a grated door. Scream as he might, it would not help him. Then she went to Gretel, shook her till she awoke, and cried: 'Get up, lazy thing, fetch some water, and cook something good for your brother, he is in the stable outside, and is to be made fat. When he is fat, I will eat him.' Gretel began to weep bitterly, but it was all in vain, for she was forced to do what the wicked witch commanded.

And now the best food was cooked for poor Hansel, but Gretel got nothing but crab-shells. Every morning the woman crept to the little stable, and cried: 'Hansel, stretch out your finger that I may feel if you will soon be fat.' Hansel, however, stretched out a little bone to her, and the old woman, who had dim eyes, could not see it, and thought it was Hansel's finger, and was astonished that there was no way of fattening him. When four weeks had gone by, and Hansel still remained thin, she was seized with impatience and would not wait any longer. 'Now, then, Gretel,' she cried to the girl, 'stir yourself, and bring some water. Let Hansel be fat or lean, tomorrow I will kill him, and cook him.' Ah, how the poor little sister did lament when she had to fetch the water, and how her tears did flow down her cheeks! 'Dear God, do help us,' she cried. 'If the wild beasts in the forest had but devoured us, we should at any rate have died together.' 'Just keep your noise to yourself,' said the old woman, 'it won't help you at all.'

Early in the morning, Gretel had to go out and hang up the cauldron with the water, and light the fire. 'We will bake first,' said the old woman, 'I have already heated the oven, and kneaded the dough.' She pushed poor Gretel out to the oven, from which flames of fire were already darting. 'Creep in,' said the witch, 'and see if it is properly heated, so that we can put the bread in.' And once Gretel was inside, she intended to shut the oven and let her bake in it, and then she would eat her, too. But Gretel saw what she had in mind, and said: 'I do not know how I am to do it; how do I get in?' 'Silly goose,' said the old woman. 'The door is big enough; just look, I can get in myself!' and she crept up and thrust her head into the oven. Then Gretel gave her a push that drove her far into it, and shut the iron door, and fastened the bolt. Oh! then she began to howl quite horribly, but Gretel ran away and the godless witch was miserably burnt to death.

Gretel, however, ran like lightning to Hansel, opened his little stable, and cried: 'Hansel, we are saved! The old witch is dead!' Then Hansel sprang like a bird from its cage when the door is opened. How they did rejoice and embrace each other, and dance about and kiss each other! And as they had no longer any need to fear her, they went into the witch's house, and in every corner there stood chests full of pearls and jewels. 'These are far better than pebbles!' said Hansel, and thrust into his pockets whatever could be got in, and Gretel said: 'I, too, will take something home with me,' and filled her pinafore full. 'But now we must be off,' said Hansel, 'that we may get out of the witch's forest.'

When they had walked for two hours, they came to a great stretch of water. 'We cannot cross,' said Hansel, 'I see no foot-plank, and no bridge.' 'And there is also no ferry,' answered Gretel, 'but a white duck is swimming there: if I ask her, she will help us over.' Then she cried:

'Little duck, little duck, dost thou see,
Hansel and Gretel are waiting for thee?

There's never a plank, or bridge in sight,
Take us across on thy back so white.'

The duck came to them, and Hansel seated himself on its back, and told his sister to sit by him. 'No,' replied Gretel, 'that will be too heavy for the little duck; she shall take us across, one after the other.' The good little duck did so, and when they were once safely across and had walked for a short time, the forest seemed to be more and more familiar to them, and at length they saw from afar their father's house. Then they began to run, rushed into the parlour, and threw themselves round their father's neck. The man had not known one happy hour since he had left the children in the forest; the woman, however, was dead. Gretel emptied her pinafore until pearls and precious stones ran about the room, and Hansel threw one handful after another out of his pocket to add to them. Then all anxiety was at an end, and they lived together in perfect happiness. My tale is done, there runs a mouse; whosoever catches it, may make himself a big fur cap out of it.

The End

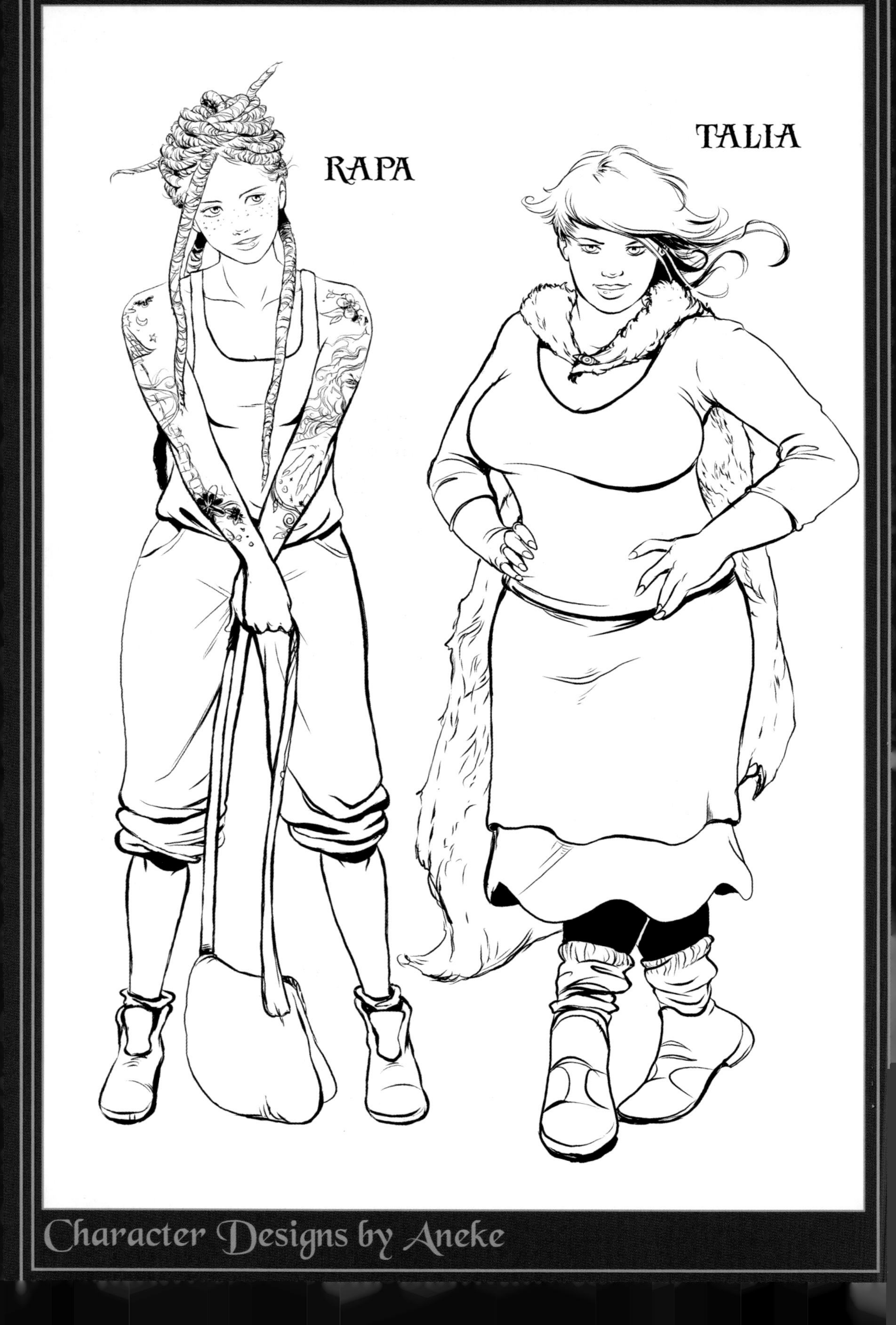
RAPA
TALIA

Character Designs by Aneke

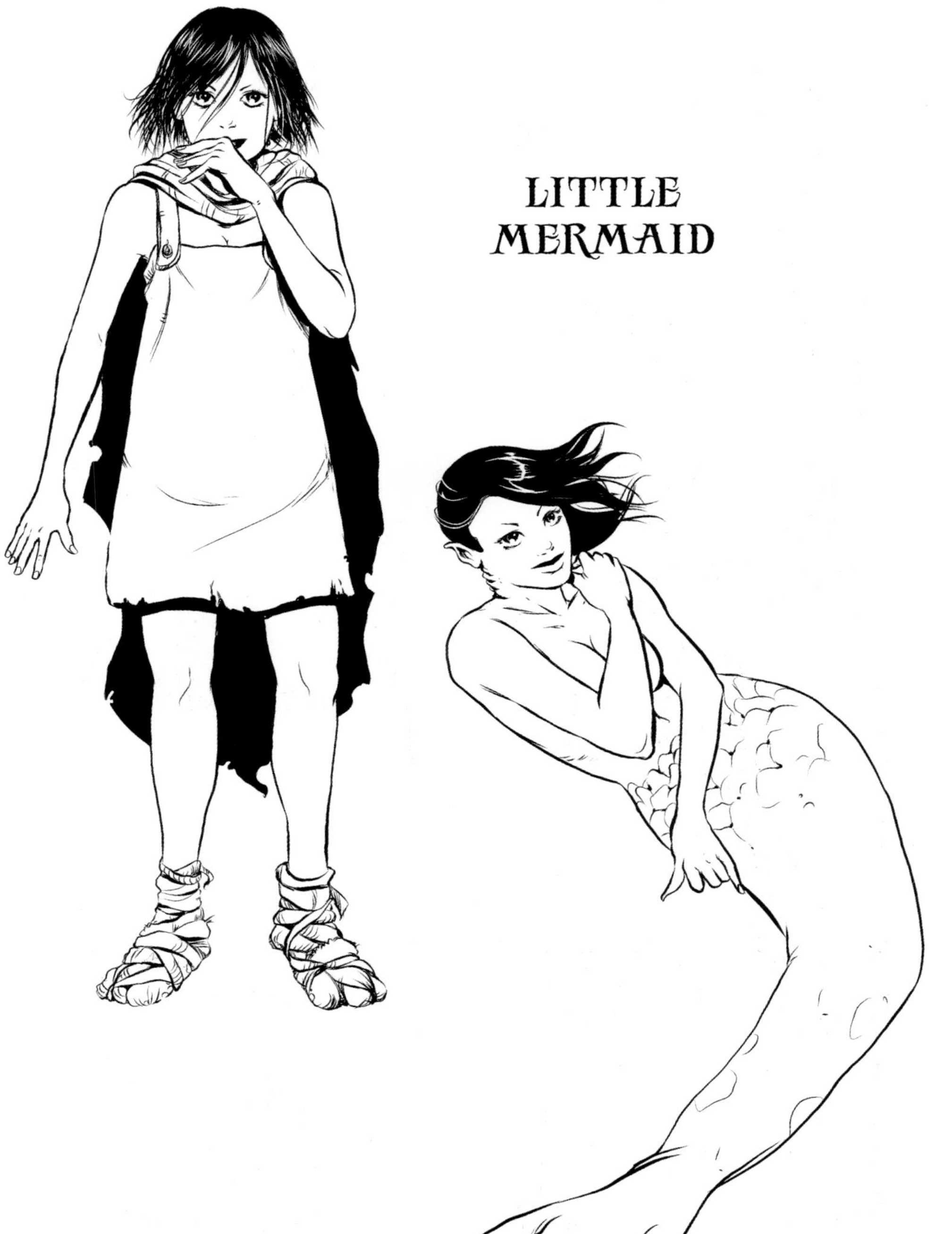
LITTLE
MERMAID

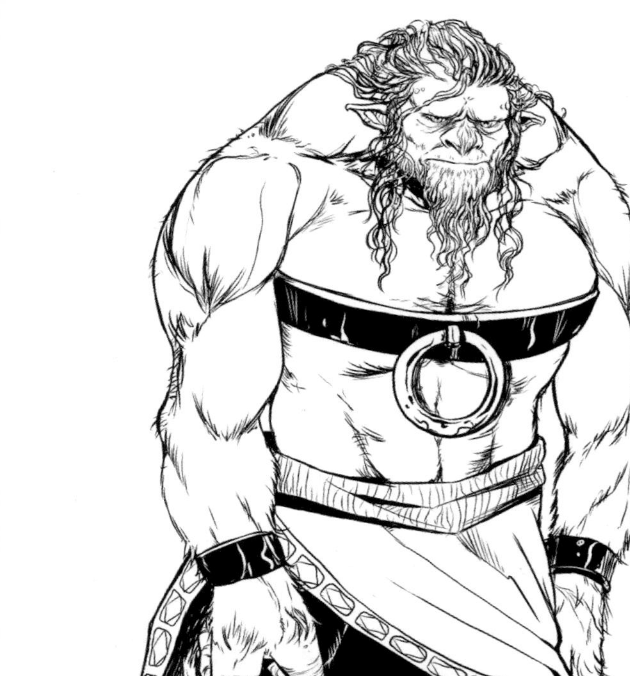

THE MONSTER KING

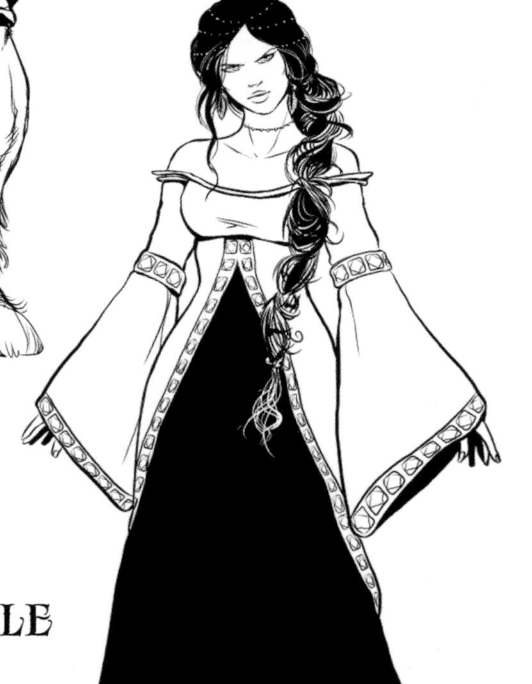

QUEEN BELLE

Character Designs Continued

KING PERSINE

QUEEN RAPUNZEL

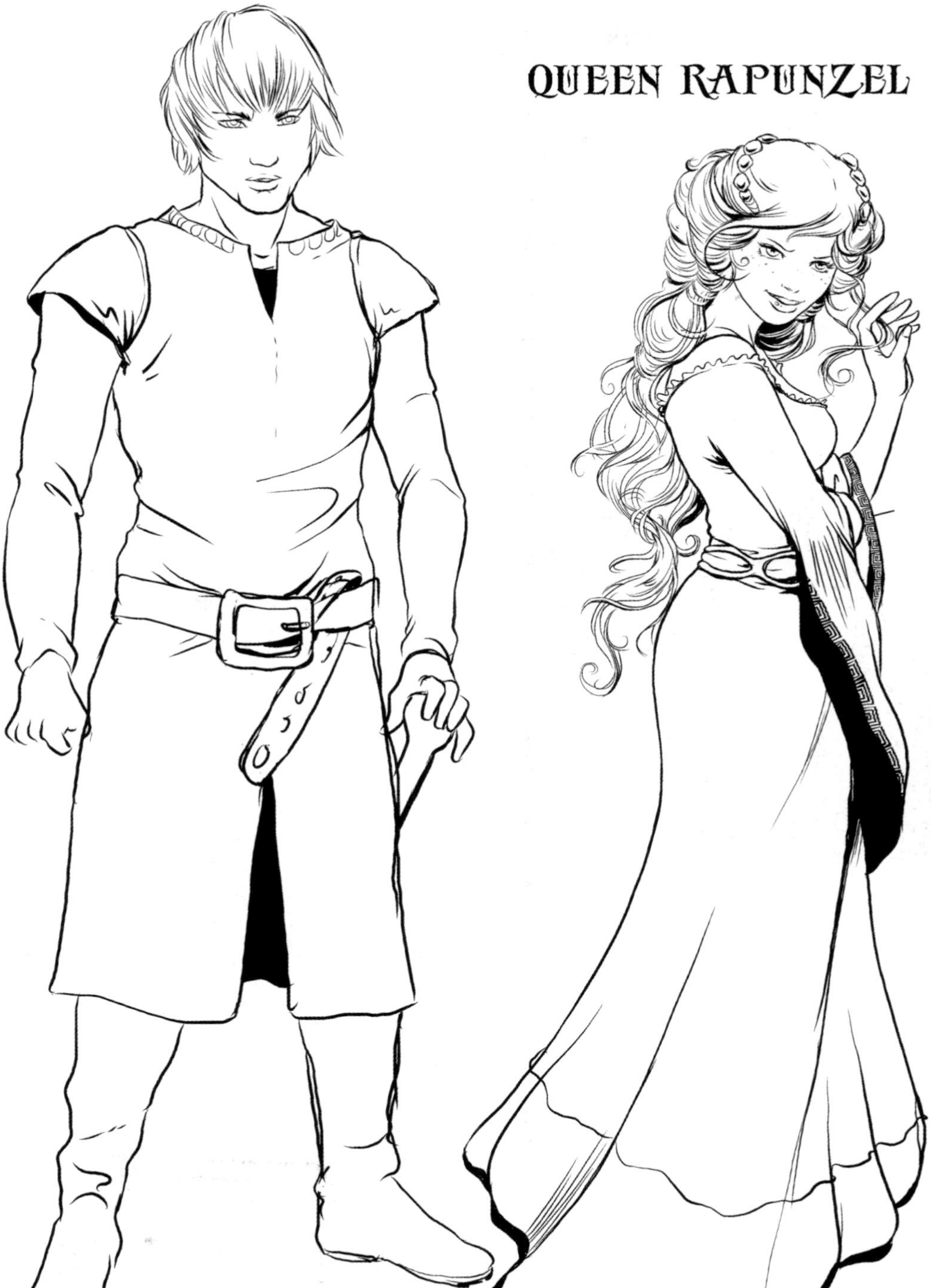